Time Out

Marrakech

timeout.com

Time Out Guides Ltd
Universal House
251 Tottenham Court Road
London W1T 7AB
United Kingdom
Tel: +44 (0)20 7813 3000
Fax: +44 (0)20 7813 6001
Email: guides@timeout.com
www.timeout.com

Published by Time Out Guides Ltd, a wholly owned subsidiary of Time Out Group Ltd. Time Out and the Time Out logo are trademarks of Time Out Group Ltd.

Previous editions 2003, 2005, 2007.

10 9 8 7 6 5 4 3 2 1

This edition first published in Great Britain in 2014 by Ebury Publishing.
A Random House Group Company
20 Vauxhall Bridge Road, London SW1V 2SA

Random House Australia Pty Ltd 20 Alfred Street, Milsons Point, Sydney, New South Wales 2061, Australia

Random House New Zealand Ltd 18 Poland Road, Glenfield, Auckland 10, New Zealand

Random House South Africa (Pty) Ltd Isle of Houghton, Corner Boundary Road & Carse O'Gowrie, Houghton 2198, South Africa

Random House UK Limited Reg. No. 954009

Distributed in the US and Latin America by Publishers Group West (1-510-809-3700)

For further distribution details, see www.timeout.com.

ISBN: 978-1-84670-326-3

A CIP catalogue record for this book is available from the British Library.

Printed and bound in China by Leo Paper Products Ltd.

The Random House Group Limited supports The Forest Stewardship Council® (FSC®), the leading international forest-certification organisation. Our books carrying the FSC label are printed on FSC®-certified paper. FSC is the only forest-certification scheme supported by the leading environmental organisations, including Greenpeace. Our paper procurement policy can be found at www.randomhouse.co.uk/environment.

Contents

36

160

122

Time Out Marrakech

Editorial
Editor Claire Boobbyer
Copy Editors Dominic Earle, Ros Sales
Proofreader Marion Moisy
Indexer Marion Moisy

Editorial Director Sarah Guy
Group Finance Manager Margaret Wright

Design
Senior Designer Kei Ishimaru
Designer Darryl Bell
Group Commercial Senior Designer Jason Tansley

Picture Desk
Picture Editor Jael Marschner
Deputy Picture Editor Ben Rowe
Freelance Picture Researcher Lizzy Owen

Advertising
Advertising (Marrakech) Jinga Media Ltd (www.jingamedia.com)

Marketing
Senior Publishing Brand Manager Luthfa Begum
Head of Circulation Dan Collins

Production
Production Controller Katie Mulhern-Bhudia

Time Out Group
Chairman & Founder Tony Elliott
Chief Executive Officer Tim Arthur
Chief Commercial Officer Kim O'Hara
Publisher Alex Batho
Group IT Director Simon Chappell
Group Marketing Director Carolyn Sims

Contributors
Marrakech's Top 20 Claire Boobbyer. **Marrakech Today** Richard Hamilton. **Itineraries** Claire Boobbyer. **Diary** Claire Boobbyer. **Marrakech's Best** Claire Boobbyer. **Jemaa Fna & Around** Claire Boobbyer (*Let me Tell You A Story* Richard Hamilton); (*Square Meals* Tara Stevens). *Restaurants, cafés & bars* Tara Stevens. *Shops & services* Mandy Sinclair. **Souks & Around** Claire Boobbyer (*The Sacred Scrubdown, Stir It Up* Tara Stevens). *Restaurants, cafés & bars* Tara Stevens. *Shopping & services* Claire Boobbyer, Mandy Sinclair. **Southern Medina** Claire Boobbyer. *Restaurants, cafés & bars* Tara Stevens. *Shopping & services* Claire Boobbyer, Mandy Sinclair. **Ville Nouvelle & Palmeraie** Claire Boobbyer (*Lunch and a Swim, Cheers!, Ville Nouvelle Galleries, Art Explosion* Tara Stevens); (*Enjoy the Outdoors* Rachel Blech); (*The Industrial Revolution* Mandy Sinclair). *Restaurants, cafés & bars* Tara Stevens. *Shopping & services* Claire Boobbyer, Mandy Sinclair. **Children** Rachel Blech. **Film** Richard Hamilton. **Gay & Lesbian** Peter Paolozzi. **Nightlife & Music** Rachel Blech. **Essaouira** Tara Stevens (*Gnawa Grooves* Rachel Blech). **High Atlas & the Sahara** Rachel Blech. **History** Hugh Graham, Richard Hamilton. **Architecture** Andrew Humphreys, Claire Boobbyer. **Hotels** Claire Boobbyer, Mandy Sinclair. **Directory** Rachel Blech.

Maps JS Graphics Ltd (john@jsgraphics.co.uk) Maps are based on data supplied by Jean Louis Dorveaux. Essaouira data supplied by New Holland Publishers.

Cover Photography Sean Randall/Getty Images

Back Cover Photography Clockwise from top left: Theatro Marrakech, Karol Kozlowski/Shutterstock.com; Suzanne Porter; La Mamounia.

Photography Pages 7, 20/21, 29 (top), 39, 41, 62 (bottom), 67, 71, 80, 82, 86, 102, 237 Suzanne Porter; 10, 12 (middle), 14/15, 18 (top), 46/47, 84/85, 229 Christian Mueller/Shutterstock.com; 12 (bottom) danileon/Shutterstock.com; 13 (bottom) TTL/Photoshot; 18 (bottom), 52, 60, 81, 95, 99, 118, 132, 135, 137, 142, 190/191, 209, 217, 218 Olivia Rutherford; 19 (top) Astudio/Shutterstock.com; 23 Karim Tibari; 24 jupiterimages.com; 24/25 Esther Quelle; 42 (top), 55, 59, 62 (top), 70, 128, 138, 145, 192, 217 (left), 219, 221, 222 Elan Fleisher; 44 Joelle Gueguen; 48 nevenm/Shutterstock.com; 50 Luisa Puccini/Shutterstock.com; 50 (bottom) Lionel B/Shutterstock.com; 51 Daleen Loest/Shutterstock.com; 53 Seleznev Oleg/Shutterstock.com; 68 Karol Kozlowski/Shutterstock.com; 74 Jan Willem Hoffwegen/Shutterstock.com; 74/75 Alarico/ Shutterstock.com; 78 Stephane Bidouze/Shutterstock.com; 87 posztos/Shutterstock.com; 106 Paradigmatik_Studio; 108 KW Photography; 126 cdrin/Shutterstock.com; 126/127 Seqoya/Shutterstock.com; 114, 115 Belinda van de Graaf; 133, 144 Alamy; 141 Elaine Sifeddine; 146 David Varga/Shutterstock.com; 146/147 Matej Kastelic/Shutterstock.com; 150 Rachid Wyatt; 153, 167 Lukasz Janyst/ Shutterstock.com; 155 Jeremy Richards/ Shutterstock.com; 156 Aerostato/Shutterstock.com; 159 Cornfield/Shutterstock.com; 160 emei/Shutterstock.com; 162 John Copland/Shutterstock.com; 164 Karol Kozlowski/ Shutterstock.com; 171 Eniko Balogh/Shutterstock.com; 173 ndphoto/Shutterstock.com; 178 Rex; 183 Getty/DeAgostini; 184 AFP/Getty Images; 189 AP/Press Association; 194 Tony Zelenoff/Shutterstock.com; 196 Jan Mastnik/Shutterstock.com; 197 Opis Zagreb/Shutterstock.com; 207 David Loftus; 225 Selman Gallery.

The following images were supplied by the featured establishments/artists:
pages 10/11, 12 (top), 13 (top), 16, 18, 20, 21, 22/23, 29 (bottom) 26/26 (bottom), 46, 58, 61, 64, 66, 72, 73, 80, 90, 91, 92, 97, 100, 105, 106/107, 109, 112, 116, 119, 120, 122, 136, 152, 157, 163, 168, 174, 200, 201, 202, 203, 205, 206, 210, 211, 213, 214/215, 216, 223, 224, 226, 227, 240, 241.

About the Guide

GETTING AROUND

Each sightseeing chapter contains a street map of the area marked with the locations of sights and museums (❶), restaurants (❶), cafés and bars (❶) and shops (❶). There are also street maps of Marrakech at the back of the book, along with an overview map of the city. In addition, there is a detachable fold-out street map.

THE ESSENTIALS

For practical information, including visas, disabled access, emergency numbers, lost property, websites and local transport, see the Essential Information section. It begins on page 198.

THE LISTINGS

Addresses, phone numbers, websites, transport information, hours and prices are all included in our listings, as are selected other facilities. All were checked and correct at press time. However, business owners can alter their arrangements at any time, and fluctuating economic conditions can cause prices to change rapidly.

The very best venues in the city, the must-sees and must-dos in every category, have been marked with a red star (★). In the sightseeing chapters, we've also marked venues with free admission with a FREE symbol.

THE LANGUAGE

Many Marrakchis speak French as well as the Moroccan dialect of Arabic, and quite a lot speak English too, especially those working in tourism. There are French and Arabic vocabulary primers on pp238-239.

PHONE NUMBERS

The area code for Marrakech is 0524. When calling within Morocco you need to dial the area code even if you are calling from the same area. For instance, to make a local call within Marrakech, you must still dial 0524. From outside Morocco, dial your country's access code (00 from the UK, 011 from the US) or a plus symbol, followed by the Moroccan country code (212), then 524 for Marrakech (dropping the initial zero) and the number. So, to reach the Maison de la Photographie, dial + 212 524 38 57 21.

FEEDBACK

We welcome feedback on this guide, both on the venues we've included and on any other locations that you'd like to see featured in future editions. Please email us at guides@timeout.com.

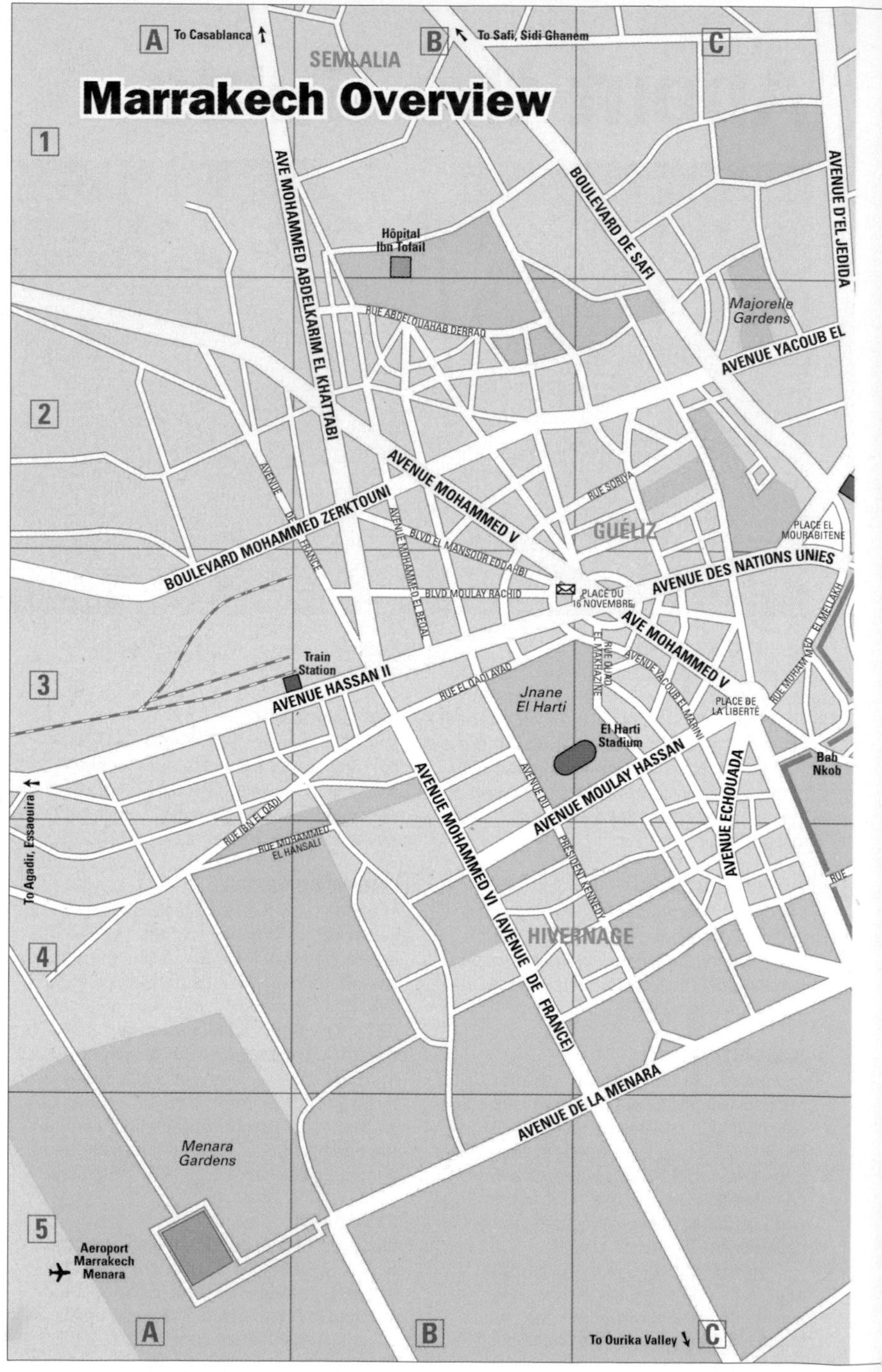
Marrakech Overview
A
To Casablanca
B
To Safi, Sidi Ghanem
C
SEMLALIA
1
2
3
4
5
AVE MOHAMMED ABDELKARIM EL KHATTABI
BOULEVARD DE SAFI
AVENUE D'EL JEDIDA
Hôpital Ibn Tofail
Majorelle Gardens
AVENUE YACOUB EL
RUE ABDELOUAHAB DERRAQ
AVENUE MOHAMMED V
BOULEVARD MOHAMMED ZERKTOUNI
AVENUE DE FRANCE
AVENUE MOHAMMED EL BEQAL
BLVD EL MANSOUR EDDAHBI
BLVD MOULAY RACHID
RUE SORIYA
GUÉLIZ
PLACE EL MOURABITENE
AVENUE DES NATIONS UNIES
PLACE DU 16 NOVEMBRE
AVE MOHAMMED V
RUE MOHAMMED EL MELLAKH
Train Station
AVENUE HASSAN II
RUE EL QADI AYAD
Jnane El Harti
RUE OUAD EL MAKHAZINE
AVENUE YACOUB EL MARINI
PLACE DE LA LIBERTÉ
El Harti Stadium
Bab Nkob
AVENUE ECHOUADA
AVENUE MOULAY HASSAN
AVENUE DU PRESIDENT KENNEDY
AVENUE MOHAMMED VI (AVENUE DE FRANCE)
RUE IBN EL QADI
RUE MOHAMMED EL HANSALI
To Agadir, Essaouira
HIVERNAGE
RUE
AVENUE DE LA MENARA
Menara Gardens
Aeroport Marrakech Menara
To Ourika Valley

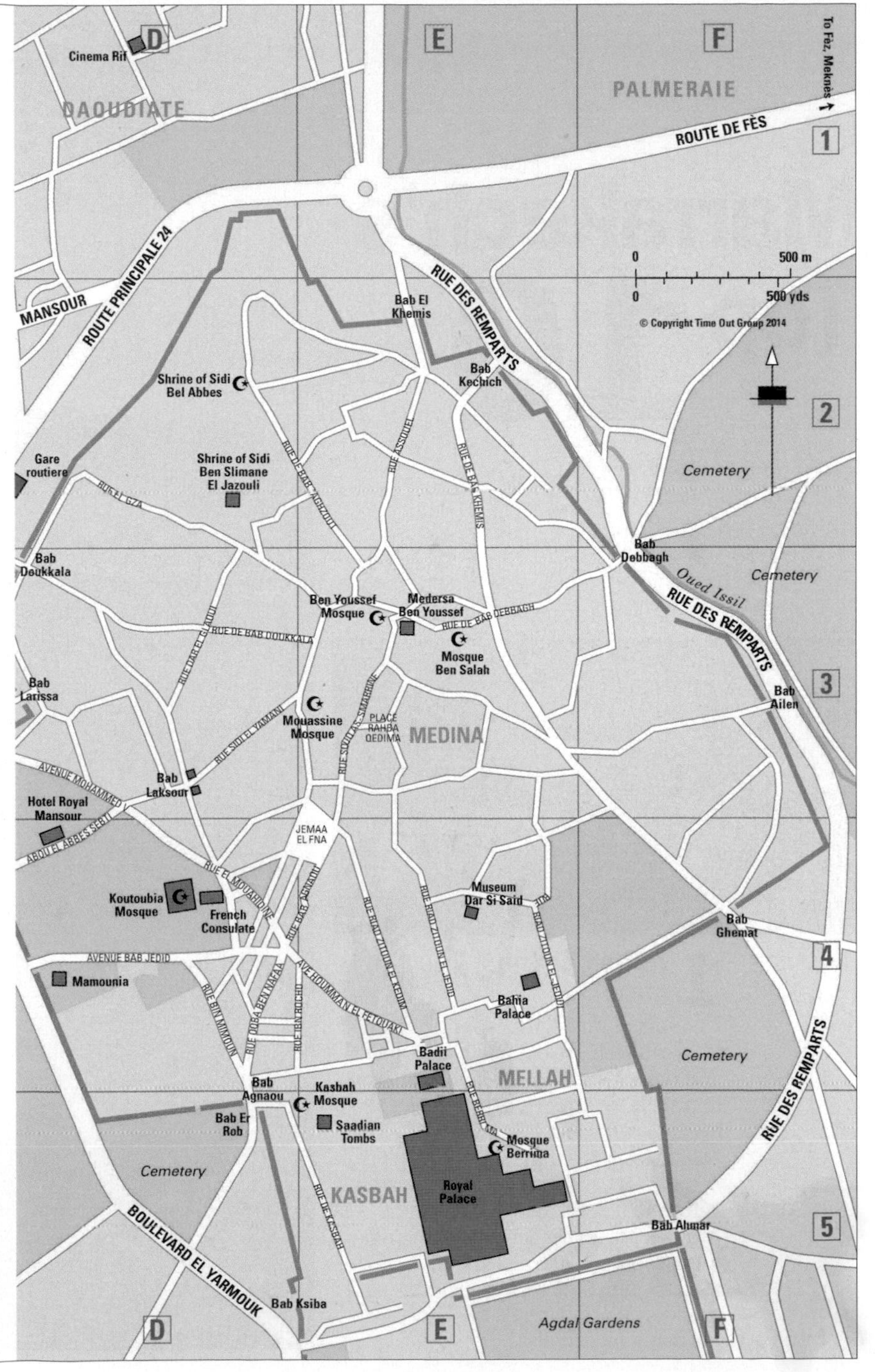
D
E
F
1
2
3
4
5
To Fèz, Meknès
Cinema Rif
DAOUDIATE
PALMERAIE
ROUTE DE FÈS
MANSOUR
ROUTE PRINCIPALE 24
RUE DES REMPARTS
Bab El Khemis
Bab Kechich
0
500 m
500 yds
© Copyright Time Out Group 2014
Shrine of Sidi Bel Abbes
Gare routiere
Shrine of Sidi Ben Slimane El Jazouli
RUE ASSOUEL
RUE DE BAB AGHZOUT
RUE DE BAB KHEMIS
RUE EL GZA
Cemetery
Bab Debbagh
Oued Issil
Bab Doukkala
Ben Youssef Mosque
Medersa Ben Youssef
RUE DE BAB DEBBAGH
RUE DE BAB DOUKKALA
RUE DAR EL GLAOUI
Mosque Ben Salah
Bab Larissa
Bab Ailen
Mouassine Mosque
PLACE RAHBA QEDIMA
MEDINA
RUE SIDI EL YAMANI
RUE SOUK AS SMARRINE
AVENUE MOHAMMED V
Bab Laksour
Hotel Royal Mansour
ABOU EL ABBES SEBTI
JEMAA EL FNA
RUE EL MOUAHIDINE
Koutoubia Mosque
French Consulate
RUE BAB AGNAOU
Museum Dar Si Said
RUE RIAD ZITOUN EL KEDIM
RUE RIAD ZITOUN EL JEDID
Bab Ghemat
AVENUE BAB JEDID
Mamounia
RUE BIN MIMOUN
RUE DOBA BEN NAFAA
RUE IBN ROCHD
AVE HOUMMAN EL FETOUAKI
Bahia Palace
Badii Palace
MELLAH
Bab Agnaou
Kasbah Mosque
Bab Er Rob
Saadian Tombs
RUE BERRIMA
Mosque Berrima
Cemetery
KASBAH
RUE DE KASBAH
Royal Palace
BOULEVARD EL YARMOUK
Bab Ahmar
Bab Ksiba
Agdal Gardens

Marrakech's Top 10

Souks, hammams and more: the very best the city has to offer.

1

1 Jemaa El Fna

(page 34)

The square that is the beating heart of Marrakech. By day, snake charmers and transvestite dancers add exoticism, and as the muezzin cranks up the evening call to prayer and a sunset pall falls on the square, the whole place becomes one big, chaotic entertainment venue. Henna artists, jugglers and hijabbed fortune tellers appear, joining the cacophony of competing musicians, all set against the backdrop of the smoky grills and trestle tables of the many food stalls.

2

2 La Mamounia scrubdown
(page 66)

Not everyone can afford to stay at La Mamounia hotel, but you can purchase a little bit of luxury for your souk-weary soul with a day pass at the spa. Descend into the subterranean chamber – past the extraordinary contemporary Murano lamps – and submit to a rigorous *gommage* in the hammam, then perhaps a massage. Post-kneading, relax in the sensually lit spa pool chamber – it was the hotel's Moroccan restaurant before its recent renovation – and then unfurl your limbs on a sunlounger and rest, cocktail in hand, by the huge garden pool.

3 The Souks
(page 46)

Saunter, survey and splurge – it's the only way to deal with the sheer quantity, the colours, the smells and the overall intoxicating exoticism of the souks. Forget the map and just follow your eyes, nose and ears. Haggling is de rigueur, but if you can't hack it, climb to the first floor of Souk Cherifia (*p64*) for gorgeous *prix fixe* designs by Moroccan and international designers.

4 Maison Arabe cooking class

(page 72)

The spices, the smells, those lentils, that salad, oh, and the tender lamb tagine, and fluffy couscous... not to mention the perfectly poured mint tea. Learning the skills of the Moroccan kitchen has never been easier – nor more enjoyable. Maison Arabe's state-of-the-art kitchen takes you through the steps needed to concoct your own classic Moroccan feast.

④

5 Majorelle Gardens

(page 90)

French painter Jacques Majorelle's flourishing homage to the plant world is a much sought-after colourful and shady retreat from the bustle of Marrakech's Medina. The lemon yellow and the striking cobalt blue (now named Majorelle blue), plus the palms, the soaring cacti and the multicoloured planters, seduce visitors in their thousands. Linger longer for the café, museum with Berber jewellery, and the cluster of shops and cafés on the garden's doorstep.

⑤

6 Ben Youssef Medersa

(page 52)

The Quranic school in the heart of the Medina is one of Marrakech's most beautiful buildings. An oblong ablutions pool in the centre of the courtyard reflects the exquisite decoration and symmetry of the surrounding arcades: bands of geometric *zelije* tiles are topped by Arabic calligraphy carved in stone. To appreciate its beauty and find time for contemplation, arrive well ahead of the tour groups, early in the morning.

⑥

7 Café Clock
(page 80)

Following in the footsteps of its Fès outpost, Café Clock has a refreshing, innovative cultural agenda. Along with the camel burgers and the coffee, Clock is reviving the art of storytelling, teaching visitors calligraphic script using bamboo pens, showcasing the music of the *gnawa*, and providing space for weekly jam sessions. It's also a cool space to hang out in – surrounded by contemporary photographic prints.

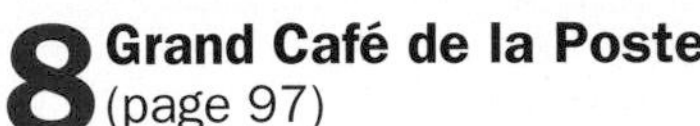

8 Grand Café de la Poste
(page 97)

Nowhere does luxe colonial quite as well as this restaurant-bar with its glamorous surroundings – it's the last word in French colonial chic. Order an aperitif at the alfresco tables on the wraparound terrace on the street, or head across the ground-floor salon, fringed with ferns in handsome planters, and up the lofty central staircase to relax into plush leather sofas and chairs.

9 Al Fassia
(page 95)

The idea with the classic Moroccan meal is not to rush. At the famous all-women run Al Fassia, you can settle into the comfortable space and feast like a king, at reasonable prices. One of the best things about Al Fassia is that you are treated to the star dishes of Moroccan cuisine but you're not obliged to eat your way through a set menu. Tuck into multiple plates of salad, slow-roasted shoulder of lamb and pigeon *b'stilla*.

10 Rahba Kedima
(page 48)

You don't see it all at first as your eyes are distracted by carpets, bottles, parasols and boxes of this and that. But look more closely, past the bunches of herbs, and you'll see them – wide-eyed live chameleons, towers of terrapins, caged birds of prey and the hanging, flapping skins of long-dead zebras. Welcome to the herbs and magic market at Rahba Kedima. Got an ache or a pain? The stallholders should be able to help.

Marrakech Today

The welcoming Red City.

So near and yet so exotic: one of Marrakech's attractions has always been that it's the Arabian Nights within easy travelling distance of Europe. Some would say it has become too easy. Budget airlines have noted Marrakech's popularity and now whisk holidaymakers to the Red City for peanuts. In 2013, more than two million tourists descended on a city of fewer than one million residents. And these numbers are set to grow, with projected figures of three and a half million visitors to the city by 2020. To accommodate them, the Moroccan government is aiming to increase total bed capacity in the city's hotels and guesthouses to 82,000 by 2020.

MMPVA.

THE QUESTION

The big question is whether Marrakech can absorb these kinds of numbers without compromising the unique qualities that attract visitors in the first place. Back in the 1960s, Gavin Maxwell wrote that 'Marrakesh has become perhaps the greatest tourist attraction of all North Africa, but the tourists, however great an impression Marrakesh makes upon them, make little impression on Marrakesh.' It's not clear that you could say the same today. While it is true that sensitive restoration means the Medina looks pretty much as it did when Maxwell was there, it is now home to hundreds of riad hotels. Back in 2006, the Moroccan government approved investment projects around the city worth two billion US dollars, mainly consisting of new five-star hotels and golf estates that will stretch water supplies to the limit. The area around the Palmeraie seems to be a permanent building site, and 100 hectares or so of land on the southern outskirts of town have been set aside as an 'international hotel zone.' The long-term effects of this on the city remain to be seen, but there is no doubt that full occupancy of the new facilities would skew the local–tourist balance still further.

LESS HASSLE

One change welcomed by all visitors is the drastic reduction of hassle and hustle. Mindful that tourists were being put off by the over-attention that was an unavoidable part of any visit to Marrakech in the past, the government formed the *brigade touristique*,

a tourist police force whose officers patrol the Medina watching over foreigners. They'll step in if they spot hassle and haul away persistent nuisances. The result is a much calmer experience. However, this is not to say that Marrakech has become a little Switzerland: it's still hard to walk from one corner of Jemaa El Fna to another without someone trying to persuade you that a photograph of you with a barbary ape on your shoulder is just what you've always wanted.

LOCAL ATTITUDES AND VISITORS

Local attitudes to the tourist influx vary. European riad and home-owners have often found locals keen to sell Medina property at inflated prices, and there is no doubt that foreign money has restored many old buildings that were on the verge of disintegration. In addition, the riad industry has done much to provide work for Marrakech's artisans, and has stimulated a revival of traditional crafts and skills. But not everyone is happy. The more traditionally minded, and particularly the Islamists, find the presence of the visitors alarming. Shortly after the Islamist Justice and Development Party (PJD), came to power in 2011, its newly elected Justice Minister took a cursory look at the nightlife, revelry and general party atmosphere of Marrakech and promptly branded it a 'city of sin'. The Tourism Ministry was alarmed and hastily put out press releases to limit the damage saying talk of alcohol bans and so on were premature.

For all the recent upheaval that increased visitor numbers have brought, it is important to remember that tourism is nothing new in Marrakech. Unlike the more conservative cities of Rabat and Fes, Marrakech has a tradition of welcoming strangers. In the days of camel caravans, the city was a gateway to the south. In the main square, Jemaa El Fna, peasants from the Atlas, Souss and Draa would mix with Senegalese traders and Tuaregs. And before the likes of Jude Law, Sienna Miller or Hugh Grant set foot on Moroccan soil, far more illustrious visitors were drawn to the city, among them Flaubert, Matisse, Orwell and Churchill. In the 1960s Marrakech was a major stop-off on the hippie trail – as exemplified in Crosby, Stills and Nash's 'Marrakesh Express'. Paul McCartney and John Lennon were seen on John Paul Getty Jr's rooftop and Cecil Beaton took snaps of Mick and Keith lounging by the pool at the Hotel Es Saadi. Paul Bowles was a frequent visitor, on one occasion turning up with Allen Ginsberg in tow. And the period saw its own property gold rush too.

THE FUTURE

The recession in Europe undoubtedly had an impact on tourism in Marrakech and many riads went out of business. (Some might argue that this is no bad thing as there had been too many in the first place.) And the 2011 bombing of the Argana Café in Jemaa El Fna (*see p35*), suspected to be the work of militant Islamists, didn't help either. But despite these setbacks, Marrakech's economy remains heavily reliant on tourism and will become more so. Today, the city is a centre for diverse holiday activities, whether it's wandering, shopping, dancing, drinking, gambling, spa treatments, eating in first-class restaurants or golfing. In addition the town is a base for trekking, skiing and more. You can even get married here. The city has always drawn outsiders. Perhaps those increased tourist numbers will merely add to the mix. We certainly hope that Marrakech doesn't become a holiday theme park, robbed of the real local life that makes it unique.

NEW DEVELOPMENTS

In 2014 King Mohammed VI announced another plan for the development of Marrakech, at a cost of around £460 million. The four-year plan – called 'Marrakech city of permanent renewal' – is intended to breathe new life into the city and reinforce its status as a magnet for tourists. It will include a music academy and a new museum of folklore, as well as schools, hospitals, swimming pools and sports centres. But aside from this plan, perhaps the most exciting and ambitious development will be the Marrakech Museum for Photography and Visual Art (MMPVA, *see p104*), currently in temporary quarters in the Badii Palace until its own building is completed.

The big question, however, is how these efforts will trickle down in terms of helping solve ever-present problems of poverty and unemployment. So far, critics argue, developments have done little or nothing to improve the wealth gap or social mobility.

Nevertheless, beyond these big official projects there is a sense that Marrakech, after a few years in the doldrums because of the world economic downtown, is on the move again. Other museums have opened, a café and cultural centre is reviving traditions in the Kasbah (Café Clock, *see p80*), and new cafés and restaurants have sprung up in the medina in recent years, giving a sense that the city really is in a state of permanent renewal, always evolving, taking on new influences with exciting, youthful and generally cool places to hang out that would have been the envy of the Stones and the Gettys.

Marrakech is still attracting the rich and famous. New hotels, such as the Four Seasons and the unspeakably expensive Royal Mansour, are attracting some of the world's richest visitors. As a 2012 article in the *New York Post* put it, 'If you are wondering where the beautiful people have gone, look no further. They are here.'

Itineraries

Plot your perfect trip to Marrakech with our step-by-step planners.

Day 1

9AM If you're staying in the Medina you'll already have been woken by the early call to prayer, but, with luck, you'll have fallen asleep again. If you're staying in a riad, feast on the standard full breakfast of coffee, juice and Moroccan *msemen* pancakes and honey before heading out to the **Ben Youssef Medersa** (*see p53*). To really appreciate this serene Quranic school, arrive ahead of the tour groups. From here, head east to the **Maison de la Photographie** (*see p53*) to view the black-and-white collection before having coffee on the gallery's roof terrace (*see p55*).

11AM Stroll south from here through the colourful souks and down **rue Semarine** (*see p48*) before emerging into the **Rahba Kedima** (*see p48*), the magic and herb market, where stacks of aromatic plants, dried chameleons and various other exotic flora and fauna are piled up on chaotic stalls.

NOON After ducking into **Souk Laghzel** (*see p48*), the women's market, head to

Clockwise from top left: **Maison de la Photographie, rue Semarine, Jemaa El Fna, Dar Cherifa**.

desert-hued **Nomad** (*see p55*) for lunch with a view. Before leaving this side of the souks, it's worth going south a few alleys to see the Moroccan pop art of Hassan Hajjij at his **Riad Yima** (*see p55*). Walking further south towards Jemaa El Fna, cut through place Bab Fteuh, just north of the square, and then north again through the less cramped rue Mouassine (*see p59*) to experience the more upmarket side of souk shopping. Pop into café and cultural centre **Dar Cherifa** (*see p60*) before delving behind the Mouassine mosque and fountain to glimpse the exquisite interior decor of the **Douiria Mouassine** (*see p60*), the restored guest reception areas of a Medina house. From here, head further north to the multistorey **Souk Cherifia** (*see p64),* home to upmarket goods with fixed prices, before a cooling lemonade and lunch in the luscious courtyard garden of nearby **Le Jardin** (*see p61*).

5PM Drop off your purchases and sip a refreshing mint tea in the cool confines of your riad before heading out to **Jemaa El Fna** (*see p34*) to marvel at the whirl of human and animal life, entertainment and commerce that is Marrakech's world-famous central square. As night falls, the daytime collection of juice sellers, snake charmers, barbary apes and transvestite dancers gives way to a cacophony of food stalls and musicians. Grab a ringside stool at one of the cafés around the square as the evening call to prayer from the Koutoubia Mosque echoes around the square. Later, take a place at a trestle table and enjoy dinner Jemaa El Fna-style (*see p40*).

Day 2

10AM Start your day in **Jemaa El Fna** (*see p34*) and walk south down rue des Banques, which leads into rue Riad Zitoun El-Jedid, a road crammed with shops and trinket stalls. A short detour leads you to the madcap collection of desert and Berber curios at **Maison Tiskiwin** (*see p83*).

NOON Back on the main road south, head under the arch into the **Bab Es Salam Market** (*see p62*) for a reviving coffee at **Caffe Internazionale** (*see p81*), before emerging and heading to the **Bahia Palace** (*see p82*) to admire the outstanding craftsmanship. Pass through the vast walls of the ruined **Badii Palace** (*see p101*) to take in the photography exhibition at the temporary home of the Marrakech Museum of Photography & Visual Arts, before heading into the heart of the old Jewish area, the Mellah. Grab an ice-cream from Café Kasbah near the **Saadian Tombs** (*see p78*) or buy a couple of 1dh macaroons from a street seller to keep you going for your visit to the tombs. Then it's time for lunch at the cultural hotspot **Café Clock** (*see p80*).

2PM

2PM Book into the Mellah's **Les Bains de Marrakech** (*see p66*) for a scrubdown in the hammam followed by a reinvigorating massage, or opt for a cooking class at Café Clock. Alternatively, head to the Ville Nouvelle for a stroll around the glorious **Majorelle Gardens** (*see p90*).

7PM Follow an early evening drink watching the storks at the Mellah's **Kosybar** (*see p80*) with a quick taxi trip to Guéliz for a sunset cocktail at the **O'Sky Bar** (*see p98*), with its commanding views down avenue Mohammed V. After dinner at one of Guéliz's many restaurants, join the crowds on the rooftop terrace at hip **Kechmara** (*see p97*), tuck into the corner bar of **Jack is Back** (*see p97*), or sink into an all-encompassing

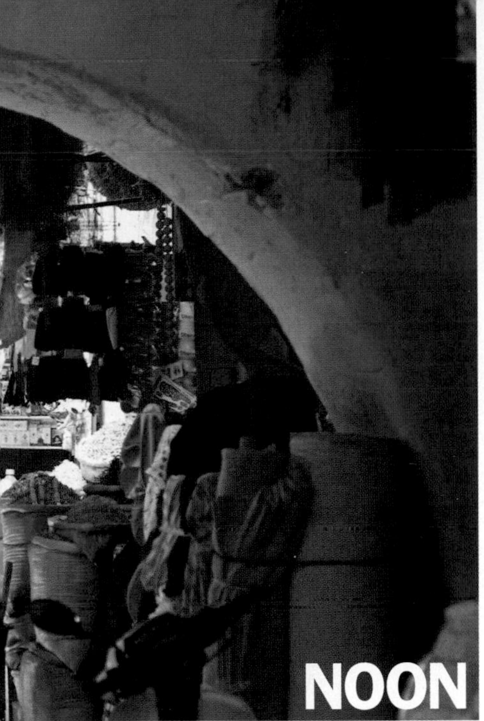

leather chair in the elegant salon of the **Grand Café de la Poste** (*see p97*). Packed your party shoes? Then dance into the night at **Silver at Jhad Madal** (*see p120*) or **Le Comptoir Darna** (*see p104*).

Clockwise from top left: **Bab Es Salam Market, Kosybar, Café Clock**.

LIFE LESSONS

Learn a new skill while on holiday.

Marrakech's popularity as a destination to learn a new skill or craft is soaring. Turn your lens on the souks with the help of a professional snapper, belly dance with a Hollywood star in the making, or add to your culinary talents with new cooking holidays.

Mosaic Palais Aziza (*see p223*) has teamed up with Moroccan-based pro photographer Terry Munson (www.terrymunsonphoto.com) to take keen snappers out into the Medina. The course, Marrakech through a Lens, costs from €745 a head including three nights' accommodation, airport transfers, one dinner and one hammam visit, but excluding international flights. **Cazenove+loyd** (www.cazloyd.com) offers a six-night photographic journey to Morocco with Chris Coe (www.chriscoe.com), photographer and founder of the Travel Photographer of the Year award, taking in Marrakech and Berber villages in the nearby Atlas Mountains. The package is priced from £2,147 per person (based on two sharing), fully inclusive and including private transfers, one-on-one tuition and all entrance fees; note that international flights are excluded.

If you fancy shimmying your way through a week's belly dancing, then there's a holiday for you. It's taught by UK expert Charlotte Desorgher (www.charlottedesorgher.com) in conjunction with **Club Dance Holidays** (www.clubdanceholidays.co.uk) in a riad just outside Marrakech.

And culinary stardom is within reach with MasterChef Travel from **Cox & King**, which takes in the souks of the Red City with Keri Moss, joint winner of *MasterChef: The Professionals* 2012. Participants explore markets, learn to cook and sample the local dining scene. Prices start from £1,195 per person including flights, accommodation and most meals. And, for drop-in cookery classes, *see p72* **Stir It Up**.

Diary

Vibrant celebrations of music, art and culture.

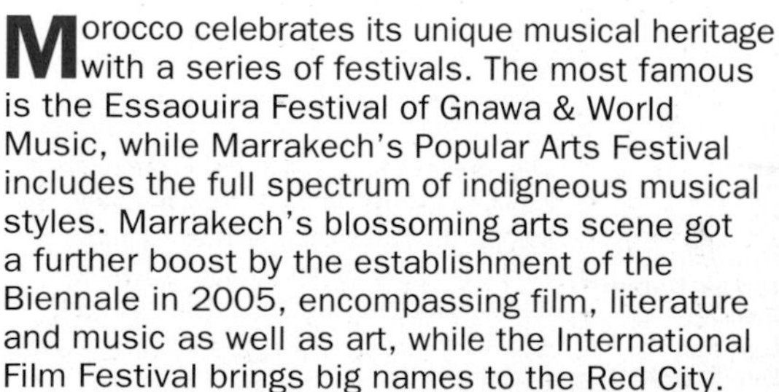

Morocco celebrates its unique musical heritage with a series of festivals. The most famous is the Essaouira Festival of Gnawa & World Music, while Marrakech's Popular Arts Festival includes the full spectrum of indigneous musical styles. Marrakech's blossoming arts scene got a further boost by the establishment of the Biennale in 2005, encompassing film, literature and music as well as art, while the International Film Festival brings big names to the Red City.

International Nomad Festival.

Spring

Marrakech Marathon

0524 31 35 72, www.marathon-marrakech.com/presa.php. **Date** late Jan.

January sees perfect running weather in Marrakech. Pull on your trainers and run with 6,000 others around the outside of the city's ancient ramparts. The full marathon (42km) and the half-marathon (21km) start within 45 minutes of each other. There's also a children's race.

Marrakech Biennale

2 Derb Moulay Abdallah Ben Hezzian, Bab el-Ksour, Medina (www.marrakechbiennale.org). **Tickets** vary. **Date** Feb-Mar.

The fifth edition of the Marrakech Biennale was held to much acclaim in 2014, in venues and public spaces across the city. *See p24*.

International Nomad Festival

M'Hamid El-Ghizlane (0662 10 47 93, http://nomadsfestival.wordpress.com). **Date** Mar.

Part country fair, part music festival, this annual gathering in the sands at M'Hamid El-Ghizlane hosts music sessions, sand hockey, camel races and exhibits of the region's produce – dates, roses, argan oil and so on.

Essaouira Festival of Gnawa & World Music.

Summer

Essaouira Festival of Gnawa & World Music

Essaouira (0522 27 26 03, www.festival-gnaoua.net). **Date** June.

Every June, around 200,000 people rock up to Essaouira for this festival – four days and nights of a carnival-like atmosphere. *See also p141*.

Marrakech Popular Arts Festival

Theatre Royal, Avenue Mohammed VI, Hivernage (0524 43 201 21, www.marrakechfestival.com). **Date** July.

MARRAKECH BIENNALE

Since it was founded in 2005 (2014 was the fifth edition), the Biennale, founded by Vanessa Branson, has become an important event, covering not just art, but film, literature and music too. It attracts visitors from all over the world, as well as an increasingly high-profile roster of exhibitors. But it's also been hugely influential in putting Moroccan artists on the map, and generating a buzz around Moroccan culture generally, including a recent surge in interest in photography and film. The Biennale played an important part in ensuring the success of the Museum of Visual Arts and Photography (*see p101*), a project by David Chipperfield Architects slated to open in 2016.

It's a sea change for a country that, until Branson appeared on the scene, had only a marginal contemporary art scene. Conservative elements felt that the only 'true' art nearly always came in painted form, but the remit of the Biennale is to promote dialogue between all the disciplines, as an expression of artists' responses to the Red City and its environs. The 2014 theme, 'Where are we now', was a showcase of the emerging arts scene in Morocco, staged in spaces as diverse as the Jemaa El Fna, the Badii Palace and the Royal Opera House and Theatre.

One of the attractions of the festival is the unique opportunity to get a glimpse of some of the city's hidden treasures, including a wealth of small-scale *dars* and riads scattered through the medina – among them Branson's own guesthouse, El-Fenn (*see p207)*, and the arts and culture residence Le 18 (www.facebook.com/dardixhuit, *see also p219*, Dar 18) set up by Laila Hida. What's more, the Biennale has paved the way for year-round activity at numerous galleries and at several major hotels, such as the Four Seasons and Sofitel. It's rare you'll show up in Marrakech and find nothing going on.

Pitching acclaimed international and national names together with young, up-and-coming talent makes for a highly stimulating environment. Rarely do you get to see an art movement blossoming before your very eyes, and that makes the Marrakech Biennale so very exciting.

For listings, *see p23*.

Date festival.

A week-long festival featuring dance troupes and bands, and the largest music festival in Marrakech. Events are staged at the Theatre Royal and at the Badii Palace and most offer free admission. Different regional folk styles are represented including *ahouache*, *issawa*, *hamadcha*, *gnawa*, *ahidous*, Arabo-Andalous and Marrakech's own percussive *deqqa*. *See also p121.*

Moussem of Setti Fatma

Date Aug.

A well-attended four-day *moussem*, an event that's both a religious celebration and a sociable fair. It's held at Setti Fatma, *see p156.*

Autumn

Date festival

Erfoud. **Date** Oct (varies according to the harvest).

As soon as the annual harvest comes around, the date festival commences. Music and dance accompany the tasting of the region's palm dates. *See p168.*

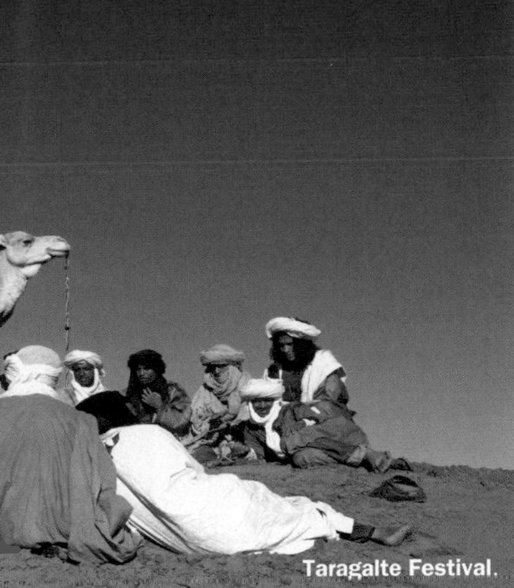
Taragalte Festival.

Festival des Andalousies Atlantiqes
Information: Association Essaouira Mogador, 10 rue du Caire 'Dar Souiri', Essaouira (0524 47 52 68, www.facebook.com/FestivalDesAndalousiesAtlantiques). **Tickets** free. **Date** late Oct-early Nov.
A festival of Arabo-Andalucian, Sephardic and flamenco music held in Essaouira amid a host of workshops and debates.

Winter

Taragalte Festival
Information: Association Zaila, Centre M'Hamid El-Ghizlane (0524 88 79 08, http://www.taragalte.org). **Date** Nov.
A desert festival that combines Saharwi and world music with films, workshops and exhibitions on the sands at M'hamid, *see p175*. There's camel racing, star gazing, and a focus on sustainable eco-practices, sustainable tourism, and cross-cultural programmes.

Marrakech International Film Festival
Various venues (0524 43 24 93, http://en.festivalmarrakech.info). **Date** Dec.
A multifaceted event with a global remit. Under the chairmanship of Prince Moulay Rachid, the festival showcases dozens of films and attracts star names and media attention. Francis Ford Coppola, Martin Scorsese, Oliver Stone, Sharon Stone, Catherine Deneuve, Juliette Binoche and Bollywood actor Shahrukh Khan have all graced its red carpets. Ninc days of screenings, competitions and lavish parties lure a global audience. Much of the excitement comes from the festival's screening venues, which include the Jemaa El Fna. Tickets are available for almost all films on a first-come-first-served basis from the cinema box offices.

HOLIDAYS

ISLAMIC HOLIDAYS

Of all the Islamic holidays, **Ramadan** is the most significant and the one that has the greatest impact on the visitor. This is the Muslim month of fasting. Many Moroccans abstain from food, drink and cigarettes between sunrise and sunset. Many cafés and restaurants will close during the day. It's also bad form to flaunt your non-participation by smoking or eating in the street. Ramadan nights are some of the busiest of the year as, come sundown, eateries are packed with large groups communally breaking their fast, a meal known as *iftar*.

The end of Ramadan is marked by the two-day feast of **Eid Al-Fitr** ('the small feast'). A few months later the feast of **Eid Al-Adha** ('the festival of sacrifice') commemorates Abraham's sacrifice of a ram instead of his son. Every family that can afford to slaughters a sheep.

Islamic religious holidays are based on a lunar calendar, approximately 11 days shorter than the Gregorian (western) calendar. This means that Islamic holidays shift forward by 11 days each year.

Note, these dates are approximate as the exact start of the celebrations depends on the sighting of the full moon.

	2015	**2016**
Ramadan	18 June	7 June
Eid al-Fitr	17 July	7 July
Eid al-Adha	23 Sept	13 Sept

PUBLIC HOLIDAYS

Morocco's six secular holidays see banks, offices and civil service institutions close, but many shops stay open and public transport runs as usual. The Feast of the Throne commemorates the present king's accession; Day of the Green March commemorates the retaking of Spanish-held Saharan territories.

New Year's Day .... 1 January
Labour Day
(Fête du Travail)............................. 1 May
Feast of the Throne
(Fête du Trône).............................. 30 July
Allegiance Day......................... 14 August
Day of the Green March
(Marche Verte)....................... 6 November
Independence Day .... 18 November

Marrakech's Best

Our hand-picked highlights.

Bahia Palace.

Sightseeing

ARCHITECTURE

Ben Youssef Medersa p53
Gaze at the *zelije* and plasterwork artistry of this sublime Quranic school.

Koutoubia mosque p42
The decorative brickwork of Marrakech's principal mosque towers over the red city.

Bahia Palace p82
Showcasing the skilled work of master craftsmen with painted wood, *zelije* tiling and intricate carved plasterwork.

Saadian tombs p78
Marble calm amid exquisite sculpted plasterwork.

Maison Tiskiwin p83
A house of curios stuffed with African masks, Berber tents, statues and jewels.

Slat Laazama Synagogue p82
The beautiful blue hues of the Mellah's only working synagogue.

Bab Agnaou p76
A perfectly symmetrical 12th-century stone gate etched in Islamic motifs.

VIEWS

Café de France/ Café Glacier p35
Peer high over the circus and the food stalls of Jemaa El Fna.

Fellah Hotel.

O'Sky Bar p98
Panoramic views over Marrakech's Ville Nouvelle to the snow-capped Atlas Mountains.

Nomad p55
The perfect elevated spot to telescope in on the exchanges in the 'magic' market.

Kosybar p80
Nesting storks on the Badii Palace walls can be spied from the top terraces of this favourite sundowner spot.

ART & CULTURE

MMPVA p101
The temporary home of avant-garde photography inside the Badii Palace.

Riad Yima p55
Eye-popping Moroccan pop art in the souks.

Musée de Palmeraie p107
A one-stop gallery of contemporary Moroccan art in a tranquil Palmeraie garden.

Le 18 p93
Performance art and cultural pop-ups amid the pillows.

Café Clock p80
Storytelling, calligraphy, and jam sessions, in one cool Mellah venue.

Masion de la Photographie p53
A photographic window into an historic Moroccan world.

Fellah Hotel p226
Pop-up events and artists' residencies at this hip out-of-town hotel.

OUTDOORS

Majorelle Gardens p90
Striking cactuses, brilliant blue walls, and Berber jewellery in this gorgeous garden rescued by Yves Saint Laurent.

Mamounia Gardens p45
Stroll the manicured walled gardens of this iconic luxury hotel.

Cyber Park Arset Moulay Abdessalam p86
A shady respite from the African sun, close to Jemaa El Fna.

CHILDREN

Kawkab Jeux p113
Ville Nouvelle playtime – and a café for parents.

Caleche rides p113
A horse-drawn carriage ride through the streets of the Red City.

Jemaa El Fna p34
Snake charmers, musicians and water carriers will enchant young ones.

Eating & drinking

Gastro MK p35
Modern Moroccan done to perfection.

Tiznit p41
No-frills eaterie cooking up superlative rabbit tagine.

Tobsil p41
A curated culinary Moroccan blowout.

Le Jardin p61
An emerald-green tiled oasis serving light dishes among the orange trees and banana fronds.

Al Fassia p95
Moroccan flagship restaurant run by female staff.

Le Loft p96
French bistro cool with a great-value lunch deal.

Le Verre Canaille p96
Much talked about chic French bistro.

Café Clock p80
Home of the legendary camel burger.

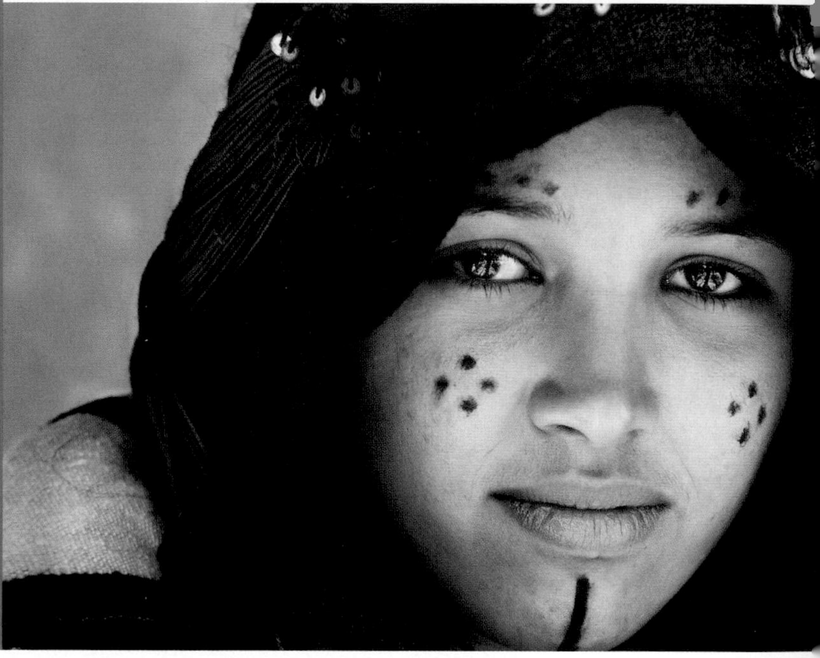

Palais Namaskar p108
Ultra-hip poolside French-Moroccan fusion.

DRINKING & NIGHTLIFE

Djellabar p97
Cocktails in a converted wedding room with pop art on the walls.

Jack is Back p97
Guéliz restaurant with an insanely popular bar tucked into a corner.

Grand Café de la Poste p97
Decadent French-colonial atmosphere in the Ville Nouvelle.

Kechmara p97
Hipster hotspot in Guéliz.

Silver at Jad Mahal p120
A dancing favourite with partygoers, with regular DJ sets.

Comptoir Darna p104
Fun-fuelled hangout for scenesters in the Ville Nouvelle.

Souk Cherifia.

Shopping

The Souks p46
From leather to lights, dates to 'diamonds', gold filigree to iron and brass: the world's headiest shopping experience.

Bazaar du Sud p56
Explore the world of carpets with the pros.

Rahal Herbes p59
Herbal remedies amid chameleons in cages and magic stalls.

Souk Cherifia p64
Fixed-price boutique stores in the heart of the souks.

Mustapha Blaoui p73
An Aladdin's warehouse of everything you could possibly want.

33 Rue Majorelle p98
Bright concept store with beautifully crafted must-have creations.

Dinanderie/Yahaya Creations p82/p104
Illumination heaven with the city's master lightmen.

Bab Es Salam Market p62
Spices and soaps at the Jewish market.

Djellabar.

Arts

Marrakech Biennale p23
A month-long festival and the city's best showcase for contemporary art.

Marrakech International Film Festival p25
A nine-day celebration of celluloid tales, attracting Hollywood stars and the glitterati.

Explore

Jemaa El Fna & Around

The soul of Marrakech lies in the amorphous form of Jemaa El Fna, market place and forum to the city almost since its foundation. Uncontained, disorderly, untainted by grandeur or pomp, untameable by council or committee, Jemaa El Fna is nothing less than bedlam. It's an urban clearing, as irregular in shape as an accident of nature, and thronged day and night with a carnival of local life – totally at odds with its name, which roughly translates as 'Assembly of the Dead'. Two hundred metres to the west, the square, towering minaret of the Koutoubia Mosque is the city's pre-eminent landmark and most recognisable icon. It is not actually very high (77 metres, 252 feet), but thanks to topography and a local ordinance that forbids other Medina buildings to rise above the height of a palm tree, it towers majestically over its surroundings.

Mamounia Gardens.

Don't Miss

1 **Jemaa El Fna** The must-see square (p34).

2 **Koutoubia minaret** Skyline symbol (p42).

3 **Mamounia Gardens** Take tea in the gardens of this iconic hotel (p45).

4 **Tiznit** No-frills tagine restaurant (p41).

5 **Café de France** Sip a sundowner at this historic café (*p35*).

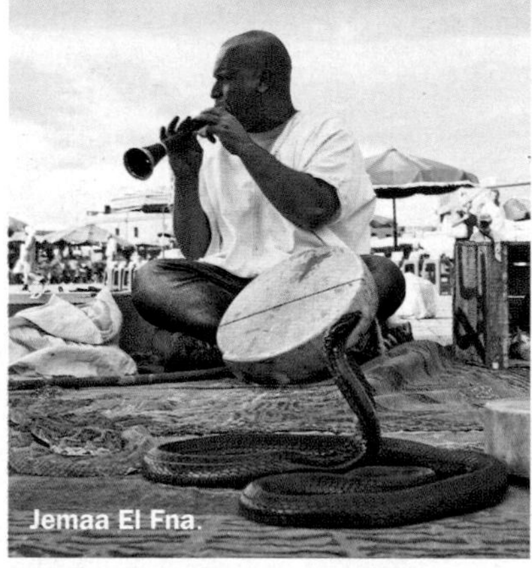

Jemaa El Fna.

EXPLORE

JEMAA EL FNA & AROUND

The square is as old as Marrakech itself. It was laid out as a parade ground by the Almoravids in front of their royal fortress (Dar El-Hajar). When the succeeding Almohads built a new palace to the south, the open ground passed to the public and became what it remains today – a place for gathering, trading, entertainment and even the occasional riot. The name (pronounced with its consonants tumbling into each other to come out something like 'jemaf'na') refers to its former role as a venue for executions, with the decapitated heads put up on spikes for public display.

In more recent times, during the 1970s, the municipality attempted to impose order with a scheme to turn it into a car park. This was opposed and defeated. Since then, thanks in part to the lobbying efforts of Spanish writer Juan Goytisolo (who has lived just off the square since the late 1970s), Jemaa El Fna has been recognised by UNESCO as part of mankind's cultural heritage and its preservation is secured.

A DAY IN THE LIFE

During the early part of the day the square is relatively quiet. The orange-laden carts of the juice-sellers line the perimeter, wagon-train fashion, but otherwise there's only a scattering of figures, seated on boxes or rugs, shaded under large shabby umbrellas. The snake-charmers are early starters with their black, rubbery reptiles laid out in front or sheltered under large drums. For a few dirhams visitors can have a photograph taken with a large snake draped over their shoulders; for a few more dirhams they can have it removed. Gaudily clad water-sellers wander around offering to pose for dirhams. Other figures may be dentists (teeth pulled on the spot), scribes (letters written to order), herbalists (good for whatever ails you) or beggars. Overlooking all, the prime morning spot for unhurried businessmen and traders is the patio of the landmark **Café de France** (*see p35*), on the square for the last 50 years.

The action tends to wilt beneath the heat of the afternoon sun, when snake-charmers, dancers and acrobats can barely manage to stir themselves for camera-carrying tourists. It's not until dusk that things really kick off.

As the light fades, ranks of makeshift kitchens set up with tables, benches and hissing flames, constituting one great open-air restaurant where adventurous eaters can snack on anything from snails to sheep's heads (*see p40* **Square Meals**).

Beside the avenues of food stalls, the rest of the square takes on the air of a circus. Visiting Berber farmers from the surrounding plains and villages join Medina locals in crowding around the assorted performers. These typically include troupes of cartoon-costumed acrobats, musicians and their prowling transvestite dancers, fortune tellers, henna artists, magicians, and boxing bouts between underage boys who can hardly lift their hands in the heavy leather gloves. The tourists and visitors who provided the raison d'être for the afternoon entertainers are now less dominant in this more surreal evening scene. Approaching midnight the food stalls begin to pack up, the performers wind down, and the crowds thin. Only the musicians remain, attended by wild-eyed devotees giddy on repetitive rhythms, helped along by hash. At the same time, the place becomes one great gay cruising ground, busy with tight-shirted, tight-trousered teens, sharp and cynical beyond their years.

SPECTATING THE SQUARE

The best place to be at any time of the day is in among it all (watch your wallet and bags), but several of the peripheral cafés and restaurants have upper terraces with fine ringside seating, among them the **Café de France** and **Argana** (for both, *see below*) and – with the best view of the lot – the Café Glacier above the Hotel CTM. Day or night, whether you choose stealthy observation from the terraces or a headlong plunge into the melée, Jemaa El Fna always remains somewhat elusive. 'All the guidebooks lie', writes Juan Goytisolo. 'There's no way of getting a firm grasp on it.'

Restaurants & cafés

Argana

Jemaa El Fna (0524 44 53 50). **Open** 5am-11pm daily. **Map** p35 C2 ❶ **Café**

Something of a Marrakech icon, even more so after a bomb detonated here in 2011, killing 17, this café on the edge of Jemaa El Fna was a perennial favourite, its terrace providing ringside seats on the action in the square below. At the time of writing, repairs were nearly completed and it was set to reopen. Stairs at the back of the ground-floor café lead up to two floors of terrace serving three-course set menus or à la carte salads, tagines and brochettes, but many just call in for an ice-cream and some people-watching.

Café de France

Jemaa El Fna (no phone). **Open** 6am-11pm daily. **No credit cards. Map** p35 D2 ❷ **Café**

The most famous of Marrakech cafés boasts a prime location and terrace fronting right on the main square. No one knows exactly how old the place is, but it crops up in Peter Mayne's *A Year in Marrakesh*, written in the early 1950s and it's a classic meeting point for locals from first light to sundown, with tourists stopping in for a breather and a strong shot of *café noir* (espresso Arabica) or *nouss nouss* (half espresso, half steamed milk) throughout the day. Expect surly service.

★ Gastro MK

14 derb Sebaai, Bab Laksour (0524 37 61 73, www.maisonmk.com). **Open** 7.30-10.30pm Mon, Tue, Thur-Sun. **Set menu** 650dh. **Alcohol served. Map** p35 B1 ❸ **Modern Moroccan**

The set-menu-only supper club at funky boutique hotel Maison K is a breath of fresh air on the Marrakech dining scene and one of the first to embrace a modern Moroccan cuisine. Chef Omar

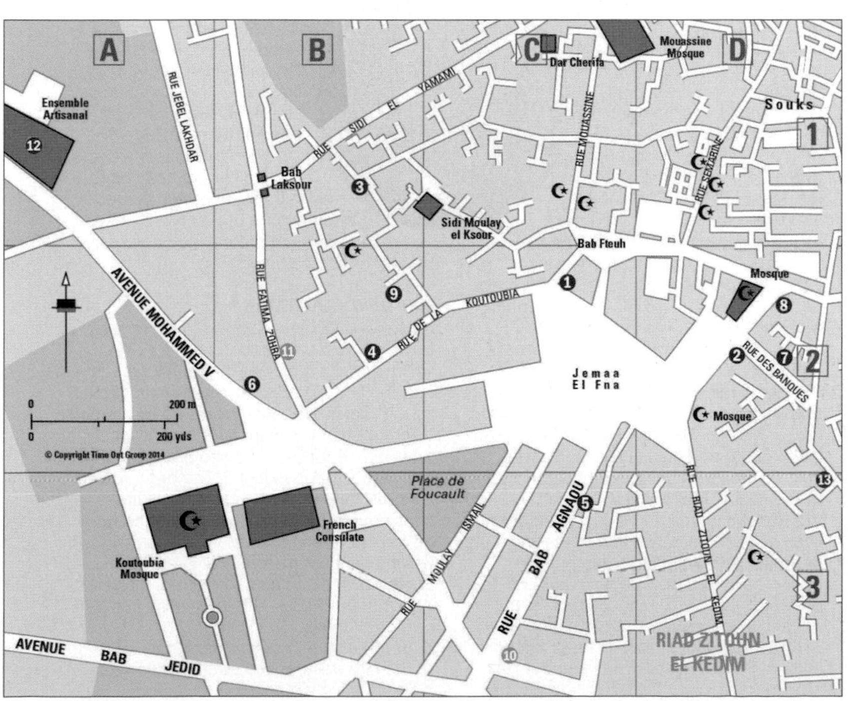

EXPLORING MARRAKECH

Get lost to find the real city.

If you want to, you can take a London-style open-top bus for a whirlwind tour of Marrakech's sights. But you'll be missing the point: 'sights' per se are not what this city is all about. For a start, conventional sights are limited and some are, frankly, disappointing. But more than that, it's just the wrong way to approach the Red City. Losing yourself is the best thing you can do here. Wander aimlessly. Explore. To sample the atmosphere of Marrakech, amble slowly down its alleyways, immerse yourself in its colours and sounds, step on some donkey droppings and smell everything from ginger and cinnamon to open drains.

THE MEDINA

The area in which to idle is the Medina (Arabic for the 'city'), the district enclosed by the old walls. This is where you will spend most of your walking hours. The city's few monuments are here, typically hidden in warrenous quarters and down dead-end, nameless alleys. There's little logic in the layout but navigation is aided by two landmarks: the minaret of the **Koutoubia Mosque**, helpfully flagging the location of the adjacent central square, the **Jemaa El Fna**. Also known simply as 'la place', it is the place you always seem to end up – the sink-hole around which Marrakech swirls.

The open space of the main square also neatly divides the Medina into two zones: north of Jemaa El Fna is commercial, with a fibrous network of souks (bazaars), and beyond them a grouping of three of the city's monuments: the **Musée de Marrakech** (*see p55*), **Koubba El-Badiyin** (*see p53*) and **Ben Youssef Medersa** (see p53). South of Jemaa El Fna is imperial, and split across two distinct neighbourhoods: the intriguing **Mellah** (Jewish Quarter) and the **Kasbah**, home to the vast **Badii Palace** (*see p78*), temporary home of the **Museum of Visual Arts and Photography** that is due to open near the Menara Gardens (*see p104*) in 2016, and location of the melancholic **Saadian Tombs** (*see p78*).

Away from tourist paths, alleys become even more shambolic. Stray into the far northern or eastern parts of the Medina to see a backstage world of Marrakech *au naturel*. Once landed in the thick of it, it helps – sort of – to remember local street etiquette: pedestrians stick to the right to make room for scooters (something of a menace and meant to be banned), pushbikes and donkeys.

THE CITY WALLS

Around 1126, in the face of threat from the aggressive Almohads, Almoravid Sultan Ali Ben Youssef encircled Marrakech with walls. He erected a circuit of ten kilometres (six miles) of ten-metre (30-foot) walls defended by 200 towers and punctuated by 20 gates. Despite extensions and repairs, the current walls follow roughly the same lines as the originals.

The walls are built of reddish pisé (dried mud mixed with lime). Although beautiful at times – especially when glowing pink under a setting sun – they are fairly featureless. A walk around the whole circuit is a slog, but a whirl in a horse-drawn calèche is fun. Carriages wait on the north side of place de Foucault. A complete circuit, heading north up avenue Mohammed V and right out of Bab Nkob, takes about an hour; state-fixed prices are posted on the carriages.

BEYOND THE MEDINA

North-west of the old walls is the 'new city', a French colonial creation of the 1930s, which goes by the name of **Guéliz** (*see pp86-104*). Old city and new are connected by the broad, tree-lined **avenue Mohammed V** (pronounced 'M'hammed Sanc'), which was named for the king who presided over Morocco's independence. The area is now a vibrant hub of modern Marrakchi life, criss-crossed by leafy streets like the rue de la Liberté and the rue Vieux Marrakchi, which crackle with life spilling out of chic European-style cafés and bistros, smart designer boutiques and increasing numbers of art galleries.

South of Guéliz and immediately west of the city walls, is the swanky **Hivernage**

Djellabar.

(*see pp104-107*) quarter, overflowing with smart villas, expensive restaurants and unimaginably luxurious hotels like the **King's Royal Mansour** (*see p199*). It's also the axis of the city's most sophisticated nightlife, especially around the avenue Echouada, where you'll find long-established haunts of the glitterati like **Le Comptoir** (*see p107*) as well as newcomers like Buddha Bar creator Claude Challe's groovy **Djellabar** (*see p97*).

On the opposite (north-east) side of the Medina is a vast oasis of palm trees known as the **Palmeraie** (*see pp107-109*). While not particularly pretty, its distance from the hoi polloi, low population density and lavish new houses have made it a favourite home of the rich – both Moroccans and foreigners – and it's the place to be if all you want to do is hole-up by a swimming pool and just dip occasionally in and out.

GETTING AROUND

The only way to tackle the Medina is on foot. It looks daunting on the map but the area within the walls isn't huge. However, the miles do add up with all the wrong turns you'll make, and many streets are too narrow for cars (watch out for motorcycles, scooters, donkeys and bikes). A taxi is sometimes handy for navigation – some hotels and eateries are so well hidden that only natives can find them – but they'll happily send somebody to get you from the nearest *bab* (gate).

Taxis are necessary for shuttling between the Medina and Guéliz, which is only a five-minute ride (roughly 30dh by day, 50dh by night; should be less but taxi drivers often don't use their meters) but a fast half-hour walk. The green horse-drawn carriages (known as calèches) are a fun way to meander, particularly for a trip round the city walls, and aren't too expensive. Rental of a two-wheeler is good for exploring beyond the walls and in the Palmeraie.

GUIDES

Do you really need a guide? The answer is definitely not. You'll almost certainly get lost but you'll never stay that way for long – any local will graciously set you back on track – and it's all part of the fun.

In any case, in a city of so many hidden surprises, there's no such thing as a wrong turn, only alternative routes where you're likely to stumble upon untold treasures. Note that many local boys think it's hilarious to point you in the wrong direction. If you are truly lost, ask a shopkeeper.

New coloured signs that have appeared on the Medina walls refer to themed routes – a project set up by the Millennium Foundation with the support of local authorities (http://visitmedina.ma/app/webroot/files/Guide/Marrakech/Guide_Marrakech_En.pdf). The five circuits are intended to provide insight into Marrakech's history, artisans and crafts through categories: iron and clay, textiles, wood, leather and earth (for building walls and ramparts).

If you have special interests or wish to hire someone whose knowledge goes beyond the confines of this book, then we can recommend Ahmed Tija, who's been guiding visitors for more than 20 years. He's fluent in English and a mine of information, anecdotes and legends of the city. He and his father were great friends of the author Gavin Maxwell, whose *Lords of the Atlas* is the definitive local history book. We've also heard good things about the other guides listed below, all of whom speak English. Expect to pay around 300-400dh per half day. Beware picking up *faux guides*/unofficial guides (official guides carry accreditation) – they're usually an expensive waste of time.

Ahmed Tija (mobile 0661 08 45 57)
Moulay Youssef (mobile 0661 16 35 64)
Mustapha Chouquir (mobile 0662 10 40 99)
Mustapha Karroum (mobile 0661 34 07 78)

combines the sweet spices and exotic flavours of his native cuisine with contemporary techniques learned at the hands of Andrew West, who trained in Gordan Ramsay's kitchens, resulting in some of the most innovative dining in the Medina. It starts with cocktails and canapés on the roof and segues downstairs into dishes such as cream of artichoke soup swirled with nutty-sweet argan oil, deconstructed chicken *b'stilla* and pan-fried duck crusted with sweet spices. Food lovers looking for a taste of the new wave need look no further.

► *For more on argan oil, see p156 Argan: Elixir of Everything.*

Jardins de la Koutoubia

26 rue de la Koutoubia (0524 38 88 00). **Open** 12.30-4pm, 7.30-10.30pm daily. **Main courses** 65dh-110dh. **Map** p35 B2 ❹ **Moroccan-Mediterranean**

Tucked away behind the garden centre on the Jemaa El Fna, this modern riad is set around a vast swimming pool (open to non-guests for 200dh per day) and makes a lovely setting for a light lunch that combines traditional Moroccan dishes with French bistro flare. Daily staples such as freshly made soups, a hearty *haricot vert* salad or a classic club sandwich served by liveried waiters lends just a *soupçon* of glamour to the whole affair. Details like a single rose on the table, deeply comfortable chairs and a well-stocked bar – remember Dubonnet? – have kept it something of a secret hideaway among resident expats, and there's also a decent Indian restaurant on the roof.

Pâtisserie des Princes

32 rue Bab Agnaou (0524 44 30 33). **Open** 5am-11.30pm daily. **No credit cards. Map** p35 C3 ❺ **Café**

A weak-kneed wobble from Jemaa El Fna, this places offers gloriously icy air-conditioning in a dim coldstore of a back room. It may sound gloomy, but, the hotel swimming pool aside, there's no better retreat on a sweltering afternoon. The front of house is taken up by glass cabinets filled with fine cakes and pastries, to be accompanied by cappuccino, English tea, orange juice or shakes. There's a large salon upstairs.

Portofino

279 avenue Mohammed V (0524 39 16 65, www.portofinomarrakech.com). **Open** noon-11pm daily. **Main courses** 45dh-180dh. **Map** p35 B2 ❻ **Italian**

Located at street level below the Pizzeria Venezia, this contemporary rival to its upstairs neighbour wins out for serving excellent pizzas cooked in a proper, wood-fired oven, along with decent pasta dishes and occasionally excellent fresh fish (check for specials). With large-screen TVs it's also a popular hangout for watching sports and wouldn't look out of place in any of Europe's big cities; its hangar-like proportions make it great for gathering a crowd. Service can be painfully slow, but comes with a smile.

Jardins de la Koutoubia.

★ Le Salama

40 rue des Banques (0524 39 13 00, www.lesalama.com). **Open** 12.30pm-1.30am daily. **Main courses & tapas** 40dh-250dh. **Alcohol served. Map** p35 D2 ❼ **Moroccan & tapas**

Spread over three floors, this is the only spot on the square where you can combine proper cocktails (they make a mean whisky sour) on the rooftop with 360° views over the city, before heading downstairs into a romantic dining room lit by a sea of giant, pierced-metal lanterns. Part of the Fakir Collection, owned by local entrepreneur Nourredine Fakir, this is where you'll find movers and shakers like Paloma Picasso and Roberto Cavalli when they're in town, feasting on superlative traditional Moroccan dishes including a sensational lamb *mechouia* (spiced and

SQUARE MEALS

How to eat on Jemaa El Fna.

Dinner on the Jemas El Fna is one of the highlights of any trip to Marrakech, the place where you get the biggest sense of its history and culture through the stew of human life. As the sun sets, musicians, snake charmers, acrobats, dancers, dentists, herbalists and henna ladies shift their pitches to accommodate the early-evening arrival of massed butane gas canisters, trestle tables and tilly lamps. With well-practised efficiency, it takes only an hour to set up 100 food stalls in tightly drawn rows, with benches for diners, strings of lights overhead and masses of food banked up in the middle. Stallholders fire up griddles and the smoke drifts and curls to create a hazy pall over what must be one of the world's biggest open-air eateries.

Most stalls specialise in one particular dish, and between them they offer a great survey of Moroccan soul food. Several places do good business in ladled bowls of harira (a thick soup of lamb, lentils and chickpeas flavoured with herbs and vegetables). Similarly popular are standbys of grilled brochettes (kebab), kefta (minced, spiced lamb) and merguez (spicy sausage; stall no.31 apparently sells the best in all Morocco). Families perch on benches around stalls selling boiled sheep heads, scooping out the jellyish gloop inside with small plastic forks. Elsewhere are deep-fried fish and eels, bowls of chickpeas drizzled with oil, and mashed potato sandwiches, while a row of stalls along the south side have great mounds of snails, cooked in a broth flavoured with thyme, pepper and lemon. Humblest of the lot is the stallholder selling nothing more than hard-boiled eggs.

Menus and prices hang above some of the stalls, but not everywhere. It's easy enough to just point, and prices are so low that they're hardly worth worrying about. Etiquette is basic: walk around, see something you like, squeeze in between fellow diners. Discs of bread serve instead of cutlery. For the thirsty, orange juice is fetched from one of the many juice stalls that ring the perimeter of the square.

The food is fresh and prepared in front of the waiting diners, so you can actually see the cooking process. Few germs will survive the charcoal grilling or boiling oil; plates and dishes are a different matter. The single same bucket of water is used to wash up all night, so play safe with your stomach and ask for the food to be served on paper, but don't be put off – this is one experience not to miss out on.

slow-cooked over wood) served by handsome waiting staff in velvet robes. There's a daily happy hour (4.30pm-1am).

★ Tiznit

Souk El-Kassabine no.28 (0524 42 72 04/ 0668 10 04 92). **Open** 8am-midnight daily. **Main courses** 25dh-60dh. **No credit cards. Map** p35 D2 ❽ **Moroccan**

Tucked away in the far north-eastern corner of Jemaa El Fna, Tiznit is one of the few deeply authentic places left on the square. Climb the narrow staircase and you'll discover a tiny little dining room clad in white tiles and lit by fluorescent strip bulbs, where photos of the royal family decorate the walls and small mountains of tagines are piled up behind the kitchen counter. The robust flavours of thick chunks of lamb and potato and the house special, rabbit with caramelised onions and raisins, is as authentic as it comes, lovingly prepared by a smiling father and son team. No alcohol.

Tobsil

22 derb Abdellah Ben Hessaien, Bab Ksour (0524 44 40 52). **Open** 7.30-11pm Mon, Wed-Sun. **Set meal** 625dh. **Alcohol served. Map** p35 B2 ❾ **Moroccan**

Considered by some to be Marrakech's premier traditional restaurant, Tobsil offers a lesson in local gastronomy. There is no menu. On being led by a uniformed flunkey to the door (the place is otherwise impossible to find), diners are greeted by owner Christine Rio, then seated either downstairs in the courtyard or upstairs in the galleries to await an extravagant and seemingly never-ending succession of courses. Aperitifs (included in the price of the meal, as is the wine) are rapidly followed by a swarm of small Moroccan salads, pigeon *b'stilla* (a crisp, flaky pastry pie dusted with icing sugar and cinnamon), followed by something like a lamb tagine with fresh figs, couscous, and finally fruit and tea or coffee accompanied by an array of cakes or pastries. Chef Fatima Mountassamim's cooking is delicious and the experience is well worth having to get a sense of that legendary Moroccan hospitality, but be sure to come hungry.

Bars

Grand Tazi

Hotel Grand Tazi, corner of avenue El-Mouahidine & rue Bab Agnaou (0524 44 27 87). **Open** 7-11pm daily. **No credit cards. Map** p35 C3 ❿

The Tazi is something of a Marrakchi institution – it used to be the only place in the central Medina where the weary and footsore could kick back with a cheap beer. Times have changed, but it's still the cheapest place in town for a Special Flag (the local brew) and, despite its rather gloomy interior (we recommend heading straight for the roof terrace), it's still got a bit of a nostalgic cult following if you're not too fussy about the company you keep and don't care about designer surrounds.

Rock 'N' Kech

Rue Fatima Zohra (0643 22 14 70). **Open** 5pm-2am daily. **Map** p35 B2 ⓫

As locals go, this newcomer to the Medina scene is a breath of fresh air among the rather more salubrious places to cadge a beer. The charcoal grey terrace with furnace-black planters, parasols and palm trees has a modest buzz about it, has fabulous views of the Koutoubia Minaret and plays decent music, and the drinks are reasonably priced to boot. All of which is something of a rarity in a country where you pay a premium for alcohol. The Magaluf go-kart course fake black rock walls need a serious rethink, though.

Shops & services

Ensemble Artisanal

Avenue Mohammed V (0524 38 66 74). **Open** 8.30am-7.30pm daily. **Map** p35 A1 ⓬ **Homewares/accessories**

Rock 'N' Kech.

EXPLORE

Koutoubia Mosque and Gardens.

EXPLORE

The second major tourist stop after photo ops at the Koutoubia, the Artisanal Ensemble is another state-sponsored crafts mini-mall like the Centre Artisanal in the Kasbah district – but far more popular because of its central location. All the artisans selling within are purportedly here by royal appointment, selected as the best in their field (a licence therefore to charge higher prices, which are non-negotiable). Expect everything from fine embroidered table linen (first floor at the back) to jewellery, clothing, lamps and even knock-off European handbags.

Warda La Mouche

127 rue Kennaria (0524 38 90 63). **Open** 9am-8pm. **Map** p35 D3 ⓭ **Fashion**

If sarouel-pants and flowing tunics are your style, then head to French-owned Warda La Mouche for reasonably priced fashion in a range of bright colours and patterns. Down a few steps is great sale rack (to the right) and a children's section (to the left), where the girls' sarouels in the sweetest patterns are simply irrestible.

KOUTOUBIA MOSQUE & GARDENS

The mosque is one of the city's oldest buildings. The original structure, built in 1147, was demolished because it was not correctly aligned with Mecca. It was rebuilt, and its new minaret was constructed more than half a century later under the patronage of the Almohad Caliph Yacoub El-Mansour.

The name Koutoubia is derived from *elkoutoubiyyin* – Arabic for booksellers – since a booksellers' market once filled the surrounding streets. The mosque's exterior is of red stone, but it's thought to have originally been covered with plaster. The tower is 13 metres (43 feet) wide. Six rooms, one above the other, constitute the interior; leading around them is a ramp by way of which the muezzin could reach the balcony – it was supposed to be wide enough for him to ride a horse to the top. The Koutoubia is built in a traditional Almohad style and the

SOMETHING DIFFA: THE MOROCCAN MENU

Moroccan cuisine evolved from Persia via the Arabs, from Andalucía with the returning Moors and from the colonial French – but the overriding principle is to throw all the ingredients into a dish and then leave it to cook slowly. Prime exhibit is the national dish of **tagine**. Essentially a slow-cooked stew of meat (usually beef, lamb or chicken, but can be camel) and vegetables, with olives, preserved lemon, almonds or prunes adding complexity and sweetness, and warm spices like cinnamon, cumin and ginger adding depth. The name describes both the food and the pot it's cooked in – a shallow earthenware dish with a conical lid that traps the rising steam and stops the stew from drying out. It is not to be confused with the Marrakchi speciality of **tangia**, which comprises an earthenware urn filled with the same meats as tagine, a glug of oil and a handful of whatever spices the butcher has to hand, then covered in parchment paper and slow-cooked for several hours in the embers of the hammam. **Tangia Street**, just off Jemma El Fna, is a great place to try one.

The other defining staple is **couscous**, commonly served on Fridays with a thin broth with seven vegetables. The coarse grains of semolina flour are steamed three times and topped with the vegetable broth and possibly also a rich meat stew, not unlike that of a tagine. It's a main course, not a side dish.

Don't expect a menu in most upmarket traditional Moroccan restaurants. Once customers are seated, the food simply arrives, banquet-style, in a parade of dishes known as a *diffa*. It always starts with a selection of small hot and cold **salades marocaines**, of carrots, peppers, aubergine, tomatoes and the like, each prepared differently, along with delicacies like spiced, fried offal. **Briouattes** – little envelopes of paper-thin *ouarka* (a bit like filo) pastry wrapped around ground meat, rice or cheese and deep-fried, might come next, or **b'stilla** (or pastilla), the same *ouarka* pastry filled with shredded pigeon or chicken, almonds, boiled egg and spices, baked until crisp and then dusted with cinnamon and powdered sugar. Next, a tagine of beef, lamb or chicken and, just in case you are still hungry, a great mound of couscous. Desserts consist of flaky pastry drizzled with honey or *crème anglaise*, and seasonal fruit platters piled high and served with limitless mint tea poured from huge silver teapots.

The entire *diffa* experience is set up to honour the guest with extreme generosity, and of course, to show off the talents of the kitchen. That a great portion of it is inevitably sent back to the kitchen almost untouched may sit uncomfortably, but culturally this is the norm. Uneaten food is eaten by staff, or in extreme cases distributed to the poor. Rest assured that nothing is wasted. There are plenty of *diffa*-style dining experiences to be had around town, but if you want to escape the large tourist groups follow locals to their favoured upmarket dining spots like **Dar Zellij** (*see p67*) at Sidi Ben Slimane and the legendary all women's co-operative **Al Fassia** (*see p95*) in Guéliz.

Tagine.

LET ME TELL YOU A STORY

Richard Hamilton investigates Marrakech's storytelling tradition.

Café Clock.

In the 1970s, there were 18 storytellers in the Jemaa El Fna; now you'd be extremely lucky to find a single one. Their profession was perhaps as old as the city itself, maybe even older. The storytellers, or *hlaykia*, would memorise hundreds of traditional tales from *A Thousand and One Nights*, the Old Testament and Moroccan folklore. For a few coins, they would recite these narratives to a circle of spellbound listeners known as the *halka*. It was entertainment at its most pure and simple.

Even if you didn't understand a word of Arabic or Berber, it was still an experience, as Elias Canetti described in *Voices of Marrakesh*. 'Their words come from farther off and hang longer in the air than those of ordinary people. I understand nothing and yet whenever I came within hearing I was rooted to the spot by the same fascination. They were words that held no meaning for me, hammered out with fire and impact: to the man who spoke them they were precious and he was proud of them.'

In a culture where few could read and write, the oral tradition provided more than just entertainment; it was a vital means of passing down information, ideas, values and philosophies, like an early form of newspapers. Even today, around 40 per cent of Moroccans are illiterate. But there is no doubt that after perhaps a thousand years, the art and practice of storytelling in the Jemaa El Fna is on the brink of extinction. Young Marrakchis would rather watch Egyptian TV soap operas or play computer games than listen to a storyteller – let alone become one. And it is a great loss because in most cases the stories have never been written down. There is a saying in Marrakech that 'when a storyteller dies, a library burns.'

But help is at hand. In 2001, UNESCO named the 'cultural space' of Jemaa El Fna as one of 19 'proclaimed masterpieces of the oral and intangible heritage of humanity.' And the new **Café Clock** (*see p80*) in the Kasbah has started storytelling sessions on Thursday evenings. Let's hope this little jewel of the world's oral heritage can be saved for posterity.

Richard Hamilton is the author of The Last Storytellers: Tales from the Heart of Morocco, *IB Tauris 2011.*

minaret is topped with four copper globes; according to legend, these were originally made of pure gold. There were also supposed to have been only three of them: it is said that the fourth was donated by the wife of Yacoub El-Mansour as compensation for failing to keep the Ramadan fast by eating four grapes. As penance, she had her gold jewellery melted down to fashion the fourth globe. Hardly more credible is the claim that only blind muezzins were employed because a sighted person would have been able to gaze into the royal harem from the minaret.

Sunken areas on the plaza outside the mosque are the remains of reservoirs that belonged to the Dar El-Hajar, a fortress built by city founder Youssef Ben Tachfine towards the end of the 11th century, and the first permanent structure in the encampment that became Marrakech. The fortress was short-lived, destroyed by the conquering Almohads who replaced it with the site's first mosque. The small white-domed structure on the plaza is the **Koubba of Lalla Zohra**, a shrine that used to be open to the public until the inebriated son of a former city mayor ploughed his car into the structure and, as part of the repairs, the door was sealed up.

It's possible to walk around either side of the Koutoubia, clockwise between the main entrance and the wall that encloses the grounds of the French Consulate, or anti-clockwise along the top of the Almohad ruins. Either route leads into the orange tree-filled **Koutoubia Gardens**, which spread south and west of the mosque. Across avenue Houman El-Fetouaki, south of the gardens, a high wall cuts from sight a modest crenellated building; this is the humble **Tomb of Youssef Ben Tachfine**, founder of Marrakech. A padlocked gate ensures that the great desert warrior rests in peace, his mausoleum off limits to the public.

MAMOUNIA GARDENS

'It is the most lovely spot in the whole world,' said Winston Churchill to Franklin D Roosevelt about Marrakech in the late 1940s, a period when the statesman would stay at **La Mamounia** (*see p199*) and paint. The world-famous hotel began its life with just 50 rooms, but expanded and was remodelled over the years. Its last grand renovation was in 2006, and now it's back to attracting Hollywood stars (Gwyneth Paltrow and Nicole Kidman, to name just two).

The hotel takes its name from its gardens, the Arset El-Mamoun, which predate the hotel by more than a century. They were established in the 18th century by Crown Prince Moulay Mamoun on land gifted to him by his father, the sultan, on the occasion of his wedding. A central pavilion served as a princely residence, occasionally lent out to visiting diplomats.

The **Mamounia Gardens** are designed in traditional style, on an axis, with walkways, flowerbeds, orange groves and olive trees. Non-residents who want to enjoy their splendour can visit for a buffet lunch at the poolside restaurant, take afternoon tea at Le Menzeh tea and ice-cream pavilion in the gardens, or on the back terrace overlooking the gardens, stop by the Majorelle or Churchill bars for cocktails, or indulge in an expensive dinner in French, Italian or Moroccan style. No jeans or shorts.

Mamounia Gardens.

The Souks & Around

North of Jemaa El Fna are the souks, with alleyway upon alleyway of tiny retail cubicles. This is commerce at its most intoxicating – a riot of strong colours, seductive shapes and rampant exoticism. In the most heavily touristed areas, the overwhelming number of shops is offset by the fact that most seem compelled to offer the same goods. But the further into the souks you venture, the more interesting they become – our reviews here pick out some of the highlights.

The two main routes in are rue Semarine and rue Mouassine; the former offers the more full-on blast of bazaar, the latter is a more sedate path leading to choice boutiques. In fact, Mouassine is now the smartest part of the Medina. To the north are several of the city's holy shrines; to the west, the high walls of the Dar El-Bacha lead on to rue Bab Doukkala and one of the Medina's gates. To the east, a very different experience awaits: the sights and (strong) smells of the tanneries.

Maison de la Photographie.

Don't Miss

1 Souk Cherifia The hip, fixed-price souk (p64).

2 Ben Youssef Medersa Serene and lovely (p53).

3 Maison de la Photographie Great photos, rooftop café (p53).

4 Shop the souks The essential retail experience bar none (p50).

5 Nomad Soulful food and a fab view (p55).

Rahba Kedima.

THE SOUKS

The entrance to **rue Semarine** (aka Souk Semarine) is via an elaborate arch, partially obscured by tat, one block north of Jemaa El Fna – reached via either the spice market or the egg market, both pungent experiences, one pleasant, the other not. Semarine is a relatively orderly street, broad and straight with smart new overhead trellising dappling the paving with light and shadow.

Every section of the souk has its own speciality and here it has traditionally been textiles, although these days cloth merchants have been largely supplanted by souvenir shops.

About 150 metres along, the first alley off to the east leads to a wedge-shaped open area known as the **Rahba Kedima**, or the 'old place'. The way between Semarine and the Rahba Kedima leads to a small court, the **Souk Laghzel**, formerly the wool market but now a car-boot sale of a souk where women – and only women – come to sell meagre possessions such as a single knitted shawl or a bag of vegetables. It is also lined with medicine stalls draped in the dead skins of a menagerie of African animals.

The Rahba Kedima used to be the city's open-air corn market but it's now given over to an intriguing mix of raffia bags and baskets, woollen hats and cooked snails. Around the edges are spice and 'magic' stalls (*see also p70* **A Kind of Magic**) and these days a handful of super-cool Medina cafés such as **Nomad** (*see p55*) and the **Café des Epices**, both with roof terraces from where you can watch the action in peace.

The upper storeys of the shops on the northern side of the Rahba Kedima are usually hung with carpets and textiles, an invitation to search for the passageway that leads through to the **Criée Berbère**. These days this partially roofed, slightly gloomy section of the souk is the lair of the rug merchants, but until well into the 20th century it was used for the sale of slaves, auctioned here three times weekly. According to North African historian Barnaby Rogerson, the going rate was two slaves for a camel, ten for a horse and 40 for a civet cat.

Nearby, **Riad Yima** (*see p55*) is the shop-cum-studio of Marrakech artist Hassan Hajjaj, now celebrated internationally for his bright, pop-art photography using local Medina hipsters as his models. His latest work is a short film featuring the henna ladies of Jemaa El Fna, but it's worth stopping by here to pick up some one-off originals including pierced beaten metal lanterns, flour-sack *babouches* and funky tees emblazoned with Arabic calligraphy. You can also arrange to have lunch here with a bit of advance planning, and there's always a pot of mint tea on the go.

North-east of Rahba Kedima on rue Sidi Ishak, Lucien Viola, owner of Galerie Rê, plans to open a museum of Berber art and urban Moroccan art, including ancient silk belts and antique ceramics, in 2015.

Back on rue Semarine, just north of the turning for the Rahba Kedima, the street forks: branching to the left is the **Souk El-Attarin**, straight on is the **Souk El-Kebir** (Great Souk). Between the two is a ladder of narrow, arrow-straight passages, collectively known as the **Kissaria**. This is the beating heart of the souk.

IN THE KNOW HAGGLE-FREE SHOPPING

Try the **Ensemble Artisanal** (*see p41*), **Sidi Ghanem** (*see p102*), shops in Guéliz (*see pp98-104*), or indeed at hip **Souk Cherifia** (*see p64*), which is inside the souks area – all of which have fixed prices.

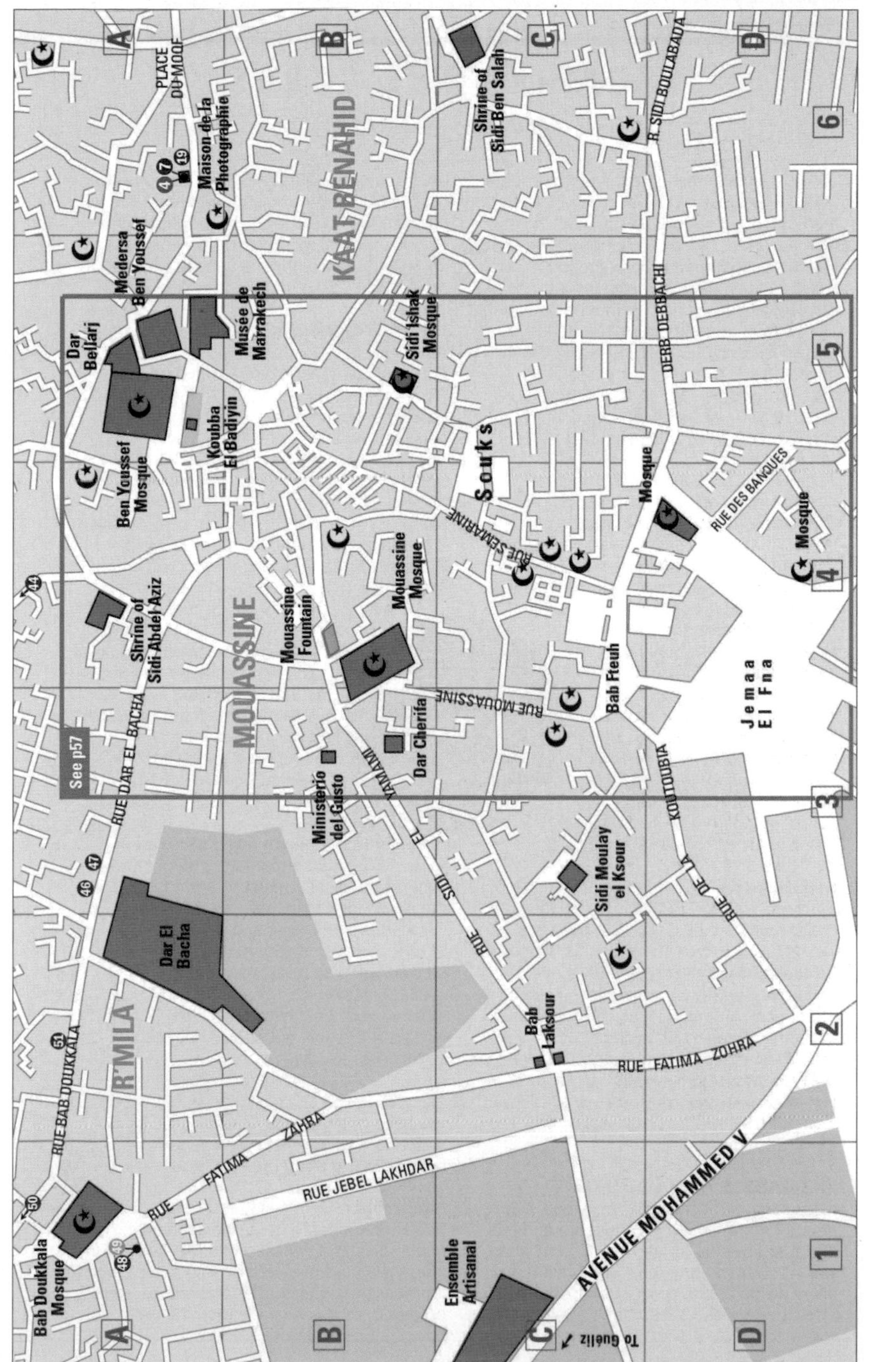
Place du MooF
Maison de la Photographie
Medersa Ben Youssef
Dar Bellarj
Musée de Marrakech
Ben Youssef Mosque
Koubba El Badiyin
Kaat Benahid
Shrine of Sidi Ben Salah
R. Sidi Boulabada
Derb Debbachi
Sidi Ishak Mosque
Souks
Rue Semarine
Mosque
Rue des Banques
Shrine of Sidi Abdel Aziz
Mouassine
Mouassine Fountain
Mouassine Mosque
Rue Mouassine
Bab Fteuh
Jemaa El Fna
See p57
Rue Dar El Bacha
Ministerio del Gusto
Dar Cherifa
Rue Sidi El Yamani
Koutoubia
Sidi Moulay el Ksour
Rue de la
Dar El Bacha
R'Mila
Bab Laksour
Rue Fatima Zohra
Rue Bab Doukkala
Rue Jebel Lakhdar
Avenue Mohammed V
Bab Doukkala Mosque
Ensemble Artisanal
To Guéliz

EXPLORE

SHOPPING THE SOUKS

What to buy and where to buy it.

The vast bazaar that spreads north of Jemaa El Fna is actually a coalescence of different markets, most specialising in one kind of item (for map, *see p57*). General handicrafts shops are scattered everywhere, but particularly on the two main souk streets of **rue Mouassine** and **rue Semarine**. An intrepid spirit brings its rewards, as the closer you remain to Jemaa El Fna, the higher the prices. Most shops are tiny holes in the wall with owners keen to attract business. If you're not interested, remain deaf to overtures of 'Just for looking' and 'I give you good price!'.

Debate rages on the issue of guides. Yes, they can zero in on the shops selling what you're looking for and haggle on your behalf, but wherever they lead it ends in a commission and that goes on your bill. A new breed of 'personal shoppers', many of them expats, may better understand what you're after and lead you to places they think you'll find interesting, working outside the traditional kickback system. The best charge from around €130 a day, so it's worth considering only if you have some very serious shopping in mind. And beware, many old-school guides are now also billing themselves as 'personal shoppers'.

Kati Lawrence *UK +44 (0)771 348 6006, Morocco +212 (0)638 41 79 03.* **Rates** €130 half day, full day €180, usually in spring and autumn. Transport not included for trips beyond the Medina or Guéliz.
Boutique Souk (www.boutiquesouk.com) offers complimentary concierge services, including shopping and dining tips, to visitors who book accommodation with the agency.
Maryam Montague, (moroccanmaryam& yahoo.com) author of *Marrakesh by Design* charges US$600 for a half day or US$900 for a 'design safari'.

THE HASSLE OF HAGGLING

It's a drag, but haggling is expected, even demanded, in the souk. There are no hard and fast rules as to how to do it, but when you've spotted something you want, it's smart to do a little scouting around and get a few quotes on similar items at other stores before making your play. Don't feel you need to go through the whole charade of offer and counter-offer like in some B-movie dialogue; simply expressing interest then walking away on being told the price is usually enough to bring about some fairly radical discounting.

THE MERCHANDISE

Antiques

Antique is a manufactured style here, and few things are as old as they might appear. Fraud is widespread too. Buy something because you like it, and if you discover it really was as old as the vendor claimed, then that's an added bonus. Bric-a-brac shops offering old but less exalted items are scattered around the souk. On **rue Sidi Ishak**, the lane leading north from the east side of Rahba Kedima, there are several where it skirts around the mosque, and another as it passes through a short tunnel. There's another on the same road south of Rahba Kedima, a short walk down on the right, and one or two on **rue Sidi El-Yamami**, just east of the Mouassine fountain. Expect a mad jumble of everything, among which a few treasures can sometimes be found.

Argan oil

Morocco's famed argan oil is rich in vitamin E and essential fatty acids. It lowers cholesterol levels, unblocks arteries, relieves rheumatic joint pain, reduces scars and wrinkles, whitens your smile, makes you horny and pays off your mortgage – or so they say. The miraculous stuff is available at herbal shops in the souk. What you buy in such places is OK as a massage oil, but should not be ingested as it's likely to have been cut with some other inferior oil. For argan oil to use as a food dressing, you need to go to a reputable outlet such as **Marjane** (*see p109*) or **Naturia Bio Shop** (*see p103*).

Babouches

The slippers come in leather, nubuck, suede or sabra (which looks like silk but is actually a kind of viscose). The sole will be leather, plastic or rubber and can be sewn on (good) or glued (not good). Yellow is the traditional Moroccan favourite, but they come in all colours and degrees of embellishment. Expect to pay around 50dh for fake leather *babouches* with glued soles, up to 150dh for the all-leather, stiched-sole variety. They're everywhere, but the obvious place to go is the **Souk des Babouches** (see map p57 C2).

Carpets

There's one simple rule when it comes to carpets: buy it because you like it, not because you've been told it's worth money. Very few carpets are antique. And ignore claims that a carpet is made of cactus silk: genuine cactus silk carpets cost ten times as much as normal ones. Bear in mind that you're unlikely to find the double of a carpet you like in another shop, as most are unique. And don't be afraid of not buying after having a guy unfurl two dozen specimens for you: it's his job – and anyway carpets have to be unrolled now and then to let them breathe.

Hundreds of different styles are produced in Morocco. Age, quality, fabric and type help to determine price. Popular carpets like Beni Ouarains (named after the Atlas people that make them) can cost up to 7,000dh for an old piece, whereas a Bouchaourite rag rug costs between 200dh and 2,000dh. *Handiras*, the popular white blankets embellished with sequins, also known as Moroccan wedding blankets, usually cost between 500dh and 1,500dh, but can cost up to 6,000dh for more intricate designs.

The main places to buy carpets are along **rue Mouassine** (try **Tapis Akhnif**, *see p64*) and **rue Semarine**, and in the **Souk des Tapis** off the Rahba Kedima, which is where you'll find **L'Art de Goulimine** (*see p56*) and **Bazar du Sud** (*see p56*).

English-speaking guide Abdelhafid Serrakh (0661 55 37 36) is an understanding local with a wealth of carpet knowledge.

Ceramics

The local style is plain terracotta glazed in bright colours. Prices start at around 60dh for a soap dish rising up to 180dh for larger plates. Green Tamegroute pottery ranges from 20dh for a small bowl up to 600dh for a large platter. As an alternative, there are *tadelakt* ceramics, which are smooth and satiny to the touch with more subdued tones. Pieces range from 80dh up to 1,000dh for a large lamp. Ceramics are everywhere, but particularly in and around the **Souk des Teinturiers** and along the lower part of **rue Mouassine** (notably **Caverne d'Ali Baba**, *see p63*). The cheapest option is to shop at the sprawling, open-air pottery market on the road just outside the south-eastern Medina gate of **Bab Ghemat** (see map p253 F6).

Lanterns

Styles range from traditional North African to art deco and avant garde – including tall, curly ones made out of decorated goatskin. The cheapest are those made of tin, whichis often rusted for colour. The price increases with the addition of glass, patterned or plain (the former more expensive). Brass and copper lanterns are also a bit more expensive but generally better finished and harder-wearing. Prices range from around 30dh-300dh for tin, and 100dh-750dh or more for copper or brass. You can find lanterns in the **Souk des Ferroniers** or the **Souk des Dinandiers** (for both, see map p57 C2).

Leather bags

Marrakech is good for leather, but be careful: some of the work is shoddy and you can end up with a bag that leaves its contents stinking or transfers its colour to your clothes (rub the bag with a wet tissue before buying).

Also popular are vintage shoulder bags. These sell for between 200dh and 400dh, or you can get modern copies for around 300dh. Contemporary handbags go for 150dh-300dh, but high-end accessories can be as much as 1,200dh. Travel luggage starts at around 400dh and goes up to 800dh, depending on the size.

You can find leatherware in the northern end of the **Souk El-Kebir** (see map p57 C3) or in the alleys of the **Kissaria** or, for something more modern and stylish, try **Lalla** and **Art/C** (for both, *see p64* **Souk Cherifia**).

Stallholders here specialise in cotton, clothing, kaftans and blankets.

Further along the Souk El-Kebir are the courtyards of carpenters and wood turners, before a T-junction forces a choice: left or right. Go left and then immediately right at the shop selling predominantly red pottery and with a téléboutique sign above to emerge once again into streets that are wide enough for the passage of cars.

Just north is the dusty open plaza of place Ben Youssef, dominated by the **Ben Youssef Mosque**, which is easily identifiable by its bright-green pyramidal roofs. The original mosque went up in the 12th century and was the grandest of the age, but what stands now is a third and lesser incarnation, dating from the early 19th century. Non-Muslims may not enter. However, in the immediate vicinity of the mosque is a cluster of tourist-friendly sights, including the decidedly average **Musée de Marrakech** (*see p55*), the enchanting **Ben Youssef Medersa** (*see p53*) and the venerable **Koubba El-Badiyin** (*see p53*).

East of the Ben Youssef Medersa, between the place Ben Youssef and the place du Moqf is the **Maison de la Photographie** (*see p53*), a handsome townhouse, which showcases photographic works from the period 1870 to 1950, and serves a top-notch, three-course lunch menu for 90dh.

Back at the fork on rue Semarine, bearing left brings you on to **Souk El-Attarin**, or the Spice Souk. Contrary to the name, this part of the souk no longer deals in spices. Instead, its traders largely traffic in tourist tat, from painted wooden thingamies to leather whatjamacallits. Almost opposite the subdued entrance to a workaday mosque is the **Souk des Babouches**, a whole alley devoted to soft-leather slippers – and their almost identical synthetic counterparts. Further along Attarin, distant ringing hammer blows announce the **Souk Haddadin**, the quarter of the ironworkers. One of the most medieval parts of the souk, it's full of dark, cavern-like workshops in which firework bursts of orange sparks briefly illuminate tableaux of grime-streaked craftsmen, like some scene by Doré.

West of Attarin three alleys run downhill into the **Souk des Teinturiers**, which is the area of the dyers' workshops. Labourers rub dyes into cured hides (to be cut and fashioned into babouches) and dunk wool into vats of dark-hued liquids. This results in brightly

Ben Youssef Medersa.

coloured sheafs of wool that are then hung over the alleyways in a manner irresistible to passing photographers. It also results in the labourers having arms coloured to their elbows. You know you're nearing this part of the souk when you start seeing people with blue or purple arms.

The three alleys converge into one, which then doglegs between a squeeze of assorted artisans' salesrooms (lanterns, metalwork and pottery) before exiting under an arch beside the Mouassine fountain and mosque (*see p59*).

Sights & museums

★ Ben Youssef Medersa

Place Ben Youssef (0524 44 18 93). **Open** 9am-6pm daily. **Admission** 50dh; 30dh under-12s. Combined entrance with the Marrakech Museum, 60dh. **No credit cards**. **Map** p57 D1 ❶

A *medersa* is a Quranic school, dedicated to the teaching of Islamic scripture and law. This one was founded in the 14th century, then enlarged in 1564 by the Saadian Sultan Abdellah El-Ghalib. It was given a further polishing up in the 1990s, courtesy of the Ministry of Culture. Entrance is via a long, cool passageway leading to the great courtyard, a serene place (before the tour parties arrive) centred on a water-filled basin. The surrounding façades are decorated with *zelije* tiling, stucco and carved cedar, all executed with restraint. At the far side is the domed prayer hall with the richest of decoration, notably around the mihrab, the arched niche that indicates the direction of Mecca. Back in the entrance vestibule, passageways and two flights of stairs lead to more than 100 tiny windowless students' chambers, clustered about small internal lightwells. Medieval as it seems, the *medersa* was still in use until as recently as 1962. The building stood in for an Algerian Sufi retreat in Gillies Mackinnon's 1998 film *Hideous Kinky*.

Dar Bellarj

7-9 rue Toulat Zaouiat Lahdar (0524 44 45 55, www.darbellarj.org). **Open** 9.30am-12.30pm, 2-5.30pm Mon-Sat. **Admission** free. **Map** p57 D1 ❷

North of the entrance to the Ben Youssef Medersa is a large wooden door in the crook of the alley emblazoned with a bird's head: this is Dar Bellarj, the 'Stork's House', so called because it was formerly a hospital for the big white birds. The stork is holy to Marrakech. There are countless tales to explain its exalted status. The most commonly repeated is of a local imam, dressed in traditional Moroccan garb of white djellaba and black robe, drunk on wine, who then compounds the sin by climbing the minaret and blaspheming. Man suffers wrath of God and is transformed into a stork. Even before the arrival of Islam, an old Berber belief held that storks are actually transformed humans.

Dar Bellarj.

Restored in 1999, Dar Bellarj now serves as a local cultural centre hosting rotating exhibitions, workshops and musical performances. Unless you're lucky enough to drop in on a happening there's little to see; the chalk white and taupe courtyard is very attractive with seating, and sweet tea is offered to visitors; it makes the perfect respite stop in this busy corner of the Medina.

Koubba El-Badiyin

Place Ben Youssef. Currently closed. **Map** p57 D1 ❸

Across from the Ben Youssef Mosque, set in its own fenced enclosure and sunk several metres below the current street level, is the Koubba El-Badiyin (also known as the Koubba Almoravide). It looks unprepossessing but its unearthing in 1948 prompted one French art historian to exclaim that 'the art of Islam has never exceeded the splendour of this extraordinary dome'. It's the only surviving structure from the era of the Almoravids, the founders of Marrakech, and as such it represents a wormhole back to the origins of Moorish building history, presenting for the first time many of the shapes and forms that remain the basis of the North African architectural vocabulary. It dates to the reign of Ali Ben Youssef (1107-43) and was probably part of the ablutions complex of the original Ben Youssef Mosque. The Koubba is currently closed. If it reopens, it's worth descending the brickwork steps and viewing the underside of the dome, which is a kaleidoscopic arrangement of a floral motif within an octagon within an eight-pointed star. *Photo p55.*

★ Maison de la Photographie

46 rue Ahl Fès, off rue Bin Lafnadek (0524 38 57 21, www.maisondelaphotographie.ma). **Open** 9.30am-7pm daily. **Admission** 40dh; free under-12s. **Map** p49 A6 ❹

Koubba El-Badiyin. *See p53.*

Patrick Manac'h's passion is plain for all to see. The photography aficionado has amassed a collection of 8,000 images that span the substantial period from 1870 to 1950; the collection, shown in rotating exhibitions, offers fascinating glimpses into the past. After surveying the collection – all original prints – climb to the top terrace for reviving drinks and a meal (*see right*) before trying to secure that winning shot: the museum's top terrace has a 270° elevated view of the city and the Atlas mountains beyond.

Musée de Marrakech

Place Ben Youssef (0524 44 18 93, www.museedemarrakech.ma). **Open** 9am-6pm daily. **Admission** 50dh; 30dh under-12s. Combined entrance with the Ben Youssef Medersa, 60dh. **No credit cards. Map** p57 D2 ❺

Inaugurated in 1997, the Musée de Marrakech is a conversion of an opulent early 20th-century house formerly belonging to a Marrakchi grandee. Entering the outer courtyard, there's a pleasant café off to one side. Within the museum, poorly curated and rag-tag exhibits rotate. The star attraction is the building itself, particularly the tartishly tiled great central court, roofed over and hung with an enormous chandelier like the mothership from *Close Encounters of the Third Kind*. The former hammam is lovely, with attractive decorative flourishes. If nothing else, the museum is a cool refuge from the blazing heat.

Riad Yima

52 derb Aarjane (0667 23 09 95, www.riadyima.com). **Open** 9am-6pm daily. **No credit cards. Map** p57 C4 ❻

The home-cum-gallery-cum-shop-cum-tea room of acclaimed Marrakchi artist Hassan Hajjaj is tucked away behind the Place Rahba Kedima (if you struggle to find it, give them a call and someone will come and get you). Though Hajjaj is primarily based in London, he can occasionally be found at work here, most recently on a film about the henna women of Jemaa El Fna. His photographs in his trademark striking bright colours and custom-made outfits fashioned from vintage textiles have been the subject of a travelling exhibition that has roved from New York to Dubai. But this is still the best place to see them, or indeed any of his quirky pieces, including pierced sardine-can lanterns, eye-popping plastic kilims, and Arabic Coca-Cola crate benches. His pop art reworking of retro Morocco has been much imitated, but it's still well worth seeking out the genuine article.

Restaurants & cafés

★ Café at Maison de la Photographie

46 rue Ahl Fès, off rue Bin Lafnadek (0524 38 57 21, www.maisondelaphotographie.ma). **Open** 9.30am-7pm daily. **Set menu** 90dh. **No credit cards. Map** p49 A6 ❼ **Café**

As well as being an absorbing gallery (*see p53*) showcasing documentary photography in Morocco, this is also one of the Medina's best-kept secrets as a lunch spot. The L-shaped, bamboo-shaded roof terrace has sensational views of the Atlas mountains, and a keenly priced *menu du jour* offering authentic Berber home-cooking. The menu changes daily and with the seasons, but keeps it simple: soups and salads to start, impeccable tagines and couscous for mains, and lovely desserts such as creamy own-made yoghurt and strawberries.

★ Nomad

Place Rahba Kedima (0524 38 16 09, www.nomadmarrakech.com). **Open** 9am-10pm daily. **Main courses** 70dh-130dh. **Alcohol served. No credit cards. Map** p57 C4 ❽ **Café**

Kamal Laftimi's latest project is, like Le Jardin (*see p61*), multifunctional. The ground floor doubles as a modern deli, run by Chabi Chic and selling local ingredients such as preserved lemons and beautifully packaged Atlas olive oil, as well as kitchen tools like olive wood spoons. Upstairs, the space is divided into a chill-out zone under a white rippling roof, and adjacent dining area padded with kilim cushions, while a second storey has shaded dining close to the zigzag-tiled bar. There's also the ultimate crow's-nest perch with fabulous views of the Koutoubia minaret and over the spice market. This time Laftimi's inspiration was groovy 1950s and '60s Morocco, typified by the Harry Bertoia-style diamond chairs on the top terrace. The menu embraces plenty of salads and vegetarian dishes alongside fish, lamb and kefta tagines. Profits from the changing dish of the day go to the Dar Bellarj Foundation (*see p53*), to help disadvantaged women in the community. Laftimi also owns the more rustic Café des Epices (on the other side of the square), a top spot for a 40dh breakfast of eggs, traditional breads, fruit, coffee and juice.

Shops & services

Akbar Delights

45 place Bab Fteuh (0671 66 13 07, www.akbardelightscollections.com). **Open** 10am-1pm, 3-7pm Tue-Sun. **Map** p57 B5 **9** **Textiles**

This upmarket French-owned boutique deals in luxury clothing and textiles from India, with some items made to their own designs, including a selection of handbags. The sister shop, Moor, in Guéliz, carries a larger selection of Moroccan home furnishings as well as a clothing line. Collections change seasonally.

L'Art de Goulimine

25 Souk des Tapis (0661 88 29 06). **Open** 9am-6.30pm daily. **Map** p57 C3 **10** **Carpets**

For something a little different try L'Art de Goulimine, which specialises in Rhamana carpets from the plains north of Marrakech. The two young dealers, Rabia and Ahmed, have a small showroom displaying choice pieces just off the main carpet souk (where you'll find plenty of all the more usual carpet types at competitive prices).

L'Art du Bain

13 Souk El-Labadine (0668 44 59 42, www.nyushashop.com). **Open** 9.30am-7pm daily. **Map** p57 C3 **11** **Soap**

French-Moroccan couple Elsa and Youssef are soap makers using local and natural ingredients. The line includes a donkey's milk soap that is said to regenerate the skin and slow ageing. Our favourites are Louise, a soap made with verbena and lemon, and Little Fatma, made with argan oil. They make a perfect gift as the packaging is as gorgeous as the product.

Art Ouarzazate

15 rue Rahba Kedima (0648 58 48 33). **Open** 10am-7pm daily. **Map** p57 D4 **12** **Fashion & Homewares**

A small, sparsely stocked shop with an interesting collection including upmarket housewares and fashion designs. Carpets and cushions are woven from leather and custom-made for each client. The clothing line is unique and blends a variety of textiles including fur, leather and floral-printed fabric. Handbags start at 600dh; a vest with faux leather starts at 1,700dh.

Au Fil d'Or

10 Souk Semarine (0524 44 59 19). **Open** 9.30am-1pm, 3-8pm Mon-Thur, Sat, Sun; 9.30am-noon Fri. **Map** p57 B4 **13** **Fashion**

It's almost indistinguishable from the multitude of small stores that surround it, but Au Fil d'Or is worth honing in on for quality *babouches* and *jellabas*. Also sold are gorgeous lounge/beach wear in the finest fabrics (1,500dh), and finely braided silk-lined jackets (2,200dh) – just the thing should one be invited to the palace. Note that the bulk of the stock is kept in the cellar-like space downstairs, accessed via a trapdoor behind the counter. Watch your head (and your spending).

Bazar du Sud

117 Souk des Tapis (0524 44 30 04, www.bazardusud.com). **Open** 9am-7pm daily. **Map** p57 C3 **14** **Carpets**

This place has possibly the largest selection of carpets in the souk, covering all regions and styles, new and old. The owners say they have 17 buyers out at any one time scouring the country for the finest examples. Although considerable effort goes into supplying collectors and dealers worldwide, staff are just as happy to entertain the novice. Prices range from 2,000dh to 350,000dh. Ask for Ismail, who speaks perfect English.

Beldi

9-11 Soukiat Laksour, Bab Fteuh (0524 44 10 76). **Open** 10am-1.30pm, 3.30-8pm Mon-Thur, Sat, Sun. **Map** p57 A4 **15** **Fashion**

Toufik studied fashion in Germany and now, back in Marrakech, he and his brother Abdelhafid have transformed the family tailoring business into what is probably the most talked-about boutique in town, and one of our favourites. They offer both men's and women's ranges in beautiful colours and fabrics, fashioned with flair and an eye to western tastes. Silk kaftans, velvet vests and cotton tunics are part of the collection that changes seasonally. Custom orders take from two weeks to one month and can be shipped internationally. There's another shop at 19 Souk des Teinturiers.

Bellawi

56 Kessariat Lossta, off Souk El-Attarin (0668 04 91 14). **Open** 9am-7pm Mon-Thur, Sat, Sun. **Map** p57 C3 **16** **Jewellery**

Abdelatif, owner of this closet-like jewellery store, is brother to the famed Mustapha Blaoui (*see p73*). Here, there's just about room for Abdelatif, his workbench and one customer. The walls are hung with beads clustered like berries, along with a fine selection of traditional-style silver bangles, necklaces and rings set with semi-precious stones. The shop is

EXPLORE

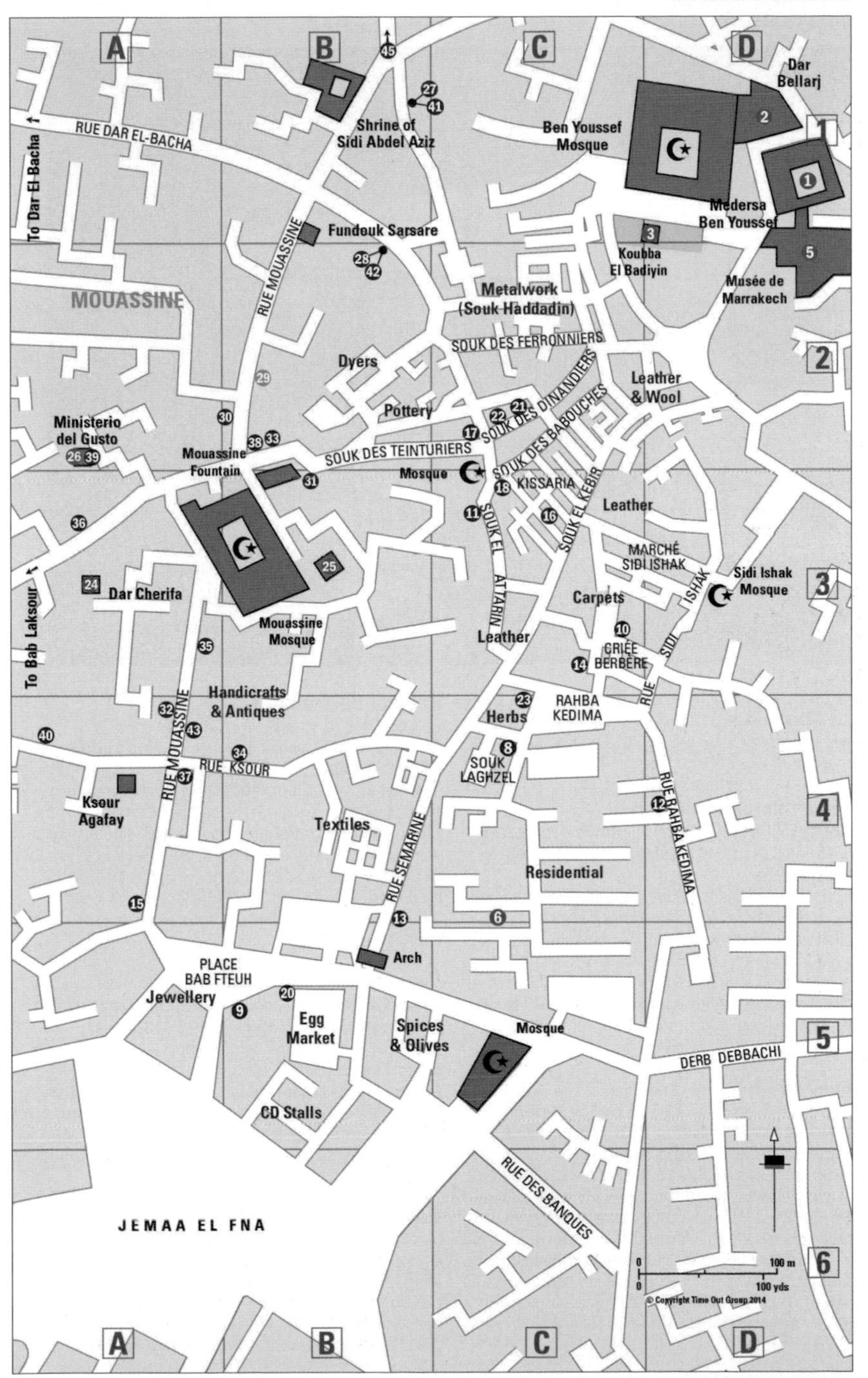

Dar Bellarj
Ben Youssef Mosque
Medersa Ben Youssef
Koubba El Badiyin
Musée de Marrakech
Shrine of Sidi Abdel Aziz
Fundouk Sarsare
RUE DAR EL-BACHA
To Dar El Bacha
MOUASSINE
RUE MOUASSINE
Metalwork (Souk Haddadin)
SOUK DES FERRONNIERS
Dyers
Pottery
Leather & Wool
SOUK DES DINANDIERS
SOUK DES BABOUCHES
SOUK DES TEINTURIERS
Ministerio del Gusto
Mouassine Fountain
Mosque
KISSARIA
SOUK EL KEBIR
SOUK EL ATTARIN
Leather
MARCHÉ SIDI ISHAK
Sidi Ishak Mosque
RUE SIDI ISHAK
Carpets
CRIÉE BERBÈRE
Dar Cherifa
Mouassine Mosque
To Bab Laksour
Handicrafts & Antiques
Herbs
RAHBA KEDIMA
SOUK LAGHZEL
RUE KSOUR
Ksour Agafay
Textiles
RUE SEMARINE
RUE RAHBA KEDIMA
Residential
Arch
PLACE BAB FTEUH
Jewellery
Egg Market
Spices & Olives
Mosque
DERB DEBBACHI
CD Stalls
RUE DES BANQUES
JEMAA EL FNA
0 100 m
0 100 yds
© Copyright Time Out Group 2014

EXPLORE

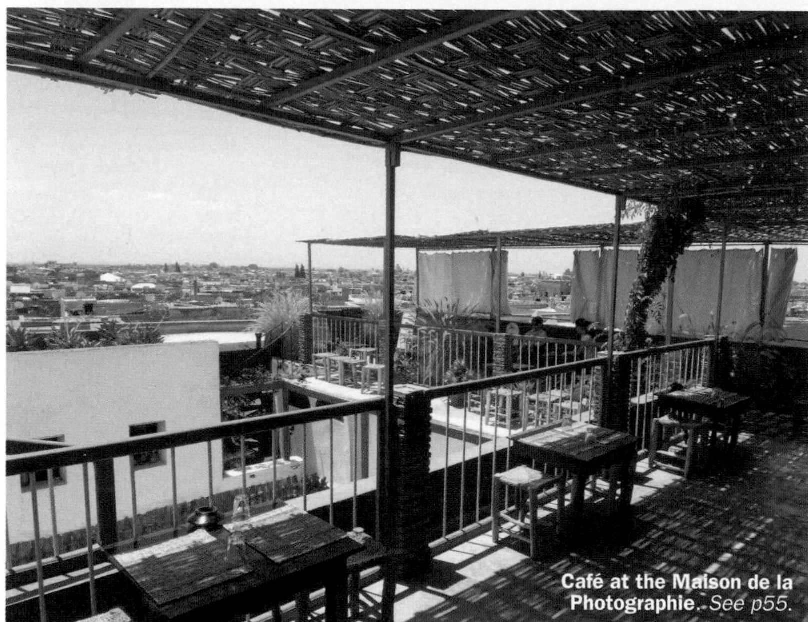
Café at the Maison de la Photographie. See p55.

along the same narrow passage as Eva/Adam (*see below*). There's no sign in English, but just ask for Abdelatif. Everyone knows him – he's been here for over 40 years.

Chez Climou et Ahmed

22 Souk Lebbadine (0648 50 60 71). **Open** 9am-8pm daily. **No credit cards**. **Map** p57 C2 ⓱ **Chess sets**

Using a small, rudimentary lathe that he spins with his bare feet, Ahmed carves chess pieces from cedar, olive and lemon wood. His designs are pleasingly solid and simple; the black pieces are created using burnt olive oil as a stain. He also sells boards and other woodcraft items, sourced from elsewhere. Step inside his small shop and he'll proudly show you a photo of Ronald Reagan's visit.

Eva/Adam

144 Souk El-Hanna (0661 08 54 91). **Open** 10am-1pm, 3.30-7pm Mon-Thur, Sat, Sun; 10am-1pm Fri. **Map** p57 C3 ⓲ **Fashion**

Practical, comfortable clothes in neutral colours, made from cotton and lightweight wool are sold here. The styles are loose-fitting yet elegant, and prices are reasonable. To find it, walk north up Souk El-Attarin just past the entrance to the mosque on the left. Look to the right for the word 'Lacoste' painted on a whitewashed arch: Eva/Adam is first on the right, with barely more than a door by way of shop frontage.

Faissal Bennouna

25 rue Ahl Fès, off rue Bin Lafnadek (0664 08 12 87). **Open** 9.30am-7.30pm daily. **No credit cards**. **Map** p49 A6 ⓳ **Textiles**

The small workshop across from the Maison de la Photographie (*see p55*) is just big enough for a loom and a bit of shelf space to sell the lovely scarves and textiles produced. Soft linen scarves in purples, pinks and oranges are perfect for summer, while heavier cottons are just right for winter. The prices are reasonable, with scarves costing from 200dh.

Fundouk Bin Chababa

Place Bab Fteuh (no phone). **Open** 9am-8pm daily. **No credit cards**. **Map** p57 B5 ⓴ **Metalware**

Just off Jemaa El Fna, heading towards rue Mouassine, is place Bab Fteuh, home to several old *fundouks* (merchants' inns). Our favourite is Fundouk Bin Chababa, piled high with metal platters, hammam buckets, candelabras and other various bits and pieces, some in better condition than others. The prices are fair.

Haj Ahmed Oueld Lafram

51 Souk Smata (0524 44 51 27). **Open** 10am-6.30pm Mon-Thur, Sat, Sun. **No credit cards**. **Map** p57 C2 ㉑ **Slippers**

Most of the souk's slipper shops are much of a muchness – look into one and you've pretty much seen them all. But Haj Ahmed Oueld Lafram offers a selection of *babouches* in a variety of styles from all over Morocco – embroidered leather ones from Tafraoute, for example – and in a variety of materials that include the likes of dyed goat fur, Italian horse leather and python skin. They're not the cheapest ones around, but the quality is excellent.

Mohammed Ouledhachmi

34 Souk El-Hararin Kedima (0666 64 41 05). **Open** 10am-8pm Mon-Thur, Sat, Sun. **No credit cards. Map** p57 C2 ㉒ **Copperware**

Mohammed does copper – copper trays, copper pots, copper kettles and so on. Only a few of the pieces are new. To find the shop, head north up Souk El-Attarin and take the second right after passing the entrance to the mosque on your left.

★ Rahal Herbes

43-47 Rahba Kedima (0524 39 03 61). **Open** 9am-8pm daily. **No credit cards. Map** p57 C4 ㉓ **Herbal remedies**

The west side of Rahba Kedima is lined with herbalists and 'black magic' stores; we recommend Rahal because of owner Abdeljabbar's fluency in English and keen interest in herbal remedies. Abdeljabbar grew up in the shop, which was originally his father's. Today it mostly sells argan oils, but have a seat and Abdeljabbar will soon share the secrets he learned from his father. Chances are you'll leave with a few natural mixtures for any aches and pains you may have.

► *For more about traditional beliefs, and what a dried chameleon can do for you, see p70 A Kind of Magic.*

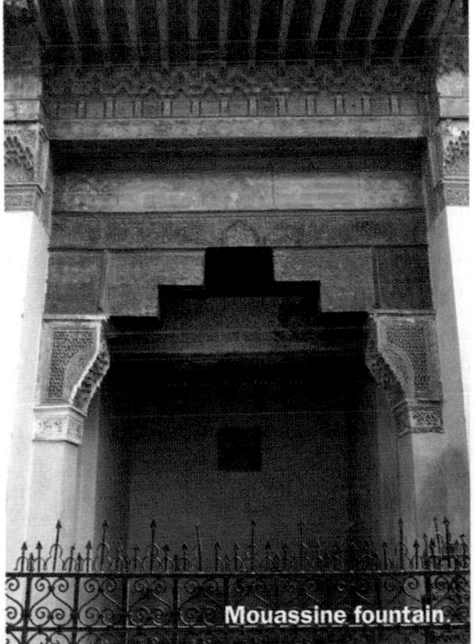

Mouassine fountain.

MOUASSINE & AROUND

Although it's far from immediately apparent, Mouassine is rapidly becoming the most chic of Medina quarters. West of the main souk area and north of Jemaa El Fna, it's home to a growing number of smart boutiques, interesting galleries and hip *maisons d'hôtes*.

Immediately on entering **rue Mouassine** from place Bab Fteuh is **Beldi** (*see p56*), a must-stop shop for the likes of Jean Paul Gaultier and sundry international fashions. West of the junction with rue Ksour, three elaborate brass lanterns above the alleyway mark the doorway of Ksour Agafay private members' club.

At the point where the street widens to embrace the walls of the **Mouassine Mosque** (which lends its name to the quarter and was erected in the 1560s by Saadian Sultan Abdellah El-Ghalib), a side street (signposted) off to the west winds left then first right to reach a large wooden doorway with a signplate reading **Dar Cherifa** (*see p60*). Inside is a stunning late 16th-century riad with filigree stucco and beautiful carved cedar detailing. It operates as a gallery and performance space, doubling as a café during the day.

Where rue Mouassine hits **rue Sidi El-Yamami**, a dim little archway under a sign reading 'A la Fibule' jogs left and right to the fantastical façade of the **Ministero del Gusto** (*see p60*), an extraordinary gallery-cum-sales space executed in an architectural style that co-creator Alessandra Lippini describes as 'delirium'.

Following rue Sidi El-Yamami west leads to the city gate **Bab Laksour**, in the vicinity of which is the Moroccan restaurant **Tobsil** (*see p41*). In the opposite direction, a few paces east of the mosque along Sidi El-Yamami is the **Mouassine fountain**, with quadruple drinking bays, three for animals and one – the most ornate – for people. It's here that the character Louis Bernard is fatally stabbed in Hitchcock's 1955 version of *The Man Who Knew Too Much* – although not so fatally that he can't first stagger half a mile to Jemaa El Fna to expire in the arms of Jimmy Stewart.

Beside the fountain is an arched gateway, beyond which is the **Souk des Teinturiers** (*see p52*). A couple of rooms within the gateway, above the arch, are now part of a boutique called **Atelier Moro** (114 place de Mouassine) run by Colombian Viviana González. It's a good place to buy funky decorative items, clothes, glass and beadwork.

Between the mosque and the fountain, the road weaves south down to the new **Douiria Mouassine** (a *douiria* is a traditional reception area of a house for male guests with a separate staircase) that shelters exquisite examples of decorative arts that were buried, before restoration, under layers of plaster; *see p60*.

Dar Cherifa.

Further north up the street are a couple of good examples of *fundouks*. A *fundouk* – in Marrakech – is the distant forerunner of the modern hotel. It was a merchant hostel, built to provide accommodation and warehousing for the caravan traders who had crossed the desert and mountains to the south to bring their wares into the marketplaces of Marrakech. A *fundouk* offered stabling and storage rooms on the ground floor, bedrooms off the upper galleries, and a single gated entrance to the street that was locked at night for security. Most of the city's surviving *fundouks* now operate as ramshackle artisans' workshops, such as the one at 192 rue Mouassine, **Fundouk Sarsare**. It also featured in the film *Hideous Kinky* as the hotel where Kate Winslet and her daughters lodged. Another grand *fundouk* across the street is thought to be the oldest surviving example of this building type in Marrakech.

At the junction of rue Mouassine and rue Dar El-Bacha, take a right and then the first right which opens out into **Souk Cherifia**, a multistorey venture with chic designers and creators based on the first floor (*see p64*), and the **Terrasse des Epices** restaurant (*see p63*) on the top terrace.

A few steps north of the *fundouks* is a crossroads: go left for the Dar El-Bacha and Bab Doukkala (*see p70*) or right for the dyers' quarter (*see p52*), but only adherents of Islam should proceed straight ahead, according to a sign that reads 'Non Moslem interdit'.

Up this particular alley is the **Shrine of Sidi Abdel-Aziz** (*see p68* **A Tour of the Backstreets**), resting place of one of the seven saints of Marrakech. Collectively known as 'El-Sebti', this group of holy men have been venerated for centuries as guardians of the city. Each has a shrine erected by Sultan Moulay Ismail in the 18th century. All the shrines are within, or just outside, the walls of the Medina and once a year they are the focus of a seven-day *moussem* (pilgrimage).

Sights & museums

★ FREE Dar Cherifa

8 Derb Charfa Lakbir (0524 42 64 63, www.marrakech-riads.net). **Open** 10am-7pm daily. **No credit cards**. **Map** p57 A3 (24)

This gorgeous townhouse is the Medina's premier exhibition space. Parts of the building date back to the 16th century and it has been lovingly restored by owner Abdelatif Ben Abdellah, who's taken great pains to expose the carved beams and stucco work while leaving walls and floors bare and free of distraction. Regular exhibitions lean towards resident foreign artists, but there have also been shows by Moroccan artists Hassan Hajjaj and Milaudi Nouiga, and lately there's been an interesting roster of cultural events, too, ranging from live music to poetry readings. The space also includes a small library, tea and coffee are served, and there's a light lunch menu.

★ Douiria Mouassine

5 Derb El-Hammam (0524 38 57 21, www.douiria.com). **Open** 10am-6pm Mon-Thur, Sat, Sun. **Admission** 30dh. **No credit cards**. **Map** p57 B3 (25)

Patrick Manac'h and Hamid Mergani of the Maison de la Photographie (*see p53*) have restored this petite reception apartment to its 17th-century glory. As you descend into a warren of alleys behind the Mouassine mosque, there is little that prepares you for encountering the exquisite decorative work within: a stunning symmetry of masterful pigmented stucco, double-stacked, decorated lintels on one side, and horseshoe doors on the other. A side room is enhanced by an arch of *muquarnas* (honeycombed architectural ornamentation) illuminated by vibrant pigments, including an irridescent peacock blue. The top terrace is a quiet refuge from the souks.

Ministero del Gusto

FREE *22 Derb Azouz El-Mouassine, off rue Sidi El-Yamami (0524 42 64 55, www.ministerodelgusto.com)*. **Open** 10am-1.30pm daily. By appointment 4.30-6.30pm daily. **Map** p57 A2 (26)

Showroom for the design talents and eclectic tastes of owners ex-*Vogue Italia* fashion editor Alessandra Lippini and Fabrizio Bizzarri, this eccentric space also hosts occasional exhibitions; when they're finished Alessandra and Fabrizio continue stocking work by the artists and designers they like. These include Essaouira-based English artist Micol, American photographer Martin H M Schreiber, the Italian multimediaist Maurizio Vetrugno, Indonesian painter Ribka and Marrakchi pop artist Hassan Hajjaj. Lippini also has a large collection of vintage fashion, much of it worn by the stars and salvaged from film sets after the wrap.

▶ *For more about the merchandise, see p64.*

Restaurants & cafés

Le Jardin

32 Souk El-Jeld, Sidi Abdelaziz, nr Souk Cherifia (0524 37 82 95, http://lejardin.ma). **Open** 10am-10pm daily. **Main courses** 70dh-150dh. **Alcohol served**. **Map** p57 B1 ㉗ **Moroccan Bistro**

Local restaurateur and all-round hotshot Kamal Laftimi opened Le Jardin as an extension to his growing restaurant empire and as an opportunity to make the most of local talent. A small grocery store at the entrance sells organic fruit and vegetables from local farmers, and one of the balcony rooms overlooking the courtyard has been taken over by Norya ayroN's glamorous kaftan shop (*see p64*). In the restaurant, the food focuses on fresh, lively dishes over the more ubiquitous stodge. Think marinated sardines (roll-mop style), a 'garden' burger, or rare-grilled duck with caramelised figs accompanied by a crisp Moroccan white. The green-tiled oasis with primrose accents is full of banana palms, lemon trees and bamboo, plus chattering canaries and resident tortoises, and makes for cooling respite from the clamour of the souks.

Terrasse des Epices

15 Souk Cherifia, Sidi Abdelaziz (0524 37 59 04, www.terrassedesepices.com). **Open** 11.30am-11.30pm daily. **Main courses** 90dh-145dh. **Map** p57 B2 ㉘ **Moroccan Bistro**

When this rooftop restaurant opened a few years ago it revolutionised life in the Marrakech Medina. All of a sudden there was somewhere quiet and hidden away to sit out of the sun; natty shaded dining booths are plumbed to spritz fresh, orange-scented water on to guests. Elephant grass down the middle of the terrace softens its edges, and the food represents an early attempt at modernising the classics. A John Dory fillet with fresh ginger and lemon is typical, but simpler dishes such as a bowl of cooling gazpacho or a caesar salad are good too. No alcohol.

Bars

Café Arabe

184 rue Mouassine (0524 42 97 28, www.cafearabe.com). **Open** 10am-midnight daily. **Map** p57 B2 ㉙

A good cocktail is not an easy thing to find in the Medina, but the Café Arabe delivers the goods. What a bonus, after dinner on the Jemaa El Fna (about five minutes' walk away), to find yourself perched at a half-moon bar on a rooftop, or kicking back on the low-slung sofas beneath the stars on a balmy night. Providing you stick to the classics – a gin and tonic, an Americano, maybe a shot of Fernet Branca – you'll find this a welcome splash of Europe with a thoroughly North African vibe.

Shops & services

Abdelhakim Keddabi

115 rue Mouassine (0670 21 68 48). **Open** 9am-7pm daily. **No credit cards**. **Map** p57 B2 ㉚ **Bags**

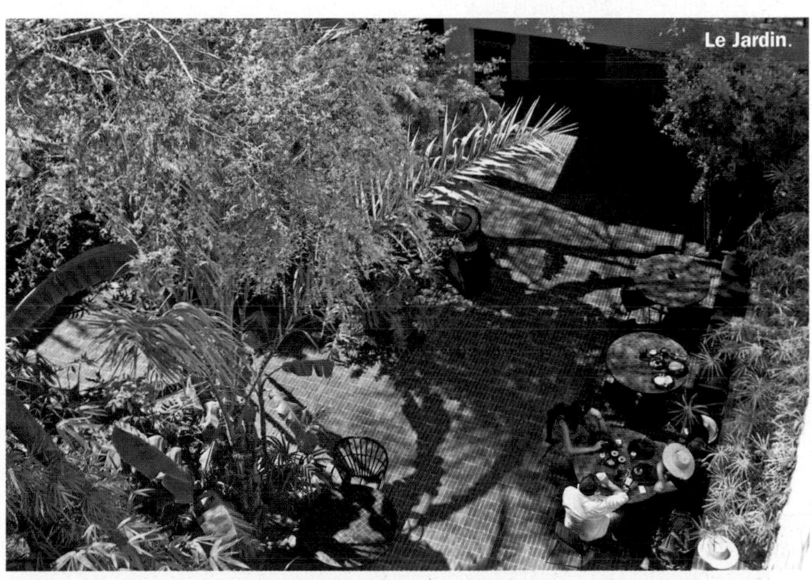
Le Jardin.

MARKET FORCES

Uncover some hidden treasures.

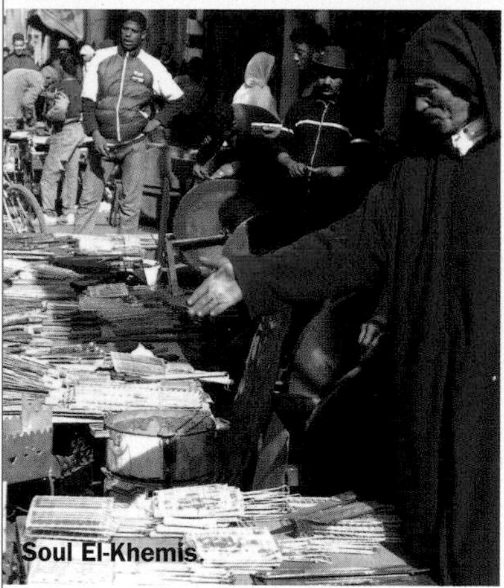

Soul El-Khemis.

Away from the souks' main lanes of concentrated commerce, small, specialised markets are worth investigating if you're looking for something a little more striking than a pair of same-same *babouches* or *tadelakt* salt-and-pepper shakers.

Just south of Rahba Kedima is **Souk Lagzhel** (map p57 C4). The site of the old slave market, it's now home to a second-hand clothes market. The piles of old garments spread out on the ground don't look like much, but you can uncover vintage kaftans and *ghondora* (robe-like tunics from the Sahara) and some great accessories. Arrive early for the best finds.

At the northern end of the Old City, just inside the Bab El-Khemis gate, you'll find the **Souk El-Khemis** (map p251 D2), which spreads chaotically through a quite handsome four-pronged hangar. The main covered area is where you'll find large-scale treasures such as antique cedarwood doors, roll-top baths and wrought-iron windows. Outside, the market spins off down unpaved roads and alleys, with commerce ranging from shops selling three-piece suites and bed frames, to blankets piled high with a pitiful heap of cast-offs – single shoes, a box of rusted bicycle gears, a bag of unravelled audio cassettes. Devotees know it, however, as a legendary treasure trove of architectural salvage. When La Mamounia underwent its last refit, the discarded sinks, light fittings and even carpets all turned up here, and when you enquire about the treasures within a particularly fine riad, chances are the owner scoped them out at Souk El-Khemis.

If you're looking for food, head to the old Jewish quarter of the Mellah, and the **Bab Es Salam market** (map p153 D7), one block east of the lively place des Ferblantiers (a good lunch spot). This market is very much a locals' affair, with traders selling jewel-bright fruit and vegetables, piles of herbs and postcard-perfect conical mounds of spices (though traders actually fake it by sticking a small amount of spice on to cardboard cones). It's the best place to stock up on freshly ground spices such as cumin, ground ginger and ras el-hanout (the legendary spice mix can feature up to 50 different ingredients if being used medicinally; most versions for cooking will have five or six). Nearby, on the south side of avenue Houman El-Fetouaki, is the **Marché Couvert** (map p253 C7), where *dadas* (private cooks) and housewives shop for meat and fish; this is where you're most likely to be brought if you sign up for a cookery class.

Bab Es Salam market.

This is one of the few storefronts with display windows in the area. From here Abdelhakim, a local Marrakchi, sells his simple handbag designs made from soft leathers. The focus is on functional designs produced in his nearby workshop. The collection includes carry-alls and totes, as well as smaller bags – all come in a range of colours.

Atelier Moro

114 place de Mouassine (0524 39 16 78/0660 54 35 20, ateliermoro@menara.ma). **Open** 9am-1pm, 3-7pm Mon, Wed-Sun. **Map** p57 B3 ㉛ **Fashion & Homewares**

This L-shaped first-floor space by the Mouassine fountain contains a cool, eclectic selection of homeware, clothes, accessories and carpets chosen by Viviana González. Some of the clothes are designed by Viviana herself and a few other items are from her native Colombia, but most of the stock is Moroccan, often the work of nameless artisans that would otherwise be lost in the souks. There's everything from inexpensive handmade scissors and Tuareg cutlery to pricey rugs, lamps made from ostrich eggs and suede or Egyptian cotton tops. The door is to the west of the fountain, just right of the arch that leads into the Souk des Teinturiers.

Caverne d'Ali Baba

17A derb Fhal Chidmi (0524 44 21 48). **Open** 9am-8pm daily. **Map** p57 A4 ㉜ **Homewares**

This huge shop is stocked with an incredible array of goods, from egg cups to lamp bases, in all imaginable colours. In fact, just about any pottery trend that has hit the Medina will very quickly be copied and put on sale here. Especially attractive are the tadelakt-finish items, which have an almost soft, leather-like appearance.

Cherkaoui

120-122 rue Mouassine (0524 42 68 17). **Open** 9am-8pm daily. **Map** p57 B2 ㉝ **Homewares**

Opposite the Mouassine fountain is this glittering Aladdin's cave, full of everything imaginable in the way of home decoration Moroccan-style (with the exception of carpets). The proprietors, one local (Jaoud) and one German (Matthias), use local artisans, 120 in fact, working in various media including wood, leather, metal and clay, to supply the store. Customers include famed hotels La Mamounia and Royal Mansour, as well as film glitterati including Gwyneth Paltrow. Any piece can be made up in eight weeks, and shipping can be arranged.

Chez Alaoui

52 rue des Ksour (0662 08 48 71). **Open** 9am-8pm daily. **Map** p57 B4 ㉞ **Ceramics**

A great place to look for ceramics in a variety of styles including Berber (which looks very African, with bold, clean shapes) and both old and new pieces from Safi, one of Morocco's main pottery-producing centres. Our favourites are the traditional green ceramics from Tamegroute near Zagora. The green glaze never comes out quite the same, so each piece is unique.

KIS Boutique

36 derb Fhal Chidmi (0524 37 82 52, www.kismarrakech.com). **Open** 10am-2pm, 3-7pm Tue-Sun. **Map** p57 A3 ㉟ **Fashion**

KIS (Keep it Secret) is a cute little hideaway. The turquoise premises hold the fashions and accessories of a handful of select designers. Up the tiled stairs, you'll find Fleur de Pirate's neon shirts, manager Abdel's 'funky Marrakech' mugs and fridge magnets, Salam's sweet pompomed children's slippers, Siroko's stuffed camel toys in bright prints, Brahim's bags and leather-fringed beach blankets, and Caroline Constancio's fashions. Not to mention potato-sack bags emblazoned with the Hand of Fatima in silver sequins. Need time out from the souks? Head for the café on the top terrace, with turquoise tables, tiki parasols and pink cushions.

La Maison du Kaftan Marocain

65 rue Sidi El Yamani (0524 44 10 51). **Open** 9am-7.30pm daily. **Map** p57 A3 ㊱ **Fashion & Homewares**

La Maison may have the unloved, run-down look of a charity shop, but it also has the widest selection of Moroccan clothing for men, women and children in the souk, housed in what sustained exploration reveals to be a vast mausoleum of a place. Stock ranges from *pantalon turque* (traditional men's trousers) to beautiful velvet jackets and vintage kaftans that go for 20,000dh. Clothing can be made to measure; it typically takes up to a week to create a tailored garment. Stock has expanded to include cushions, poufs and textiles decorated with traditional Moroccan embroidery styles.

Maktabet El Chab

rue Mouassine (0667 23 25 27). **Open** 9am-8.30pm daily. **Map** p57 A4 ㊲ **Books**

AKA the 'FNAC Berbère' bookshop, this corner kiosk claims to be 'La première librairie à Marrakech', founded in 1941. The stock of coffee table books is largely in French, but includes tomes on Moroccan interior design, cookery and the arts. Upstairs is a small café with views over the Medina.

Maktoub by Max and Jan

128 Souika Fontaine Mouassine (0524 37 55 70, www.maxandjan.ma). **Open** 9.30am-8pm daily. **Map** p57 B2 ㊳ **Fashion**

Just across from the Mouassine fountain, this concept store largely sells modern Moroccan styles in bright colours created by Agadir-based designers Max & Jan. Bright oranges, fuschias and greens, together with softer blues and browns, are common colours for the fitted dresses, *sarouel* pants, flowing kaftans and one-piece suits. The collection changes seasonally and a range of accessories is available to complete the look.

Pop-up Shop – Norya ayroN.

Ministero del Gusto

22 derb Azouz El-Mouassine, off rue Sidi El Yamani (0524 42 64 55, www.ministerodelgusto.com). **Open** 10am-1.30pm daily; also by appointment 4.30-6.30pm daily. **Map** p57 A2 ❸❾ **Homewares**

HQ to Alessandra Lippini and her business partner Fabrizio Bizzarri, the Ministerio is a surreal space – a sort of Gaudí goes Mali with a side trip to Mexico. As well as filling the role of informal social centre for friends and assorted fashionistas and creatives blowing through town, the two floors also act as an occasional gallery and a showcase for funky 'found' objects (sourced from house clearances) such as African-inspired furniture, Eames chairs and Bernini glassware, plus a vintage fashion collection, some of it salvaged from film sets.

► *For more about art at the Ministero, see p60.*

Al Nour

57 rue Laksour (0524 39 03 23, www.alnour-textiles.com). **Open** 9am-2pm, 3-7pm daily. **Map** p57 A4 ❹⓿ **Fashion & Homewares**

Socially responsible shoppers will want to check out Al Nour, which provides an embroidery workshop for disabled women, who are happy to chat as they work away on home accessories including place mats, napkins and tablecloths in colourful patterns. The children's clothing is adorable; the women's fashion line is simple and reasonably priced.

Pop-up Shop – Norya ayroN

32 Souk El Jeld, Sidi Abdelaziz, nr Souk Cherifia (0661 29 59 90, www.norya-ayron.com). **Open** 11.30am-9.30pm daily. **Map** p57 B1 ❹❶ **Fashion**

Located up some stairs inside Le Jardin (*see p61*), Algerian-French designer Norya ayroN's Moroccan-inspired womenswear is becoming a hit with the stars. Trendy, yet comfortable, colourful kaftans and one-of-a-kind robes are what Pop-up Shop is known for. Sharon Stone stopped by on a recent visit to Marrakech and her photo sits on the desk. Kaftans start at 690dh and *gandouras* cost from 1,090dh.

★ Souk Cherifia

Sidi Abdelaziz (http://souk-cherifia.com). **Open** 10am-7.30pm daily (some shops closed Tue). **Map** p57 B2 ❹❷ **Souk**

Some of the city's most exciting designers and artists have opened small, fixed-price boutiques in Souk Cherifia to sell their alluring wares and hip creations. Come with plenty of cash – or steely resistance. Beautifully soft leather handbags are sold at Lalla (0524 38 36 85, www.shop-lalla.com) – check out the classic habibi and the fringed hippy habibi (1,500dh), which come in a range of colours; at Sissimorocco (0615 22 65 20, www.sissimorocco.com) French designer Sylvie Pissard has a range of funky, stylish cushions (750dh). Also here are Artsi Ifrach's fabulous, innovative designs under his Art/C label – cartoon flamingo print kaftan, anyone? Hassan Hajjij has a small outlet here too, selling his wheat-sack *babouches*, couscous-sack totes and a reworked Barbie in a box, Moroccan style. For men there's Randall Bachner's Marrakshi Life (0659 79 73 54) with its natty threads – smart shirts and stylish scarves set against a gorgeous backdrop of blue-hued tiles. Note that only some of the boutiques take credit cards.

Tapis Akhnif

6 rue Mouassine (0524 42 60 96). **Open** 9am-9pm daily. **Map** p57 A4 ❹❸ **Carpets**

A small family business, run by a father and his two sons, Akhnif offers a wide array of carpets, raffia and wool rugs and large pouffes. There's no sales hassle and prices are fair.

NORTHERN MEDINA

North of the shrine Sidi Abdel-Aziz in Mouassine, the road zigzags east then north, then east and north again on to **rue Bab Taghzout**, which runs north to the resting place of another of the city's renowned saints, the **Shrine of Sidi Bel Abbas**. En route is the stately **Chrob ou Chouf** – 'Drink and Look' – a monumental 18th-century fountain.

Soon after widening to accommodate a local bus stop and scrubby park, the street narrows again to squeeze through the ornate gateway known as **Bab Taghzout**, with its

ON FOOT SOUK SAFARI

Allow at least two hours.

From Jemaa El Fna, head off into the entrance of the souks opposite the Café de France and walk north between the souvenirs, spices and the egg market. Make your way through an arch that leads into the main spine of the souks, **rue Semarine**. This main street is straight and easy to follow. It passes stalls selling textiles, lanterns and leather.

Rue Semarine eventually transforms itself into **Souk El-Kebir**. When wafts of varnish and wood shavings enter your nostrils, you know that you've reached the furniture-making section and are at the end of the souks. Go left at the T-junction, then immediately right and you should come on to a main thoroughfare. The open square of the **place Ben Youssef** is just up on the left ahead of you. On your right will be the **Musée de Marrakech** (*see p55*). At the entrance to the museum is a pleasant café with parasols. The museum itself has refreshingly cool rooms and a spacious main courtyard with what must be the biggest chandelier ever made.

Coming out of the museum you should see the **Medersa Ben Youssef** (*see p53*) far down on your right, and the **Koubba** (*see p53*) on your far left. The Medersa's elaborate wall carvings and beautiful proportions are superlative.

With your back to the Koubba, take a left and walk away from the museum, with the Ben Youssef Mosque on your right. Take the second left into the leather stalls and keep bearing left around the tea stall (notice the 'Clinique du Ballon', which sells and repairs ancient rugby and soccer balls); take the path to the extreme left and walk through the **Souk des Babouches** and then turn right back on yourself at an opening with a mosque door, and return to the opening where the 'Clinique du Ballon' is. Turn left under an arch marked 'Souk Belaarif' into **Souk Haddadin**.

You should come to a little mosque on your left. You then go straight over an opening and towards a T-junction. Here you can turn left into the **Souk des Teinturiers**. Remaining on the main path, the street bends right and under an arch and then left past the big mosque – the 16th-century **Mouassine Mosque** – this should be on

your left. You then walk left opposite the Café Bougainvillier and keep going straight along the pleasant **rue Mouassine**. Walk past another little mosque on the right. You should see the attractive **KIS Boutique** (*see p63*), a good place for a break.

After passing yet another small mosque on your left, you should eventually come out of the souks under an archway and on to the triangular **place Bab Fteuh**. Take the right fork here and you'll find yourself on the north-western corner of the **Jemaa El Fna**.

Keep hugging the streets on the right and proceed down **rue Koutoubia**, packed with stalls of spices and dates. Walk past the Hôtel Les Jardins de la Koutoubia on your right and the slightly unsightly rear end of the Club Med on your left until you emerge in front of the stunning **Koutoubia Mosque**.

You can then turn back towards the Jemaa El Fna with the **place de Foucauld** on your right. Viscomte Charles de Foucauld was an eccentric French aristocrat who toured Morocco at the end of the 19th century disguised as a rabbi, and who later became a hermit in the Sahara. His bizarre life is described in *The Sword and the Cross* by Fergus Fleming. By the time you've walked past place de Foucauld and the rather smelly *calèches* on your right, you're back at the Jemaa El Fna again, and definitely deserve a drink.

THE SACRED SCRUB-DOWN

Get ready to rub.

Another one of those Moroccan 'must-do' experiences, the traditional hammam remains an integral part of Medina life. Aficionados of the lavish Turkish-style bathhouses may find them something of a disappointment. These days, public hammams in Marrakech are a pedestrian lot, in most cases, and often not terribly warm or clean. That's what happens when modern life takes over and you get your own bathroom installed at home.

However, canny entrepreneurs have spotted a gap in the market for something a little more tourist-friendly and there are plenty of fairly priced day spas around town, where a *gommage* (scrub-down with black soap) in a steam room, *rhassoul* (a white clay body mask infused with essential oils) and a massage on a marble slab will cost in the region of 200dh. You'll also get warmer temperatures and maybe an ice-cold plunge pool, a prettier environment and someone to look after you properly, though the ritual and etiquette remain much the same: both men and women strip down to their pants/ boxers and your attendant provides the rest: a new mitt for scrubbing, black olive-oil-based soap and clay, shampoo and a plastic comb if you want it. Do bring your own towel and a pair of flip-flops.

Expect to spend at least an hour having your dead skin sloughed away to squeaky-clean, baby-soft smoothness, and allow some time to chill out afterwards. The more boutique places often serve tea and a biscuit, and it's amazing how dreamy you'll feel just lolling about soaking up the vibe.

At the top end of the scale, in places such as **La Mamounia** (*see p201*), the **Royal Mansour** (*see p202*) and the **Selman Hotel** (*see p226*), you'll find eye-popping design on a fantastical scale. These are some of the most sensational hammam spas in the world – if you're travelling out of season and fancy a treat (at a fraction of the cost of staying overnight), they offer good-value day passes including lunch from around 1,500dh.

Hammam El-Bacha

20 rue Fatima Zohra, Dar El-Bacha (no phone). **Open** *Men* 7am-1pm daily. *Women* 1-9pm daily. **Rates** 7dh men; 7.50dh women; massage 50dh. **No credit cards**. **Map** p49 B2.

Probably the best-known traditional hammam in town, it used to be the local soak for the servants and staff of the Dar El-Bacha opposite. The dimensions are impressive, with a six-metre high cupola, and the women who work here do a fantastic scrub-down. Just remember it's as authentic as it gets: grit, grime and all.

Hammam de la Rose

130 rue Dar El-Bacha (0524 44 47 69, www.hammamdelarose.com). **Open** 10am-8pm daily. **Rates** hammam from 250dh; massage from 500dh. **Map** p49 A3.

This pretty newcomer to the Bacha area feels more luxurious than traditional hammams. The modern interior inlaid with bottle-green tiles against olive-green *tadelakt* is soothing, while the candle-lit steam rooms, scented with rose and orange blossom oils and scattered with rose petals, are a pleasing place to decompress. High-quality products and well-executed treatments make it one of the best deals in town.

Les Bains de Marrakech

2 derb Sedra, Bab Agnaou, Kasbah (0524 38 14 28, www.lesbainsdemarrakech.com). **Open** 9am-7.30pm daily. **Rates** hammam 170dh; massage 370dh. **No credit cards**. **Map** p77 A4.

French-born Kader Boufraine was among the first to open a boutique hammam in the Medina, and the first to offer dual massage and steam rooms so that couples could enjoy that floaty experience together. It's built around an exterior courtyard with a decent-sized swimming pool at its heart, with several hammam, massage and treatment rooms leading off it (including a mud-therapy room). Cream-coloured *tadelakt*, pierced lanterns, stained glass and gold-threaded textiles create a luxurious atmosphere that belies the price and begs you to linger.

Souk Cherifia.

six-inch thick wooden doors. This was one of the original Medina gates until the walls were extended in the 18th century to bring the shrine within the city.

Through the gateway and a few steps to the right is an even more elaborate arched gateway, executed in carved alabaster. Beyond is an arcade that was once lined with herbalists, faith healers and quack doctors here to minister to/prey on the sick drawn to the tomb to bask in its saintly *baraka* (blessings). Such beliefs remain strong, and the courtyard of the shrine – adorned with supposedly Marrakech's only sundial – is always filled with the crippled and infirm. If things don't work out, a shaded arcade on the south side harbours a decrepit gathering of largely blind characters, all of whom belong to a sect specialising in the ministering of last rites. The sanctuary itself is off limits; instead depart the courtyard on the western side where a large open plaza affords a photogenic view of the shrine's pyramidal green roofs.

Returning back through Bab Taghzout, a right turn leads down to the **Shrine of Sidi Ben Slimane El-Jazuli**, another of the patron saints of Marrakech. Active in the 15th century, he was an important Sufi mystic and his *Manifest Proofs of Piety* remains a seminal mystical text.

Restaurants & cafés

Dar Yacout

79 rue Ahmed Soussi, Arset Ihiri (0524 38 29 29, http://yacout.ma). **Open** 7pm-1am Tue-Sun. **Set meal** 700dh dinner. **Alcohol served. Map** p49 A4 ㊹ **Moroccan**

Yacout's fame rests more on its decor and sense of theatre than it does on the food it serves, but for design lovers it's completely worth it. The building is all show, a madcap mansion designed by American interior designer Bill Willis, who lived in Marrakech for 40 years prior to his death in 2009. There are flowering columns, candy striping and fireplaces in the bathrooms. Guests are invited up to the yellow crenellated rooftop terrace or into the first-floor lounge for pre-dinner drinks, before being taken down, past the swimming pool and across the courtyard, to be seated for dinner at great round tables, which are inset with mother-of-pearl. Reservations are essential. *Photo p70.*

Dar Zellij

1 Kaasour, Sidi Ben Slimane (0524 38 26 27, 0524 37 54 41, www.darzellij.com). **Open** 7.30pm-1.30am Mon, Wed, Thur; 12.30-2.30pm Fri-Sun. **Set menus** 350dh, 450dh, 600dh. **Alcohol served. Map** p57 B1 ㊺ **Moroccan**

More pared-back than many of the traditional riad restaurants, Dar Zellij has four dining rooms arranged around a regal courtyard of cool white plaster columns and orange trees, and an open-air lounge on the roof (for pre-dinner drinks). Dinner is a romantic affair; tables are scattered with rose petals, painted wood ceilings add colour to the minimalism, and fireplaces and candles create a warm glow. The food is excellent too, and attracts a mix of well-heeled Moroccans and discerning travellers. They come for Moroccan cuisine that goes beyond the usual tagines and couscous to include pristine seafood *b'stilla* and a memorable *trid royale* (plump pigeon wrapped up in tender, buttery pastry leaves), and an excellent wine list. Discreet local musicians add to the vibe without dominating it.

DAR EL-BACHA & AROUND

West of the Mouassine quarter and the city's holy shrines is the high-walled former residence of the most unsaintly Thami El-Glaoui, self-styled 'Lord of the Atlas' and ruler of Marrakech and southern Morocco throughout much of the first half of the 20th century (*see p184* **Glaoui Power**). Known locally as Dar El-Bacha

ON FOOT A TOUR OF THE BACKSTREETS

Allow two and a half to three hours. This walk – recommended by the tour guide Ahmed Tija (*see p37*) – takes you off the beaten tourist track.

Start in **Jemaa El Fna**. Standing with your back to the Café de France (*see p35*), take a right and head down the busy derb Dabachi for about 700 metres or five minutes. You are heading right, or east, of the square in the rough direction of the tanneries. Take a left turn (at a series of *teleboutiques*) towards the **Sidi Ben Salah** shrine and mosque. This road has a traditional dentist on the left. Walk on, noticing the Moroccan wedding shop on your right: everything for the traditional wedding party can be hired here, from elaborately decorated kaftans to singers.

Just before arriving at Ben Salah square is the first of several **fundouks** (merchants' hostels). On your right is **Fundouk Lahana**, which is more than 200 years old. It looks tatty but from the inside you have an excellent view of the **Sidi Ben Salah Mosque**, and if you walk up the stone steps on your right you can peer into some fascinating old wokshops, including one belonging to a traditional *djellaba* maker. The mosque is on the east side of the picturesque Ben Salah square. In another corner, up on the left, is one of the weirdest houses in Marrakech – a sort of tiled penthouse piled on top of other flats.

From the square, take a right and an immediate left and follow the street as it bends in a slight zig-zag past another *teleboutique*. The road then veers left and heads northwards. By this time you have come into the quarter known as El-Moqf. The street turns into a covered market area. Before heading north, on the right is a door (between a stationery shop and a seeds and grains store) that opens into one of the oldest *fundouks* in Marrakech, dating from the 16th century.

When you come out of this covered section, take the first left through the place and keep left (Souk Ahl Fès) passing the **Maison de la Photographie** (*see p53*) and head towards the Medersa Ben Youssef and the Foundouk restaurant. As you pass the restaurant, you can see yet another old 18th-century *fundouk*. At this point, walk towards a mini-fork in the road and keep to the right, walking past other dilapidated *fundouks* where you can see woodworkers.

As you follow the street around you will see in front of you a series of keyhole arches leading towards the Medersa Ben Youssef. Don't go this way. Instead, turn right and follow the alleyway, which bends left. As you walk on from here, you go under an arch. On emerging, head straight across the crossroads and towards the **Shrine of Sidi Abdel-Aziz**. An 18th-century doctor famed for his ability to help the mentally ill, Abdel-Aziz promises help for modern sufferers too and people come here hoping for a cure.

After you've seen the mausoleum, retrace your steps for a little way and turn right down **Riad El-Arous**. Continue for several minutes, bear right down **rue Sidi Ben Slimane**, passing the pâtisserie Marocaine on your left, and you should be able to see the mosque and shrine of **Sidi Ben Slimane El-Jazuli** (one of Marrakech's seven holy men) ahead of you. Take the next right turn and then left again at the T-junction into **rue Bab Taghzout**, which opens up into **Bab Taghzout square**, which provides a handy landmark for taking your bearings and has a taxi rank – useful if you're getting tired.

Now walk left towards the mosque and mausoleum of **Sidi Bel Abbas** (the greatest

Ben Youssef Mosque.

EXPLORE

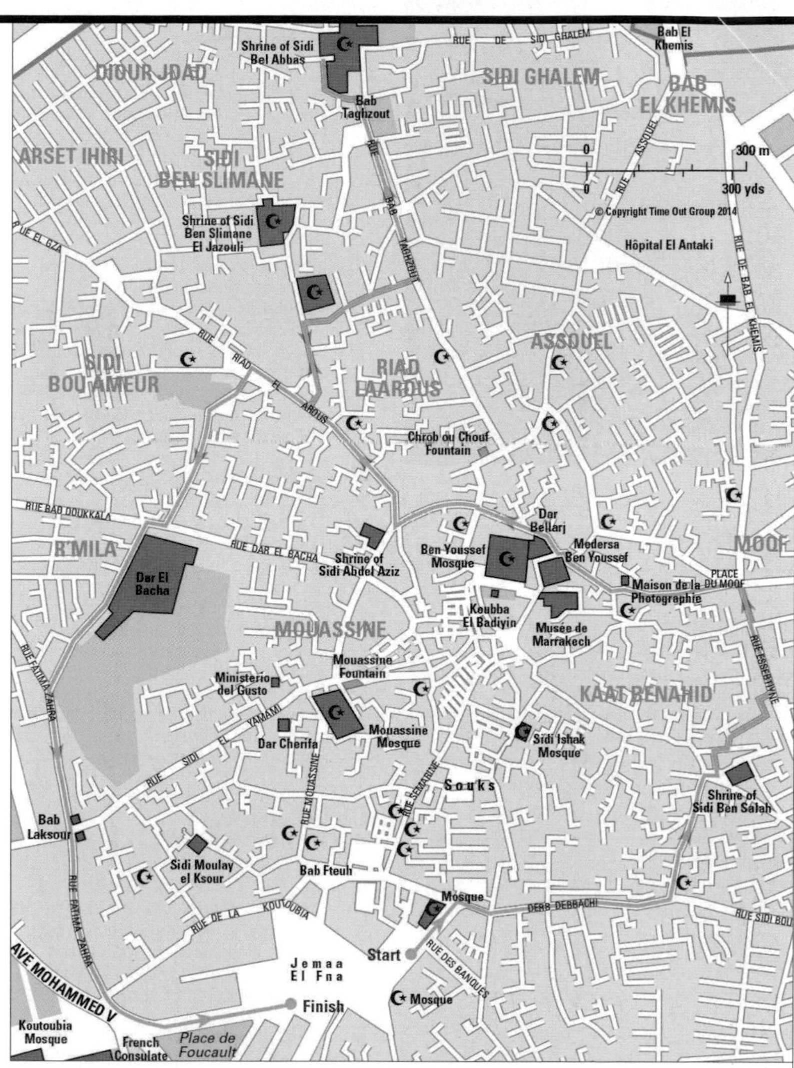

of the city's holy men). Walk under an archway and turn immediately right where you will be able to enter the courtyard of the mausoleum. Here, blind people gather to ask for alms. Walk through more courtyards and you can take an alleyway, off to the left, that goes round the whole building and takes you back to rue Bab Taghzout.

From here you will have to retrace your steps back towards Ben Slimane. From the small square of Riad El-Arous, take another right turn and then a left and walk towards **Dar El-Bacha** (House of the Pasha – it belonged to the notorious despot, Thami El-Glaoui).

Bear left, keeping the high walls of the palace on your left, and head down the long stretch of **rue Fatima Zahra**. On your right is Marrakech's most famous hammam: **Hammam El Bacha** (*see p66*). Rue Fatima Zohra eventually leads back towards the Koutoubia Mosque and Jemaa El Fna.

Dar Yacout. See p67.

('House of the Lord'), and also as Dar El-Glaoui, the residence dates from the early 20th century and is where the Glaoui entertained luminaries such as Churchill and Roosevelt, as well as the women his agents collected for him, scouring the streets for suitable prizes.

Facing the side wall of the Dar El-Bacha is another property with pedigree – owned »previously by the chamberlain of the Glaoui, later by French couturier Pierre Balmain ('dressmaking is the architecture of movement') and now the premises of Dar Moha, a lavish restaurant arranged around a turquoise pool, these days favoured by large tour groups.

Shops & services

Librairie Dar El Bacha

2 rue Dar El-Bacha (0524 39 19 73, www.darelbacha.com). **Open** 9am-1pm, 3.30-7pm daily (occasionally closed Sun). **Map** p49 A3 ㊻ **Books**

This small shop mostly stocks coffee-table books about Morocco and Marrakech, but there's also a decent selection of guidebooks and reproductions of old tourist posters. Books are available in both French and English.

★ Topolina

134 rue Dar El-Bacha (0651 34 57 95).
Open 9.30am-2pm, 3-7pm daily. **Map** p49 A3 ㊼ **Fashion**

This store is popular with shoppers who like one-of-a-kind fashion. Made with retro fabrics and bold patterns, the boho-chic collection includes colourful dresses and vintage handbags. Dainty pastel and floral patterned loafers are available for women (starting from 750dh), with more masculine colours available for men. A small seating area at the entrance is perfect for contemplating purchases.

BAB DOUKKALA

From Dar El-Bacha, **rue Bab Doukkala** runs due west for half a mile to the gate of the same name. At nos.142-144 is **Mustapha Blaoui** (*see p73*), venue for some of the best shopping in the Medina, and diagonally across the way is a recovery and refreshment stop, the **Henna Café** (www.hennacafemarrakech.com, open noon-evening), with profits being reinvested in the local community.

The major monument round here is the **Bab Doukkala Mosque**, built in 1558 by the mother of the Saadian sultans Abdel-Malek and Ahmed El-Mansour. It's fronted by the Sidi El-Hassan fountain, now dry, fenced around and under restoration. Behind the fountain a hand-painted 'WC' signposts the city's oldest toilets, built at the same time as the Doukkala Mosque opposite. They're still in use.

Across from the fountain, a small rose-pink building houses a 400-year-old hammam (men only) with a fantastic cedarwood ceiling in the reception area. Enter an alley, between no.141 rue Bab Doukkala and a bike shop, to witness the medieval scene behind the hammam. In a cavernous blackened pit at the end of the alley, men darkened by smoke shovel woodchips into the enormous oven that stokes up the heat for the hammam. The westernmost stretch of rue Bab Doukkala is mostly the domain of the butchers and vegetable sellers. It verges on the macabre, with prominent displays of decapitated heads and mounds of glistening offal. Note that all the hanging bits of carcass display testicles:

IN THE KNOW
A KIND OF MAGIC

Looking around the Rahba Kedima (*see p48*), you may wonder just what those jars of leeches and dried chameleons are for. The answer is magic. Many Moroccans hold fast to a cosmology that embraces Islam, local saints and the *djinn* – spirits. Mentioned in the Quran, *djinn* are generally invisible to humans, but humans appear clearly to the *djinn* and, what's more, *djinn* can possess people. In Moroccan mythology they're very often creatures of the dark side. But humans have weapons they can use against them and their malice – and they're found in the market. There are incenses and compounds for all kinds of situations, and chameleons are useful to ward off the evil eye. Toss one into a wood-fired oven and walk around it three times. If it explodes, you're free. If it melts, you're still in trouble.

Moroccans don't eat female meat, so butchers are mindful to prove the masculine provenance of their produce. The massive Almoravid gate of **Bab Doukkala** is now bypassed by a modern road that breaches the city walls. There's a *petit taxi* rank at the foot of the gatehouse.

Restaurants & cafés

★ Maison Arabe

1 derb Assehbe (0524 38 70 10, www.lamaison arabe.com). **Open** 7-11pm daily. **Set meal** 350dh (drinks not included). **Alcohol served**. **Map** p49 A1 ㊽ **Moroccan & Asian Fusion**

The original Maison Arabe was opened by two French women at the end of World War II. It was the first foreign-owned restaurant in the Medina and fast became a social hub for the city's illustrious visitors – film stars, artists and politicians among them. The place has expanded (it's also a hotel, *see p211*) and changed hands a few times since then, but under the directorship of its latest owner, Fabrizio Ruspoli, Maison Arabe has regained much of its glamorous lustre. If you can't stay the night, at least come for supper. There are two restaurants – one serving exquisite Moroccan haute cuisine in a room lavishly decorated with antique textiles and filigree lanterns by celebrated local designer Yahya Rouach, the other a more casual eaterie alongside the pool that fuses Mediterranean and Asian ingredients – as well as an atmospheric Piano Bar. Booking is recommended.

Bars

Piano-Jazz Bar

Maison Arabe, 1 derb Assehbe (0524 38 70 10, www.lamaisonarabe.com). **Open** 3-11pm daily. **Map** p49 A1 ㊾

The leather-panelled walls, club chairs and sofas, tribal rugs, a fire in the hearth, imposing big-game art (an elephant in oils) and a tinkling piano make this bar feel utterly *Out of Africa*. Best of all is Rachid, who's been head barman here since anyone can remember and whose take on service is to make everyone feel like a long-lost friend, whether he's delivering an expertly mixed bloody mary or his secret remedy, hot ginger shot (if he spots you've got a cold). Cocktails start at 85dh, a glass of house wine at 70dh and a beer at 40dh. Lebanese bar snacks are a welcome touch too, and the platter of houmous, red pepper relish, spiced cucumber, baba ganoush and labneh is a good deal at 130dh. *Photo p73.*

Shops & services

Aswak Assalam

Avenue du 11 Janvier (0524 43 10 04, www.aswakassalam.com). **Open** 9am-10pm daily. **Map** p49 A1 ㊿ **Food & Drink**

Across from the *gare routière* at Bab Doukkala, this decent-sized supermarket offers the closest good

Topolina.

EXPLORE

STIR IT UP

Learn to cook Moroccan-style.

One of the greatest ways to get to know a culture is through its food. Moroccan culinary culture is extremely rich, and cooking and eating remains a deeply entrenched community-based activity. Signing up for a cookery class offers the opportunity to spend quality time with someone from Marrakech and to view the city and its food through their eyes.

Nearly all teachers are happy to take students on a shopping expedition to local markets before starting the class, to provide tips on selecting spices and buying produce, for a first-hand explanation of traditional cooking equipment such as the *gsaa* used to knead bread, or to visit the *ferran* (community oven) where it is baked. You may even stop by a butcher (the traditional makers of *tangia*; *see p43*) with a terracotta urn to drop off at the hammam, while you do the rest of your class.

The long-established cooking classes at **Maison Arabe** (*see p71*) were the first to arrive on the scene and remain among the best for getting a handle on the preparation and cooking of traditional Moroccan dishes. Classes are structured around traditional Moroccan feast classics: a couple of starters (soups and salads) and a main course (tagine or couscous), or a main course and a dessert. Prices start at around 600dh per person for a group of four to ten (800dh for smaller groups; private one-on-one classes are also available).

The classes are held in the hotel's swanky new culinary studio in a lush garden just outside town – and it's state-of-the-art stuff. Everyone gets their own station, with a small flat-screen TV to show what the *dada* is doing up close, and courses are big on details that include a potted history of Moroccan gastronomy and visiting a local bakery, right through to making edible flower-shaped garnishes (food presentation in Morocco can be exquisite). Kids are welcome to join in and if you're finding the buzz of Marrakech a bit too much, it makes for a wonderfully stimulating, but more relaxed, day out.

The new kid on the block is Clock Kitchen at **Café Clock** (*see p80*). Situated in the Kasbah, it's a modern, light-filled space on the roof terrace and it brings a fresh angle to the established cookery class routine. Because it's some distance away from the main produce markets, shopping trips can be done by *calèche* (horse and carriage) and there's lots of opportunity for more specialised workshops, including bread-baking, pastry-making and foods cooked in community ovens. Most classes (maximum eight students) take a half day, though it is possible to sign up for more if you have the enthusiasm. Classes take place around a central island, allowing for lots of social interaction and highly personalised attention from the chef. While much of the conversation drifts around food and eating in Morocco, there's plenty of laughter and banter to keep it light-hearted.

For a taste of the new wave, the tailor-made private classes with chef Omar at **Maison MK** (*see p205*) are a boon for enthusiasts who have already worked their way around the various salads, couscous and tagines, though you can learn about these too. Because classes are limited to two people, there's more flexibility, and Omar is happy to consult about the kind of things you're interested in making, and to put together a customised menu that might include dishes such as a deconstructed pigeon *b'stilla*, or a contemporary dessert of spiced cucumber sorbet with mint foam. The price for a full morning of cooking with lunch is 2,000dh for two.

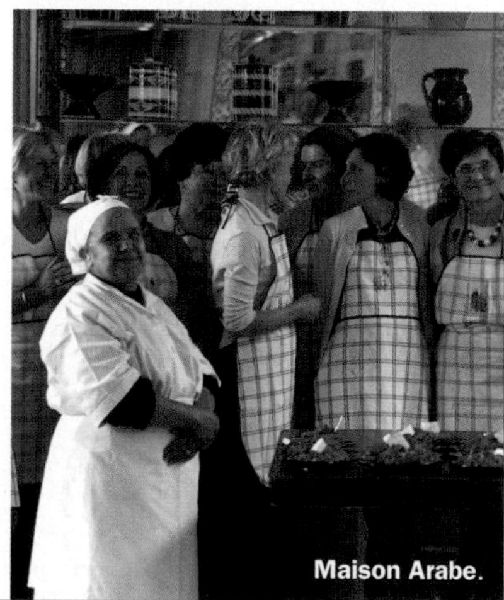

Maison Arabe.

grocery shopping to the Medina. Note that there's no booze here though. It has less choice than Marjane (*see p109*) and Carrefour and is pricier, but it's also much more convenient for anyone without a car.

★ Mustapha Blaoui

142-144 rue Bab Doukkala (0524 38 52 40, tresordesnomades@hotmail.com). **Open** 9am-7pm daily. **No credit cards. Map** p49 A2 ⓫
Homewares

This is the classiest, most loved 'best of Morocco' depot in town. It's a warehouse of a place: crammed, racked, stacked and piled with floor-to-ceiling irresistibles – lanterns, dishes, pots, bowls, candlesticks, chandeliers, chests, tables and chairs… If Mustapha doesn't have it, then you don't need it. He supplied a lot of the furnishings for both the Villa des Orangers (*see p202*) and the nearby Riad Noir d'Ivoire (*see p213*). Even people who don't own a hotel will find it almost impossible to visit here and not fill a container lorry. Added to which, Mustapha is a real sweetheart, his staff are ultra-helpful and shipping here is a cinch.

Piano-Jazz Bar. *See p71.*

THE TANNERIES

To experience Marrakech at its most raw, not to mention most pungent, take a taxi to the place du Moqf and walk east along rue de Bab Debbagh to the tannery district. The tanners have been here since the city was founded and legend has it that they are descended from demons who lived under a black king. He condemned them to their vocation for failing to obey his rules. Some workers still believe that the tanneries are inhabited by *jinns* or spirits.

The tanners use hundreds of concrete vats to process the skins that are bought at the city's markets. The treatment of the skins remains a pre-industrial process. First, hair and traces of flesh are removed. To do this the skins are soaked in vats of quicklime and water to bring the skins 'back to life'. They are then washed and pressed in other vats. After that, the skins are placed in a vat of water and blood, which strengthens them. They are believed by some to gain a male and a female soul during the tanning process, which leads to their 'rebirth'. Workers separate and wring the skins, which are suspended over one of the vats. In order to dye the skins, they are rubbed with pomegranate powder to colour them yellow. Olive oil is then used to make them shiny. Other traditional products, such as bark, saffron, henna and poppy are also used to dye the skins. The vats used to dye the skins are kept covered to prevent the sunlight from affecting the process. Stretched-out skins are then left to dry in the sun beside the tanneries. This whole complex process takes 20 days.

Many of the workers and their families live around the tanneries, an area traditionally considered marginal; the tanners themselves are also considered to be on the edges of society despite the skill required for the job, and the apprenticeship process required to acquire those skills. The work makes tanners prone to arthritis, and they often have to retire in their 40s, at which point their sons are inducted into the family trade.

The tanneries can be tricky to find but some loitering youth will always approach unaccompanied foreigners and offer his services as a guide. One is easy to find, though: just before **Bab Debbagh**, on the right and opposite the Au Rêve Berbère shop, is an arch marked 'Fin XI siecle' and a sign 'Association Sidi Yacoub pour les tanneurs'.

The tanneries fill large yards and, with rows of lozenge-shaped pools of various hues, look like giant paintboxes. However, closer up, the bubbling pits are more like cesspools of floating, bubbling crud; the hides piled up beside look like rancid tripe. Pity the poor labourers who wade in the noxious fluids ladling the skins from one pit to another. Guides sometimes hand out sprigs of mint to hold under your nose to block out the reek of pigeon shit (used to soften the hides). The animal hides are mostly sheep and goat, although cow and camel are sometimes used for bigger items. At one time antelope hide was tanned to order, but no more, and the trade in lion skins has dwindled since the last Atlas lion was shot dead in 1942.

The results of the process can be seen and purchased at the leather shops near the gate, but you may prefer to get the hell out of the quarter and purge yourself in the nearest hammam. Taxis can be caught outside the Bab Debbagh (where a stair inside gives access to the roof of the gatehouse) on the route des Ramparts ringroad.

Southern Medina

Almost since the founding of Marrakech, the area south of Jemaa El Fna has been the domain of sultans and their retinues. Today it houses the museum-palaces of the city. The present Royal Palace is built on the site of the earliest Almohad palaces and covers a vast area, equivalent to a whole residential quarter. Morocco's king, Mohammed VI, a little more modest in his requirements, has had a much smaller residence built nearby. Neither of these two modern-day royal precincts is open to the public, but visitors are allowed to explore two 19th-century palaces, the Bahia and the Dar Si Said, as well as the impressive ruins of the Badii Palace (the temporary home of the new Museum for Photography and Visual Arts). Also in the area is the Mellah, historically Marrakech's Jewish quarter, now known as the Hay Assalem quarter.

Saadian Tombs.

Don't Miss

1 Saadian Tombs A calm marble sanctuary (p78).

2 Bahia Palace A 19th-century grand vizier's ornate palace (p82).

3 Bab Es Salam Market Wander the stalls of the Mellah's market (p81).

4 Slat Laazama Synagogue A reminder of the dwindling Jewish community (p82).

5 Café Clock Stories and camel burgers (p80).

Bad Agnaou.

EXPLORE

THE KASBAH & AROUND

The pedestrianised rue Bab Agnaou, which runs south-west off Jemaa El Fna, is a honey pot for budget tourists, with banks, ATMs, moneychangers, internet centres and numerous dodgy eateries. At the far end is the **Grand Tazi** (*see p41*), famed for decades as a roost for impecunious travellers and one of the few places in the Medina where it's possible to get a cheap beer. South of the Tazi, the street runs in the shadow of high walls: these are not the city walls, but a wall that formerly sectioned off the royal Kasbah (palace precincts) from the rest of the Medina.

The traditional entrance to the Kasbah is via the gorgeous **Bab Agnaou** (Gate of the Gnawa), named after the black slaves brought from sub-Saharan Africa. The gate was built on the orders of the Almohad Sultan Yacoub El-Mansour in 1185. It's one of the very few stone structures in this otherwise mudbrick city, and has weathered in such a way that the aged limestone now resembles heavily grained wood. Across the street from Bab Agnaou is the original southern gate to the Medina, the **Bab Er Rob**, now filled by a pottery shop and bypassed by traffic, which exits through a modern breach in the walls.

A short distance inside the Agnaou gate is the **Kasbah Mosque**, constructed in 1190, again during the reign of Sultan Yacoub El-Mansour (hence its alternative name of El-Mansour Mosque). It has been renovated on numerous occasions since (most recently during the reign of Hassan II, father of the current king), but the cut-brick-and-green-tile decoration on the minaret is original. The plaza in front is popular at night with women and playing children and in the day it's busy with guide-led tourist groups. They're not here for the mosque (non-Muslims are forbidden to enter Marrakech mosques), but for what lies hidden in the lee of its southern wall: the **Saadian Tombs** (*see p78*).

In the early 1920s the French authorities noticed two green-tiled roofs rising above the shanty quarters. Inquiries made of the locals were met with evasive answers. The persistence of one curious official was eventually rewarded when he discovered a narrow, dark lane, wide enough for a single person, that ended in a tiny arched door. He pushed through to enter a courtyard garden and saw what apparently no infidel had ever seen before – the holy tombs of the Saadian sultans. According to the account in a 1928 travelogue, *The Magic of Morocco*, the Frenchman was then accosted by a wizened guardian who said, 'You have discovered our secret, but beware what you do with the knowledge. You cannot make it a mere show for your people to come and gaze at.' Well, tough luck, because that's exactly what has happened: the tombs are possibly the most-visited site in Marrakech.

Exiting the tombs, a left turn on to rue de Kasbah eventually leads to the Grand Méchouar, or parade grounds of the Royal Palace, but the way is closed when the king is in town. Instead it's perhaps more interesting to duck into the warren of alleys behind the tombs, where a small square at the conjunction of four alleys hosts a morning market of fruit, vegetable, meat and fish vendors. A grander market – the **Marché Couvert** – is to the north-east of the Tombs, at the end of avenue Houmann El-Fetouaki, opposite the Badii Palace.

Barely 400 metres east of the Saadian Tombs is the city's other great monument of that era, the **Badii Palace** (*see p78*). While secrecy preserved the sultans' mausoleums intact, the scale and ostentation of their triumphal residence marked it out for special attention and it survives only as a denuded ruin. The

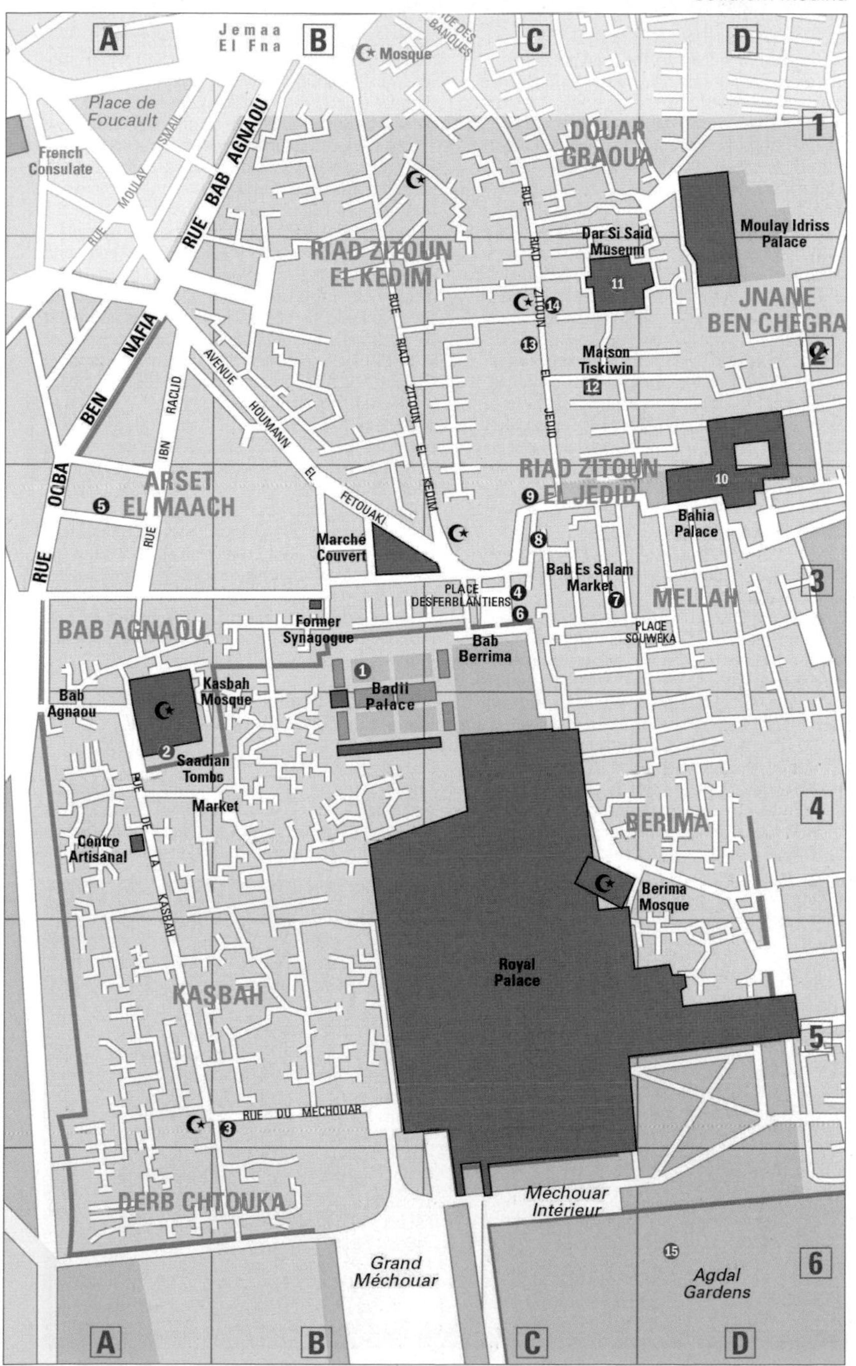

Jemaa El Fna
Mosque
Rue des Banques
Place de Foucault
French Consulate
Rue Moulay Ismail
Rue Bab Agnaou
Douar Graoua
Rue Riad Zitoun El Jedid
Riad Zitoun El Kedim
Rue Riad Zitoun El Kedim
Dar Si Said Museum
Moulay Idriss Palace
Jnane Ben Chegra
Rue Ben Nafia
Avenue Houmann El Fetouaki
Rue Ibn Raclid
Maison Tiskiwin
Rue Ooba
Arset El Maach
Riad Zitoun El Jedid
Bahia Palace
Marché Couvert
Bab Es Salam Market
Place Desferblantiers
Mellah
Bab Agnaou
Former Synagogue
Place Souweka
Bab Berrima
Kasbah Mosque
Badii Palace
Saadian Tombs
Market
Rue de la Kasbah
Centre Artisanal
Berima
Berima Mosque
Royal Palace
Kasbah
Rue du Mechouar
Derb Chtouka
Méchouar Intérieur
Grand Méchouar
Agdal Gardens

EXPLORE

palace is approached via the open plaza of place des Ferblantiers and a canyon-like space constricted between two precipitous walls; the outer one was intended to keep the Medina at a respectful distance from the royal domains.

In the south-east corner of the Badii Palace, a gate leads through to a newly reconstructed pavilion housing the **Koutoubia Mosque minbar**. This was the original minbar (stepped pulpit) in the city's great mosque. It was fashioned in the early 12th century by Cordoban craftsmen and the 1,000 decorative panels that adorn the sides supposedly took eight years to complete – the word 'ornate' falls somewhere short. It was removed from the mosque in the early 1960s for restoration and after a spell at the Dar Si Said Museum has ended up here. Next to the minbar pavilion are the excavated remains of troglodytic chambers and passages.

Sights & museums

Badii Palace

Place des Ferblantiers (no phone). **Open** 9am-4.45pm daily. **Admission** 10dh; 20dh minbar pavilion. **Map** p77 B3 ❶

Constructed during the reign of Sultan Ahmed El-Mansour (1578-1607), the palace was funded by wealth accrued through victories over the Portuguese. Walls and ceilings were encrusted with gold from Timbuktu (captured by El-Mansour in 1598), while the inner court had a massive central pool with an island, flanked by four sunken gardens filled with scented flowers and trees. At the centre of each of the four massive walls were four pavilions, also flanked by arrangements of pools and fountains. It took some 25 years for the labourers and craftsmen to complete the palace. Surveying the achievement, the sultan is said to have invited opinion from his fool and received the prophetic response that the palace 'would make a fine ruin'. And so it does. The sultan was spared that vision because barely were the inaugural celebrations over before the ageing ruler passed away. His palace remained intact for less than a century before the Merenid sultan, Moulay Ismail, had it stripped bare and the riches carted north for his new capital at Meknès.

The former main gate is collapsed and gone, and entrance is through a gaping hole in the fortifications directly into the great court. It's a vast empty space the size of a couple of football pitches, ringed around by pockmarked mudbrick walls that act as apartment blocks for pigeons and have stork nests along the battlements. The sunken areas that were once gardens still exist, as does the great dry basin that was the ornate central pool. On the west side are the ruins of the Pavilion of Fifty Columns; a small area of mosaic remains on the floor, but the colours are badly dulled by exposure to the elements.

One of the palace bastions remains intact at the north-eastern corner of the great central court. Steps lead up to a rooftop terrace with fine views of the site and the surrounding quarter. You can also get up close and personal with the many nesting storks.

In the south-east corner of the palace, a gate leads through to a pavilion housing the Koutoubia Mosque minbar (*see above*).

★ Saadian Tombs

Rue de Kasbah, Bab Agnaou (no phone). **Open** 9am-4.45pm daily. **Admission** 10dh; free under 12s. **Map** p77 A4 ❷

Entrance to the tombs is via a constricted passage first 'discovered' 80 years ago (*see p76*) and it gives access to an ancient walled garden, the use of which far predates the time of the Saadians. There are a

Saadian Tombs.

ON FOOT PALACES AND TOMBS

Allow at least two hours.

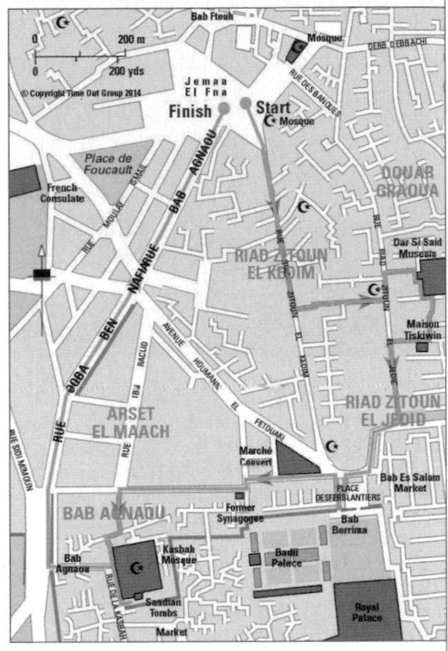

Begin on the east side of Jemaa El Fna. Turn so that you can see the Café des Glaciers on your right and a small mosque on the left. Walk under an arch and head down the colourful **rue Riad Zitoun El-Kedim**. Pass Riad Jnane Mogador on your right and an alleyway that leads to Casa Lalla on your left. A pleasant place for a tea is **Dar Mimoun Salon de Thé** on the left.

After this, walk under an arch and take a left; written above the arch in green are the words 'Musée Dar Si Said'. You will pass several shops selling traditional remedies. Turn left at the T-junction on to **rue Riad Zitoun El-Jedid**, passing a small mosque on the corner. Then, almost immediately, take a sharp right under a small arch (marked Earth Café, also a good stop for a reviving carrot and ginger juice), then a right down **Derb Si Said**. (Just before walking under the arch, head to 175 Riad Zitoun El-Jedid, on the left, to see a traditional baker, who bakes *khobz* bread for a dirham each). This narrow street bends left and then right, leading to the **Dar Si Said Museum** (*see p83*).

After the museum, walk straight ahead and then take a right at the T-junction. Twenty metres further is the entrance to the fascinating **Maison Tiskiwin** (*see p83*) – definitely worth a look inside.Leaving the house, walk under an arch that will bring you back on to rue Riad Zitoun El-Kedim and a square-turned-car park. Go left past the Hammam Ziani and head towards the **Bahia Palace** (*see p82*), whose courtyards and orange groves provide a welcome respite from the heat and dust.

For a short detour into the alleyways of old Jewish quarter, the **Mellah** (*see p81*), you can take an immediate left at the Palais de Bahia exit. Otherwise from the Bahia Palace grounds you head into a square opposite and continue to walk in the direction of the Badii Palace. Notice the storks nesting on the old walls – they have lost their migratory instincts and stay in Marrakech all year round.

Very shortly afterwards you arrive in the **place des Ferblantiers**. Carry on through the **Bab Berrima** (Berrima Gate) to the **Badii Palace** (*see p78*). If you need a rest at this point, the **Kosybar** (*see p80*), on your left just before the gate, has a restaurant and roof terrace. When you re-emerge through Bab Berrima, turn left into another square and an open section of road with taxi ranks.

Keep left at this point, with the Marché Couvert on your right. Continue for about two hundred metres until the road kinks slightly to the left. This brings you on to a long straight stretch of road, heralded by an old mustard-coloured synagogue (look for the Star of David) with some cafés on your left. Keep going for another 500m metres or so, until you reach a wide newly paved opening on your left. Turn left and walk for about 50 metres towards a large mosque. Follow the walls around to the entrance of the **Saadian Tombs** (*see p78*) on your left.

On exiting, turn right past the Kasbah Café, and follow the road around to the left, going through the double arches of **Bab Agnaou**. Turn right back on to **rue Oqba Ben Nafia**. Notice the walls of the king's new palace on your left. Where the road forks, keep to the right, remaining on rue Oqba Ben Nafia. This turns into **rue Bab Agnaou** (also known as rue des Princes), and is the most direct route back to Jemaa El Fna; it's about ten minutes' walk.

Kosybar.

great many early mosaic graves dotted around the shrubbery; the identity of those interned is long lost. Attention instead focuses on the three pavilions constructed during the reign of Saadian Sultan Ahmed El-Mansour. Despite drawing so many visitors, it's far from spectacular, and the setting is so modest that it reminds one of an English parish churchyard.

First on the left is the Prayer Hall, which was not intended as a mausoleum but nevertheless holds numerous graves, mainly of Alaouite princes from the 18th century. Their resting places are marked by what look like marble offcuts from a mason's yard. Next to it is the Hall of Twelve Columns, a far more ornate affair with three central tombs surrounded by a dozen marble pillars. The tomb in the middle is that of Sultan Ahmed El-Mansour, flanked by those of his son and grandson. A third, stand-alone pavilion has ornate Andalucian-style entrance portals.

Restaurants & cafés

★ Café Clock

Derb Chtouka, no number (0535 63 78 55, http://cafeclock.com). **Open** 10am-10pm daily. **Main courses** 45dh-95dh. **Map** p77 B5 ❸ **Café**

The baby brother of the phenomenally successful Café Clock Fez, Mike Richardson's Marrakech branch, housed in an old schoolhouse, opened in March 2014 to widespread cheer. Richardson has made clever use of the building's clean, blocky lines to create a thoroughly contemporary space. It doubles as a cultural centre and exhibition room for local artists and photographers as well as providing a great cup of coffee, date milkshakes (no alcohol is served) and his now-legendary camel burger. Among a roster of constant innovations are storytelling workshops (with translations) from the *hlaykia* storytellers of the Jemaa El Fna on Thursdays, Sunday evening Gnawa concerts, and calligraphy, Arabic and cooking lessons (*see p72* **Stir it Up**). *Photo p44.*

► *For more on Marrakesh storytelling, see p44 Let Me Tell You a Story.*

Kosybar

47 place des Ferblantiers (0524 38 03 24, www.kosybar.com). **Open** 11am-1am daily. **Main courses** 70dh-150dh. **Alcohol served. Map** p77 C3 ❹ **Japanese-Moroccan**

One of the early adopters of the Marrakech-chic style, Kosybar has dark, sultry lounges and dining rooms lined in yellow ochre tadelakt with animal-skin rugs on the floor. These spin off a central staircase rising steeply to the roof, where most people spend their time. And why wouldn't you when it affords such wonderful ringside seats of the antics of the storks who hang out on the ramparts of the Badii Palace, and you get to kick back with a glass of wine over lunch? The place belongs to the son of the owner of some of Morocco's best wine estates, and it has one of the best wine lists in town (if you're serious, ask to go off-menu). The Moroccan-style mezze is perfectly good, but the best thing to order here is spanking fresh, impeccably made sushi and sashimi by chef Nao Tamaki.

Shops & services

Lup 31

11 rue Okba bnou Nafia, Sidi Mimoun (0524 39 00 08, www.lup31.com). **Open** 10am-1.30pm, 2.30-6pm Tue-Thur; 10am-1.30pm, 3.30-6pm Fri; 9am-1pm Sat; Mon am by appointment only. **Map** p77 A3 ❺ **Homewares/accessories**

Bab Es Salam Market.

Stylist, designer and decorator Ludovic Petit is hot property in Marrakech. His work appears at Peacock Pavilions (*see p225*), Le Palais Paysan (*see p227*) and a host of other riads and *dars* in town. You can have a glorious rummage at his workshop for finds covering the homewares (and financial) spectrum: embroidered cushions, canvas totes, Mondrian-style cushions, oil-drum tables, beaded lamps, pouffes made from wheat sacks, metal scrap picture frames and gorgeous brightly coloured laptop bags. You can also find his work at 33 rue Majorelle, *see p98*.

Zwin Zwin

Place des Ferblantiers (0524 37 83 22, www.zwinzwinmarrakech.com). **Open** 10am-8pm daily. **Map** p77 C3 ❻ **Accessories**
Located in the place des Ferblantiers, just across from Kosybar, this little shop is the place for trendy accessories. Our favourite is the pochette made from recycled grain bags with a vintage photo sewn on the front – funky, yet practical. The pochettes are fashioned in all sorts of colours and sizes – from change purses to laptop bags.

THE MELLAH

Hugging the eastern walls of the Badii Palace are the narrow gridded alleys of the Mellah, the old Jewish quarter. The name translates roughly as 'Place of Salt', a reference either to the Jews' historic monopoly on the trade in mineral salts from the Atlas Mountains, or to their landing the job of salting the heads of decapitees before they were hoisted on spikes. Although the number of Jews in Marrakech is now negligible (*see right* **Exodus**), evidence of Jewish heritage is abundant to anyone who knows where to look. Several houses in the neighbourhood have external balconies, which was peculiar to Morocco's Jewish population. Some have Hebrew letters on the metal grills above the doors and there's even an occasional Star of David.

Diagonally across the road from the Bahia Palace entrance, an arch leads through into the **Bab Es Salam Market**, also known to locals as the Jewish market. Following this south and east, past stalls of gaudy beaded necklaces (made in China), bright pyramids of spices (the tallest of them are actually clever cardboard fakes), and windows of the lurid sweets known as Pâte Levy, leads deep into the Mellah. The streets here are some of the narrowest and poorest in the Medina and in places crude scaffolding keeps the houses from collapsing. In among the narrow lanes, on Derb Tijara, is the new **Caffe Internazionale** (0610 99 89 11, open 8am-8pm daily), a handsome home-turned-café painted in bold letterbox red.

At the heart of the quarter is a small square, **place Souweka**, now disfigured by a badly

EXODUS

Shifting demographics.

Talk about population shifts: according to the Paris-based Alliance Israélite Universelle, in 1905 there were 15,700 Jews living in Marrakech; the current total is 150, according to Jacky Kadoch, president of the Israeli community of Marrakech-Essaouira.

Jews have been present in Morocco since Phoenician times. Later, protected by the walls and gates of their own quarter, and by the express patronage of the sultans (who valued their abilities in trade, languages and crafts), the Jews flourished as middlemen between visiting Christian merchants and local Muslims. Many of the latter viewed them with mistrust, especially in times of strife, but that didn't prevent the community from growing. However, from the end of the 19th century the pull of Zionism and the struggle for a homeland in Palestine (culminating in the creation of Israel in 1948) triggered mass emigration.

King Mohammed V (who during World War II had resisted implementing the Vichy regime's anti-Semitic decrees) passed laws to prevent a mass exodus, fearing adverse effects on the economy. But Mossad, the Israeli secret service, smuggled out 18,000 Jews between 1958 and 1961. Arab-Israeli conflicts in 1956, 1967 and 1973 engendered such bad blood that even non-Zionists felt it wise to relocate. Jews with money went to Canada, France and Israel. For many who arrived in the latter it was out of the frying pan and into the firing line – they were settled on the northern border with Lebanon to absorb missile attacks. Those less well off sought refuge in the more cosmopolitan climes of Casablanca, where the remaining Jewish community now thrives as part of the upper middle classes. The only Jews to stay in Marrakech were too poor or elderly to move, hence the decrepit state of the Mellah today.

sited concrete building. At no.36 Derb Manchoura, along the street that runs north just beyond the square, is one of Marrakech's two last working synagogues (once there were 29). The **Slat Laazama Synagogue** (0668 95 44 13, open 9am-6pm Mon-Fri, Sun) occupies a large hall off the beautiful open courtyard, striped in Majorelle blue, of a well-maintained community centre. Judging by the plentiful supply of new prayer books and other contemporary trappings, the synagogue is kept alive by remittances from Marrakchi Jews abroad.

On the very eastern edge of the Mellah is the extensive **Miâara Jewish cemetery**; the sheer number of modestly marked graves (tens of thousands) is probably the best remaining testament to the one-time importance of Jewish life in Marrakech.

Shops & services

★ Art C

Derb Saka (0660 03 62 46, www.art-c-fashion.com). **Open** by appointment only. **Map** p77 C3 ❼ **Fashion/homewares**

Fashion creative Artsi Ifrach has turned his family's old Mellah home into a showroom for his eclectic fashion pieces and his collectibles. The former ballet dancer, who was born in Israel after his parents left the Mellah in the 1960s, is self-taught. He has worked in Paris and only visited his parents' home town for the first time three years ago. His signature style sees him reinterpreting clothes that are one-offs: you'll find a gorgeous deer tapestry in deep bordeaux refashioned as a dress, trousers embellished with *handira* blanket sequins, shoes made from carpets, a vintage linen piece crowned with a fur collar and the non-kosher pig print dress. Everything in his beautifully tiled Mellah home is for sale. Artsi's work (sold at Anthropologie) is also on sale at his shop in Souk Cherifia (*see p64*).

Miâara Jewish cemetery.

Aya's

11 bis Derb Jedid Bab Mellah (0524 38 34 28, http://ayasmarrakech.com). **Open** 10am-1pm, 2.30-4.30pm Mon-Sat. **Map** p77 C3 ❽ **Fashion**

Nestled under the archway leading past Le Tanjia restaurant, Aya's stocks a beautiful collection of kaftans and tunics made from the finest textiles and featuring exquisite embroidery. From evening wear to casual, modern and traditional, the quality of the authentic products is second to none. A photo display of rich and famous customers attests to this.

Dinanderie

6-46 Fundouk My Mamoun (0524 38 49 09). **Open** 8am-7pm Mon-Sat. **Map** p77 C3 ❾ **Metalwork**

Moulay Youssef is one of the country's handful of elite artisans. If you need something extravagant wrought from metal – and if you have the money – then Moulay is your man. The bulk of his work is made to order, but adjacent to his workspace is a crowded gallery of smaller pieces. A little difficult to find, the Dinanderie atelier fills an alley immediately west of the small rose garden across from the place des Ferblantiers.

RIAD ZITOUN EL-JEDID

The Mellah is connected to Jemaa El Fna (a distance of just under a kilometre) by **rue Riad Zitoun El-Jedid**, a name also used for the area. It means the 'new olive garden' but the only olive trees in the vicinity these days are in the modern rose garden at the very southern end of the street.

Just to the north of the Mellah is the **Bahia Palace**. This place will mean much more to you if you've read Gavin Maxwell's *Lords of the Atlas*, but even if you haven't, its shady courtyards and blue mosaic walls still make a pleasant break from the hot bustling streets outside.

Also down at this end is the Préfecture de la Medina and a narrow arch giving entrance to the Derb El-Bahia and **Maison Tiskiwin** (*see p83*), with its collection of southern Moroccan crafts and decorative arts. Following a couple of twists to the north is the **Dar Si Said Museum**, the former home of the brother of Ba Ahmed, builder of the Bahia, and home to another collection.

Sights & museums

★ Bahia Palace

Riad Zitoun El-Jedid (0524 38 91 79). **Open** 9am-4.30pm daily. **Admission** 10dh; 3dh children. **Map** p77 D3 ❿

EXPLORE

The palace was built principally by Bou Ahmed, a powerful vizier to the royal court in the 1890s and a man of 'no particular intelligence, but of indomitable will, and cruel' (*Morocco That Was*, Walter Harris; 1921). Entered via a long garden corridor, it's a delightful collection of paved courtyards, arcades, pavilions and reception halls with vaulted ceilings. The walls are decorated in traditional Moroccan *zelije* tiling, with sculpted stucco and carved cedarwood doors. The fireplace off to the right of the main courtyard is quite impressive too. The palace includes extensive quarters that housed Bou Ahmed's four wives and twenty-four concubines.

On Bou Ahmed's death – probably poisoned by the sultan's mother, along with his two brothers – the palace was completely looted by Sultan Abdel-Aziz. Caravans of donkeys staggering under the weight of furniture, carpets and crates made their way the short distance from the Bahia to the Royal Palace. Between then and now it served as the living quarters of the French *résident généraux*; Edith Wharton stayed here at this time, described in her 1927 book, *In Morocco*, and it's still occasionally used by the current royal family.

Dar Si Said Museum

off rue Riad Zitoun El-Jedid (0524 38 95 64). **Open** 9am-6.45pm Mon, Wed-Sun. **Admission** 10dh; 3dh children. **Map** p77 C2 ⓫

This palace, whose interiors are a showcase for Moroccan artisanship, is home to a large collection of crafts and woodwork. Among all the ceramics, leather and weapons are numerous beautiful examples of carved cedar, rescued from the city's lost dwellings – among them, polychromic painted doors, window shutters and fragments of ceilings. One room is devoted to 'rural' woodwork, including some primitively worked and painted Berber doors. Such items are very much in vogue with collectors these days and change hands for vast amounts of cash. Captions are mostly in French.

Maison Tiskiwin

8 Derb El-Bahia, off rue Riad Zitoun El-Jedid (0524 38 91 92, www.tiskiwin.com). **Open** 9am-12.30pm, 2.30-6pm daily. **Admission** 20dh; 10dh children. **Map** p77 C2 ⓬

On display in this private house, owned by the veteran Dutch anthropologist Bert Flint, is his fascinating collection of crafts and decorative arts from southern Morocco and the Sahara. He has donated all of these artefacts to the University of Marrakech but you can still see them at the Tiskiwin. The exhibition is designed to show Morocco's connection to sub-Saharan Africa and is a geographically laid-out collection that takes you on a journey across the Sahara, as if you were following an old desert trade route from Marrakech to Timbuktu. Exhibits include masks from as far afield as Mali and an entire Berber tent made of camel hair. This is one of Marrakech's hidden gems.

Shops & services

Cordonnerie Errafia

Rue Rad Zitoun El-Jedid (mobile 0662 77 83 47). **Open** 9am-8pm daily. **No credit cards.** **Map** p77 C2 ⓭ **Accessories**

In a little workshop opposite the Préfecture de la Medina, artisan Ahmed cobbles together classic loafers out of raffia for gents, with more extravagantly coloured and cut stylings for women. Given a few days, he can also make to order.

Mr Goodyear

26 rue Riad Zitoun El-Jedid (no phone). **Open** 10am-9pm Mon-Sat. **No credit cards.** **Map** p77 C2 ⓮ **Accessories**

Not just Goodyear – there's Firestone, Pirelli and Michelin too. Abdou creates his hardy black accessories – handbags, purses, bracelets, rings and bowls – from rubber tyres. There are actually a couple of 'rubber craftsmen' in the souks but Abdou, 22, who discovered his talent after a woman commissioned him to make a rubber dress, has a very neat and alluring line in earrings, bracelets and hats. He will also make to order.

AGDAL GARDENS

Laid out in 1156-57 by the Almohads, the royal Agdal Gardens are several hundred years older than those most celebrated of Islamic gardens at the Alhambra. They cover a vast 16 hectares (40 acres), stretching south for a couple of kilometres from the back door of the Royal Palace. At the centre of the Agdal is a massive pool, the **Sahraj El-Hana**, so large that the sultan's soldiers used it for swimming practice. In 1873 Sultan Mohammed IV drowned in it while boating with his son; the servant who managed to swim to safety was executed on the spot for failing to save his lord.

The rest of the area is divided into different kinds of orchards and gardens, including an orange grove, vineyards, areas of pomegranates and figs, masses of walnut trees and palm groves. With an eye on safety, we recommend not walking in these groves alone. There are several ornamental pavilions, and it's possible to climb a dilapidated building for an impressive view of the gardens and the High Atlas beyond.

To get to the Agdal, take the path off the south-western corner of the Méchouar Intérieur, or more sensibly, get a taxi to the entrance on route d'Agdal.

Agdal Gardens

Open 7.30am-6pm Fri, Sun. Closed if the king is in residence at the Royal Palace. **Admission** free. **Map** p77 D6 ⓯

Ville Nouvelle & the Palmeraie

Guéliz is the heart of the *ville nouvelle*, or new town of Marrakech. Built during the French protectorate, with some interesting modernist buildings, it's known for 1930s elegance, though it's marred by concrete blocks, tourist coaches and a McDonald's. With the influx of the tourist euro however, it's undergoing a renaissance, and is emerging as the most fashionable spot in Morocco, especially around streets such as the leafy rue de la Liberté and rue Vieux Marrakchi, as well as a corner at the southern end of avenue Mohammed V. The Guéliz of 2014 is a vibrant and cosmopolitan neighbourhood, home to the city's most interesting galleries, designers and restaurants, and increasingly, trendy bars and cocktail lounges. To the south, in Hivernage, lie the city's fanciest hotels and dance clubs, while the Palmeraie is home to some of North Africa's priciest real estate.

Majorelle Gardens.

Don't Miss

1 Rue de Vieux Marrakchi Elegant boutiques (p86).

2 Al Fassia Grande dame of Moroccan food (p95).

3 Majorelle Gardens Glorious, colourful and deservedly popular (p90).

4 Galleries Moroccan contemporary art in modern spaces (p92).

5 New Town cocktails Marrakech's best (p97).

Carré Eden shopping complex.

HOLY BEGINNINGS

The 'new city' came into being shortly after December 1913 – the arrival date of Henri Prost, the young city planner imported to assist in the schemes of French résident général Marshal Lyautey. One of Prost's early sketches shows how he took the minaret of the Koutoubia as his focal point and from it extended two lines: one north-west to the Guéliz hills; the other south-west to the pavilion of the Menara Gardens. In the pie slice between these lines (which have since become avenue Mohammed V and avenue de la Menara) is the original nucleus of the new European city.

One of the first buildings was the church, or *église* – a word that was corrupted into the name Guéliz. This wasn't the first church in Marrakech; in 1908 a French priest consecrated a house in the Medina near what is now the Dar Si Said Museum. A Christian cross fashioned into the wrought-iron grill over one of the windows survives as evidence. The priest, however, lasted nowhere near as long, murdered within two years of setting up shop.

The Guéliz *église* is now the Catholic Church of St Anne, barely a communion queue from the northern walls of the Medina. It is a modest affair, with a bell tower deliberately overshadowed by the taller minaret of a mosque built next door after independence.

Straddling the Ville Nouvelle and the Medina, the **Cyber Park Arset Moulay Abdelsalam** is a welcome and lushly planted space that provides a peaceful location with plenty of shade to catch up on your email (there's free Wi-Fi).

GUELIZ

The focal point of Guéliz used to be the Marché Central on avenue Mohammed V, and it was here that the expats and middle-class Marrakchis gathered for groceries, booze, flowers and gossip. However in a mystifying piece of town planning, it was demolished in 2005, and has been replaced by the brand new Carré Eden shopping complex, featuring Starbucks and high-street brands, while the fresh produce market has been replaced by a much more sterile affair just east of the nearby place du 16 Novembre.

At the junction of **avenue Mohammed V** and fashionable **rue de la Liberté** is an elaborate colonial building with pavement arcades, art deco lines and Moorish flourishes. It dates to 1918 and is just about the oldest surviving building in Guéliz. This was the address (30 rue de la Liberté) of the city's first tourist office. A fading gallery of ancient hand-painted scenes of Morocco decorates the hallway.

North off the eastern stretch of rue de la Liberté is the chic shopping street, **rue des Vieux Marrakchi**. At the western end of the

GREEN GARDENS FOR A RED CITY

Urban oases for a desert town.

Menara Gardens.

In a hot, dusty city where the predominant colour is pink and red, it's a relief to contemplate water and see serene greens and blues. Some of the classic picture-postcard photographs of Marrakech are taken in two of the city's most famous gardens, the **Menara** (*see p104*) and the **Majorelle** (*see p90*). These little urban oases – and others around the city including the well-tended gardens of hotels in the Palmeraie – provide peace and calm away from the buzz of mopeds, the fumes of exhausts and the chatter of street hawkers. So should you start to feel that Marrakech is doing your head in, we recommend you escape to any of these tranquil spots.

Desert dwellers know how to manage water. When the Almoravids moved out of the Western Sahara to found Marrakech in the 11th century, they brought in water from the Ourika Valley by means of *khettaras*, long irrigation pipes made of baked mud, the remains of which can still be found in the Palmeraie on the outskirts of the city. They used the water to nurture *jnane* (market gardens) and *agdal* (walled private gardens), as well as abundant public gardens. The *khettaras* were eventually replaced by a system of artesian wells and reservoirs.

The Menara Gardens, for instance, date back to the 12th century and the era of the Almohads, as do the royal **Agdal Gardens** (*see p83*). When the Saadian Sultan Ahmed El-Mansour built the show-stopping Badii Palace in the late 16th century, visitors marvelled at its architecture, but more than anything they were awestruck by its multilevel gardens and 700 fountains.

Neither were gardens the preserve of royals. Wealthy merchants, judges, master craftsmen and petty officials dwelt in riads, townhouses built around courtyard gardens. These were usually designed symmetrically: four beds planted with trees, underplanted with perfumed flowers, and arranged around the all-important central fountain. The microclimate thus created provided shade, cooled the air, gave off sweet smells and encouraged songbirds.

All credit to the French, who continued the horticultural tradition under the Protectorate. In Guéliz, many of the boulevards are lined with jacaranda trees that bloom in electric blue each spring. Bougainvillea and vines clothe the boundary walls of villas and hibiscus flowers add spots of vibrant colour. Then there are the orange trees. The streets of Guéliz are lined with them. The combination of blue sky, pink walls, green leaves and orange fruit is a knockout; it's like walking through a landscape by Matisse. All this and free fruit too? But that would be just too perfect, and the oranges are in fact too sour to eat or juice. Instead, the prize is the blossom, highly valued for its scent. In recent years the municipality has embarked on a scheme to green the city even more. Large-scale planting of trees and flowers along the airport and Medina ring roads has already been completed and the ramparts are now surrounded by beds of roses, hibiscus and jasmine. The **Jnane El-Harti** park (*see p90*) in Guéliz was completely replanted and re-landscaped, as was the **Arset Moulay Abdelsalam** (*see p89*) on the edge of the Medina, now with free Wi-Fi.

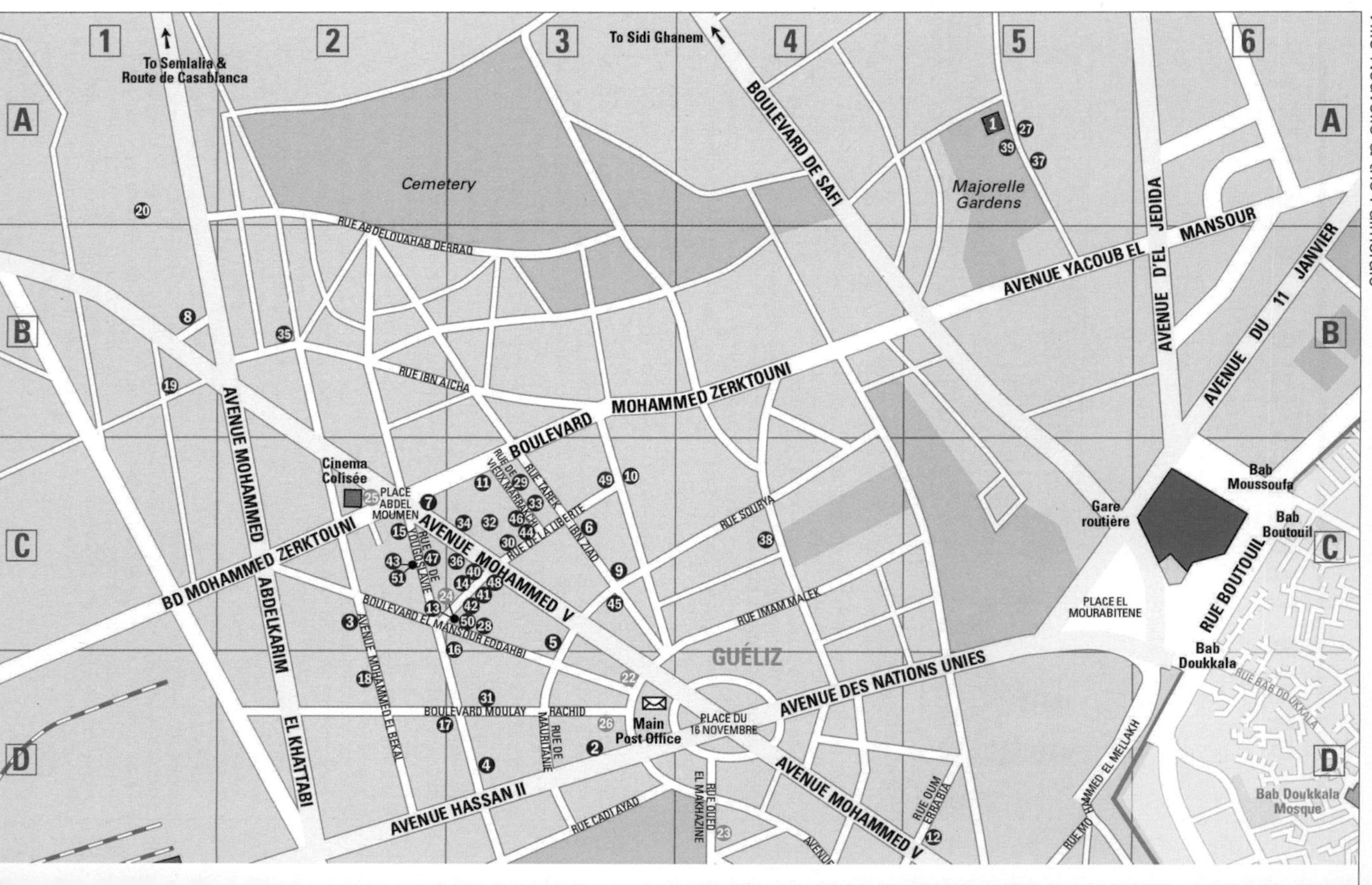
To Semlalia & Route de Casablanca
To Sidi Ghanem
Cemetery
RUE ABDELOUAHAB DERRAQ
BOULEVARD DE SAFI
Majorelle Gardens
AVENUE YACOUB EL MANSOUR
AVENUE D'EL JEDIDA
AVENUE DU 11 JANVIER
RUE IBN AICHA
BOULEVARD MOHAMMED ZERKTOUNI
AVENUE MOHAMMED ABDELKARIM EL KHATTABI
Cinema Colisée
PLACE ABDEL MOUMEN
RUE DE VIEUX MARRAKCHI
RUE TAREK IBN ZIAD
RUE DE LA LIBERTE
RUE DE YOUGOSLAVIE
AVENUE MOHAMMED V
BD MOHAMMED ZERKTOUNI
BOULEVARD EL MANSOUR EDDAHBI
AVENUE MOHAMMED EL BEKAL
BOULEVARD MOULAY RACHID
RUE DE MAURITANIE
RUE SOURYA
RUE IMAM MALEK
GUÉLIZ
Main Post Office
PLACE DU 16 NOVEMBRE
AVENUE DES NATIONS UNIES
AVENUE HASSAN II
RUE CADI AYAD
RUE OUED EL MAKHAZINE
RUE OUM ERRABIA
RUE MOHAMMED EL MELLAKH
Gare routière
PLACE EL MOURABITENE
Bab Moussoufa
Bab Boutouil
RUE BOUTOUIL
Bab Doukkala
RUE BAB DOUKKALA
Bab Doukkala Mosque

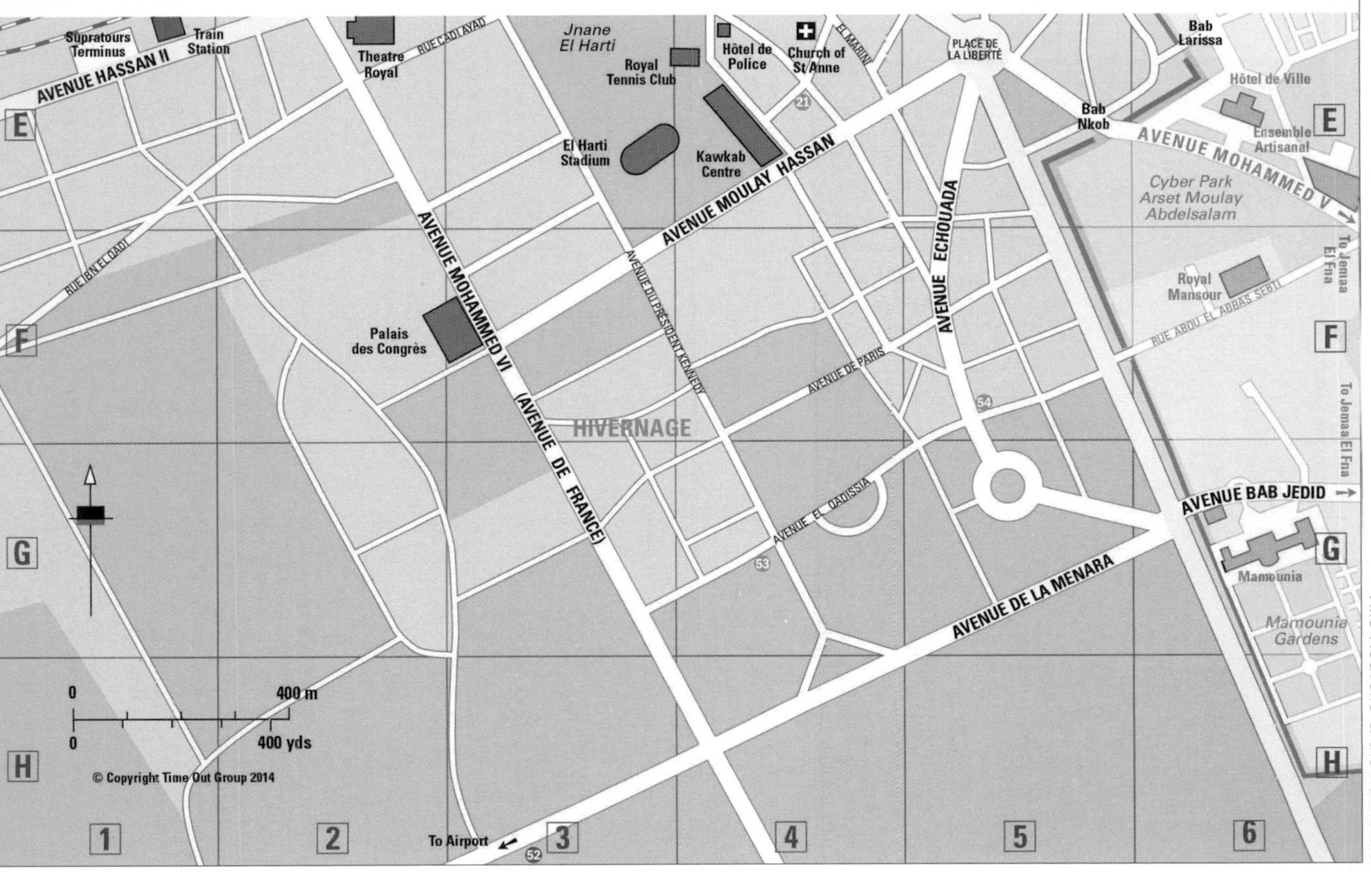

Supratours Terminus
Train Station
AVENUE HASSAN II
Theatre Royal
RUE CADI AYAD
Jnane El Harti
Royal Tennis Club
Hôtel de Police
Church of St Anne
EL MARINI
PLACE DE LA LIBERTÉ
Bab Larissa
Hôtel de Ville
Bab Nkob
Ensemble Artisanal
AVENUE MOHAMMED V
Cyber Park Arset Moulay Abdelsalam
To Jemaa El Fna
El Harti Stadium
Kawkab Centre
AVENUE MOULAY HASSAN
AVENUE ECHOUADA
Royal Mansour
RUE ABOU EL ABBAS SEBTI
RUE IBN EL QADI
AVENUE MOHAMMED VI (AVENUE DE FRANCE)
AVENUE DU PRÉSIDENT KENNEDY
Palais des Congrès
AVENUE DE PARIS
HIVERNAGE
To Jemaa El Fna
AVENUE BAB JEDID
AVENUE EL QADISSIA
Mamounia
Mamounia Gardens
AVENUE DE LA MENARA
0
400 m
0
400 yds
© Copyright Time Out Group 2014
To Airport
E
F
G
H
1
2
3
4
5
6
21
52
53
54

EXPLORE

Amaia.

street, beyond the **Kechmara** bar (*see p97*) and where it meets rue de Yougoslavie, is a forgotten bit of Marrakech history: a narrow alley planted with mulberry trees and crammed with single-storey dwellings daubed in pink with the odd splash of Majorelle blue and navy blue. This is the old Spanish quarter, a reminder of the city's once significant Hispanic population.

In the middle of Mohammed V is the **place du 16 Novembre**, which is the main hub of high-street fashion chains and fast food outlets, plus a sprinkling of iconic cafés and bars such as the **Grand Café de la Poste** (*see p97*) and newcomer Level 5. To the south of place du 16 Novembre, and connected to it by its north-east corner, is the **Jnane El-Harti** park, originally laid out as a French formal garden and a zoo. The park was relandscaped and now boasts fountains, ponds and a children's play area with two pale blue dinosaurs.

North of place du 16 Novembre, **place Abdel Moumen** marks the start of the restaurant district proper, with old stalwarts like the **Café les Négociants** (*see p94*) where grouchy uniformed waiters serve coffee so strong you can stand a spoon in it, grand dame **Al Fassia** (*see p95*) serves brilliant traditional Moroccan food, and the **O'Sky Bar** provides a secret hideaway for sundowners.

From place Abdel-Moumen, it's a 20-minute walk to the glorious **Majorelle Gardens** (*see right*). To get to the garden, walk from central Guéliz (it's about two kilometres east along boulevard Mohammed Zerktouni) or take a taxi. Note that picnics, unaccompanied children and dogs are not allowed. The area outside the garden entrance on the renamed rue Yves Saint Laurent is now buzzing with the opening of the **33 Rue Majorelle** concept store (*see p98*), other boutiques, and the **Café Kaowa** (open 9am-7pm) which serves reviving vegetarian wraps, smoothies and coffees.

Sights & museums

★ Majorelle Gardens

Rue Yves Saint Laurent (0524 31 30 47, www.jardinmajorelle.com). **Open** 8am-5.30pm daily. **Admission** 50dh; free under-9s. *Berber Museum* 25dh. **Map** p88 A5 ❶

Now privately owned by the Fondation Pierre Bergé-Yves Saint Laurent – but open to the public – the gardens were created in the 1930s by two generations of French artists, Jacques and Louis Majorelle. Although small in scale and out on the edge of the New City, the gardens are often packed well beyond comfort. The juxtaposition of colours is striking; plants sing against a backdrop of the famous Majorelle blue, offset with soft yellows and terracottas. Bamboo groves rustle in the soft breeze and great palms tower over all, sheltering huge ancient cacti. Rills lead into pools floating with water lilies and flashing with golden carp, terrapins paddle languidly and frogs croak. Great pots overflow with succulents and birds sing. For the botanically curious, everything is clearly labelled. Yves Saint Laurent's memorial, a rather incongruous and unkempt broken classical column, has been placed against the back wall of the garden.

Jacques Majorelle's former studio has been turned into a beautiful small Berber museum, with well curated rooms of traditional jewellery, tools, and a fine collection of mannequins draped in traditional dress. Air-conditioned and dimly lit, the museum is a welcome refuge from the intensity of light and colour outside; exhibits have English labelling. Beside the museum is a bookshop (now with its own publishing house), and opposite is the YSL Galerie Love (featuring poster designs from YSL's New Year greetings cards), a small boutique selling 100% Moroccan-made goods: T-shirts, leather goods, *babouches*, pottery, Majorelle paint, *zelije* tiles and cushions. The pretty Bousafsaf café behind the museum offers refreshing drinks and snacks.

Restaurants & cafés

See also **Jack is Back** (*p97*).

Amaia

84 avenue Hassan II (0524 45 71 81). **Open** 10am-midnight Mon-Sat. **Main courses** 75dh-120dh. **Alcohol served. Map** p88 D3 ❷ **French/Italian/South-east Asian**

Usually when a restaurant has such an eclectic menu alarm bells ring, but Eric Garozzo was born in Casablanca to Sicilian parents and his wife has roots in Vietnam, so their menu of French, Italian and South-east Asian dishes is, in fact, completely authentic. Most are based on old family recipes, cooked with lashings of love. The restaurant is an intimate space of rich chocolate browns made sexy by gauzy, champagne-hued cubes that deflect light from chandeliers, and modern wooden table lamps that mean you can actually see what you're eating. Add a little funked-up jazz and a European-Moroccan wine list, all of which is available by the glass, including champagne for 650dh per bottle (very reasonable for Morocco), and this is exactly the sort of neighbourhood joint you'll wish you had around the corner back home.

Amandine

177 rue Mohammed El-Bekal (0524 44 96 12). **Open** 7am-9pm daily. **No credit cards. Map** p88 C2 ❸ **Café**

This smart pâtisserie is banked on two sides by floor-to-ceiling windows to optimise views of a long, sparkly glass display cabinet piled high with sculpted cakes, highly decorated pastries and pastel-coloured macaroons. You can buy a box to go, but the height of Marrak-chic is to snag one of the candy-coloured armchairs at the front of the shop and order up afternoon tea. They also do a good line in buttery croissants, toasted sandwiches and other savouries.

★ Association Amal

Corner rues Allal Ben Ahmed & Ibn Sina, quartier l'Hopital Ibn Tofail (0524 44 68 96/0604 23 88 60, http://hope-amal.org). **Open** 8am-5pm Mon-Sat. **Main courses** from 25dh. **No credit cards. Moroccan**

Association Amal.

EXPLORE

ART EXPLOSION

Marrakech discovers its own artistic voice.

Le 18.

The last few years have seen the scope of and interest in art in Marrakech go from strength to strength. 'It all changed with the launch of Vanessa Branson's Biennale,' says Hassan Hajjaj, one of the country's leading living artists. Not only is the Biennale (*see p23*) now a serious art event, but also artists in Marrakech are embracing street art, photography, video and other multimedia with a gusto that is unprecedented.

European painters first began showing up in North Africa in the 19th century and were captivated by Morocco's clear light and rich colours. It also helped that pictures of fearsome desert warriors and dusky harem girls sold well back home. The 80 or so canvases produced by Eugène Delacroix on a visit to Morocco and Algeria in 1832 diverted French painters from the traditional pilgrimage to Italy and set them scurrying all over North Africa instead.

Delacroix defined the style that became known as Orientalism; look out for the Delacroix prints that will be displayed in the meticulously restored Douiria Mouassine (*see p60*), run by the Maison de la Photographie. Although the subject matter in these days of political correctness is widely derided for treating its subjects as colourful curiosities, it did motivate Henri Matisse to settle in Tangier for a productive stint, now regarded as the culmination of his Fauve period. Matisse protégé Raoul Dufy travelled to Marrakech and painted the typically cartoony *Couscous With the Pasha of Marrakech*, but few other painters made it this far south.

The notable exception was Jacques Majorelle, a tuberculosis sufferer who came on the advice of his doctor. He settled here in 1923, building a villa and later adding the gardens that perpetuate his name. Majorelle's work still falls under the heading 'Orientalist' but is redeemed by his apparent empathy with his subjects; that and a superbly graphic sense of line and colour. Some of the most striking works were posters to promote exotic Maroc. He's also noted for his attachment to a particularly intense shade of cobalt that now goes by the name Majorelle Blue.

It was only after independence in 1956 that Moroccan artists began to emerge with their own styles, mostly abstract, naïve or calligraphic, and mostly in the north and on the coast. Many were trained at the fine arts school in Tetouan. Tangier used to have cash and international connections, and still has one of Morocco's only two contemporary art museums. Nearby Asilah hosts an annual art festival, hitting its 37th edition in August 2015 with three weeks of exhibitions and workshops. But there's never been a Marrakech school or style, until recently, when the city is becoming increasingly celebrated for a uniquely Islamic take on street art that embraces calligraphy, among other traditional forms. Check out the works of Larbi Cherkaoui (www.larbicherkaoui.com) at the **David Bloch Gallery** (*see p100*), and pop art like Hajjaj's striking films and photographic compositions of Medina figures in funky renditions of traditional textiles that he makes himself. A good range of his work can be seen at **Riad Yima** (*see p55*).

Many of the interesting new studios and galleries are choosing the Medina over the Ville Nouvelle as their base, seeing it as being closer to the pulse of Marrakchi creativity. Laila Hida's **Le 18** project (https://fr-fr.facebook.com/dardixhuit) has become a hub for young artists, photographers, dancers and film makers. Part venue for artists in residence, part place to stay (*see p219*), part studio, part cultural centre, Le 18 hosts regular film screenings, contemporary dance workshops and readings as well as providing work and exhibition space for visiting artists. Hida is currently exploring an exchange programme to further advance artistic dialogue between Morocco and the rest of the world.

It's also worth heading out of town to the Dar al-Ma'mum project at the **Fellah Hotel** (*see p226*), which dedicates one of its riads to visiting artists in residence, has an extensive library and runs cultural events and local education programmes.

Check out http://diptykblog.com, too, the only magazine dedicated to the arts in Morocco.

Nora Belahcen Fitzgerald's philantrophic project of a women's training centre offers courses in cooking and general hospitality skills, ranging from food hygiene to service, as well as English lessons and a kids' activity centre. The women who come here – many travelling a fair distance from surrounding villages – get paid for their efforts, and punters are treated to some of the best country cooking in the city. Daily specials such as *seffa* (a Fassi dish of steamed vermicelli with chicken, saffron and ginger) combine with lighter meals like niçoise salads and a zingy home-made lemonade.

Azar

Rue de Yougoslavie (corner boulevard Hassan II) (0524 43 09 20, www.azarmarrakech.com). **Open** 12.30-4pm, 7.30-11pm daily. **Meze** 40dh-70dh. **Mixed meze platters** 180dh-790dh. **Alcohol served. Map** p88 D3 ❹ **Lebanese**

The jaw-dropping design of this upmarket Lebanese lounge and restaurant was done by the talented Marrakechi designer Younes Duret, and it's well worth coming for a cocktail just to admire it. Soaring ceilings, lanterns with contemporary Islamic cut-out motifs and custom-made tables and chairs lend a real sense of glamour to the place, and it makes for good eating too, especially for large groups where platters of six to 16 kinds of meze means nobody has to think too hard. Classic crowd-pleasers like houmous, *moutabal* (roast aubergine with lemon and sesame), tabbouleh and *kebbe* (minced lamb with pine kernels) combine with more exotic fare like *sawda djaj* (chicken livers in pomegranate juice), *shanklish* (goat's cheese with tomatoes and green onion), and *mouhalabieh* (Lebanese milk pudding with orange syrup and pistachios) to provide a real feast for the senses.

Bar L'Escale

Rue de Mauritanie (0524 43 34 47). **Open** 11am-10.30pm daily. **Main courses** 35dh-80dh. **No credit cards. Beer served. Map** p88 C3 ❺ **Moroccan**

Beloved by Moroccan men in search of a cheeky cold one, L'Escale is also the best *grillade* (barbecue) in town. Staff still cook over a wood fire and the lemon grilled chicken is superlative, as are the spicy merguez sausages and lamb kebabs, all served with a chopped tomato and onion salad, a dish of shoestring fries and a basket of bread for mopping up. There's a back room specifically for dining, but the top spot is at one of the six sun-shaded tables out on the pavement, where you can happily pass a couple of hours watching the world drift by.

Café du Livre

44 rue Tarek Ibn Ziad (0524 44 69 21). **Open** 10am-11pm Mon-Sat; 12.30-11pm Sun. **Alcohol served. Map** p88 C3 ❻ **Café**

Those who know Sandra Zwollo's sophisticated first-floor café-cum-vintage bookshop may feel the

EXPLORE

Café du Livre has seen better days, but it's still very much the meeting point for anyone new in town. It's slightly scruffy around the edges, and very smoky at times, but the books and magazines are still here, as are plenty of sofas to sink into, free Wi-Fi and most of the international newspapers. There's also the added lure of a happy hour that lasts from 7pm to 9pm, Tuesday to Sunday. The menu majors in salads and sandwiches. It's one of the few places in town that have beer on tap, and there's often live music or a pop quiz at the weekend.

Café les Négociants

Place Abdel-Moumen, avenue Mohammed V (0524 43 57 82). **Open** 6am-11pm daily. **No credit cards. Map** p88 C2 ❼ **Café**

Far classier than the endearingly sleazy Café Atlas, which it faces across the road, Les Négociants is a Parisian boulevard-style café with acres of rattan seating and round glass-topped tables crowded under a green-and-white striped pavement awning swinging with chandeliers. It's a glamorous spot for breakfast: *café au lait*, orange juice and croissants, plus the papers from the international newsagent across the road.

Le Cuisine de Mona

Residence Mamoune 5 no.115B, Quartier El-Ghoul cite OLM (0618 13 79 59). **Open** noon-3pm, 8-11pm daily. **Main courses** 35dh-75dh. **Alcohol served. Map** p88 B1 ❽ **Lebanese**

There's no missing the eye-boggling, hot pink and acid apple decor of this cute little eaterie (cross over Mohammed V at Restaurant L'Avenue and walk about ten metres down this residential side-street to find it). The doll's-house sized terrace outside is the top spot on a sunny day, but it gets busy with regulars who come for a dose of Mona's home-style Lebanese cooking. There may be smarter places for this type of cuisine, but nobody does baba ganoush, tabbouleh and chargrilled lamb kebabs better.

Catanzaro

42 rue Tarek Ibn Ziyad (0524 43 37 31). **Open** noon-2.30pm, 7.30-11pm Mon-Sat. **Main courses** 60dh-95dh. **Alcohol served. Map** p88 C3 ❾ **Italian**

This simple, hacienda-style French-run Italian bistro (red-checked tablecloths, wagon wheel lanterns, wood-beamed ceilings) has a homely air and reliable cooking. It's been going strong for years and remains as popular as ever. White-hatted chefs work in an open kitchen with a big wood-fired oven turning out excellent thin-crust pizzas. There's also lasagne and steaks, as well as slightly more exotic dishes such as rabbit in mustard sauce, osso bucco and a glorious pannacotta. Waiters flit about in red-velvet waistcoats greeting customers old and new with enthusiastic affection and work a labyrinthine series of dining rooms, though we think the best place to eat is at the heart of the action, in front of the kitchen.

EXPLORE

CHEERS!

The best in local beer, wine and cocktails.

Curiously, for a dry country, quite a lot of the good stuff is made nationally. Beers such as Flag and Flag Spéciale are brewed in Tangier; Stork comes from F`ès. Casablanca, the finest and most expensive brew in the country, and marketed as 'the legendary beer from the legendary city', is self-explanatory.

Local wines (predominantly from Meknes) are getting better all the time, and there are some exceptional vintages made by boutique wineries such as Volubilia and the Vall d'Argan, near Essaouira. Among the best accessibly priced reds are Cabernet du Président, Domaine de Sahari and La Ferme Rouge. Gazelle de Mogador (from the Vall d'Argan vineyard) is a deliciously crisp and refreshing white, and the country's very pale rosé wines (known as *gris*), by Larroque and Volubilia, are delightful on a hot day.

In the last couple of years, Marrakech has started to embrace cocktail culture too, and there are some decent mixologists about. The **Maison Arabe** (*see p71*) is great for a Sunday morning bloody mary, and the bar on the circular rooftop of the **Pearl Hotel** in Hivernage (corner avenue Echouhada & rue du Temple, 524 42 42 42, www.thepearlmarrakech.com) mixes a mean Moroccan martini. For more sophisticated sipping with a view, the **O'Sky Bar** (*see p98*) atop the Rennaissance Hotel offers 360-degree panoramas across the city and beyond; it's a sensational spot from which to watch a sunset.

Alcohol is heavily taxed, however. Expect to pay above the odds for beer, wine and cocktails (a bottle of Moët champagne, for example, costs easily in excess of €100). And don't forget that standalone bars close for the duration of the holy month of Ramadan, and some hotel bars (though not the more upmarket places) stop serving alcohol: for dates, *see p25*.

Al Fassia.

Chez Joel

12 rue Loubnane (0524 43 15 49). **Open** noon-midnight daily. **Main courses** 40dh-110dh. **Alcohol served. Map** p88 C3 ⑩ **French**

Chef Jaouad Kazouini learned his trade in Chicago and still has his first restaurant there. He returned home in mid 2013 eager to bring a touch of US laid-back style to Marrakech. This sleek little bistro, with elephant-grey walls framing black- and-white photos from the mothership across the water and newspaper print wallpaper, has fast become the haunt of Marrakchi businessmen and savvy expats exchanging gossip over lunchtime specials like mussels and fries with a beer, or platters of Oualidia oysters followed by beef carpaccio and caesar salads at night. A keenly priced wine and beer list is the icing on the cake.

★ Al Fassia

55 boulevard Zerktouni (0524 43 40 60, www.alfassia.com). **Open** noon-2.30pm, 7.30-11pm Mon, Wed-Sun. **Main courses** 100dh-150dh. **Alcohol served. Map** p88 C3 ⑪ **Moroccan**

Some things never change, and Al Fassia is one of them. Thirty years old in 2015, the restaurant was set up as a women's co-operative headed by chef Halima Chaab and her sisters, and it remains, hands down, the best traditional food in Morocco. It employs only women, and the business has gone from strength to strength, now having two restaurants and a hotel to its name. The best place to eat, however, is here at the mother ship, where elegantly sumptuous surrounds and a pretty garden are complemented by a mind-boggling array of dishes from traditional Moroccan salads, to steamed vermicelli with pigeon and slow-roasted shoulder of lamb with almonds and caramelised onions. Reservations essential.

Katsura

Rue Oum Errabia, behind Hotel Le Marrakech (0524 43 43 58/0667 12 68 63). **Open** noon-midnight daily. **Main courses** 45dh-75dh. **Alcohol served. Map** p88 D5 ⑫ **Asian**

The best of a number of pan-Asian restaurants in town, Katsura's funky geometric design splashed with vibrant orange, combined with a lively atmosphere and good cooking at reasonable prices, ensures it always draws a crowd. California rolls, *ikura* (salmon roe) *maki*, top-grade tuna and *chirashi* (sashimi-topped bowls of rice) as well as some pleasing Moroccan twists such as *temaki* (seaweed cones) stuffed with eel, avocado and mint combine well with decent *yakitori* (Japanese skewers) and nicely made Thai noodles and curries.

★ Kechmara

3 rue de la Liberté (0524 42 25 32). **Open** 9am-1am Mon-Sat. **Main courses** 80dh-140dh. **Alcohol served. Map** p88 C3 ⑬ **International/Moroccan**

For many, this was the bar that changed Marrakech. For a long time it was the only bar (in the hip, European sense) in the city and wowed locals with its fresh approach. Brothers Pascal and Arnaud Foltran revamped an old villa, turning it into a seductive mid-century modern bar and restaurant, serving beer on the rooftop and top-notch burgers with skinny fries. As the hipsters discovered it the menu expanded with a celebration of local produce, including a sensational Oualidia spider-crab salad. These days there are continuously changing art and photography exhibitions, and bands on a Wednesday night. The brothers' refusal to conform to the fickle trends of Marrakech means their place remains as hot as ever.

EXPLORE

★ Le Loft

Rue de la Liberté (0524 43 42 16, www.loft-marrakech.com). **Open** noon-late daily. **Main courses** from 120dh. **Alcohol served. Map** p88 C3 ⓮ **French**

Sleek teak panelling, colonial ceiling fans and cane furniture give Le Loft a distinctly colonial feel, although the food is solid French bistro and the aspiration New York. No matter, since it has a lively, lived-in vibe that makes you want to spend time here. The lunch combo is a good deal (110 dh) and there's a good range of starters like home-made pâté with cornichons and caesar salad, as well as slowly cooked lamb shank, duck leg confit and grilled prawns.

O'Cha Sushi

43 rue de Yougoslavie (0524 42 00 88, www.ocha-sushi.com). **Open** noon-midnight daily. **Main courses** 45dh-95dh. **Map** p88 C2 ⓯ **Japanese**

O'Cha has a deserved reputation for serving the best sushi and sashimi in town. The long, glass-fronted chill counter houses impeccable, freshly made pieces. Ergonomic fibreglass chairs, lichen-green leather banquettes, lime-green walls and modern enamelled lanterns lend a contemporary freshness that you'll enjoy if you eat in, but we prefer to take our sushi and picnic in one of the nearby parks.

Rôtisserie de la Paix

68 rue de Yougoslavie (0524 43 31 18). **Open** noon-3pm, 6.30-11pm daily. **Main courses** 60dh-180dh. **Alcohol served. Map** p88 C3 ⓰ **Rôtisserie**

Flaming for decades, the 'peaceful rôtisserie' is a large garden restaurant with seating among palms and bushy vegetation. Simple and unpretentious, it's utterly lovely, whether lunching under blue skies (shaded by red umbrellas) or dining after sundown when the trees twinkle with fairy lights. (In winter, dining is inside by a crackling log fire.) Most of the menu comes from the charcoal grill (kebabs, lamb chops, chicken and merguez sausages) but there are also delicacies such as quail, and a selection of seafood. We recommend the warm chicken liver salad, listed as a starter but easily a meal in itself.

Snack Al Bahriya

No.2/69 bis, Avenue Moulay Rachid (0678 76 82 43). **Open** noon-late daily. **Main courses** 25dh-90dh. **No credit cards. Map** p88 D3 ⓱ **Fish**

If a good old-fashioned fish fry is what you crave, look no further than Al Bahriya, a heaving great canteen of a place with wonderfully friendly staff that's always rammed. The draw? Pristinely fresh fish and seafood, clean fryers and a real charcoal grill capable of doing justice to some of the freshest produce in the country. Mixed platters include prawns, mussels, squid and a couple of whole grilled fish that you eat with your hands on a couple of pieces of paper with hot sauce for dipping.

Trattoria de Giancarlo

179 rue Mohammed El-Bekal (0524 43 26 41, www.latrattoriamarrakech.com). **Open** 7.30-11.30pm daily. **Main courses** 120dh-180dh. **Alcohol served. Map** p88 D2 ⓲ **Italian**

Just about clinging on to its reputation as Marrakech's finest Italian restaurant, Trattoria serves good food in enchanting surroundings. The Felliniesque interiors (lush, occasionally lurid and more than a little louche) were designed by late local legend Bill Willis and are a delight – in fact, it's worth a visit just to see the decor. The best tables are those overhung by oversized greenery out on the tiled garden terrace, beside a large, luminous pool. In the evening the place is lit by lanterns and candles to ridiculously romantic effect. While the menu is hardly extensive, it holds plenty of broad appeal (a variety of salads, several vegetarian pastas, and an array of meat and seafood dishes). Service is excellent, verging on obsequious: 'Would Sir like his beer with a head or without?' Reservations are recommended.

Le Verre Canaille

Corner of route de Targa & rue Capitaine Errigui (0650 92 97 42). **Open** 12.15-2.15pm, 7.15-11pm Mon-Sat. **Main courses** from 130dh. **Alcohol served. Map** p88 B1 ⓳ **French**

With its natty, retractable roof-covered terrace, oyster-grey banquettes and olive wood tables and chairs to match the olive tree planters, Bruno Gomes Tmim's little French bistro is a chic addition to the scene. Candles, French crooners on the stereo and a decent French wine list add to the Little Paris vibe, but it's the food that has Marrakchi resident expats clamouring to get in. It's excellent and unapologetically French, featuring such classics as home-made pork terrines, Grandmama's egg salad, *côte de boeuf* with béarnaise, veal tongue in ravigote sauce, *pain perdu* and chocolate mousse, all done to perfection.

Wok Bangkok

No 14 Residence Amira 1, rue Ben Ali Benihaj Complexe al Ghoule (0642 99 95 53). **Open** noon-late daily. **Main courses** 39dh-59dh. **No credit cards. Map** p88 A1 ⓴ **Thai**

Chef Pee worked a couple of Marrakech's better Thai places before setting up on his own, and this out-of-the-way little eaterie feels as if it dropped straight out of the sky from the streets of Bangkok. The makeshift kitchen at the back of a small, simply decorated dining room belies the standard of the cooking. There are spicy authentic dishes such as spiced beef and cucumber salad, *larb gai* (green chilli-spiked chicken salad with mint), *tom yam goong* (hot and sour prawn soup), *pla rad prik* (fried fish with hot sauce), green curries and phad thai (noodles) at prices that are straight out of South-east Asia too.

Bars

See also **Bar L'Escale** (*see p93*).

★ Djellabar

2 rue Abou Hanifa, Villa Bougainvillée (0524 42 12 42, www.djellabar.com). **Open** 7.30pm-late daily. **Map** p89 E4 ㉑

This rather bonkers-looking converted wedding room literally drips in garish colour, carved plaster, fake jewels and Moroccan pop art featuring everyone from Elvis and Ray Charles to the present-day King Mohammed VI in a fez. The music strays wildly from Arabic pop to Latin tunes and 1970s disco and funk but it's a reliably fun night of dancing and decent cocktails – and there's always the possibility of an appearance by the bar's creator, Claude Chaulle, formerly of the Buddha Bar in Paris, in a madcap outfit.

★ Grand Café de la Poste

Place 16 Novembre, behind post office, (0524 43 30 38). **Open** 7.30am-midnight daily. **Map** p88 D3 ㉒

Long before the hotels, the fashionable bars and the sexy French bistros there was the Grand Café de la Poste. Situated right behind the post office, with wrap-around terraces shielded by plants and bamboo screens, the Grand Café was a reliable spot for an afternoon snifter, while the black-and-white tiled dining room was the smartest place in town for lunch. There's still a decent line in salads, club sandwiches and aperitifs, though the main reason to come today is to soak up the atmosphere of a bygone era and to have cocktails upstairs at the most sophisticated cocktail bar in town. A central fireplace (open on all sides), leather chesterfields, plush woven pouffes, animal rugs, African art and lush, deep green plants make it a place in which to linger.

★ Jack is Back

10 Rue Oued El-Makhazine (0524 43 38 90). **Open** 8pm-2am daily. **Map** p88 D4 ㉓

Technically, Jack is Back is more restaurant than bar. The food, such as a bone marrow and parsley salad and artichoke-topped pizzas, is superb, with about two-thirds of the space given over to a mixture of round and oblong tables, slouchy booths and sofas, and a high table presided over by a portrait of a fried breakfast. That's Jack, his tongue firmly in cheek and a regular for years on the Marrakech night scene. This is his latest offering and the little bar at the front of the house teems with regulars, fellow bar owners and scenesters who all come for a taste of his special brand of unpretentious, grown-up fun, a funky sound track, killer cocktails, and reliably good company.

Kechmara

3 rue de la Liberté (0524 42 25 32). **Open** 9am-1am Mon-Sat. **Map** p88 C3 ㉔

A café by day and restaurant by night, Kechmara is also a lively bar lacking the kind of wannabe pretention that Marrakech has a certain penchant for. There's a long bar counter downstairs, a solid drinks list and beer on tap. Top-quality bands play on Wednesdays, many of them guests in from Paris or Barcelona. Drinks on the roof is a treat in summer.

EXPLORE

Djellabar.

O'Sky Bar
Renaissance Hotel, 89 boulevard Zerktouni, corner avenue Mohammed V (0524 33 77 77, www.renaissance-hotel-marrakech.com). **Open** 11am-1am daily. **No credit cards. Map** p88 C2 ㉕
Perched at the top of the Renaissance Hotel, O'Sky Bar has one of the best views in the city with a 360° panorama of the ring of mountains that surround Marrakech. It's brilliant for a cheeky afternoon pick-me-up, or a drink at sunset, when you'll be left in no doubt how the 'red' city earned its moniker. Comfortable grey sofas sprawl against blood-red terracotta walls and cactuses in planters painted Majorelle blues and yellows. The music is much calmer than the throbbing techno of most night spots – funk, soul, blues and jazz – and the cocktails aren't insanely priced either (90dh-100dh for the classics, up to 200dh for champagne cocktails).

Le Studio
85 Avenue Moulay Rachid (0524 43 37 00, www.restaurant-lestudiomarrakech.com). **Open** noon-2.30pm Mon; noon-2.30pm, 7.30-11.30pm Tue-Fri; 7.30-11.30pm Sat. **Map** p88 D3 ㉖ **French/wine bar**
On a street better known for grilled meat on a stick, this is a bistro-wine bar but also one of the few places you can go just for a glass of wine. You need to get in early if you want to perch at the bar with a drink, though. By 7.30pm the place is heaving with a largely French contingent merrily drinking, chain-smoking and carrying on. There's a good selection of wines by the glass, and if you just want a small nibble to go with it, there are plates of cheese and charcuterie.

Shopping

★ 33 Rue Majorelle
33 rue Yves Saint Laurent (0524 31 41 95, www.33ruemajorelle.com). **Open** 9.30am-7pm daily. **Map** p88 A5 ㉗ **Fashion/accessories/homewares**
A bright and breezy concept store showcasing more than 100 Moroccan and foreign designers, intended to lure you in once you've wafted around the Majorelle Gardens. The brainchild of Yehia Abdelnour and designer Monique Bresson, it has become a highly fashionable one-stop shop. Must-haves in the bright emporium include funky rubber-tyre bags, rice-sack *babouches*, Hassan Hajjaj's (*see p92*) recycled wares, Orenzo Design's vibrant cactus metal dishes, slick oil-drum tables, Lup 31's stylish make-up bags, cute baby accessories from l'Etoile de Jasmin, and Robert Merloz's reversible satin kaftans in gorgeous jewel colours. In the same complex, along with the Kaowa Café, is Chabi Chic, selling hip kitchenware. Next door is Hadaya, selling colourful leather handbags from Spanish designer María Bazan under her Wildeve label.

IN THE KNOW NIGHTCLUBBING

For music and nightlife, check out the acts at **African Chic** (*see p120*), or **Kechmara** (*see p97*) on Wednesdays. After dinner, the city's groovers and shakers head to fun-loving **Jack is Back** (*see p97*) for cocktails in lively surroundings, **Djellabar** (*see p97*) to shake it down to disco, funk and soul, and **Comptoir Darna** (*see p104*) for club tunes. The mega-clubs are all located out of town, mainly in La Palmeraie. They include the lavish Brazilian spectacle at **Fuego Latino** (*see p120*), which attracts visitors from far and wide, or, more obviously, **Pacha** (*see p120*) on the route d'Ourika.

Amazonite
94 boulevard El-Mansour Eddahbi (0524 44 99 26). **Open** 10am-1.30pm, 4-7.30pm Mon-Sat. **Map** p88 C3 ㉘ **Acccesories**
This is a cramped, three-storey repository of all manner of *objets d'art*, top quality Berber jewellery, a stunning collection of ancient silk carpets, plus miscellaneous ethnic trappings, including old marriage belts. Head down to the basement for a collection of antique kaftans. A place for serious buyers in search of rare finds at fixed prices.

Atelier Nihal
16 rue de Vieux Marrakchi (0671 16 01 62). **Open** 10am-1pm, 3-7pm Mon-Sat. **Map** p88 C3 ㉙ **Homewares/accessories**
From her workshop in Sidi Ghanem, Marion Verdier works with local artisans to create unique hand-woven cushions, other home-decor items and even handbags, which she sells in this chic Guéliz store. Working on looms, the artisans create tightly woven carry-alls, in both leather and cotton, with prices starting at 800dh; smaller clutches sells from 400dh.

Atika
35 rue de la Liberté (0524 43 64 09). **Open** 8.30am-12.30pm, 3-7.30pm Mon-Sat. **Map** p88 C3 ㉚ **Fashion**
This is where well-heeled residents and enlightened tourists flock for stylish and affordable men's and women's ranges – everything from classic loafers to natural leather sandals and stylish beige canvas mules. Prices start at 390dh and go up to 790dh for the Tods-style moccasins for which this place is known. It also carries children's shoes and a small selection of handbags.

El Badii
54 boulevard Moulay Rachid (0524 43 16 93). **Open** 9am-6pm Mon-Sat. **Map** p88 D3 ㉛ **Antiques**
Two floors of museum-quality antiques, hand-picked by owners Najat Aboufikr and her husband

VILLE NOUVELLE GALLERIES

A round-up of Guéliz art spaces.

Galerie 127.

Of all the recent gallery openings, the **David Bloch Gallery** (*see p100*) pushes the envelope the most. Set in a contemporary industrial-style space, the focus is on Morocco, North African and Middle Eastern street artists. Large picture windows, steel struts painted charcoal, and white-washed brick provide the frame for bold works that fuse neon, neo-calligraphy and geometrics by collectible artists like Larbi Cherkaoui, Mohamed Boustane and Yassine 'Yaze' Mekhnache.

Noir Sur Blanc Gallery (*see p103*) is a sprawling place spread through several rooms of a smart townhouse showcasing the work of 25 predominantly Moroccan contemporary artists. It covers all mediums, from painting and sculpture through to photography and video art, and provides an important meeting point hosting regularly changing exhibits and formal openings. Comfortable sofas and armchairs in the interior patios keep the dialogue flowing between artists and art-lovers on a day-to-day basis.

When Nathalie Locatelli opened **Galerie 127** (*see p100*) in February 2006 it was the very first photo gallery in the Maghreb. It's an appealingly simple space – a converted apartment with tall windows and walls left unsurfaced – and it got off to a good start with an opening show by Tony Catany. The king bought 30 of the photographs. Locatelli has continued with work by other big names in contemporary photography, mostly French or France-based, with work including portraits by Carole Bellaiche and Gérard Rondeau, Alejandra Figueroa's images of ancient statues, and Bernard Faucon's 'staged photography'.

Prominent art collector Lucien Viola commissioned the specially designed venue for **Galerie Rê** (*see p101*) in 2006. Part gallery, part theatre, the long, tall building has a floor-to-roof glass frontage to maximise natural light within. A sleek, central staircase provides a focal point, while museum-quality lighting and a high definition sound system ensures that each work, no matter the medium, gets maximum exposure. The collection is based primarily on contemporary works by Moroccan and Mediterranean-rim artists, and aims to open cross-cultural exchange and dialogue across those areas.

The **Matisse Art Gallery** (*see p101*) is a decent space devoted to solo shows by young Moroccan artists such as calligraphy painters Nouredine Chater and Nouredine Daifellah, and figurative painter Driss Jebrane. More established names are also exhibited, such as Farid Belkahia and Hassan El-Glaoui (the son of the former 'Lord of the Atlas' who is devoted to painting horses). Upstairs are some vintage Orientalist canvases.

Galerie Rê.

EXPLORE

33 Rue Majorelle

Mohamed Bouskri, owners of Riad Kniza (*see p213*), featuring a dazzling array of gold and silver jewellery, unusual lamps, carved Berber doors, ornate mirrors and a huge choice of carpets. In pride of place are antique ceramics from Fès, in traditional yellow and cobalt blue. Photos of Brad Pitt, Will Smith and Ronald Reagan browsing here tell you about well-known customers, but the fixed prices and warm welcome are for everyone.

Creazen

32 Galerie de la Liberté, rue de la Liberté (0524 43 22 33, www.creazenspirit.com). **Open** 9.30am-1.30pm, 3-7.30pm Mon-Sat. **Map** p88 C3 ㉜ **Fashion**

For ten years designer Sophie Rouault has crafted the collections here to reflect a European style with Asian and Moroccan influences. Her friendly approach ensures a personalised shopping experience for her customers. Using cottons and linens, the pieces, produced in Marrakech, can be mixed and matched to create an individual look. Rouault's collection changes regularly, as does her line in accessories.

★ David Bloch Gallery

8 bis rue des Vieux Marrakchis (0524 45 75 95, www.davidblochgallery.com). **Open** 3.30-7.30pm Mon; 10.30am-1.30pm, 3.30-7.30pm Tue-Sat. **Map** p88 C3 ㉝ **Gallery**

See p99 **Ville Nouvelle Galleries**.

Entrepôt Alimentaire

117 avenue Mohammed V, Guéliz (0524 43 00 67). **Open** 8am-noon, 3-10pm Mon-Sat; 8am-noon Sun. **No credit cards**. **Map** p88 C3 ㉞ **Wine**

This dusty little place may appear disorganised, and service may not always be so friendly, but it does have one of the best selections of wine (Moroccan and French) in town. If you can't see what you're looking for, just ask.

Founoun

119 rue Mohamed El-Bekkal (0524 44 88 41). **Open** 10am-1.30pm, 4-7.30pm Mon-Sat. **Map** p88 B2 ㉟ **Leather goods**

For ready-to-wear leather goods, head to Founoun, where jackets, skirts and vests and handbags are designed by young Marrakchi owner Kenza. Inspired by Moroccan style, Kenza's collections include updated versions of traditional clothing. The leather desk accessories are also unique and stylish. Custom orders can be completed in three days. Expect to pay from 2,700dh for a leather coat.

Galerie 127

127 avenue Mohammed V (0524 43 26 67, www.galerienathalielocatelli.com/galerie127). **Open** 3-7pm Tue-Sat or by appointment. **Map** p88 C3 ㊱ **Gallery**

See p99 **Ville Nouvelle Galleries**.

Galerie Birkemeyer

169 rue Mohammed El Bekal and 2 rue Yves Saint Laurent (0524 44 69 63, www.galerie-birkemeyer.com). **Open** 8.30am-12.30pm, 3-7.30pm Mon-Sat; 9am-12.30pm Sun. **Map** p88 A5 ㊲ **Leather goods**

A long-established haunt for leather goods, from handbags and luggage to shoes, jackets, coats and skirts, with a sportswear section of international designer labels. You may stumble across a good bargain, such as a beautifully crafted purse for 800dh. Founder Ms Birkemeyer no longer has anything to do with the place. (She now owns Intensité Nomade, *see p101*).

Galerie Rê

Résidence Al Andalous III, corner rue de la Mosquée & rue Ibn Toumert 3 (0524 43 22 58, www.galeriere.com). **Open** 10am-1pm, 3-8pm Mon-Sat. **Map** p88 C4 ㊳ **Gallery**
See p99 **Ville Nouvelle Galleries**.

Heritage Berbere

Rue Yves Saint Laurent (0524 30 88 41, www.heritageberbere.com). **Open** 9.30am-6.30pm daily. **Map** p88 A5 ㊴ **Perfumery**

This place sells lovely scents for the home with reed diffusers and room sprays in a variety of distinctive varieties, including Oud and Dynamic Green Tea. There are also perfumes for men and women, starting at 320dh for men and 340dh for women.

Intensité Nomade

139 avenue Mohammed V (0524 43 13 33). **Open** 9.30am-1pm, 3-7.30pm Mon-Sat. **Map** p88 C3 ㊵ **Fashion**

Intensité Nomade features owner-designer Frédérique Birkemeyer's own chic 'nomad' line of colourful kaftans, suede skirts, comfy raffia slippers, men's cotton shirts, leather jackets and a host of relatively inexpensive accessories. Pickings are mixed, but the place draws a glitzy local clientele, poking around the racks for casual prêt à porter.

Jeff de Bruges

17 rue de la Liberté (0524 43 02 49, www.jeff-de-bruges.com). **Open** 9am-1pm, 3.30-8pm Mon-Sat. **Map** p88 C3 ㊶ **Chocolatier**

Not real Belgian chocolates, but still the best chocolates in Marrakech. They make a great gift if you're invited to dinner at a local home (Moroccans are notoriously sweet-toothed), but don't expect to get a share because they'll be hoarded away for later. The place to go for treats.

L'Orientaliste

11 & 15 rue de la Liberté (0524 43 40 74). **Open** 9am-1pm, 3-7.30pm Mon-Sat. **Map** p88 C3 ㊷ **Antiques/homewares**

A small street-front boutique and a huge basement space hidden just around the corner make up L'Orientaliste. The former is stuffed with piles of inexpensive items – Fès ceramics, filigree metal containers, painted tea glasses, scented candles and perfume bottles, some filled with essences. The latter is crammed with pricey antique furniture, early 20th century Moroccan paintings and engravings.

Matisse Art Gallery

61 rue de Yougoslavie, no.43 passage Ghandouri (0524 44 83 26, www.matisse-art-gallery.com). **Open** 9am-1pm, 3.30-8pm Mon-Sat. **Map** p88 C2 ㊸ **Gallery**
See p99 **Ville Nouvelle Galleries**.

Michele Baconnier

12 rue du Vieux Marrakchi (0524 44 91 78, www.michele-baconnier.net). **Open** 9am-1pm, 3-7pm Mon-Sat. **Map** p88 C3 ㊹ **Fashion/homewares**

Thrifty shoppers might want to steer clear of Michelle Baconnier's treasure trove in the chic rue du Vieux Marrakchi. Her petite shop is a visual feast of textiles, textures and gorgeous threads. Beautifully light and whimsical organza sun hats

EXPLORE

NEW MUSEUMS

New collections with a focus on the arts.

With a growing number of artists' studios and the increasing international profile of the **Marrakech Biennale** (*see p23*), Marrakech's reputation as an artistic hub will be sealed by three big museums in the next few years.

The **Marrakech Museum for Photography & Visual Arts** (MMPVA, www.mmpva.org), designed by British architect Sir David Chipperfield, will occupy a site next to the Menara Gardens. The cool, cubist brick museum will showcase historic and contemporary Moroccan, North African and international photography, and also house a theatre, bookshop, café and educational facilities. Until the new building is unveiled in 2016, the MMPVA is temporarily squatting inside the Badii Palace (*see p82*) with a changing roster of exhibitions.

Also in the pipeline, on the other side of town, the **Al Maaden African Contemporary Art Museum** (MACAAL), funded by Fondation Alliances (www.fondationalliances.org), is a new cultural venue designed by architects Omar Alaoui from Morocco and Nieto Sobejano from Spain. The museum's collection will be drawn mostly from the holdings of the foundation's president, Alami Lazraq, a hotels and housing investor.

Finally, exciting news for the world of haute couture is the proposed **Yves Saint Laurent Museum of Fashion**, to be built near the Majorelle Gardens. Information is scant – the folks from the Fondation Pierre Bergé (www.fondation-pb-ysl.net), who look after the legacy of YSL, are being very coy about the details.

THE INDUSTRIAL REVOLUTION

Venture beyond the souks for yet more shopping.

If you've arrived in Morocco and have fallen in love with everything in your riad, chances are it came from the **Industrial Zone of Sidi Ghanem**, if it wasn't sourced at Mustapha Blaoui (*see p73*) that is. Beautiful linens, gorgeous pottery, scented bath products and even lanterns, Sidi Ghanem is the place for those who want to take large pieces of Morocco home with them.

About eight kilometres (five miles) north of town, it doesn't have the most romantic of locations, the streets have no names and the showrooms are housed next to busy workshops. But this old industrial and warehousing area, built on an ordered, linear street pattern, offers space that can't be found in the Medina or Guéliz. As a result, more and more Marrakech-based designers are establishing studios and showrooms here and most accept credit cards.

Be warned that it's a long walk from one end of the main street to the other, with minimal shade. If you take a taxi out here, you won't want to let it go – it's not easy to find another one in these parts. If you ask a driver to wait or to shuttle you from shop to shop, agree an hourly rate; 50dh-60dh is a fair price. Or book a driver through your riad and expect to pay up to 600dh. Bus no.15 departs Bab Doukkala every half hour (4dh per passenger), passing by Majorelle Gardens before eventually winding its way through the industrial zone.

We recommend having the taxi drop you off at the roundabout, near Bo Luminaire, where several shops are located. Pick up a copy of the free map or download it at http://sidighanem.net. Most shops are closed Saturday afternoons and Sundays.

FASHION

The Marrakech showroom of Tangier-based fashion designer **Salima Abdel-Wahab** (no.315, 0618 29 90 18, www.salima abdelwahab.com, open 10am-6pm Mon, Wed, 10am-1pm, 2-6pm Tue, Fri, 10am-1pm Sat) features her fabulous collection of unique designs created using local textiles including kilims. **Topolina** (*see p70*) also has a large, funky workshop and showroom here at no.436 (0651 34 57 95, open 9.30am-2pm Mon-Fri, afternoons and Sat by appointment), with a huge selection of vintage and vintage-inspired boho-chic styles in bright colours and striking patterns.

Topolina.

HOMEWARES

If industrial-style interior design is your look, check out **Ardevivre** (no.437, 0524 33 66 10, www.ardevivre.com, open 9.30am-12.30pm, 2.30-6.30pm Mon-Fri, 9am-1pm Sat, no credit cards), a large showroom with all kinds of goodies. Next door at no.437, **W.Home** (0524 33 61 28, www.w-homemaroc.com, open 9.30am-1pm, 2-6.30pm Mon-Fri, 9am-1pm Sat, no credit cards) also features a wonderful selection of lamps and unique interiors pieces. **Design&Co** (no.166b, 0524 33 50 47, http://designandcookmarrakech.com, open 9am-6pm Mon-Sat) curates a collection of unique artwork, furniture and home accessories and regularly features new artists. **La Boutique de l'Atelier** at no.315 (0524 33 52 67, open 10.30am-6pm Mon-Fri, 10am-1pm Sat) has a wonderful selection of upcycled furnishings in bright metals and one-of-a-kind designs by two interior designers.

COSMETICS AND PERFUME

For cosmetics, our favourite is **Les Sens de Marrakech** (no.17, 0524 33 69 91, www.lessensdemarrakech.com, open 8.30am-6pm Mon-Fri, 8.30am-4pm Sat). The argan oil sold here is some of the best we've found. Expect to pay around 197dh for a 125ml bottle. Further up the road, it's also worth checking out **Keros** (no.238, 0524 33 63 30, www.kerosfragrances.com, open 9.30am-5.30pm Mon-Fri, 9.30am-1pm Sat) for beautifully scented perfumes and room sprays. **Nour Bougie** (No.231, 0524 33 57 18, www.nourbougie.com, open 8.30am-6.30pm Mon-Sat) provides the ingredients to create an exotic ambience: candles in all shapes, colours and sizes as well as cut-out containers for creating magical patterns when lit.

CERAMICS
Further up the street, the **Loun** showroom (no.109, 0524 33 60 68, www.loun marrakech.com, open 10am-6pm Mon-Fri, 10am-3pm Sat, no credit cards) features beautiful ceramics produced in its workshop on the route d'Ourika. There are coffee and tea sets, plus tagines in various sizes and styles, priced from 35dh to 550dh, and vases from 250dh to 1750dh.

LIGHTING
For lighting options head to Henry Cath (no.139, 0524 33 88 30, open 9am-12.45pm, 2.15-6.30pm Mon-Fri, 9am-1pm Sat), where custom-made lamps and lanterns of the finest quality are produced. Each piece takes five weeks to make.

ONE-STOP SHOPPING
Fenyadi (no.219, 0524 33 62 01, open 9am-7pm Mon-Sat) has an extensive pottery collection on its ground floor, with modern takes on classic Moroccan shapes, from tagines to tea glasses, as well as pick 'n' mix dinnerware, mostly in fantastically rich colours. It changes the range every year, but keeps older designs in stock so that broken pieces can be replaced. Head upstairs for luxurious Egyptian cotton bedlinen, all in white and embellished with simple, coloured embroidered detailing. You can specify colours with an order, and commission calligraphic embroidery to your specifications. Big white towels and towelling bathrobes round off the range. On a higher floor is a small selection of scented candles and intricately designed candleholders in leather and metal.

EATING
With limited options in the area, **Le Zinc** (no.517, 0524 33 59 69, www.durand-traiteur.com, noon-3.30pm Mon-Sat, open for dinner from 8pm Thur, Fri, no credit cards) is centrally located, serves wine and is popular at lunchtime. **Café Leon** (no.24, 0526 71 65 45, open 9am-4pm Mon-Fri, no credit cards) is perfect for a light lunch (no alcohol) or a wonderful café au lait.

sitalongside heavier, but no less beautiful, Turkish textiles wrapped around leather boots, which make for stylishly embroidered footwear. The St Tropez-based owner is equally inspired by Indian pieces as she is by Moroccon crafts and her Guéliz shop is hung with brightly patterned Indian bedspreads. Her Moroccan pumps for women in jewel colours and silver are adorned with sequins, spirals or bows and are the perfect flats for shopping the streets of the Red City.

Mysha & Nito

Rue Sourya, corner rue Tarik Ibn Ziad (0524 42 16 38). **Open** 9.30am-1pm, 3.30-8pm Mon-Sat. **Map** p88 C3 ㊺ **Fashion**

On the ground floor you'll find womenswear by local designers. In the basement is a large collection of kaftans and djellabahs, reinvented as evening-wear in a variety of fabrics – including chiffon, gingham, simulated leather and imitation snakeskin – and priced anywhere between 1,000dh and 25,000dh. There are also T-shirts, bags, slippers and belts for those on a smaller budget, including hats by Le Chapelier.

Naturia Bio Shop

9 rue des Vieux Marrakchis (0524 43 00 00). **Open** 9am-1pm, 3.30-7.30pm Mon-Sat. **Map** p88 C3 ㊻ **Health foods**

This small shop is the go-to place for travellers with special dietary requirements. The shop stocks a selection of natural foods, including gluten-free products, all-natural snacks and herbal teas. Cosmetic, organic argan oils are also available. A naturopath and nutritionist are available for consultation once a week, free of charge, but check with the shop in advance as appointment times vary.

Noir Sur Blanc Gallery

A l'étage 48, Immeuble Adam Plaza, rue de Yougoslavie (0524 42 24 16, www.galerienoir surblanc.com). **Open** 3-7pm Mon; 10am-1pm, 3-7pm Tue-Sat; by appointment Sun. **Map** p88 C2 ㊼ **Gallery**

See p99 **Ville Nouvelle Galleries**.

Place Vendome

141 avenue Mohammed V (0524 43 52 63). **Open** 9.30am-1pm, 3-7.30pm Mon-Sat. **Map** p88 C3 ㊽ **Fashion/accessories**

Owner Claude Amzallag is known for his custom-designed buttery leather and suede jackets, and sleek line of handbags and wallets in every colour from forest green to hot pink. The suede shirts for men and stylish luggage are also big hits with the fortysomething crowd.

Scènes de Lin

70 rue de la Liberté (0524 43 61 08, www.scenes delin.com). **Open** 9.30am-1.30pm, 3.30-7.30pm Mon-Sat. **Map** p88 C3 ㊾ **Fabrics**

EXPLORE

A chic fabric store that specialises in linens and also offers a huge range of soft woven cloth or delicate pastel organdie in a range of brilliant hues. Custom-made curtains, tablecloths or place settings are available. There are plenty of other top-quality textiles, including luxurious bathrobes and towels, cushions with Fès embroidery, and even natural essential oils (including argan oil) and tableware. Downstairs is a small selection of Moroccan couture, including a sale rack with end-of-season stock reduced by up to 50%.

Vita

58 boulevard El-Mansour Eddahbi (0524 43 04 90). **Open** 9am-12.30pm, 3-7.30pm Mon-Sat. **No credit cards**. **Map** p88 C3 50 **Florist**

A Western-style florist and garden centre with a decent stock of cut flowers and ready-made bouquets. It also does delivery (local and Interflora).

★ Yahya Creation

49 passage Ghandouri, off rue de Yougoslavie (0524 42 27 76, www.yahyacreation.com). **Open** 9.30am-1pm, 3-7.30pm Mon-Sat. **Map** p88 C2 51 **Homewares**

Yahya Rouach's mother is English and Christian, his father is a Jew from Meknes, and he's a Muslim convert brought up in the UK and now resident in Marrakech. He designs extraordinary items, such as lanterns, torches and screens, all made from finely crafted metals. His pieces are unique, often stunning, one-offs. Most of them are big too: conversation pieces for a chic sheikh's Dubai penthouse, perhaps? This arcade outlet is a showroom rather than a shop, where customers drop in to place commissions, joining a client list that includes Harrods and Neiman Marcus.

EXPLORE

HIVERNAGE

South-west of place Abdel-Moumen, Guéliz peters out at the expanse of avenue Mohammed VI (formerly known, and still often referred to, as the avenue de France). Here, and to the south, is the area known as Hivernage. A showcase of colonial planning, it's a garden city for winter residence. On curving suburban streets, hidden in greenery, luxury hotels sit next to modernist villas. In the shade of a well-groomed hedge, soldiers indicate a royal in residence. The junction with avenue Hassan II is lorded over by the monumental **Theatre Royal**, designed by local star architect Charles Boccara. An open-air theatre is used for occasional performances but the opera house, behind, remains a shell. Hivernage is where you'll find popular nightclubs (*see pp119-121*) and the **Menara Gardens**. To reach the gardens, take a *petit taxi*, which should cost about 30dh from anywhere in the Medina. They'll try to charge you more to come back.

Sights & museums

Menara Gardens

FREE *Avenue de la Menara (0524 43 95 80).* **Open** 7am-5pm daily. *Picnic pavilion* 9am-5pm daily. **Admission** free. *Picnic pavilion* 10dh. **Map** p89 H3 52

Coming in to land at Aéroport Marrakech Menara, alert passengers may notice a large rectangular body of water to the east. This is the basin of the gardens from which the airport takes its name. They've been there since around 750 years before man took to the air – like the Agdal, the Menara Gardens were laid out by the Almohads in the 12th century. Later they fell into neglect and their present form is a result of 19th-century restoration by the Alouites. The highly photogenic green-roofed picnic pavilion that overlooks the basin was added in 1869. Climb to the upper floor for a wonderful view over the water or, better still, stroll around to the opposite side for the celebrated view of the pavilion against a backdrop of the Atlas. Great ancient carp live in the basin; buy some bread, toss it in and watch the water churn as the fish go into a feeding frenzy. Next to the Menara Gardens is the site of the new starchitect-designed photography museum due to open in 2016 (*see p101* **New Museums**). Soft drinks and ice-creams are available.

Bars

La Casa

Hotel El-Andalous, avenue Président Kennedy (0524 44 82 26, www.elandalous-marrakech.com). **Open** 8pm-2am daily. **Map** p89 G4 53

A bar that thinks it's a club, La Casa mixes food, music and dance to great effect. It is primarily a bar, dominated by a huge central serving area, surrounded on all sides by tables and seating. Above the counter hangs a giant rig of multicoloured lights fit for a Pink Floyd gig. Much flashing and strobing occurs in accompaniment to a heavy Arab/Latin beats soundtrack. There's no dancefloor, but then there's none needed, as everyone just lets go where they are. Around the stroke of midnight expect an 'impromptu' performance of dancing from the chefs in the corner kitchen area. Berber columns cloaked in purple drapes and characters from the ancient Tifinagh alphabet highlit in ultraviolet add the thinnest veneer of Moroccan theming.

Comptoir Darna

Avenue Echouada (0524 43 77 02, http://comptoirmarrakech.com). **Open** 4pm-1am Mon-Thur, Sun; noon-1am Fri, Sat. **Map** p89 F5 54

Marrakchi socialites will tell you that Comptoir is sooo over, but on the right night it's still the best party in town. From the outside, it's a well-behaved little villa on a quiet residential street, but inside the place buzzes with dressed-up diners on the ground floor, while upstairs is a sizeable lounge filled each

LUNCH AND A SWIM

Souks overdose? Time to relax with a poolside lunch.

Jnane Tamsna.

Stimulating as it is to spend time in Marrakech, there comes a time when you just want to chill out by a pool for the afternoon, especially in the heat. Fortunately, there are plenty of country options within a half-hour taxi ride from the Medina, as well as a couple of lesser-known getaways within the city itself.

Several roads lead out of town towards the Atlas mountains, Fès or into the Palmeraie, and it's here that many of the bigger hotels, and various clubs, have taken advantage of the wide-open spaces that surround the city. If it's views of the Atlas you seek (particularly sensational in spring, when snow still caps those powerful peaks), head down the rue d'Ourika.

Le Bled (*see p108*) is located within several acres of olive and citrus groves. The former farmhouse is now a simple country hotel, painted in bright Majorelle blues, buttercup yellows and hot pinks, and its swimming pool is open to day guests (200dh lunch plus pool pass). It's blessedly free of the thumping techno that besieges many of Marrakech's so-called 'beach' clubs; and you can have lunch anywhere you fancy, from poolside to a quiet corner beneath an olive tree. Wine and beer is served, and a *petit taxi* will bring you here for 50dh if you negotiate hard.

More upmarket is the **Beldi Country Club** (*see p108*). With several long, deep, midnight-coloured pools surrounded by salmon pink *pisé* buildings, richly scented rose gardens and pergolas shaded in jasmine and bougainvillea, it's every inch the Arabian Days fantasy and doesn't cost the earth (370dh lunch plus pool pass). The food is superb and you can also grab a hammam, massage or facial.

Heading into La Palmeraie, the **Jnane Tamsna** (*see p224*) is owned by entrepreneurial designer, restaurateur and hotelier Meryanne Loum-Martin and her ethnobotanist husband, Gary. Between them they've created a true oasis filled with soaring palms and native Moroccan and Mediterranean species including a wide range of aphrodisiac and healing plants. Stroll around the sensational gardens before indulging in one of chef Bahija's creative healthy lunches before collapsing by the pool (300dh lunch plus pool pass). The couple are keen art lovers, and the pool house has rotating art exhibitions and its own shop; afternoon tea is also available.

If you're staying in the Medina, **Les Jardins de la Koutoubia** (*see p205*) is one of the city's best-kept secrets for an elegantly peaceful lunch combined with a dip (200dh for lunch plus pool pass). The courtyard swimming pool is vast but tends to be busy with families, so head to the smaller rooftop pool which gets more sun and has the best view of the Koutoubia minaret.

Finally, for a real taste of the high life, treat yourself to a day or weekend Spa Pass (500dh-1,800dh, not including lunch) at **La Mamounia** (*see p201*), which gives access to the spa (not including treatments) and the outdoor swimming pool. It's a great way to indulge in the luxurious surrounds without committing to the cost of an overnight stay.

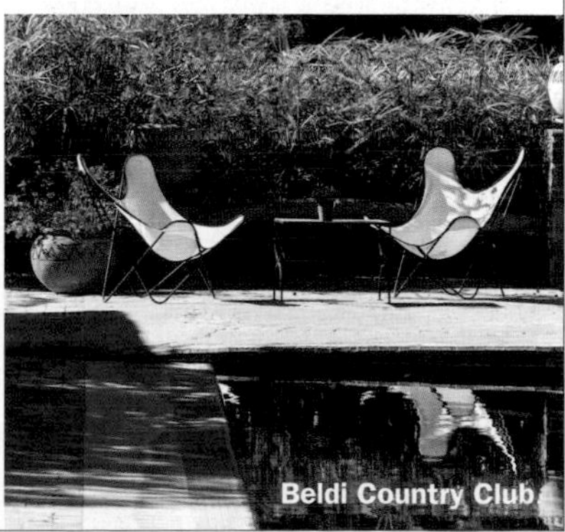
Beldi Country Club.

ENJOY THE OUTDOORS

Adventurous activities around Marrakech.

Ciel d'Afrique.

No trip to Marrakech is complete without a camel ride – anything from a few minutes to a full day's trip through the oases. If you just want a quick photo op, there are several places in the Palmeraie where camels are tethered waiting for the tourists. A half-day trip plus mint tea pit stop in a village can be arranged through **Touareg Quad** (Bab Atlas, route de Fès, opposite Hotel El Dorador, 0660 64 64 92, www.maroc-quad-buggy.com) at 250dh per half-day (no under-10s). Its Touareg Day package includes camel, quad and buggy riding with lunch, for 1,100dh per person.

Camel treks for younger kids are available through **Dunes & Desert Exploration** (route de Palmeraie, 0524 35 41 47, www.dunesdesert.com), a one-stop adventure shop with English-speaking staff. The company also offers quad bikes and buggies, from half-day trips around Marrakech to multi-day adventures further afield.

Grand Prix champion wannabes should try go-karting. **Atlas Karting** (route de Safi, km8, Ouhat Sidi Brahim, 0524 33 20 33, 225dh for 15 mins, 650dh for 1hr) is a challenging course on the outskirts of Marrakech, set up by an ex-pro rally driver. Day packages, with karting in the morning, quad-biking in the afternoon and lunch, cost 2,100dh.

Horse-riding is popular among expats and wealthy Moroccans. **Les Cavaliers de L'Atlas** (0672 84 55 79, www.lescavaliersdelatlas.com) is a French-run equestrian centre five kilometres out of town on the route de Fès. A half-day ride in the Palmeraie costs 350dh; a trek in the countryside near Lalla Takerkoust is 770dh per person.

Stunning scenery and clear skies for most of the year make ideal conditions for aerial adventures. Hot-air ballooning is organised by **Ciel d'Afrique** (Immeuble Ali A, route de Targa, Guéliz, 0524 43 28 43, www.ceildafrique.info), which has been taking tourists skywards in style for decades. An early-morning 'Classic' flight costs from 2,050dh per person. For paragliding, try

Touareg Quad.

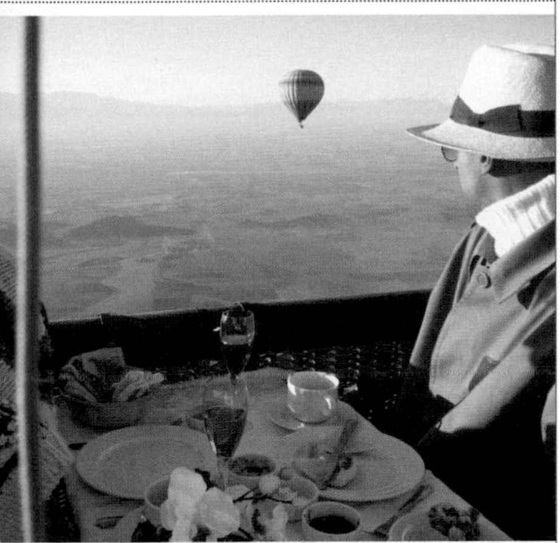

Evolution2 Marrakech (Residence Ali B, avenue Mohammed VI, Guéliz, 0524 45 76 88, www.evolution2ma.com).

At a more sedate pace, golfers are well catered for on the newly manicured plains surrounding the city. Marrakech has been promoting itself as a world-class golfing destination in recent years and there are currently seven courses to choose from; two more are opening later in 2014. The **Royal Golf Club** (Ancienne route de Ouarzazate, km2, 0524 40 47 05) is the oldest course in Morocco, built in the 1920s by the Thami El-Glaoui to impress his guests, while the **Al Maaden Golf Resort** (Sidi Youssef Ben Ali, 0525 065 065, www.almaaden.com), flaunts its modernity with angular bunkers, water features and outdoor sculptures. Golf package agencies include **Golf in Morocco** (www.golfinmorocco.co.uk). Green fees are usually around 800dh for 18 holes, with club hire on top and optional caddy service.

For rafting, canyoning, zip-lining, rock climbing, cycling, hiking, camel-trekking and sand-boarding and other activities, you need to head out of town (*see p150* **Adventure!**).

Whatever activity you choose, make sure you have adequate travel insurance and that the operator provides training, safety gear and a competent guide and possesses civil responsibility insurance.

weekend night to within a whisper of health and safety crisis. The crowd is a mix of good-looking locals, sharper expats and wide-eyed tourists delighted to have stumbled on the Marrakech they'd always heard about. Drinks are pricey but the nightly belly-dancers are hilarious.

THE PALMERAIE

Legend has it that the huge Palmeraie north-east of the Medina was born of the seeds cast away by date-chomping Arab warriors centuries ago. A nice story, but it fails to accord due credit to the clever minds that designed an underground irrigation system to carry melted snow water all the way from the High Atlas and enable a palm oasis of several hundred thousand trees. The ancient *khettra* system now has only historical curiosity value because the water supply is guaranteed by several reservoirs and a network of artesian wells.

It's not what you'd call a pretty oasis: many of the palms are the worse for wear and the ground is dry, dusty and lunar-like, with much of the scrappy land turned over to building sites. Even so, this is some of the most desirable real estate in all North Africa. Ever since the 1960s, when King Hassan II first granted permission for it to be sold, Palmeraie land has been the choice for the rich – it's the Beverly Hills of Morocco. Land is available only in parcels of more than one hectare and buildings must not interfere with the palms. Narrow lanes slalom between copses, occasionally squeezing beside high walls surrounding the typically massive grounds of very discreet residences.

Other than pricey homes, there isn't much to see in the Palmeraie (other than the odd ramshackle village, grazing camels and building sites). You might venture out here for a combination lunch and swim (*see p105* **Lunch and a Swim**), or you might choose to stay in this part of town, taking advantage of the luscious gardens of some of the city's most luxurious hotels (*see pp223-225*).

Sights & museums

Musée de Palmeraie

FREE *Dar Tounsi, route de Fès (0661 09 53 52, www.museepalmeraie.com).* **Open** 9am-6pm daily. **Admission** free.

Abderrazzak Benchaâbane's museum is rather like a small sanctuary. His private collection of modern and contemporary art from the 1950s to the present day hangs in large, bright galleries. Benchaâbane has collected the work of painters, photographers, sculptors and calligraphers, and showcases the work of Moroccan artists including Larbi Cherkaoui and Nourredine Chater, with stunning calligraphy and henna work on paper by Nourredine Daifallah, paintings by Hassan El-Glaoui and Farid Belkhahia, and

EXPLORE

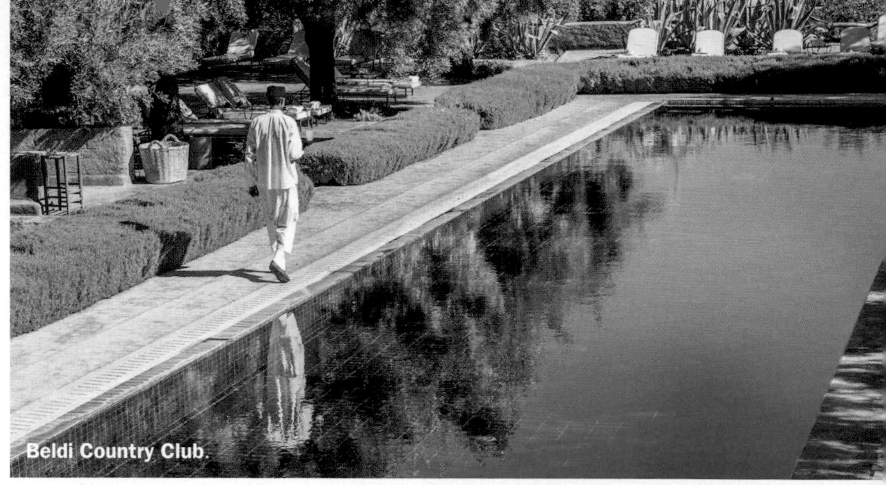
Beldi Country Club.

more. Considering that there is no contemporary art museum in Marrakech, it's worth the trip out here, although labels are in French so if you're not fluent it might be better to organise a tour in advance. Benchaâbane, a university ecology teacher with a science and botanical background, runs a small perfume atelier in his garden with one-hour workshops (50 euros per person). After that you can swan around the cactus garden and take tea in a little domed pavilion in the grounds.

EXPLORE

Restaurants & cafés

★ Jnane Tamsna

Douar Abiad (0661 24 27 17 www.jnane.com). **Open** 12.30-2.30pm, 7-9.30pm daily. **Main courses** 75dh-150dh. **Alcohol served. Moroccan**

It's well worth making the trek out to the Palmeraie from the Medina for lunch and a prowl around the gardens at Jnane Tamsna. It's much more than just a restaurant. Meryanne and Gary Loum-Martin built the house back in the early 1990s and set about creating their very own Garden of Eden with acres of native plants, home-grown fruit and vegetables, olive groves and, of course, those all important palms. With so much pristine fresh produce at her fingertips, chef Bahija, who's been with the family since the start, offers an inventive and healthy spin on traditional Moroccan dishes from a menu that changes twice daily. She also does cooking classes. After lunch, bask by the pool for a couple of hours, but don't forget to pop into the gallery-cum-tearoom to admire Meryanne's own collection of homewares (her scented candles are droolworthy) and works by some of the country's best artists.

Palais Namaskar

Route de Bab Atlas, no.88/69, Province Syba (0524 29 98 00, www.palaisnamaskar.com). **Open** 12.30-2.30pm, 7pm-late daily. Bar opens 5pm. **Main courses** from 120dh. **Modern Moroccan**

Heading deeper into La Palmeraie, you'll find this aptly named, contemporary 'palace' hidden away behind thick pink pisé walls and surrounded by perfectly manicured gardens and reflecting pools. Complete with turrets and golden domes, sweeping staircases and swimming pools peeking out from frilly arches, it's one of the prettiest restaurants in the city, and chefs Antoine Perray's and Nicolas Warot's modern Moroccan cooking is some of the country's best. Have a sundowner before dinner at the Nomad bar to enjoy magnificent views across the oasis to the Atlas, though fashionistas may prefer to don their summer dresses and head out for the Sunday Garden Party (788dh excluding drinks).

OUT OF TOWN

Restaurants & cafés

Beldi Country Club

Route de Barrage km6, Cherifia (0524 38 39 50, www.beldicountryclub.com). **Open** noon-1am daily. **Main courses** 110dh-250dh. **Alcohol served. Mediterranean**

There's no shortage of places just outside of Marrakech serving up bone-jiggling techno poolside. It's rather more difficult finding a peaceful retreat for the afternoon where you can combine a swim with a top-flight lunch. Beldi Country Club scores highly on all counts as a suave, sophisticated, summer hangout. Impeccably landscaped rose gardens provide the backdrop for three generously proportioned pools (one for kids, one heated year round, one for everyone) and several different alfresco dining areas dishing up healthy Mediterranean-inspired fare such as spinach, tomato and basil tart, spaghetti vongole and vanilla-strawberry pannacotta.

► *For more venues for lunch and a swim, see p105.*

Le Bled

Douar Coucou, Oasis Hassan II, Taseltanet (0524 38 59 39, www.lebledmarrakech).

Open 10am-10pm daily. **Pool & lunch** 200dh. **Alcohol served. Moroccan**

Out on a dusty highway about 20 minutes from Marrakech (a *petit taxi* should cost around 40dh), this low-key, organic farm hotel and swimming pool set amid acres of citrus orchards and olive groves is a welcome newcomer to the pool-lunch scene. It is owned by Dar Moha restaurant in the city and is a popular day out for Moroccans looking for peace and quiet. Here, the laid-back ambience means there's nothing so formal as a restaurant, but the kitchen is happy to lay tables or picnic blankets for you to eat anywhere you like on the grounds: under a shady tree, poolside, or in the cool internal courtyard. The home-grown menu offers authentic home cooking and fabulous home-made ice-cream and pastries.

► *For more venues for lunch and a swim, see p105.*

Touco Café

Fellah Hotel, route de l'Ourika km13, Tassoultante, Canal Zabara (0525 06 50 00, www.fellah-hotel.com). **Open** 8am-11pm daily. **Main courses** 160dh-230dh. **Alcohol served. Moroccan.**

It's worth the 20-minute taxi ride out of town to spend time at the Fellah, one of the most inspiring philanthropic projects to hit Morocco in recent years. It wears various hats, as home to the Ma'mun Art Foundation, which runs artists-in-residence programmes, and as a community based project that employs local villagers to organically farm their land and run the Touco Café, which serves authentic regional street food. The retro, mid-century-modern dining room and bar are set around a large, deep-blue swimming pool with the Atlas mountains as a backdrop and, unusually, dining guests are welcome to take a dip for free. If you're staying for the evening bring something sparkly, because Le Salon Mahler is one of the hottest tickets in town, shaking things up with live piano recitals, visiting DJs, film screenings and killer cocktails.

► *For more venues for lunch and a swim, see p105.*

Shopping

Marjane

Route de Casablanca, Semlalia (0524 31 37 24, www.marjane.co.ma). **Open** 9am-10pm daily. **Supermarket**

This massive hypermarket is popular with the city's middle and upper classes. It combines a supermarket (food and booze, clothes, household items, electronics, white goods, computers) with a McDonald's, plus Lacoste, Yves Rocher and other franchises, plus ATM machines, Méditel and Maroc Télécom, and a pharmacy. It's about eight kilometres north of town; a *petit taxi* will cost around 30dh each way from the Medina.

Myriam Roland-Gosselin

6 Rue de l'Aeroport, sign indicating La Ferme Zanzibar (0659 05 31 **66,** *www. myriamroland gosselin.com).* **Open by appointment only. No credit cards. Glassware**

Roland-Gosselin has a studio in a tranquil garden just off the airport road, where she makes delicate hand-blown glass objects for the home. Her collection, exhibited at MyArt (Place 16 Novembre, angle rue Tarek Ibn Zyad, Guéliz, 0524 44 91 81, open 9.30am-1.30pm, 4-8pm Mon Sat) includes tumblers, bells, candleholders and small lamps. Colour schemes tend to be warm ambers and oranges that bring to mind fiery Moroccan sunsets. For custom orders, call Myriam for an appointment in her studio.

Touco Café.

EXPLORE

Arts & Entertainment

Children

Marrakech may not seem, at first glance, a child-friendly town. There's chaotic traffic, broken pavements, seething crowds and virtually nothing in the way of attractions dedicated to children. That said, most youngsters will be enthralled by the city's exotic charm and leave with memories of great adventures. Making life easier is the fact that Moroccans generally adore children – doting on other people's offspring as much as their own. Exploring the souks with your young family can put you at an advantage, as traders tend to be more generous and respectful when children are around. Inside the largely car-free Medina, local children play in the maze of alleyways, but with mopeds a persistant hazard it's more relaxing to head to the city's gardens to let off steam and escape the crowds.

GETTING OUT AND ABOUT

Sightseeing with small children is difficult, particularly in the summer when temperatures can reach over 40°C (104°F). Avoid the noon sun and be sure to take the usual precautions: light, loose cotton clothes, sun hats, high-factor sun cream and plenty of fluids. Apart from cafés, there are few places to rest within the Medina, and amenities such as toilets and baby-changing areas are scarce. It's worth making use of toilets in hotels and restaurants wherever possible, and carrying a toilet roll just in case. Drink only bottled water, avoid uncooked food, such as salads, and be sure to peel or wash fruit and veg. Diarrhoea and stomach complaints are common; children are more susceptible than adults, so pack rehydration sachets.

IN THE KNOW
CHILD CAR SEATS

If renting a self-drive car or chartering a taxi, don't expect child seats to be provided. Some larger rental companies and tour operators may have them, but check beforehand. For long journeys, pack extra water and food – shops (and toilets) may be few and far between on the open road.

ACTIVITIES & OUTDOORS

You'll need to head out of the city for the high-octane fun stuff (*see p106* **Enjoy the Outdoors**). However, most children will be just as fascinated by the unfamiliar sights, sounds and smells of Marrakech as their parents – and it's not as if the city has any shortage of visual stimulation. Among the city's parks and open spaces, the **Menara Gardens** (*see p104*) is the most appealing to kids. There are camel and pony rides by the entrance and a big water-filled basin full of greedy fish at its centre. Children can buy bags of bread from a kiosk to feed them. In Guéliz, **Jnane El-Harti** (*see p90*) has a play area with sandpits, climbing frames and model dinosaurs, while nearby, the ever-popular **Kawkab Jeux** is a supervised play-park for kids aged two to nine, with electric kiddy-carts, rides, slides, trampolines and a café. Central Marrakech also offers **carriage rides**, the **Marrakech Bus Tour** and the fun of the **Jemaa El Fna**.

About 30 minutes drive out of town, **Jarjeer Mules Sanctuary** makes for an ideal family outing: little ones can ride donkeys, help care for the mules, ride bikes, swim and have lunch (by arrangement) at this British-owned donkey sanctuary. The luxury **Fellah Hotel** (*see p226*) also offers cultural day workshops for children aged four to 16, even if they are not staying at the hotel (550dh per person). Need to cool off? Head to **Oasiria**, a water park just a few kilometres out of town, for slides, wave pools, cafés and green spaces. A free minibus shuttle runs from near the Koutoubia and from opposite McDonald's in Guéliz.

Carriage rides

Place de Foucault, Medina. **Map** p252 B6.

A ride in a brightly painted horse-drawn carriage (calèche) is great fun. They seat four to five people and can be hired for a circuit of the walls or for a tour through the Palmeraie. The ramparts tour takes about two hours and should cost no more than 500dh; the Palmeraie tour takes three hours (700dh). Hourly charges per carriage are 200-250dh per hour, but be prepared to negotiate. Pick the calèche up on the north side of place de Foucault, midway between the Koutoubia Mosque and Jemaa El Fna.

Jarjeer Mules Sanctuary

Rue d'Amizmiz, km24, Oumnass (0524 48 39 84, www.marrakechmules.com). **Open** 8am-7pm daily. **Admission** by donation.

Jemaa El Fna

Map p250 C5.

Children love the Jemaa El Fna. During the day there are monkeys, snake charmers, acrobats and brightly clad, bell-ringing water carriers. At night it transforms into a giant sizzling barbecue offering all kinds of strange things to eat. Berber musicians and intriguing sideshows will enchant the kids before bedtime, but beware of pickpockets in the audience. *See also pp32-45.*

Kawkab Jeux

1 rue Imam Chafaï, Kawkab Centre, Guéliz (0524 43 89 29, www.kawkab-jeux.com). **Open** 12.30-9pm daily. **Admission** from 20dhs per child. **No credit cards.**

Marrakech Bus Tour

The red double-decker open-top bus tour is perfect for tired little legs. Hop on and hop off at Place de Foulcault and main city attractions. Day passes cost 145dh adults, 75dh 6-13s; under-fives go free.

Oasiria

Route d'Amizmiz, km4 (0524 38 04 38, www.oasiria.com). **Open** *Pool* 10am-6pm daily. *Slides & wave pools* Apr-Oct 10am-6pm daily (closed Nov-Mar). **Admission** from 120dh.

RESTAURANTS

Most restaurants will offer reduced prices for children's portions, but not a separate children's menu. **Café 16** (Marrakech Plaza, Guéliz, 0524 33 96 70, www.16cafe.com) has a limited kid's menu of pasta or hamburgers. **Les Jardins de Guéliz** (rue Oued Makhzine near Jnane El-Harti, 0524 42 21 22) is also ideal for children, with a garden and self-service buffet. Nearly all café-restaurants serve pizza, and the global fast-food giants can all be found in Guéliz. High-chairs and baby-changing facilities are rare.

SHOPPING

Nappies, UHT and powdered milk are widely available. For prepared baby foods you'll need to trek to supermarkets **Marjane** (*see p109*) or **Acima** (109 boulevard Abdelkrim El-Khattabi, Guéliz). For beautiful kids' kaftans, go to **Alrazal** (55 Rue Sourya, Guéliz, 0524 43 78 84), or for funky modern designs by **ZidZid Kids**, visit the 33 Rue Majorelle boutique (opposite Majorelle Gardens, *see p90*).

ACCOMMODATION

When planning a visit with children, think carefully about where to stay. Although riads are popular, not all are well suited to young children. They tend to be peaceful, intimate spaces, with rooms arranged off a central courtyard and no space to play – fine if you have a quiet, well-behaved child. For larger boisterous families, renting an entire riad in the Medina or a private villa in the Palmeraie, with on-site staff, can be a suitable choice. A more economic option is to go for one of the larger hotels in the Hivernage district with modern facilities, gardens and pool – and, crucially, a free shuttle service to the Medina to avoid expensive taxi transfers. Boutique hotel **Dar Zemora** (*see p224*) in the Palmeraie can accommodate families in its self-contained pavilion with private pool and terrace. The nearby resort hotels of **Palmeraie Golf Palace** (Circuit de la Palmeraie, 0524 33 43 43, www.pgpmarrakech.com) or **Club Med Marrakech La Palmeraie** (Sidi Yayha La Palmeraie, 0524 42 58 00, www.clubmed.co.uk) both have a free Medina shuttle service, ample sports facilities, organised activities and kids clubs for all ages. Budget hotels may not have en-suite bathroom facilities or adequate heating/air-conditioning.

BABYSITTING

Most riads and hotels can provide babysitters upon request. Most won't speak English, but the language of play is universal.

Film

The 2006 movie *Babel*, starring Brad Pitt and Cate Blanchett, was that rare phenomenon – an international film in which Morocco appears as itself. Generally, it's playing somewhere else – an alter ego. This identity crisis goes back a long way: David Lean's 1962 classic, *Lawrence of Arabia*, was partially shot in Morocco.

The Moroccan film industry is doing better than it was 20 years ago, however, with subsidies now generating around six million euros a year for local movies, and more than half a dozen young directors making home-grown films. There is also a film school in Marrakech, the ESAV (Ecole Supérieure des Arts Visuels), with around 100 students.

MOROCCO AS A SCENIC BACKDROP

In recent years, Morocco has been an adaptable backdrop for a number of foreign filmmakers. It stood in for Tibet in Martin Scorsese's *Kundun*, Somalia in Ridley Scott's *Black Hawk Down* and Paul Greengrass's *Captain Phillips*, and Ethiopia in Renny Harlin's *Exorcist: The Beginning*. It was a generic North Africa for Matthew McConaughey and Penélope Cruz in *Sahara*, for Jean-Claude Van Damme in *Legionnaire* and for Ridley Scott's *Gladiator*. It's also a popular substitute for the Holy Land: Ben Kingsley took the lead role in *Moses*, Willem Dafoe was Jesus in *The Last Temptation of Christ*, and there always seems to be some biblical epic in production in Ouarzazate.

The aftermath of 9/11 has accelerated this phenomenon of Morocco as a handy substitute for more dangerous locations in the Middle East and the Islamic world. Casablanca appeared as Beirut in Paul Gaghan's *Syriana*, and Greengrass used the Atlas mountains as Afghanistan (although they were later discarded) in *United 93*. Morocco reappeared as Afghanistan in Mike Nicholls' 2007 hit *Charlie Wilson's War* starring Tom Hanks. A year later it turned into Jordan for Ridley Scott's *A Body of Lies*. In 2010, Tangier doubled as Mombasa in Christopher Nolan's *Inception*. That same year the stars of *Sex and the City 2* descended on Marrakech, pretending it was Abu Dhabi. Morocco also masqueraded as Saudi Arabia when production began in 2014 on *A Hologram for the King*, also starring Tom Hanks.

So, *Babel* aside, when has Morocco actually been Morocco? Bertolucci's adaptation of Paul Bowles's *The Sheltering Sky* was shot in Tangier as well as the Sahara, and Gillies Mackinnon brought Esther Freud's *Hideous Kinky* to the screen. Tangier was indeed Tangier in Greengrass's *Bourne Ultimatum* in 2010. After that we have to go back to 1956 and Hitchcock's *The Man Who Knew Too Much*. Morocco's signature image on screen is, of course, *Casablanca*. But Rick's Café never existed, and Bogart and Bergman never left the Warner Bros backlot.

SWORDS, SANDALS AND SAVINGS

The $457-million, multiple-Oscar-winning success of *Gladiator* inspired a flurry of sword-and-sandal epics. Wolfgang Petersen's *Troy* might have relocated to Mexico after jitters about the Iraq War, but Ridley Scott flew back in for *Kingdom of Heaven*, and Oliver Stone turned up to shoot *Alexander*.

Appearing at the 2004 Marrakech International Film Festival, Stone grandly declared: 'Without Morocco there would be no film. It is the place where East meets West.'

He went on to elaborate the more prosaic reason Morocco is attractive: cost. 'We tried to make the film in Hollywood. But when we factored in all the unit costs in California we were way over budget. In Morocco we could run 500 to 2,000 extras a day. It's not possible to do this kind of movie in America.' In America, an extra earns $100 a day. In Morocco it's $15.

MOROCCO'S GAINS AND LOSSES

What's good for Hollywood is also good for Morocco. A major production such as *Alexander* brings an investment of around $60 million, and up to around 10,000 people get work as extras and crew. Not to mention the £30,000 bar bill that leading man Colin Farrell supposedly clocked up at Marrakech's Le Meridien.

Enlightened government policies regarding foreign filmmaking in Morocco have also boosted the indigenous film sector. To receive a production licence, at least one producer must be Morocco-based. In addition, ten per cent of all domestic box office revenue goes towards funding Moroccan movies. The central body for filmmaking in Morocco, the CCM (Centre Cinematographique Marocain) has followed a French model and now subsidises local movies to the tune of six million euros a year, with each film receiving between €300,000 and €500,000. This means that about 20 feature films and 30-40 short films are made every year in Morocco. The Moroccan director Faouzi Bensaidi says this has made a huge difference to the national film industry, compared to when he started out 20 years ago. At that time, he says, it was a real struggle as there was no funding at all. There are now more than half a dozen young directors, among them Nabil Ayouch, Narjiss Nejar, Laila Marrakchi, Nour-Eddine Lakhmari and Hicham Lasri (*see p116* for a selection of some of their films), a sort of bratpack of young Moroccan artists. Since the late 1990s they have been breaking artistic boundaries and social taboos to deal with subjects such as sex, religion and extremism. According to Bensaidi, the film industry is holding up a mirror to Moroccan society and helping with a process of modernisation and liberalisation partly encouraged by King Mohammed VI. There is also a film school in Marrakech, the ESAV (Ecole Supérieure des Arts Visuels), with around 100 students. Foreign productions also provide locals with an opportunity to learn and hone their cinematic skills, although in some cases local technical expertise has been lured away from Morocco.

Save Cinemas in Morocco.

The local industry does, however, face some difficulties. Moroccan films can rarely pay for themselves. Nor does it help that the local Arabic dialect is not widely understood beyond Morocco and Algeria. Many Moroccan films are French co-productions and are often in French. Not surprisingly, emigration to Europe is a common theme (in 2001's *Au-delà de Gibraltar*, for example), as are the difficulties of love in an Islamic society and of life in general in a desperately poor one. They are popular with local audiences but sometimes struggle to get much international attention outside of the festival circuit. Nabil Ayouch's *Ali Zaoua* and Laila Marrakchi's *Marock* are both unusual in having broken through to achieve wider distribution in Europe.

Filming in Morocco was hit by the knock-on effect of the financial crisis in Europe and the rest of the world. On top of that, production companies have complained about the difficulties with Moroccan bureaucracy when trying to obtain permits and so on. This has meant that many walk-on actors and craftsmen working on sets in Ouarzazate have struggled to find work.

CINEMAS

Thirty years ago there were 280 cinemas in Morocco; in mid 2014, there were only 35. In an effort to stem the flow, Save Cinemas in Morocco (Residence Zineb Rue Mauritania, Guéliz, 0661 58 00 90, www.savecinemasinmarocco.com) was created to try to preserve movie theatres such as the Eden. The association organises cultural tours for movie buffs who want to peek inside some of the Medina's disused classic auditoriums.

Marrakech today has less than a handful of city-centre cinemas, plus a new multiplex. Films are usually dubbed into French, with Arabic subtitling. Unless you can speak one or read the other, your experience is likely to be disappointing, especially as

REEL MOROCCO

Moroccan movies that have made their mark.

Death for Sale.

AL HALL (AHMED EL MAANOUNI, 1981)
Released abroad as *Trances*, this documentary tracks the history of Nass El-Ghiwane, the pioneering group who merged traditional influences with protest lyrics.

UN AMOUR À CASABLANCA (ABDELKADER LAGTAÂ, 1991)
This gritty, daring love story depicted a Casablanca of sex, prostitution, drugs and alcohol, that no one had seen on screen before. It won two prizes at the 1991 Meknès film festival, and opened up a new way of seeing and filming Morocco.

À LA RECHERCHE DU MARI DE MA FEMME (MOHAMMED ABDERRAHAM TAZI, 1995)
A comedy about a man who repudiates his third wife and then tries to get her back, *Looking for My Wife's Husband* was the biggest-grossing Moroccan film ever.

MEKTOUB (NABIL AYOUCH, 1997)
Thriller in which a doctor's wife is kidnapped and raped in Tangier. Her husband gets involved in a revenge killing, and the couple rebuild their relationship on a trip to the south.

KEÏD ENSA (FARIDA BEN LYZIAD, 1999)
Women's Wiles is a traditional tale adapted for the cinema, in which a young woman marries a sultan and, after an argument, finds herself a prisoner in the harem.

ALI ZAOUA, PRINCE DE LA RUE (NABIL AYOUCH, 2000)
A compelling mix of compassion, realism and sentiment earned this tale of young Casablanca street kids (played by homeless children) 44 film festival prizes and an international release.

MAROCK (LAILA MARRAKCHI, 2005)
Deft coming-of-age love story in which an Arab girl and Jewish boy fall for each other in the milieu of the wealthy, French-speaking Casablancan middle-class.

WHAT A WONDERFUL WORLD (FAOUZI BENSAÏDI, 2007)
Writer/director Bensaïdi plays a hitman who has a phone affair with a traffic cop in a Casablanca of disillusion and vast contrasts. Inventive visuals compensate for an occasionally stuttering narrative.

FEVERS (HICHAM AYOUCH, 2011)
Thirteen-year-old Benjamin is a troubled soul who has been in and out of foster homes. When his mother is sent to jail she reveals that Benjamin has a father. After leaving foster care he decides to live with his father in the suburbs of Paris but finds new dangers lurk there.

DEATH FOR SALE (FAOUZI BENSAIDI, 2012)
Three desperate petty criminals try to flee a life of poverty in Tetouan. One is in love with a prostitute and works for a corrupt police

inspector, another is a drug pusher, and the third embraces fundamentalism. Their last resort is to try to rob a jewellery store. Scorsese was so impressed with this project that he helped to fund the film. *Death for Sale* premiered at the Toronto Film Festival and was selected as Morocco's entry for best foreign film at the 85th Academy Awards.

KHALF ALABWAB ALMOGHLAKA (BEHIND CLOSED DOORS) (MOHAMMED AHED BENSOUDA, 2013)
Samira is an attractive young Moroccan woman who is happily married to a banker. But their lives are turned upside down with the appointment of a new boss at her workplace who begins to harass her. The film was premiered at the Marrakech International Film Festival in 2013.

THEY ARE THE DOGS (HICHAM LASRI, 2013)
Majhoul is a political prisoner who was jailed in 1981 during riots in Morocco. Thirty years later he is released in the middle of the Arab Spring. A TV crew doing a report on the unrest in Morocco decides to follow Majhoul, who is suffering from amnesia. *Variety* magazine praised it for having 'a certain cool vibe' but complained that it was 'an unsubtle and uneasy meld of satire and political commentary.'

KANYAMAKAN (SAID NACIRI, 2014)
When a robbery goes wrong, Amir steals the gang's loot and flees to the desert, taking refuge in a village among the dunes. He meets Shahin, the head of an old desert tribe. The film spent three years in post-production largely due to its ambitious special effects. It was the first Moroccan movie to be shown in the Jemaa el Fna as part of the International Film Festival. The director described it as a cross between *El Mariachi* (a Mexican action movie), *Indiana Jones* and *Once Upon a Time in the West*.

Marrakchis are notorious for making a lot of noise during the screening.

The Cinema Eden in Riad Zitoun El-Kedim is a sad testament to the decline of movie-going in Marrakech. This tiny auditorium opened in 1926, but audiences dwindled and it closed in 2009. This is hardly surprising since locals can buy pirate DVDs for about 5dh, while it costs at least 25dh to go to the cinema. There was talk of restoring the Eden to its former glory, but so far, at the time of writing, this has come to nothing. Mind you, its former glory was not really that glorious, with a crowd-pleasing selection of Westerns, Bruce Lee vehicles and Bollywood romances. Spanish novelist Juan Goytisolo, a long-time resident of Marrakech, remembered it as a flea pit with a concrete floor covered in peanut husks, empty food cartons thrown down from the upper circle and, at one time, a nasty smell from a drunk who had urinated in the front stalls.

In addition to the cinemas listed below, films are shown about twice a week at the Institut Français (Route de la Targa, Jbel Guéliz, 0524 44 69 30, www.ifm.ma, tickets 20dh), which has a more eclectic programming remit.

Cinéma le Colisée

Boulevard Mohammed Zerktouni, Guéliz (0524 44 88 93). **Tickets** from 25dh. **Map** p254 A2.
This place trumpets itself as 'the best cinema in Morocco' and it's certainly the best in Marrakech – a comfortable, modern venue with excellent sightlines.

Cinema Mabrouka

Passage Prince Moulay Rachid, Jemaa El Fna & Around (0524 44 33 03). **Tickets** from 25dh. **No credit cards**.
A charming restored 1950s cinema just south of Jemaa El Fna. The Mabrouka shows Hong Kong action movies, Bollywood comedies and Egyptian films but it also joins in the fun at the Marrakech International Film Festival (*see p25*). It has been described as loud, testosterone-filled and not great for females on their own.

Cinéma Al Massira

Off rue Palestine, Hay Mohammadi, Daoudiate (0524 30 94 59). **Tickets** from 25dh.
A very popular, comfortable and modern cinema in the new town.

Megarama

Avene de 7eme Art, off route d'Ourika, Jardins de l'Agdal (0890 10 20 20, www.megarama.info/marrakech). **Tickets** from 50dh.
Marrakech enters the multiplex era with this nine-screen complex, catering for 1,350 filmgoers, just behind the Pacha nightclub. The building, a concrete hulk topped with Berber-style crenellations, is like a pre-Saharan version of Californian mall architecture; inside, you could be just about anywhere.

Gay & Lesbian

Gays have long been attracted to Marrakech and the feeling is mutual... just as long as nobody finds out. Tennessee Williams, Joe Orton, William S Burroughs and Paul Bowles all visited, and more recently many high-profile, openly gay men have felt the spell of Marrakech. But the irony is that homosexuality is illegal in Morocco, with Article 489 of the penal code outlawing 'lewd or unnatural acts with an individual of the same sex', punishable with a jail term of up to three years and a fine. In practice convictions are rare.

Meanwhile, Moroccan LGBT rights groups operate from outside the country, unable to gain legal recognition at home.

Sex among men in Morocco may be common, but few would identify themselves as gay. Here, the rules are different and so are the facilities. There are no gay bars, clubs or cafés. In fact, any place marketing itself explicitly as such would risk being closed down. There are also no openly gay riads, despite many being gay-owned, mainly by foreigners. (However, staying as a couple in a double room, whether you are gay or straight, is unlikely to raise even an eyebrow in Marrakech.)

Moroccan men make contact in the streets and cash-rich foreign tourists are considered a particularly good catch. That warm, open, friendliness can often be followed up with a quick tug at the nether regions, just to make intentions clear. Much has been written in the West about the willingness of young Moroccans to engage in gay sex. Rules about no sex before marriage are cited as a reason, yet heterosexual prostitution is rife. So why are so many Moroccan men keen to have sex with tourists? Perhaps it's because they leave after a few days.

Moroccan men approach, chat and try to pick up without being too explicit. In Marrakech, gay sex is everywhere. The key is not to get caught. Walking through the Jemaa El Fna, flirtatious eyes are keen to make contact. The square is a gay pick-up joint, but this goes unnoticed by the hordes. Sitting in a café overlooking Jemaa El Fna, a packet of cigarettes open and pointing out towards passers by is a code. It reveals the smoker is open to meeting men. Walking on a particular part of the pavement up avenue Mohammed V in front of the Koutoubia Mosque discloses the same thing. Cars stop, drivers wind down their windows, men chat and then drive off together. To anybody walking past, they could simply be friends. That's gay Marrakech: it's everywhere and nowhere. Visiting lesbians are are also likely to go unrecognised, though in this case it's because many Moroccans simply don't know they exist. (When young Moroccans are asked about lesbians, they often say 'we don't have any'.)

There is a small but growing group of Moroccans who identify as gay in the same way as Europeans, and North Americans. Young, professional and relatively affluent, these men often feel at odds with their country, believing they have to choose between their family or their sexuality. Most end up living a double life, getting married and hiding a secret sexuality – just like European or American men did during the 1940s or '50s. Young Moroccan author Abdellah Taïa has published autobiographical novels on the difficulties of growing up gay in Morocco, written from his adopted home in France.

Nightlife & Music

A sleepless night in Marrakech is known as '*une nuit blanche*' and, more often than not, is spent enjoying the city's vibrant cabaret and nightclub scene. Nights without sleeping of a more traditional nature can also be brought about by a good old-fashioned Berber knees-up, rocking the Kasbah until sunrise. And Moroccans like their music loud... very loud.

Marrakech is a highly diverse city, where ragged mule carts vie with Mazeratis, and the designer shops of Guéliz take on the artisan crafts of the souks. It's a place of deep-rooted traditions and conservative religious values, but one where hedonism and consumerism are booming. And this mix has a soundtrack – Arabic pop in the supermarket, Berber folk music in the taxi, Western jazz in city bars, and DJ sets in the clubs.

NIGHTCLUBS

The opening of the enormous **Pacha** complex in 2005 went some way towards putting Marrakech on the international clubbing map. The mega-club draws international devotees of the brand for weekend parties and has inspired a host of others to set up shop along the same strip on the outskirts of town. One of these is the cavernous **555**, which has gathered momentum targeting a largely home-grown crowd as well as tourists. The ever-popular **Théâtro** is now entering its second decade with a reputation as one of the hottest places in town. Each night an extravagant floorshow of costumed dancers, aerialists and fire-jugglers intermingle on the dancefloor.

At these clubs, look out for big-name guest DJs such as David Guetta, who played Pacha in 2013, and superstars like Algerian *rai* legend, Khaled, who has performed live at 555.

Aside from the full-on nightclubs, there is a growing trend towards inclusive dinner-cabaret venues, with live shows, musicians and DJs. Even though the food may be expensive, it is not always obligatory to dine. In the dinner-cabarets listed (*see p120*) you can turn up after 10pm and just buy overpriced drinks at the bar in return for your night of fun.

The city's more upmarket nightlife tends to be concentrated in Hivernage. Here, for example, the **So Lounge**, annexed to the Sofitel, attracts wealthy Moroccans, visitors and expats, as does the **Lotus Club**, which has a Vegas-style nightly cabaret with great live music.

Over in Guéliz, the clubbing waters are rather murkier, but come with a cheaper price tag. A recent French news report dubbed Marrakech the 'Bangkok of Africa' – and that wasn't a reference to its Thai restaurants. Prostitution is rife here, and Guéliz is its epicentre, so don't be surprised to see working girls (and boys) at some of the clubs.

555 Famous Club Marrakech

Boulevard Mohammed VI, Zone hôtelière de l'Aguedal (0678 64 39 40, www.beachclub555.com).
Admission 200dh. **Open** 11pm-5am daily.
New kid on the block 555 opened in 2012, playing house, R&B and hip hop. Seemingly desperate to attract female clientele, Ladies Nights run Monday to Wednesday, with no charge for groups of four or more. The huge dancefloor only really fills up at weekends. Expect loads of dry ice and ultraviolet

beams, exuberant young Moroccans and pounding decibels. While drinks prices may be excessive, free nibbles are provided, and the rooftop Sky5 bar is a popular spot where you can also eat tapas.

African Chic

6 Rue Oum Errabia, Guéliz (0524 43 14 24, www.african-chic.com). **Admission** free. **Open** 7.30pm-3am daily. **Map** p254 C3.

Not a nightclub as such, but a bar with late live music and a thumping dancefloor – and, in 2014, much improved from previous years. A Latin and Salsa ensemble from Spain, Morocco and Venezuela rocks the house from 11.30pm Monday through Saturday. A backing-track singer warms up the crowd, and a DJ takes over at 1.30am. Dark wood, zebra-painted niches and carved masks create the 'African' effect, but the 'Chic' is sadly lacking.

Pacha

Boulevard Mohammed VI, Zone hôtelière de l'Aguedal (0524 38 84 00, www.pachamarrakech.com). **Open** midnight-5.30am Tue-Sun. **Admission** 200dh; 250dh Fri, Sat.

Pacha is an enormous complex which, apart from the club itself, also includes two restaurants, a chill-out lounge and swimming pool. The dancefloor and bars can accommodate up to 3,000 smiley souls. International guest-DJs play at weekends, but resident DJ Daox is one to watch out for too. The club is some seven kilometres south of town, so getting there and back can be pricey.

Silver

Downstairs at Jad Mahal, 10 rue Haroun Errachi, Hivernage (0663 73 15 42, www.silvermarrakech.com). **Admission** 200dh. **Open** midnight-5am daily. **Map** p254 C4.

If you've spent the evening at Jad Mahal, head underground for after-hours into the shiny, industrial space of Silver. Glittering disco balls, pumping techno and soulful house remixes fill this former cabaret venue and attract a youthful, blinging crowd of partygoers. Guest DJs from Europe regularly perform. Free entry if you've spent your evening at Jad Mahal.

So Lounge

Sofitel, rue Haroun Errachid, Hivernage (0660 12 34 10). **Admission** 250dh (free to hotel guests and restaurant clients). **Open** 11pm-4am daily. Map p254 C4.

The So Lounge space in the Sofitel is carved up into four sections: restaurant So Food; chill-out lounge So Zen; So Nice, an alcohol-free outdoor shisha garden; and So Fun, the dancefloor and music stage. On Wednesdays there are belly dancers and an 'oriental' theme until 1am. Otherwise, there's live soul, R&B and a funk band, plus DJs. The decor is contemporary and cool and the place attracts a more mature crowd of tourists, expats and locals. For groups, it can work out cheaper to make a dinner reservation.

Théâtro.

Théâtro

Rue Ibrahim El-Mazini, Hivernage (0524 33 74 00, www.theatromarrakech.com). **Admission** 150dh. **Open** 11.30pm-5am daily. **Map** p254 C5.

Going strong since 1952, the dramatic Théâtro was originally a variety theatre, attracting such illustrious names as Maurice Chevalier and Josephine Baker. Completely revamped in 2005, it is still the best place in the city for proper dancing. The vast space makes room for all sorts of shenanigans from pole dancers to cabaret style performances, men on stilts, jugglers and fireeaters. As well as Morocco's funkiest DJs, the venue attracts guest stars from abroad. There are different themed parties every night of the week; Tuesday is (free for) Ladies Night.

Music & dinner cabarets

Le Blokk

Lotissement Ennakhil, Palmeraie (0674 33 43 34, www.leblokk.com). **Open** 8pm-1.30am daily. **Show** 8.30pm.

Blues, jazz and R&B singers take to the stage to accompany dinner before the acrobats start falling from the rafters at around 11pm. Then the party gets in full swing, with a mix of Arabic and Western pop music filling the small dancefloor. The chic restaurant attracts smartly dressed Moroccans and foreigners, but non-diners are also welcome to drink at the bar and dance to the live acts and DJs.

Fuego Latino

Hotel Palmeraie Palace (0619 27 29 45, www.palmeraiemarrakech.com). **Open** 7pm-2am daily. **Set meal** from 350dh. **Show** 11pm.

After you've eaten your fill of barbecued *churrascaria* meat and fish, it's carnival time. Sip a caipirinha as you watch the *capoeiristas* perform the traditional Brazilian martial arts dance. And there's more Latin-themed entertainment with samba drummers and exotic dancers. Book for dinner to get the best view of the catwalk stage. Entry to the bar area is free, but drinks are expensive.

Lotus Club

Rue Ahmed Chawki, Hivernage (0524 42 17 36, www.lotusclubmarrakech.com). **Open** 7.30pm-2am daily. **Main courses** 180dh-450dh. **Show** 9pm. **Map** p254 C4.

Costumed dancers with feathers aplenty take to the stage in a Vegas-style cabaret revue called *Oh La La*. There's also a pop, soul and funk band from England and Moroccan virtuoso guitarist Mahmoud 'Mood' Chouki. 'Mood' gives a captivating performance in a kaleidoscope of world music styles. The intimate restaurant-bar area has an elegant art deco feel. Turn up after 9pm to view from the bar, but for a table near the stage book for dinner (there are Mediterranean, Japanese and Moroccan menus).

MUSIC

Long before the words 'world' and 'music' got friendly with each other, Morocco was one of the few developing countries whose music had any kind of audience in Europe or America. Paul Bowles toured the country in the late 1950s with a tape recorder and a commission from the US Library of Congress, aiming to capture examples of endangered music from all regions. Another Tangier resident, Brion Gysin, established diplomatic relations with Berber Sufi trance group the Master Musicians of Joujouka, who famously went on to work with Brian Jones of the Rolling Stones, beat poet William Burroughs, and Ornette Coleman. Robert Plant and Jimmy Page also were inspired to record their *No Quarter* album in Marrakech with local *gnawa* masters back in 1994. But despite this ongoing Maroc 'n' roll dialogue, pure undiluted Moroccan music remains relatively unknown outside of the country, and is very hard to find as a visitor.

Record labels such as World Music Network in the UK and the Paris-based Institut du Monde Arabe have brought forth quality recordings of both contemporary and traditional Moroccan artists, but with the absence of an organised music industry or many performance venues, lack of copyright protection and rampant piracy, it is almost impossible for Moroccan musicians to make a living at home. Paradoxically, the CD stalls are brimming with pirated recordings of popular performers like Abdelaziz Stati, Mohamed Rouicha, Najat Aatabou and Abdellah Daoudi, who can fill stadiums when they appear at festivals but whose names remain unknown to Western audiences.

There is a rich tradition of Berber music and Arab music, Jewish music and the music of the descendants of African slaves, music for dancing, music for storytelling, music for harvest festivals and music for circumcision rituals, classical music rooted in medieval Andalucía and pop music that belongs to the urbanised Arab cultures of today. But there aren't many easy ways to hear it live. To help you find it, *see p122* **Seeking Live Music**.

BERBER SOUNDS & CEREMONY

With its own instruments and tunings, rhythms and sounds, Berber music is entirely different from the more formal Arabic music. It's rootsy, rural stuff that's traditionally performed at community celebrations, especially harvest and religious festivals. Just as different parts of Morocco have their own Berber dialects, so the different regions all have their unique sounds, dances, costumes and instruments – typically the banjo-like *luthar*, the one-string violin or *r'bab*, *nai* flute, the *bendir* frame drum and other small hand-drums. In the High Atlas Mountains, nearest to Marrakech, the most

MUSIC FESTIVALS

Festival National des Arts Populaire (www.marrakechfestival.com, June) is Marrakech's single major music festival. Those coming to Marrakech to seek out its music should synchronise their visit with this festival or a handful of other well-established festivals sprinkled across the kingdom. In order of proximity to Marrakech, the key music festivals are as follows:

Festival of Gnawa and World Music Essaouira (*see p141*, June), with *gnawa*, world and jazz fusions.

Festival des Andalousies Atlantiques Essaouira (Nov-Dec), with Arabo-Andalucian, Sephardic and flamenco sounds.

Mawazine Festival Rabat (www.festivalmawazine.ma, May), with popular Western artists, Berber and Arabic big names.

Timitar Festival Agadir (www.festivaltimitar.ma, June), with Berber music.

Fes World Sacred Music Festival Fes (www.fesfestival.com, June).

Taragalte Festival M'Hamid El-Ghizlane (www.taragalte.org, Nov), with Saharwi and world music.

International Nomad Festival M'Hamid El-Ghizlane (www.nomadsfestival.org, Mar), with local traditional music and international acts.

Tanjazz Tangier (www.tanjazz.org, Sept).

SEEKING LIVE MUSIC

Movers, groovers and shakers.

Café Clock.

You can't go down the usual Western routes to find live music in Morocco, a country with few music venues and no culture of going out to concerts, despite a rich musical heritage. To really discover Moroccan music in Marrakech, you'll need to do a bit of research to uncover festivals (*see p121*), organised cultural events or venues where there may be sporadic performances. It may get easier soon: the government is investing in cultural provision in the city, and plans include renovating the Theatre Royal and establishing a music conservatoire.

In the meantime, the **Institut Français** (05 24 44 69 30, www.if-maroc.org/marrakech) puts on occasional concerts of jazz, world and contemporary music, either in the small auditorium or in an outdoor amphitheatre, and there's more – occasional – classical music at the **Theatre Royal** (*see p104*), which is also a venue for the **Festival National des Arts Populaires** (*see p121* **Festivals**). And classical music devotees in Marrakech have created the **Association des Amis de la Musique Marrakech** (www.aammarrakech.com), which organises chamber music recitals in luxurious riads, usually involving a buffet dinner. Membership, available online, is obligatory and costs 300dh a year.

For music of a more home-grown variety there's a buzz around the 2014 opening of **Café Clock** (*see p80*). Café Clock in Fès has already established itself as a cultural insitution and its sister café is aiming for a similar role. Sunday evenings sees traditional acts and young local bands, including *gnawa* groups and Berber musicians, play. Keep an eye, too, on the **Mint Collective** (mintcollectivemb5.com) and **Le 18** (05 24 38 98 64, email le18marrakech@gmail.com), creating screenings, sound-art and multimedia pieces. Both were kickstarted by the Marrakech Biennale 2014 (*see p24*). The **Dar Bellarj** cultural centre (*see p53*) hosts informal performances with traditional ensembles in its courtyard around the festivals of Ramadan and Ashura.

Bars with worthwhile bands include **Jad Mahal** (*see p120*). Then there are the late-night cabarets with Western and Moroccan music at **Le Blokk** (*see p120*) and **Lotus Club** (*see p121*). **Fuego Latino** (*see p120*), meanwhile, is a Brazilian-themed extravaganza. Ironically, the samba band leader is the son of a famous *gnawa* master and a *gnawa* musician himself, but working the clubs is a more lucrative career.

Finally, of course, the **Jemaa El Fna** (*see p34*) hosts clusters of Berber musicians every night of the week, hustling for a few dirhams to play a tune. Most so-called '*gnawa*' in the square are little more than beggars in fancy dress, though – for a better *gnawa* experience ask your riad to book a professional troupe.

common folk music form is a courtship dance called *ahouache*. Men in long white robes and yellow babouches stand shoulder-to-shoulder opposite a line of brightly costumed Berber women. Accompanied by *bendir* drums and clapping, the men sing their praises and the women call their response. A male leader signals the steps: firstly, the line of men shuffles forward in unison stamping rhythmically, then the women respond. Heavy and ornate costume jewellery adds a percussive sound. The *ahouache* ritual is ancient and can last until dawn. It may be encountered by chance in a village context during religious holidays or *moussems*, or at an organised music festival (*see p121* **Music Festivals**).

On the streets of Marrakech you may come across groups of young men clapping, singing and playing small goblet *tarija* drums. Their quick-fire rhythms and songs are called *daqqa marrakchia* and celebrate the seven spiritual guardians of the city. You are most likely to hear it around the time of *achoura* – the tenth day of the Islamic new year.

VIVE LE TRANCE

If Berber music comes across as elemental, bordering on mystical, it's got nothing on *gnawa*. The name refers both to the music and to its practitioners. The *gnawa* trace their ancestry back to the Sudan and sub-Saharan Africa – '*gnawa*' may derive from the same root as Ghana or Guinea – whence they were dragged to Morocco as slaves. To reflect their difficult history, the *gnawa* claim spiritual descent from Bilal, the Ethiopian slave who suffered much before becoming the Prophet's first muezzin. *Gnawa* communities are concentrated mostly in Marrakech and Essaouira – though they exist all over the country. A strong oral tradition has kept alive the culture of their ancestors, and *gnawa* is the best-preserved manifestation of the black African aesthetic within Morocco.

At its simplest, *gnawa* is just drum and bass. The *guimbri*, a long-necked lute, is the main component, combining a fat acoustic bass sound with a metallic rattle. Accompaniment comes from the insistent clatter of chunky iron castanets, *karakeb*. Bigger ensembles add drums, call-and-response vocals, and lots of dancing. It's repetitive, hypnotic stuff, built around looping riffs. At their most authentic, *gnawa* performances are part of all-night healing rituals involving trance and possession. Different powers in the *gnawa* spirit world are denoted by different colours (seven in all), and the different colours by different music. At a *lila* (from the Arabic word for 'night') ritual, one of the musicians will play until whatever colour is dominating proceedings reveals itself.

Back in the mundane world, *gnawa* lyrics are riddled with references to the pain of slavery and exile, and the turmoil of dislocation. In this sense *gnawa* is similar to both blues and reggae, speaking the universal language of suffering. But it also has much in common with European trance or techno, in which music becomes one enveloping continuum of sound and rhythm.

GLOBAL GNAWA

Although marginal in Moroccan society, *gnawa* has made an impact on both the local and global music scenes – particularly since the Essaouira **Festival of Gnawa and World Music** (*see p141* **Gnawa Grooves**) gave it an annual focus and international respect.

A music of loops, spaces and extended durations, *gnawa* lends itself easily to fusion experiments and collaborations. Attempts to merge *gnawa* with other musics have been going on since the 1970s. The torch was lit by Casablancan five-piece Nass El Ghiwane, who played traditional instruments and fused *gnawa* with elements of popular Egyptian and Lebanese song. That, and a political edge, gave them Bob Marley-like status across North Africa. The original band leader died in a plane crash in the 1980s, but the group restructured and play on under the same name.

Gnawan fusionist Hassan Hakmoun cut his teeth playing around Jemaa El Fna, before moving to New York in the mid 1980s, where he made the impressive *Gift of the Gnawa* (1991), featuring legendary trumpeter Don Cherry and avant-garde composer Richard Horowitz. *Gnawa* fusion also made radical moves forward with Arabic techno pioneers Aisha Kandisha's Jarring Effects during the 1990s. More recently bands springing from the Maghrebi diaspora living in France, such as Gnawa Diffusion and Orchestre National de Barbès, blend *gnawa* with ragga and reggae. In the UK, Rabat-born DJ U-Cef mixes samples of Moroccan music with just about anything, but most recently mixing dub with the traditional *gnawa* approach of Marrakech's Maâlem Said Damir. In 2011, *guimbri* player Aziz Sahmaoui took *gnawa* fusion up a further notch with the album *University of Gnawa*. He blended traditional *gnawa* songs, new songs and street sounds, and brought West African musicians and their instruments into the mix.

Finding *gnawa* music in its authentic and intended context is hard; there are very few *lila* rituals and the ones that do take place happen behind closed doors. Local *gnawa* musicians make their living by other means or may play for tourists in the lobbies of hotels and restaurants, but it's nowhere near the real deal. Your best bet is to head to a festival.

Escapes & Excursions

Essaouira

Southern Morocco's most interesting coastal town – and the one most easily reached from Marrakech – offers both a contrast and an escape. Here, the pink and green of Marrakech is replaced by blue and white, and the town is cooled by refreshing Atlantic breezes. It's around three hours away by bus, quicker by car or taxi, and, while just about doable as a day trip, travellers tend to linger here enjoying its chilled-out charms.

Sandy-coloured ramparts shelter a Medina built around French piazzas, carved archways and whitewashed lanes and alleys. The fishing port provides a constant fresh catch for local restaurants, while the wide, sandy beaches to the south – combined with high winds – have put Essaouira on the international windsurfing map. Essaouira can also claim to be one of the cleanest Moroccan towns, with no vehicles in the Medina and regular street sweeping.

Ramparts.

Don't Miss

1 Hammam Pabst Scrub down at one of Morocco's oldest hammams (p144).

2 Val d'Argan Local wines, lovely surroundings (p139).

3 Tangaro For an afternoon poolside (p144).

4 Ramparts Enjoy a stroll as the setting sun dips over the Atlantic (p129).

5 Caravane Café Dinner with music, magicians and fire jugglers (p136).

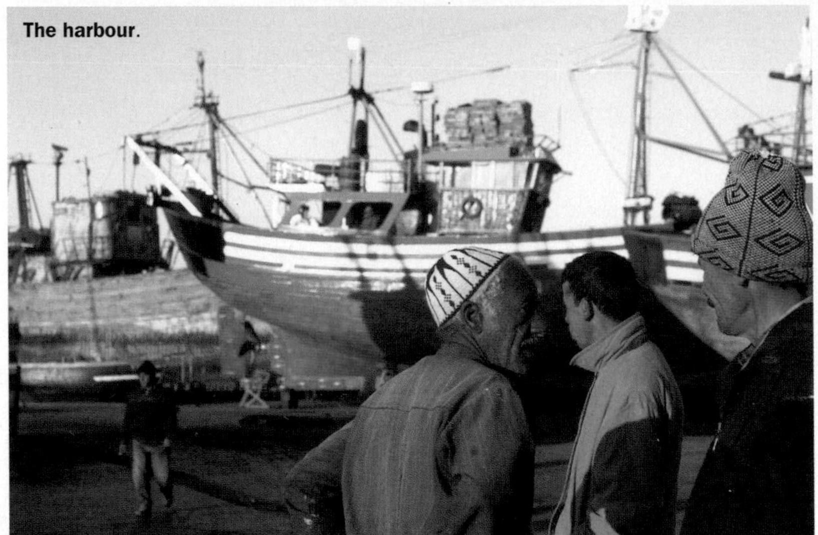
The harbour.

HISTORY AND CULTURE

In 1878 British consul Charles Payton observed of the locals that 'they are a tough and hardy race these Moorish fishermen, bronzed and leathery of skin, sinewy of limb and yet not too fond of hard work… They would rather smoke the pernicious hasheesh in a foul and frowsy den of the back slums of the Moorish quarter than live out on the rippling sea.'

The westerners arriving in ever-increasing numbers today may still note the locals' talent to be comfortable doing nothing, even when they're not smoking the pernicious weed, though this relaxed attitude is being challenged by the pace of change. The town's designation as a UNESCO World Heritage Site has put it on the map for culture seekers, and more than ten per cent of the Medina's 16,000 houses – some 1,700 properties – are now owned by Europeans. The accompanying upswing in property prices is pushing the poorest Souiris out to the city limits. But locals know that the town is now largely dependent on tourism and this reinforces their instinctive tolerance – Essaouira is said to have the most integrated Moroccan-foreigner population in the country.

Travellers have been coming to Essaouira since the seventh century BC, when the Phoenicians established their furthest outpost in Africa on one of its islands. During the first century BC, King Juba II extracted purple dye from Essaouira's murex (a form of tropical sea snail) shells for the Romans. The dyeworks were on what are still known as the Iles Purpuraires. In the 15th century, the Portuguese occupied Mogador, as it was then called, and built fortifications around the harbour. The town was one of their major bases until they abandoned it in 1541. Sir Francis Drake ate his Christmas lunch on the Ile de Mogador in 1577.

In 1765 local ruler Sultan Sidi Mohammed Ben Abdellah captured a French vessel and hired one of its passengers – French architect Théodore Cornut – to redesign the place. The sultan wanted a fortified southern base to counter trouble from the port of Agadir to the south, threatening revolt at the time; but he also wanted an open city for foreign traders. A grid street layout was drawn up and the sultan shipped in black slaves from the Sudanese empire to begin building what was to become the most important port on the North African coast. The *gnawa* brotherhood of mystic musicians first set foot on Moroccan soil as part of this shackled workforce. With the work completed, Mogador became Essaouira. (It was to revert to Mogador again when the French arrived in 1912, and then become Essaouira again at independence in 1956.)

A sizeable Jewish community was welcomed, numbering around 9,000 at its peak, and British and European merchants were drawn by protected trade status and a harbour free from customs duties. For a long time, Essaouira was the only Moroccan port on the Atlantic coast that was open to European trade, and it prospered greatly until the French arrived in 1912. It is said that Morocco's first French Résident-Général, Marshall Lyautey, visited Essaouira on a Saturday when the Jewish community was at prayer, took one look at the deserted streets, and decided to make Casablanca the principal port. Trade began slipping away. The town slid into further decline with the departure of all but a handful of the Jewish community following independence in 1956.

CLAIMS TO FAME

Orson Welles stayed here on and off in 1949-50, shooting much of his wonderful *Othello*. There are many scenes on the ramparts, and the murder of Rodrigo was staged in Hammam Pabst (*see p144*). Locals pitched in as extras, earning two dirhams a day, plus bread and a tin of sardines. In 1992, after a special screening of the restored version attended by King Mohammed VI (then Crown Prince), a small park outside the Medina's south-west corner was officially named place Orson Welles. The Prince also unveiled a memorial sculpture by local craftsman Samu Mustapha that is curiously unrecognisable as either Welles or Othello. More recently, Essaouira was used as a location for both Ridley Scott's *Kingdom of Heaven* and Oliver Stone's *Alexander*.

In the late 1960s, Essaouira and the neighbouring village of Diabat were inked on the hippie map. Celebrity visitors included Tennessee Williams, Margaret Trudeau and Cat Stevens, who, now Yusuf Islam, still returns each summer. Most celebrated of the lot, though, was Jimi Hendrix, whose brief visit in 1969 has generated a wealth of myth (*see p133* **Castles Made of Sand**). Otherwise, the influence of the hippies lingers on in the school of naïve painters and in the annual music festival in June, which sees 200,000 revellers descend upon the town (*see p141* **Gnawa Grooves**).

As in Marrakech, Essaouira has next to nothing in the way of formal sights such as monuments and museums. The **Medina** itself is one big sight, with highlights including the **ramparts**, the **souks** and the **Mellah**. You can march from one end to the other in ten minutes; a more leisurely exploration, however, can take days and the influx of cool little places to eat and drink makes it ever more attractive as a place for R&R. The port is a separate entity, worthy of at least a stroll. Connecting the two is the **place Moulay Hassan**, the town's social nexus, which you'll pass through at least a dozen times a day.

Arriving by car from Marrakech, you'll most likely enter the Medina through the arch of **Bab Sbaâ**, one of five gates. (By bus, you'll enter through **Bab Marrakech**.) Beyond Bab Sbaâ, avenue du Caire has the town's fairly ineffective tourist information office on the left, and the police further down on the opposite side. The few cross streets around here also contain several hotels, galleries and restaurants and a rowdy Moroccan bar, but it's a strangely detached corner of town, separate from both the Kasbah area and the rest of the Medina.

The narrow, shady avenue du Caire intersects the broad, open avenue Oqba Ibn Nafia, the spine of the Medina. Left, this leads out to the port. Right, it dips under an arch, changes its name to avenue de l'Istiqlal, and becomes Essaouira's main commercial thoroughfare. Opposite avenue du Caire, the arch in the wall leads into the Kasbah district and, bearing left, to place Moulay Hassan.

Near the Bab Marrakech you'll find the **Artisan Centre** (1 rue Ibn Batouta) – being renovated in mid 2014, but scheduled to be open by the time you read this, providing a solid overview of what crafts are available locally and what you should be paying for them. And near Bab Sbaâ, **Dar Souiri** (avenue du Caire, www.association-essaouiramogador.org, open 9am-12.30pm, 3-7pm) is a cultural centre with permanent exhibition of Gnawa Festival posters plus 1st floor changing exhibits of exceptionally high-quality local photographers.

PLACE MOULAY HASSAN AND THE PORT

Connecting the Medina to the port, **place Moulay Hassan** is Essaouira's social centre. You can sit at any of the cafés and watch the theatre of the town unfolding. Early in the morning, fishermen pass by on their way to work, and the first wave of itinerant musicians and shoe-shine boys appears. By 10am or 11am the café tables have begun their secondary function – as alfresco offices from which most Souiris conduct business at some time or another. Purveyors of sunglasses, watches and carpets sweep from table to table, only occasionally selling something. By now tourists have started to appear, buying the previous day's international newspapers from **Jack's Kiosk** (*see p140*).

Apart from the cafés at street level, place Moulay Hassan is also overlooked by the terrace of **Taros** (*see p138*), the city's premier spot for a sundowner overlooking the ocean. The port comes to life in the late afternoon when the fishing fleet rolls back into the harbour and the catch is auctioned between 3pm and 5pm at the market hall just outside the port gates. Fresh fish are grilled and served up at stalls (*see p135*) on the port side of place Moulay Hassan and makes for fun picnicking.

If you want to go boating yourself, **Essaouira Sailing Tour** (0661 62 63 13) is located on the quayside near **Chez Sam** (*see p137*) and organises trips of 1.5-3 hrs (300dh per person; minimum two people).

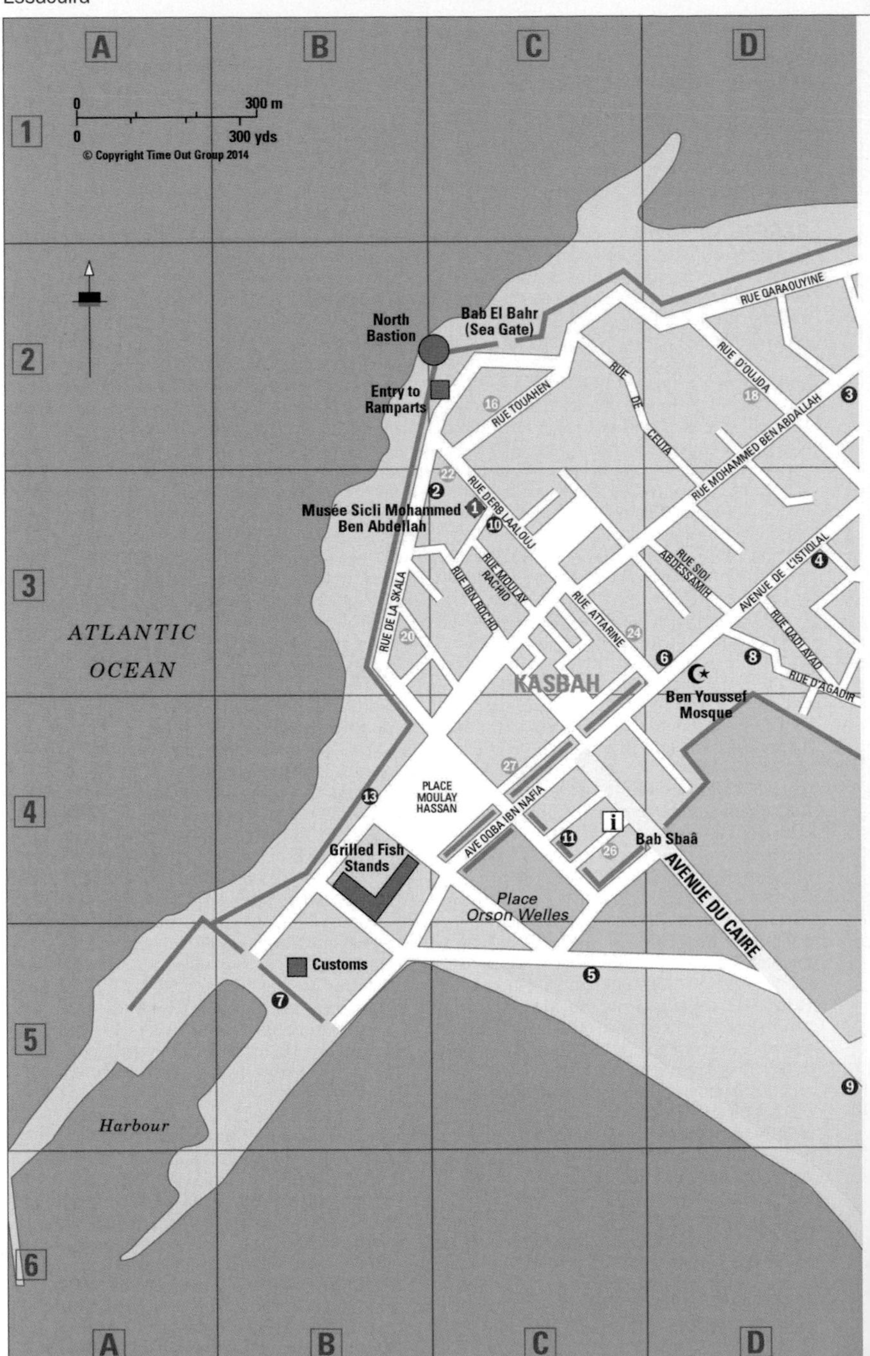
A
B
C
D
1
2
3
4
5
6
0
300 m
0
300 yds
© Copyright Time Out Group 2014
ATLANTIC
OCEAN
Harbour
North
Bastion
Bab El Bahr
(Sea Gate)
Entry to
Ramparts
RUE QARAOUYINE
RUE D'OUJDA
RUE DE CEUTA
RUE TOUAHEN
RUE MOHAMMED BEN ABDALLAH
Musée Sicli Mohammed
Ben Abdellah
RUE DERB LAALOUJ
RUE MOULAY RACHID
RUE IBN ROCHD
RUE DE LA SKALA
RUE SIDI ABDESSAMIH
AVENUE DE L'ISTIQLAL
RUE ATTARINE
RUE QADI AYAD
RUE D'AGADIR
KASBAH
Ben Youssef
Mosque
PLACE
MOULAY
HASSAN
AVE OQBA IBN NAFIA
Bab Sbaâ
AVENUE DU CAIRE
Grilled Fish
Stands
Place
Orson Welles
Customs

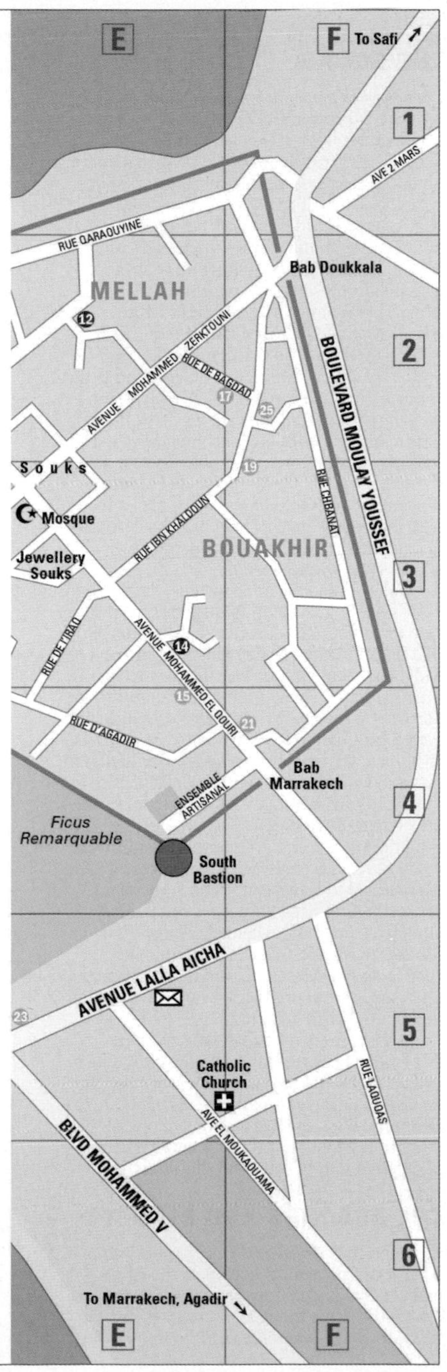

COAST, MOUNTAINS & DESERT

SKALA DE LA VILLE

The narrow rue de la Skala leads from place Moulay Hassan along the inside of the sea wall. It's also possible to get here by ducking through the spooky tunnel-like alley that leads off place Moulay Hassan by the Café de France.

Rue de la Skala leads to the **Skala de la Ville**, where you can walk on top of the ramparts. There is one ramp up to the top near the junction with rue Ibn Rochd at the southern end, and another near the junction with rue Derb Laâlouj at the northern end. Locals gather here to watch the sunset and lovers cuddle in the crenellations, where ancient cannon offer places to perch. At the far end is the tower of the North Bastion, the top of which offers good views across the Mellah and Kasbah.

Painters lay out their work for sale on and around the ramparts. Artisans sculpting thuja – a local coniferous hardwood with a smell like peppery cedar – have their workshops in the arches below and here you can find all manner of carvings and marquetry.

From near the North Bastion, rue Derb Laâlouj leads back into the heart of the Medina, past a variety of handicraft and antique shops, a handful of restaurants, and Essaouira's lone museum, the **Musée Sidi Mohammed Ben Abdellah**.

At one time Essaouira was known as the Sanhedrin (Jewish cultural centre) of North Africa. As recently as the 1950s the city still claimed 32 official **synagogues**. One that still functions remains at 2 Derb Ziry Ben Atiyah, which is the last lane on the right off rue Derb Laâlouj before it intersects with avenue Sidi Mohammed Ben Abdellah. The synagogue was founded by British merchants from Manchester; at the height of Essaouira's importance this section of the Kasbah was the location of various consulates and administrative buildings.

Musée Sidi Mohammed Ben Abdellah

7 Derb Laâlouj (0524 47 23 00). **Open** 8.30am-6pm Mon, Wed-Sun. **Admission** 10dh. **Map** p130 C3 ❶

This renovated 19th-century mansion was used as the town hall during the Protectorate and hosts a fairly boring collection of weapons, woodwork and carpetry. There are also *gnawa* costumes and musical instruments and a few pictures of old Essaouira.

THE MELLAH

British merchants outnumbered other nationalities during the 19th century to the extent that 80 per cent of the town's trade was with Britain and sterling was the favoured currency. The sultan brought in Jews from all over the kingdom to deal with trade with

Europe; by 1900 they outnumbered the locals. All but the wealthiest lived in the Mellah district between the North Bastion and Bab Doukkala, an area that has been neglected since most of the Jews emigrated to Israel in the 1950s and '60s.

The Mellah can be found by following the alleys just inside the ramparts beyond the Skala de la Ville – turn down rue Touahen off rue Derb Laâlouj – or by following avenue Sidi Mohammed Ben Abdellah. When the shops and businesses start to peter out, the Mellah begins. These days its alleys are grubby and dilapidated; some houses look ready to fall down. It was always a gloomy quarter; until the end of the 19th century it was even locked up at night and it's still not a place to wander alone. The family of Leslie Hore-Belisha, British Minister of War in 1939 and inventor of the belisha beacon, lived at 56 rue de Mellah. These days there are at most perhaps two dozen Jews left in Essaouira.

At the northern end of the Mellah is Bab Doukkala. Just outside of the gate is the **Consul's cemetery**, another reminder of the town's cosmopolitan past. It's crammed with the graves of British officials from the days when Mogador had as many links with Manchester as with Rabat. Over the road, tombstones are packed tightly together in the old **Jewish cemetery**, where graves are reputed to be five layers deep.

THE SOUKS

Leading south-west from Bab Doukkala, **avenue Mohammed Zerktouni** is a busy commercial street of butchers and vegetable stalls. The narrow lanes of the Chabanat district on the eastern side are full of tiny workshops.

In the centre of the Medina, the souks are in cloistered arcades around the intersection of avenue Mohammed Zerktouni and avenue Mohammed El-Qouri, another busy street leading at right-angles towards **Bab Marrakech** and the hotels **Casa Lila** (*see p142)* and **L'Heure Bleue** (*see p143*).

First on the left as you come under the arch from avenue Mohammed Zerktouni is the cobbled grain market. Slaves were auctioned here until the early 20th century. Now it's brimming over with hip, sunshine-filled café terraces where visitors and Souiris bask in the sun. The next cloistered square along, the Joutiya, comes to life between 4pm and 5pm for a daily auction hawking the detritus of daily life: old alarm clocks, fishing reels, slippers and transistor radios.

On the other side of the avenue, the fish and spice souk is a fascinating insight into long-held and lingering Moroccan beliefs. It is here that Souiri women come to buy chameleons, hedgehogs and various weird and wonderful plants for use in sorcery and magic, and where you can buy your own fish and vegetables and have **Chez Karim** (*see p135*) across the street cook them for you (simply leave your haul with him and tell him what time you'll be back to eat).

Beyond this point, avenue Zerktouni turns into avenue de l'Istiqlal. The jewellery souk is on the left, curling around the outside of the mosque. It's a surprisingly quiet corner where it's possible to browse in peace. Avenue de l'Istiqlal offers Essaouira's most upmarket stretch of shopping, where you'll also find **Mogador Music** (*see p140*). Turn down rue Malek Ben Morhal to find the traditional pharmacy, Azurette, and left into rue d'Agadir to find the **Elizir** restaurant (*see p137*).

After the arched Kasbah gate, avenue de l'Istiqlal changes names again, becoming avenue Oqba Ibn Nafia. We are now back in the neighbourhood around Bab Sbaâ. **Galerie Damgaard** (*see p139*), a commercial gallery that has nurtured Essaouira's naïve school of painters, can be found on this stretch.

THE BEACHES AND DIABET

Essaouira has wonderful beaches, but the north-westerly winds, known as the Alizés, make it cold and choppy for bathing. It's ideal for windsurfing, though (*see p136* **Wind City Afrika**). The area to the north of town is fast

CASTLES MADE OF SAND

Jimi Hendrix was here.

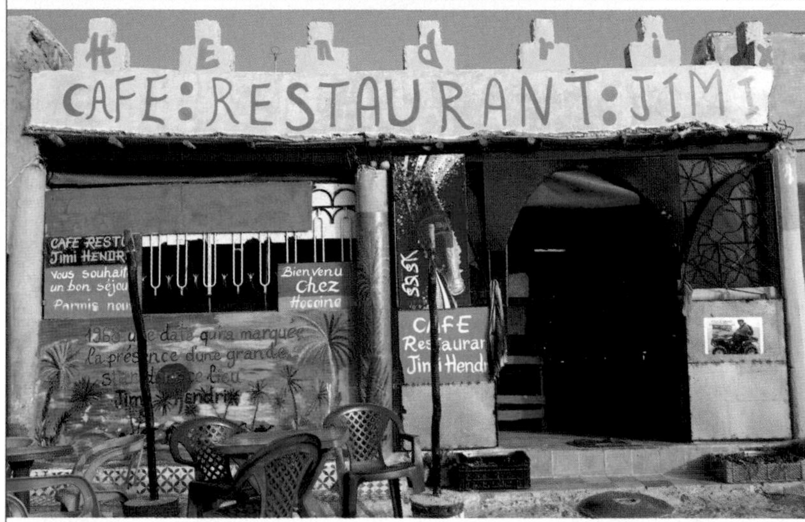

'Welcome to the village of Jimi Hendrix!' So runs the patter of shoeshine boys and dope dealers. 'Hendrix stayed here!' is the proud claim of at least two hotels. In nearby Diabat, where Jimi supposedly spent time with the hippie community, there is a Café Hendrix and a Hotel Hendrix, both overlooking the decidedly unrocking new golf resort.

Orson Welles may have a square named after him, but Hendrix is Essaouira's claim to street cred. The stories pour forth. Jimi jammed with the gnawa! He tried to buy one of the islands! He met with Timothy Leary! The most enduring tale is that he was inspired to write 'Castles Made of Sand' (which melt into the sea, eventually) by the ruins of the Borj El-Berod. It seems almost plausible. The Borj El-Berod is a small, ruined fort at the ocean's edge, quite clearly melting into the sea. But the story has one small snag. 'Castles Made of Sand' appeared on the *Axis: Bold as Love* album, released on 1 December 1967. And Jimi didn't visit Morocco until July 1969.

Just ten days long, it was the only vacation Hendrix ever took. Stressed out after the break-up of the Jimi Hendrix Experience, moving from London to New York, getting busted by the Mounties in Toronto, and rehearsing a new band, Jimi accepted his friend Deering Howe's suggestion that they go to Morocco, and ran off in defiance of his management. The pair flew to Casablanca in late July, where they met up with two Moroccans they knew from New York, Stella Douglas and Colette Mimram. They stayed at the Casablanca Meridien, the Mamounia in Marrakech and the Hotel des Iles in Essaouira, travelling by limo and doing tourist things – eating out, smoking kif, shopping for clothes. Far from jamming with local musicians, Hendrix enjoyed his anonymity and kept a low profile. He had a spooky fortune-teller experience, conducted a romance with Colette Mimram, and spent an evening in Essaouira with a couple of actors from the Living Theater. But he didn't meet Timothy Leary, bought no islands, probably didn't visit Diabat, certainly didn't stay at the Riad Al Madina, and likely never even saw the Borj El-Berod.

It's a lot of myth from a short visit, but that's what you get from a good rock legend. By 6 August Hendrix was on his way back to New York, stopping off in Paris to shag Brigitte Bardot. Twelve days later, he was playing Woodstock.

becoming known as the Guéliz of Essaouira because of its funky beach scene with various cafés and bars like **Beach and Friends** (0524 47 45 58, 11am-11pm daily) and **Tamouziga** (0524 47 45 78), a popular expat haunt for a Sunday lunch of sardine tagine or a great pizza. At this end, the **Plage de Safi** can be dangerous when it's blowy, but it's nice when it's warm and usually less crowded than the main beach.

The main beach stretches for miles to the south, backed by dunes once the town peters out. Closer to the Medina it serves as a venue for football. There's always a game going on and at weekends there are several played simultaneously, their kick-offs timed by the tides. You'll also find guys with camels, or they will find you, insistently offering rides. It can be fun to trek around the bay to the ruined old fort of **Borj El Berod**, but wait until you find a camel guy you feel comfortable with, and agree a firm price before setting off.

The village of **Diabat** is a few miles further south and a little inland, on a ridge overlooking the scrubby dunes. In the late 1960s it hosted a hippie community, and legends of a visit made by Jimi Hendrix abound (*see p133* **Castles Made of Sand**). Any lingering flavour of those times is, however, rapidly being obliterated by the enormous golf resort between the village and the ocean. Diabat's main street now overlooks one of the fairways, and there is further large-scale development occurring along the coast. A whole new town, **Essaouria Al Jadida** (meaning 'New Essaouria'), is going up near the airport; and the small surfer haven of **Sidi Kaouki** (*see p136* **Wind City Afrika**), 25 kilometres (15.5 miles) south of Essaouira, has expanded too.

RESTAURANTS, CAFES & BARS

Traditionally the best budget lunch in town was fresh fish from a stall, charcoal-grilled and eaten outside on the quayside, but these days you'll rarely see locals eating there. They will tell you to go to the fish souk, nab a catch of your own and take it to a local café, such as **Chez Karim** (open 10am-11pm daily) and have them cook it for you. It's extremely popular with large Moroccan families and arguably the most authentic dining experience in Essaouira.

If you can't resist the allure of the fish stalls, there is now a list of fixed prices posted on a signboard (it's at the end furthest away from the water and includes a number for complaints, 0524 784 033), and it's all much of a muchness. Prices range from 10dh for a plate of sardines to 400dh per kilo of lobster, with squid, sole, shrimp, bass, red mullet, urchin and crab

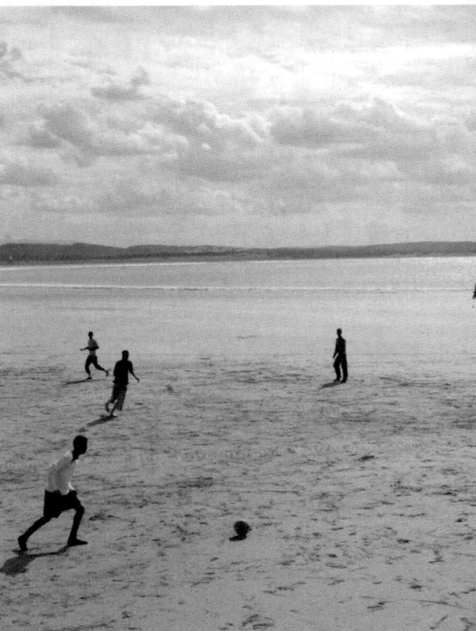

costing anything in between and includes a slice of lemon and half a baguette. A 60dh set meal includes a selection, plus salad, but no alcohol is served. Stalls are open from 11am until 4pm every day.

On place Moulay Hassan, the **Café de France** (open 9am-late daily) has an interestingly dated interior and you can get a decent ice-cream at **Gelateria Dolce Freddo** (open 11am-10pm daily). Groovier these days than the place Moulay Hassan is the walled, cobbled Grain Market square, a sun-trap with good protection from unrelenting winds, filled with hip little cafes like **Safran** (0600 60 50 31, open 11am-late daily), a sunny spot for fresh, simply grilled fish, salads, tagines and pastillas.

For an out-of-town lunch in an open-sided café in gardens, visit **Tangaro** at Diabet (*see p144*).

Les Alizés Mogador

26 rue Skala (0524 47 68 19). **Open** *Lunch* noon-3pm daily. *Dinner* 1st service 7pm, 2nd service 9pm, daily. **Set meal** 95dh. **No credit cards. Map** p130 C3 ❷ **Moroccan**

Opposite the wood workshops under the ramparts, and blessedly sheltered from the winds that lend the restaurant its name, Les Alizés has a stone-arched interior, a friendly, candlelit atmosphere, and hearty portions of good, reasonably priced Moroccan home-cooking from a set menu. This place has a reputation as one of the best budget restaurants in town. You can't reserve, so there may be a wait for a table.

WIND CITY AFRIKA

Windsurfing central.

With frequent high winds between March and September, Essaouira is Morocco's capital of windsurfing and has begun to market itself as such under the rubric 'Wind City Afrika'. Known as the Alizés, the north-westerly winds really are strong; wetsuits and sturdy sails are necessary. In winter, surfers can also be found on the town's broad and sandy beaches.

A 20-minute walk along the seafront (or short cab ride from Bab Smaâ), **Ocean Vagabond** (boulevard Mohammed V, www.oceanvagabond.com, open 8am-6pm daily, no credit cards) is the best place to hire equipment and receive instruction from a friendly French and Moroccan team. They offer surfing, windsurfing and kite-surfing; windsurfing tuition starts at €120 for a six-hour starter course, including equipment. It's also a good beach café for breakfasts, salads and pizzas with the sun on your face and your toes in the sand.

There is more hardcore windsurfing at **Sidi Kaouki**, 25 kilometres (15.5 miles) to the south of Essaouira, where a broad beach stretches for miles. The village here is also popular with non-surfers in search of peace and quiet. There are several reasonable places to eat such as **La Mouette et Les Dromadaires** (0678 44 92 12, open 11am-5pm Wed-Sun), or **Beach and Friends** (Corniche Sud Plage d'Essaouira, 0524 47 45 58, www.beachandfriends.com, open 11am-11pm daily), where groovy surfer types gather to chat over beachy chill-out tunes, fuel up on burgers and generally look cool, and small hotels, including the **Auberge de la Plage** (0524 47 66 00, www.kaouki.com), which also has horses and can arrange trekking. The No.5 bus runs regularly to Sidi Kaouki from outside Bab Doukkala. It's also possible to get there via *grand taxi*.

La Mouette et Les Dromadaires.

COAST, MOUNTAINS & DESERT

La Cantina

66 Rue Boutouil (0524 47 45 15). **Open** 10am-5pm Mon-Sat. Closed most of Jan. **Mains** from 35dh. **Map** p130 D2 ❸ **International/Mexican**

Situated on shady Place Taraa, the English-owned La Cantina has a vaguely Mexican edge and is a good bet for true vegetarians, with a solid range of meat-and-fish-free dishes including a properly spicy vegetarian chilli and veggie burgers. Breakfasts are excellent too, as are the home-made cakes and scones for an afternoon pick-me-up.

Caravane Café

2 bis, rue du Qadi Ayyad (0524 78 31 11). **Open** 12.30-2.30pm, 6.30-10.30pm Tue-Sun. **Set meal** 95dh. **No credit cards**. **Map** p130 D3 ❹ **Moroccan/French**

The former home of artist Didier Spindler and partner Jean-François – a traditional house with a central courtyard – was converted into a restaurant a couple of years ago. It now comprises several eclectically decorated dining rooms packed around a lushly planted patio and roof terrace, with Spindler's trademark brightly coloured oils on the walls, romantic lanterns on every table, and vases festooned with flowers. The food on a regularly changing menu is always excellent and might include king prawns in a saffron sauce, tender beef brochette dressed with argan oil, blood sausage on baked apples, and a brilliant lemon meringue pie. But there's more: a dangerously strong house punch of rum, pineapple and cinnamon; nightly live music from local bands; a convincing magician, and fire jugglers.

Chalet de la Plage

1 boulevard Mohammed V (0524 47 59 72, www.lechaletdelaplage). **Open** 6.30-10pm Mon; noon-2.30pm, 6.30-10pm Tue-Sat; noon-2.30pm Sun. **Main courses** 70dh-180dh. **Map** p130 C5 ❺ **French/seafood**

Built in 1893 entirely out of wood, this iconic beach-side institution serves a solid, unfussy menu. The fish is good, there's beer and a small wine list, and the overall vibe is friendly and efficient. Best of all, you can sit outside on the terrace and admire that tremendous panorama of the bay all the way around to the ruins of the Borj El-Berod on the headland.

Chez Jalila

Avenue Istiqlal (0606 84 53 01). **Open** 9am-late daily. **Meals from** 25dh. **No credit cards. Map** p130 D3 ❻ **Café**

Situated on the main drag, this cheery little place is a delight. Filled with turquoise chairs topped with tangerine-coloured cushions, it provides a veritable splash of sunshine with your breakfast omelette and morning coffee. The rooftop is a perfect sun trap if you want to escape the souks with a book, and the home-made ice-cream served in summer is the best in town.

Chez Sam

Port de Peche (0524 47 65 13/0661 15 74 85, email chez_sam@live.fr). **Open** noon-3pm, 7-10.30pm daily. **Set menus** 85dh-250dh. **Main courses** from 80dh. **Map** p130 B5 ❼ **Seafood**

Abutting the harbour walls, this waterside wooden shack is designed like the hull of a ship, with a wood-panelled interior, portholes that allow you to see the fishing boats bringing in the catch, and a small conservatory dining room that seems to float out over the water. The fish and seafood is decent enough, particularly the sea bass or bream baked in salt so it stays succulent and juicy, but the main reason to come here is the atmosphere – a throwback to the Essaouira of yore.

Elizir

1 rue de Agadir (0524 47 21 03). **Main courses** 90dh-120dh. **Open** from 6pm daily. **No credit cards. Map** p130 D3 ❽ **Moroccan/ Mediterranean**

One of the first of the hip newcomers, Elizir opened back in 2006 with a Moroccan-Mediterranean menu and an atmosphere of idiosyncratic cool. Slink up the narrow staircase from the street and you'll find yourself in a pair of dining rooms that combine traditional Moroccan tiles with vintage finds from local flea markets. Striking portraits adorn the walls, and the food is straight out of the early 1990s, piled up in moulds with glazes streaked like paint across the plate, but it can be very good. The fish of the day is always excellent, as is the richly flavoured balsamic beefsteak. In winter, ask for a table in the room with the open fire; in warmer months, go for the sheltered roof terrace. The louche, jazzy playlist sounds good wherever you're sitting.

Fanatic

Boulevard Mohammed V (0524 47 50 08, email fanatic-essaouira@menara.ma). **Open** 9am-9pm daily. **Mains** 75dh-115dh. **Map** p130 D5 ❾ **Moroccan/seafood**

Located midway along the beach between Essaouira port and Diabat, Fanatic stands out as a slightly smarter beach bar than the rest with esparto grass sunbeds and shades laid out neatly in the sand, a comfortably shaded terrace dining area and a largely French clientele (always a good sign food-wise). Looking straight across the water to the Purple Isles, it's a blissful spot for a long lunch, especially if you have kids in tow (there's a play park next to the sunbathing areas). Try the mixed fish fry (easily enough for two) with home-made tartare sauce and a bowl of hot, crunchy chips.

One-Up

1 Derb Laalouj (0610 09 82 03). **Open** 11am-late daily. **Main courses** 40dh-200dh. **Map** p130 C3 ❿ **Moroccan/Mediterranean**

Housed in what were once offices of the British Consulate, this clubby first-floor restaurant and bar feels light and airy, with a vintage, lived-in look. Dining furniture from the 1940s and '50s, plus plaid armchairs and turquoise leather sofas, mix well with Moroccan crafts against oyster-grey zelije-tiled walls and Vivienne Westwood wallpaper in dazzling red flame. The mix of styles is spread across several rooms, including a lounge with a glittering fireplace. Casual dining – a fusion of Mediterranean and Moroccan tapas, fish and chips in a paper cone and burgers – is paired with killer cocktails. There's a chill-out lounge on the roof, too.

La Table Madada

7 rue Youssef El Fassi (0524 47 11 06, www.latablemadada.com). **Open** 12.30-2.30pm, 7.30pm-late daily. **Main courses** from 150dh. **Map** p130 C4 ⓫ **Seafood**

Elizir.

This sleek and stylish restaurant sprawled beneath sturdy stone arches is now widely regarded as the best in town. Giant lampshades direct light over linen-clothed tables, cream-coloured banquettes and comfortable armchairs, a large, corner fireplace keeps chilly nights at bay and the buzz created by popping champagne corks (110dh a glass), clinking platters of Dahkla oysters and general bonhomie could have you believe you've landed somewhere far more cosmopolitan than little old Essaouira. Local seafood is put to good use here in the form of tiger prawn risotto, grilled John Dory, and sea bream ceviche. The cooking classes at L'Atelier de Madada next door are a great way to fill an afternoon.

Tara Café

5 rue Boutouil, Place Taraa (0524 78 30 64). **Open** 8am-7pm daily. **No credit cards.** **Map** p131 E2 ⓬ **International**

Wedged into the arches of a sturdy old townhouse, with tables and chairs spilling out into the square, this is a reassuringly homely little place and a top spot for satisfying breakfasts and lunches. Soothing jazz and piano music emanate from the dining room while the owner, Abdou, floats about in a cream djellaba looking after his customers personally. The food is superb, too, with a varied menu ranging from boat-fresh fish and seafood to Lebanese mezze and a comforting shepherd's pie.

Taros

Place Moulay Hassan (0524 47 64 07, www.taroscafe.com). **Open** 11am-4pm, 6pm-midnight Mon-Sat. **Main courses** 90dh-160dh. **Map** p130 B4 ⓭ **Bar/Mediterranean/ Moroccan**

Perched above the town's main square on a corner overlooking the sea, Taros is a multipurpose venue with a prime location. It has a first-floor salon and library, where you can drink tea and read quietly in the afternoons or have a beer and listen to live music in the evenings (Thur-Sat). Then there's a cocktail bar on the fine roof terrace with tables and bar stools looking out to sea. And, of course, food, with a seafood focus and European and Moroccan dishes.

Vague Bleu

2 rue Sidi Ali Ben Abdellah (0611 28 37 91). **Open** noon-3pm, 6.30-9pm Mon-Thur, Sat, Sun. **Main courses** 40dh-75dh. **No credit cards.** **Map** p131 E3 ⓮ **Italian**

Possibly the smallest restaurant in the world, Vague Bleu is built into a triangular recess with just five or six tiny tables. It was formerly owned by an Italian chap who employed local husband-and-wife team Brahim and Fadma to help him, teaching them all he knew before heading back to the motherland. They've gone from strength to strength, serving what is probably the best Italian food in the country. Daily specials such as prawn and courgette lasagna are chalked up on a blackboard, but it gets rammed so get here early or be prepared to wait.

SHOPS & SERVICES

As with its bars and restaurants, Essaouira's shops are becoming more diverse and sophisticated. The town has all the variety of Marrakech packed into an infinitely more manageable space, with local specialities such as argan oil, found only in Morocco, and the best wine in the country.

Taros.

To find these treasures in situ, hop in a taxi to **Lalla Abouch Organic Farm and B&B** (Tidzi, 0661 32 27 91, www.darattajmil.com), which works with local families to make argan oil for both cosmetic and edible purposes, and has simple, charming accommodation too. Then head to **Le Val d'Argan Winery** (Ounagha, Route de Casablanca, 0660 24 18 93, www.valdargan.com) owned by Charles Melia, a respected winemaker in the Châteauneuf du Pape region of France, who's transferred his skills here. Tastings with lunch cost 200dh and showcase a good cross-section of wines from the bright, refreshing La Gazelle de Mogador white to the flagship Le Val d'Argan Rouge. Should the mood take you, you can also snag a room at the vineyard in simple but comfortable stone cottages (www.riaddesvignes.com) arranged around a swimming pool.

Afalkay Art

9 place Moulay Hassan (0524 47 60 89).
Open 9am-8pm daily. **Gallery**
Searching the wood workshops under the ramparts might turn up the odd different item, but pretty much anything they can make out of fragrant thuja wood – from tiny inlaid boxes to great big treasure chests, toy camels to bathroom cabinets – can be found somewhere in this big barn of a place opposite the cafés of place Moulay Hassan. Staff speak English and are used to shipping larger items.

Azurrette

12 rue Malek Ben Morhal (0524 47 41 53).
Open 9.30am-8pm daily. **No credit cards. Herbalist**
At some remove from the hassle and hustle of the spice souk, this traditional Moroccan pharmacy has the largest herb and spice selection in the Medina and also offers perfumes, pigments, remedies, incense and essential oils. The big, cool space is lined with shelves of common condiments, exotic ingredients, mysterious herbs and colourful powders, all in glass jars or baskets. English is spoken by amiable young owner Ahmed, who's happy to explain what's what.

Bokado

Rue Laalouje (no number). **Open** 8am-8pm daily. **No credit cards. Fabrics**
Abdullilah started out as a herbalist, but while waiting for customers he found himself with idle hands and, somewhat unusually for a Moroccan man, got into sewing. The reason, he says, is that the Sufis became masters of patchwork because they travelled from place to place in one djellaba; and the more patched it got the richer the experience they had to share. He recycles vintage fabrics into a unique collection of hand-stitched patchwork quilts, cushions and bags costing up to 2,400dh for a double bedspread.

Chez Boujmaa

1 avenue Allal Ben Abdellah (0524 47 56 58).
Open 8am-midnight daily. **No credit cards. Food & drink**
The place to stock up on deliciously flaky Moroccan pastries as well as English teas and biscuits. There's also a range of Italian pasta and parma ham, and French cheeses, if you're hankering for a taste of Europe. Staff will make up a sandwich for you at the basic deli counter if you just want something easy to take to the beach.

Elahri Mohamed Tisserand

181 souk El-Gouzel (0655 09 74 14). **Open** 9am-8pm daily. **No credit cards. Fabrics**
This tiny family-run weaver's shop still has a working loom at the back, where weavers make bespoke textiles as well as their own designs. The influence of European taste is evident in the beautiful soft cotton throws in muted tones of ash green, dusky pink and duck-egg blue, and heavier sheep's wool and camel blankets edged with pompoms, as well as the flashier silk fabrics often favoured by Moroccans.

Espace Othello

9 rue Mohammed Layachi (0524 47 50 95).
Open 9am-8pm daily. **Gallery**
The extremely mixed bag of work by artists from Essaouira and beyond includes some small pieces as well as large paintings and sculptures. There's some interesting stuff here, but you have to poke around a bit to find it. The gallery's architecture is worth a look in its own right. It's behind the Hotel Sahara.

Galerie Damgaard

Avenue Oqba Ibn Nafiaa (0524 78 44 46, www.galeriedamgaard.com). **Open** 9am-1pm, 3-7pm daily. **Gallery**
Danish expat Frédéric Damgaard opened the town's only serious commercial gallery in 1988 and helped to develop the work of around 20 local artists – who came to be known as the Essaouira School. It's bright and colourful, almost hallucinogenic work, heavy with folk symbolism and pointillist techniques. Gnawa artist Mohammed Tabal is the star: his 'paintings of ideas' are inspired by the *gnawa* trance universe of colour-coded spirits. We also like the paint-splattered wooden furniture sculptures of Saïd Ouarzaz and the dreamlike canvases of Abdelkader Bentajar.

Histoire de Filles Concept Store

1 rue Mohamed Ben Messaoud (0524 78 51 93, email contact@histoiresdefilles.com).
Open 10am-8pm daily. **No credit cards. Gifts & souvenirs**
Arguably the smartest shop in the Medina, this top-notch collection of clothing, accessories and interior design items points to a modern Morocco. Quality contemporary kaftans, elegant locally made straw Panama hats, impeccably cut stuffed camels

COAST, MOUNTAINS & DESERT

and chic hessian lampshades, leather pouches and scented candles make for easy gift-buying.

Jack's Kiosk

1 place Moulay Hassan (0524 47 55 38). **Open** 9.30am-10.30pm daily. **No credit cards. Books**

In a key location on the square, Jack's is the place to find the previous day's international newspapers and other foreign periodicals, complemented by a small selection of new and second-hand English, French, German and Spanish books – mostly guides and bestsellers. Jack also rents sea-view apartments by the ramparts.

Mashi Mushki

89-91 rue Chbanat (www.facebook.com/mashimushki). **Open** 11.30am-6.30pm Tue-Sun. **No credit cards. Gifts & souvenirs**

An extension of Project 91 (*see right*), located across the way, Mashi Mushki – meaning 'no problem' – sells a carefully selected range of boutique Moroccan handicrafts and trinkets. Many of them are made by local women's co-operatives with the help of local designers who lend the crafts a more contemporary edge. Modern striped cushion covers and throws in browns, creams and charcoals with natty neon zips look just as good when you get them back home as they looked in the shop.

Mogador Music

52 avenue de l'Istiqlal (0670 72 57 79). **Open** 10am-10pm daily. **No credit cards. Music**

Gnawa, arabo-andalusian, *grika*, bellydance, *rai*, desert blues – Mogador Music is well stocked with all varieties of North African and West Saharan music on CD and cassette. If you can't find it here you probably won't find it anywhere: owners Youssef and Azza know their stuff and distribute to all the other music shops.

Other location 1 place Chefchaouen (0661 72 83 62).

Othman Shop

86 rue Laalouj (0666 09 05 28, email othmanshopp@hotmail.com). **Open** 10am-8pm daily. **No credit cards. Clothing/jewellery**

On first inspection this seems to be a small hole-in-the-wall shop specialising in antique Berber jewellery with the odd bit of nicely made Indian silver thrown in. On closer inspection, however, you'll also discover beaded masks from the Cameroon and owner Kamal Ottmani's lovingly hoarded collection of antique kaftans from 1960s and 1970s. His father, something of a local legend, sells knitted skull caps on the next corner.

Ouchen Mohamed

4 rue El Attarine (0524 47 68 61). **Open** 9am-9pm daily. **No credit cards. Leatherwork/gifts & souvenirs**

On a corner by the Riad Al Madina (*see p143*), Ouchen Mohamed is our favourite of the various leatherwork shops. It's good for pouffes, bags and belts, but there's also a big slipper selection and a few non-leather items, such as boxes, mirrors and old musical instruments.

Project 91

79 rue Chbanat (www.p-91.com). **Open** 11.30am-6.30pm Tue-Sun. **No credit cards. Clothing/gifts & souvenirs**

The clever concept at work here allows visitors to 'leave their wardrobe' and recycle items through this social enterprise shop, which also provides work experience for young people. The UK-based charity was created with the aim of helping young people in Essaouira find jobs and new skills through small grants for schooling, vocational training and supporting other organisations. As well as second-hand clothes, you'll find handwoven blankets and throws, flour sack totes and other low-cost gifts. The full 100% of the shop's profits is invested in the charity.

Riri d'Arabie

66 rue Boutouil (0524 47 45 15). **Open** 10am-7pm daily. **No credit cards. Bric-à-brac**

French exile Richard Brecquehais accumulates intriguing bric-à-brac, some of which he sells on as *objets trouvés*, some of which he arranges in his own eccentric way, matching pictures to frames or ornaments to shelving units. The result is a small curiosity shop of old postcards, framed mirrors, ancient signs, out-of-date toys and a scatter-brained sense of comedy. If you feel like sitting down, he also sells juices (10dh) and a few hot snacks (35dh).

Trésor

57 avenue de l'Istiqlal (0664 84 17 73). **Open** 9am-8.30pm daily. **Jewellery**

On the Medina's main avenue, jeweller Khalid Hasnaoui speaks good English and offers a more discerning selection than that found in the nearby jewellers' souk. It's a mixture of Berber, Arab, Tuareg and other pieces – some old, some new, and some new but using old designs. Look out for work in the local filigree style, traditionally made by Essaouiran Jews.

HOTELS

The bar is continuously being raised for Essaouira accommodation, but if you've got your heart set on a particular guesthouse it's essential to book, especially if you want to secure anything at all over Christmas or Easter and during the *gnawa* festival in late June (*see p141* **Gnawa Grooves**). There are rooms to suit all budgets and there's no such thing as a bad location – most places are a few minutes' walk from the central place **Moulay Hassan** and the fishing port.

GNAWA GROOVES

Celebrating one of Morocco's cultural treasures.

Every June, around 200,000 people flock to Essaouira for the **Festival of Gnawa and World Music** – a heady four days and nights of carnival-like atmosphere. Renowned musicians from across the globe and members of the *gnawa* brotherhood from all over Morocco converge for what has been described as 'one of the world's biggest jam sessions'. Each year the festival draws together Morocco's most revered *gnawa* masters, or *maâlems*, together with contemporary jazz, world and blues musicians. Old hands like Hamid El-Kasri and Mahmoud Guinea have traded licks with Pat Metheny, Wayne Shorter and Salif Keita – each of them exploring and uncovering a common musical language. One year, the acrobatic leaping of *gnawa* dancers was brilliantly mirrored by a balletic troupe of Georgian cossacks, and in another, the ecstatic qawali trance of Pakistan's Faiz Al-Faiz fused perfectly with the hypnotic gnawa groove.

The *gnawa* are descendants of slaves from sub-Saharan Africa, now constituted as a itinerant brotherhood of healers and mystics. Their music is rooted in trance and possession rituals, where spirits are represented by colours, and colours are represented by music. These spirits, or *mlouks*, are invoked during the all-night ritual ceremonies. It's compellingly rhythmic stuff played on bass drums, clattering iron castanets and a sort of bass lute called a *guimbri*. True *gnawa* music is reserved for spiritual ceremonies and the masters seen performing in Essaouira will be called upon in their home towns when required – they are not professional gigging musicians per se. The music was never intended for entertainment, but the festival in Essaouira provides an exception and all the greatest maâlems will come to perform.

Essaouira is bursting at the seams with Moroccans and foreign visitors for this annual party, keeping the *gnawa* flame burning bright. Young Moroccan artists such as Aziz Sahmaoui have given the tradition a contemporary twist, and DJ-producers like London-based U-cef fuse *gnawa* with hip hop and dub to take it in a new direction. Once looked down upon and regarded with suspicion, the *gnawa* are now seen as one of Morocco's cultural treasures.

Thankfully, in recent years, crowd safety issues have been addressed and the event is less concentrated inside the Medina. There is one main stage on place Moulay Hassan, another out on the beach, with some ticketed smaller events inside the Medina. In addition, festival-goers can buy stage-passes to allow access to a limited-capacity standing area in front of each stage. Otherwise the big outdoor concerts are still free.

For more on the music of the *gnawa* *see p123*. For the latest festival news and programme, visit www.festival-gnaoua.net.

COAST, MOUNTAINS & DESERT

Old Essaouira houses are set around open courtyards and tend to be smaller and less fussy than their Marrakchi equivalents, although the boutique hotel is on the rise here. Only a very few places own ocean views or roof terraces with cinematic vistas of sea and sky, which you'll soon come to realise is not such a bad thing once you've battled breakfast in high winds. Those same ocean breezes can make the town cold and damp too, and you will be glad of a log fire or central heating in winter – so double check that heating is provided. Keenly priced apartments of one sort or another can be found via **Jack's Kiosk** (*see p140*).

Casa Lila

94 rue Med El-Qorry (0524 47 55 45, www.riadcasalila.com). **Rates** 825dh-1,600dh. **Map** p131 E4 ⑮

Halfway between the souks and Bab Marrakech, this tasteful, unfussy maison d'hôte has eight rooms and suites, plus one two-bedroom apartment, ranged around the central courtyard. Most of the rooms have baths (three just have showers) and all except the apartment have open fires. Common areas include a salon off the courtyard and a rambling roof terrace. It's all nicely decorated in bold pinks and purples with lots of grey tadelakt in the bathrooms, complemented by a few well-chosen knick-knacks.

Dar Adul

63 rue Touahen (0524 47 39 10, www.dar-adul.com). **Rates** 550dh double-1,200dh suite. **Map** p130 C2 ⑯

Houses on the ocean side of the Medina need a lot of maintenance if they're not to fall into decline, and the four bedrooms of this former notary's house were recently renovated by the house's owners – who also own the Caravane Café (*see p136*). Given a new lease of life thanks to lavish colours, deeply comfortable beds and a quirky roof terrace complete with its own ceramic crocodile, it's a welcome addition to otherwise fairly samey options in this price bracket. Heating is supplied. Downstairs, a restaurant occupies the ground-floor rooms and courtyard, decorated with rich textiles, jugs of roses, flamboyant oil paintings and papier mâché sculptures. Everything's for sale and the daily-changing 150dh-200dh lunch menu is excellent value.

Dar Beida

0667 96 53 86/07768 352 190 in UK, www.castlesinthesand.com). **Rates** £300 per person per week. **Map** p131 E2 ⑰

For something a bit special, consider 'the White House'. Deep in a corner of the Medina, a twist or two off the tourist trail, this is a wonderful 200-year-old house owned by English partners Emma Wilson and Graham Carter. They've renovated and furnished with playful good taste, mixing Moroccan materials and flea-market finds with imported antiques and a retro vibe. The result manages to be both idiosyncratically stylish and unpretentiously comfortable (there are plug-in electric heaters). It can sleep up to four couples, has two bathrooms, two roof terraces, a lounge, a small library, open fires and a well-equipped kitchen, and comes with two amiable cats for £300 per person per week, with a minimum booking of three persons.

Dar Maya

Rue d'Oujda (0524 78 56 87, www.riaddarmaya.com). **Rates** €120-€170. **Map** p130 D2 ⑱

Of all the chic newcomers, Gareth Turpin's Dar Maya has the most design gravitas. Rising upwards to an elegant roof terrace with, unusually for Essaouira, a small plunge pool, the soft, sand-coloured hues and gentle curves of the place give it the air of a contemporary sandcastle. Light breezy balconies connect one room to another, and rooms are made interesting by contrasting textures and carefully chosen bespoke pieces of furniture, such as the cube-shaped pouffes made of old flour sacks. Bedrooms are pared back, with spacious bathrooms and fireplaces, and while there's no formal restaurant (breakfast is served wherever and whenever you like), there's always someone around ready to help you with a glass of wine and something to nibble.

Dar Mouna Mogador

44 Rue Ibn Khaldoun (0524 78 32 56/0666 40 95 48, www.darmouna.com). **Rates** 600dh-700dh double. **Map** p131 F3 ⑲

Dar Beida.

IN THE KNOW NAÏVE ART

The naïve school of painting for which Essaouira has become famous began in the 1950s with the mystical painting and sculpture of local artist **Boujemaâ Lakhdar** (1941-1989). During the 1960s, visiting hippies painted psychedelic murals (none have survived) and this undoubtedly encouraged the Souiris to pick up their brushes and experiment with bright colours of their own. **Galerie Damgaard** (*see p139*) is the place to see the most serious results, but you'll find paintings and sculpture on sale all over town – sometimes alongside handicrafts, sometimes in tiny artists' studios-cum-shops. And locals will tell you that one of the best places to see authentic naïve work is at the Sunday **Joutiya** (flea market) in the neighbouring village of **La Scala**.

Easily spotted by the colourful mural at the entrance, this cheap and cheerful bolthole is run by gregarious Australian expat Jane Folliott, a fountain of information not just about the local area but for all of Morocco. Her five homey rooms are spread over three fairly steep floors and decorated in a shimmer of purple and orange textiles. There's simple furniture, objets d'art by local artisans and gas heating. There's a sweet, sheltered roof terrace where Jane serves a hearty breakfast of fresh fruit, yoghurt, eggs, goat's cheese and olives, along with as much juice and coffee as you can drink.

Dar Ness
1 rue Khalid ben Oualid (0524 47 68 04, www.darness-essaouira.com). **Rates** 655dh double. **No credit cards. Map** p130 B3 ⑳
This is a bright little spot located just off the place Moulay Hasssan. Bare brick in places lends a lived-in feel to the place. It has a couple of pleasant living rooms with real wood fires off the courtyard, and spotless bedrooms, their only down side being the hand-held showers. Still it's good value for the price.

L'Heure Bleue
2 rue Ibn Batouta, Bab Marrakech (0524 78 34 34, www.heure-bleue.com). **Rates** 3,080dh double; 3,300dh-3,900dh suite. **Map** p131 F3 ㉑
Although this has long been considered the poshest spot in town, you can end up feeling just a tad abandoned, thanks to erratic opening hours of the bars, rooftop terrace and restaurant and service that ranges from welcoming to aloof. A renovated private mansion of 16 rooms and 19 suites arranged around a lovely, leafy courtyard, its big draw is a rooftop pool with fab views. The standard rooms (on the first floor) are spacious and African-themed – black marble, dark wood, zebra-patterned upholstery. Suites are on the second floor, and have Portuguese (blue and white), British colonial (19th-century engravings) and 'Eastern' (gold and burgundy) themes. The British colonial-style bar has big armchairs and mounted animal heads, but it's pot luck as to whether you'll get served.

La Maison des Artistes
19 rue Derb Laâlouj (0524 47 57 99/mobile 0662 60 54 38, www.lamaisondesartistes.com). **Rates** 650dh-970dh double; 1,200dh-1,450dh suite. **Map** p130 C3 ㉒
A characterful French-run guesthouse that makes the most of its oceanfront location and the slightly eccentric taste of its original owners. It has six comfortable rooms, three overlooking the sea, three facing on to the patio, all furnished differently and some boasting intriguingly odd pieces. The suite is splendid, with the ocean on three sides and lording over it, the roof terrace like the bridge of a ship. It's pretty exposed, however, and can get a bit rattly in high winds, though there is heating. La Maison seems to be a home from home for an assortment of young and vaguely arty French folks, and whether you'll like it here depends greatly on whether you get on with the crowd. Manager Cyril is also proud of his 'Judeo-Berber' kitchen and lunch or dinner (150dh per person, non-residents 200dh, booking necessary) can be served on the terrace with the ocean view.

Ocean Vagabond Guest House
4 boulevard Lalla Aicha (0524 47 92 22, www.oceanvagabond.com). **Rates** 1,300dh-1,680dh double. **Map** p131 E5 ㉓
In a modern villa on the seafront, just a short walk outside the old city walls, Ocean Vagabond boasts a few features alien to converted medina houses, such as a garden and a pool. Opened by the crew from the Ocean Vagabond café and surf station, it's a breath of fresh air in all senses. Common areas are bright, stylish and simple, and the place has heating. The 14 rooms are themed ('Bali' is vaguely Indonesian, 'Geisha' vaguely Japanese, and so on). Try to get one of the four ('Dogon', 'Felluca', 'Pondichéry' and 'Inca') that have balconies with an ocean view (two others have balconies with a view of the Medina – and the post office). A garden bungalow is the place for pampering: it houses a hammam and rooms for massage, beauty treatments and a hairdresser.

Riad Al Madina
9 rue Attarine (0524 47 59 07, www.riadalmadina.com). **Rates** 664dh double. **Map** p130 C3 ㉔
Once the location of the Hippy Café, this is a good-value hotel that trades on the myth that Jimi Hendrix, Frank Zappa and Cat Stevens all once hung out here. The beautiful courtyard is one of the nicest

breakfast spots in town, with wraparound balconies spilling over with geraniums and ferns, and a restaurant and bar area that hosts Gnawa musicians on Wednesday and Saturday evenings. The rooms have all been recently renovated so the overall feel is clean and fresh, though if you're tall you might want to avoid the low ceilings of the mezzanine rooms. The hotel has heating.

Riad Remmy

29 Daoud Ben Aicha (0653 23 61 92/0676 08 09 55, www.riadremmy.co.uk). **Rates** 550dh-600dh (whole house rental available). **No credit cards.** **Map** p131 F2 ㉕

Run by gregarious Manchester expat Sandra Cripps, this is a bright, thoughtfully decorated boutique B&B with a chill-out lounge in the courtyard warmed by a big fireplace, and five rooms spread out over the next three floors. A pale palette brightened with colourful local textiles keeps things easy on the eye, and the natural-coloured tiles, stripped-back wood and lush ferns give the place a relaxed ambience. On the second floor a small communal kitchen is available for guests to make their own tea, coffee and light meals, and there's a pleasant roof terrace for catching a few rays.

Tangaro

Diabat (0524 78 47 84, www.aubergetangaro.com). **Rates** €70-€120. **Open** 10am-8pm daily. **Set meals** from 250dh. **Day passes for pool & lunch** 250dh.

This 100-year-old former farm has recently become the hip hang-out of local groovers and shakers. Situated at the top of a hill in Diabat, it has fabulous ocean views, swimming pool access, a yoga studio and a breezy massage room created from pale driftwood, along with a chic, open-sided

PAMPERVILLE

The best spas, hammam and massage experiences.

For total indulgence in gorgeous surroundings, visit **Mumtaz Mahal** (5 rue Youssef el Fassi, 0524 78 53 00, www.riadmumtazmahal.com), the most lavish and luxurious of all the city's hammam experiences. Jewel-like zelije, marble columns and a vigorous scrub-down will soon have you feeling like new. For a spa experience in contemporary surroundings, **Azur** (Place Moulay Hassan, 15 rue Khalid Ben Walid, 0524 78 57 94, www.azur-essaouira.com, open 10.30am-7.30pm daily) is a sleek outfit with creamy tadelakt, state-of-the-art facilities, massage and other beauty treatments and a cute place to chill in the sun when it's all done.

For a more conventional Moroccan experience, **Les Massage Berbere** (135 avenue Mohamed El Quorry, 0524 47 31 30, www.lesmassagesberberes.com) has well-trained therapists and offers a two-hour massage in clean, comfortable rooms with deeply moisturising argan oil for 350dh. And if you really want to keep it real, there's **Hammam Pabst** (rue Ennasr). This is the oldest public baths in Essaouira and was used for the murder scene in Orson Welles' *Othello*. It's one of the best places in the country for a scrupulously clean, intensely hot, supremely traditional *gommage* (scrub down with black soap). It costs 10dh for the hammam, plus 50dh for someone to do the *gommage* for you, and is open daily until 9pm for women, and after 9pm for men.

Villa Maroc.

café for lunch or sunset cocktails followed by electricity-free, candlelit dinners. The handful of rustic rooms are scattered across the rambling eucalyptus-scented gardens, simply decorated but all with working fireplaces.

Villa de l'O

3 rue Mohamed Ben Messaoud (0524 47 63 75, www.villadelo.com). **Rates** 1,700dh-2,700dh. **Map** p130 C4 ㉖

Indulge in a little colonial-edged glamour at this richly decorated luxury retreat. From the cane furniture of the planted courtyard to the sultry bar with its leather sofas and Louis XVI-style armchairs, to the ample roof terrace with endless sea views, chill-out areas, sun beds and a bar, this place feels just as grown up as its competitors, minus the stuffiness. In the rooms, ceiling fans, fireplaces and rich velvet throws contrast pleasingly with fun extras like telescopes for all those sea views. Add impeccable service and a decent restaurant and it's easy to see why this place has fast established itself at the top of the high-end hotel roster.

Villa Maroc

10 rue Abdellah Ben Yassine (0524 47 61 47, www.villa-maroc.com). **Rates** 1,050dh double; 1,350dh-1,700dh suite. **Map** p130 C4 ㉗

The first boutique hotel in Morocco when it opened back in 1990, the Villa Maroc is now a mature, well-known establishment. It's nicely located just inside the walls of the Kasbah quarter, its roof terraces conveniently overlooking the square and the fishing port. Twenty rooms and suites are furnished in appealing style and arranged around an intriguing warren of open terraces, narrow staircases and small, secluded spaces – the result of knocking together four old merchants' houses. Dinner is 200dh and the food, served in one of several small salons, uses ingredients from the owners' farm. Non-residents are welcome for the lunchtime barbecue and pool access.

GUIDED TOURS & EXCURSIONS

Morocco Made Easy

(info@moroccomadeeasy.com, 0666 40 95 48). Jane Folliott runs guided tours of Essaouira and the surrounding area that get visitors off the beaten track. She also offers bespoke itineraries of Morocco.

GETTING THERE

By bus

Supratours (0524 43 55 25) runs a bus service from its depot next door to Marrakech railway station; the timetable changes frequently so check times. In summer, buy tickets (one-way 70dh regular coach, 100dh *confort plus*) at least a couple of days before travelling as the service for the three and a half hour journey gets busy. You can buy tickets in advance from www.marrakechtraintickets.com. In Essaouira buses arrive at and leave from the south side of the big square outside Bab Marrakech, where tickets are sold at a kiosk (0524 47 53 17) next to the **Telecom building**. Again check for times.

By taxi

Shared grand taxis from Marrakech (80dh per person) leave from Bab Doukkala. Coming back, they leave from outside Essaouira's *gare routière*. You can also hire your own taxi for around 700dh.

By air

At the time of writing, **Royal Air Maroc** (www.royalairmaroc.com) was running three daily flights from Paris and thrice-weekly flights from **Casablanca** to the tiny **Aéroport de Mogador**.

The High Atlas & Sahara

The south was always the unruly part of Morocco. Few Europeans dared venture into the High Atlas or journey through the expanse of the Moroccan Sahara before the French Foreign Legion built roads and garrisons in the 1920s and '30s. To ascend into the dramatic mountain valleys and pass through the lush oases of the South is still somehow to venture into another world. Even if you're never off the mobile phone network and stay only in tasteful riads, the desert can still be a raw and salutary experience, and the Atlas sometimes might as well be Tibet. Coming back, tired and dusty, from the point where civilisation peters out in the desert sands, makes Marrakech feel like New York City.

Camel ride.

5 Highlights

1 Camel ride into the Sahara dunes of **Erg Chegaga** (p175) or **Erg Chebbi** (p168).

2 Jaw-dropping views from the **Tizi-n-Test** pass (p155).

3 **Drâa Valley Oasis** in October when the palms droop with ripened dates (p172).

4 Sunrise on **Mount Toubkal** (p151).

5 The climb to the top of the kasbah at **Aït Benhaddou** (p159).

WHERE TO GO

South of Marrakech, there are two main passes over the High Atlas. The **Tizi-n-Test** (*see p155*), to the south-west, runs up past the 12th-century mosque of Tin Mal, snakes over the spectacular pass, and hairpins down to the Souss Valley and the pre-Saharan town of Taroudant. The **Tizi-n-Tichka** (*see p159*), to the south-east, zig-zags over the mountains via the Col de Tichka at a 2,260-metre (7,415-feet) altitude, and then down to Ouarzazate and the edge of the Sahara. In between the two, another road follows the **Ourika Valley** (*see p156*) into the High Atlas as far as the village of Setti Fatma and its waterfalls. This is the easiest journey from Marrakech and it's a popular day trip.

Ouarzazate is basically the gateway to the desert, and here it's possible either to head further south down the palmeraie of the **Drâa Valley** (*see p172*) until both road and river sink into the sand at M'Hamid, or bear east along the rugged **Dadès Valley** (*see p163*), taking in the Dadès and Todra gorges. Further east lies the great **Tafilelt Oasis** and the dunes of **Merzouga** (*see p168*), which can be reached from either the Drâa or Dadès valleys.

Whichever route takes your fancy, there are basically two kinds of country south of Marrakech: the colourful mountains of the High Atlas, and the stony plains and lush oases of the Moroccan Sahara.

The landscape may sometimes seem inhospitable but in most places people are unbelievably friendly. They're also unbelievably poor, and often the former is a result of the latter – they're happy to make contact with you in case it leads to a money-making transaction. But then, if it doesn't, they're happy to talk to you anyway. It's depressing to see children begging or ingeniously trying to scam a few dirhams, but our advice is never to hand out money, instead encourage kids to stay in school and finish their education. A gift of a ballpoint pen – *un stylo* – will still bring beaming smiles.

THE HIGH ATLAS

There are some serious peaks in the Atlas. At 4,167 metres (13,667 feet), Jebel Toubkal is the highest mountain in North Africa. But you don't need to be a climber to enjoy the spectacular landscape, and various valley roads take you into some of the most interesting areas.

Rugged and remote, throughout history the Atlas has been home to an assortment of Berber tribes, and every now and then one of them has come galloping down to conquer the rest of the

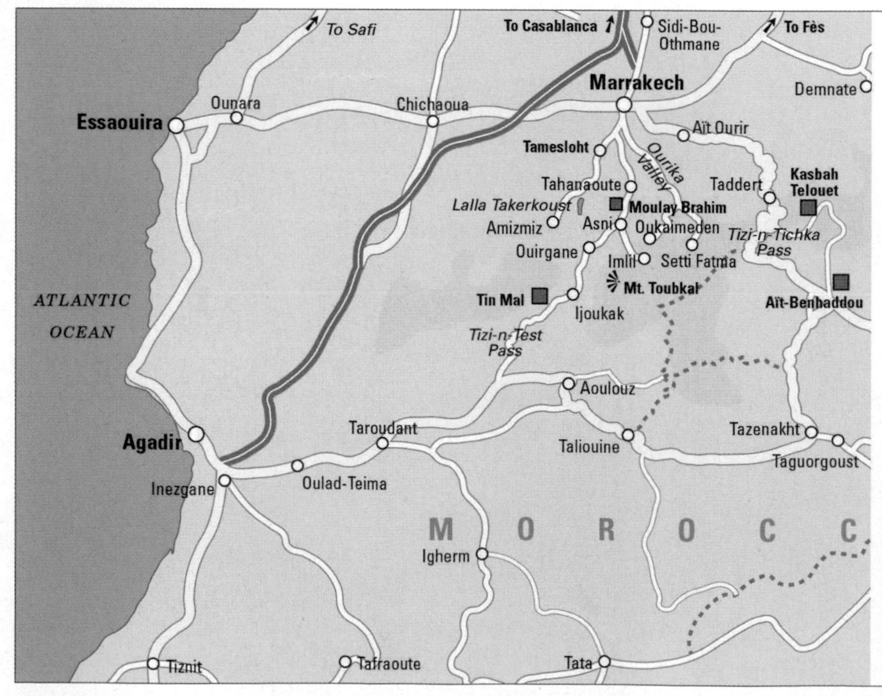

country and establish a new dynasty. These tribes were never really conquered by anyone, and their traditions are very different from those of urban Moroccans. The women, for example, wear headscarves but are never veiled and have skirts in bright, clashing patterns. They also seem to do all the work: you see them carrying huge bales of brushwood on their backs while the men sit around smoking and talking.

These tribes live in villages up on the valley sides looking on to clear streams, rugged skyscapes, wriggling roads and verdant valley floors. In spring, like the clothes of the women, it's all one big patchwork of colour.

THE SAHARA

Strictly speaking, the area south of the Atlas is the pre-Sahara, rather than the full-blown desert itself, but the aridity is palpable the minute you cross the watershed, and the pattern of lush oases separated by barren stretches begins just beyond the town of Ouarzazate.

An oasis – called a palmeraie in Morocco – is an area of densely cultivated land, anchored by palm trees, with other crops grown beneath. In the palmeraies you'll also find *ksour* (fortified tribal villages) and kasbahs (fortified family mansions) made out of pisé mud and straw. Most of these aren't anywhere near as old as they look (feudal days ended less than a century ago) and they decay fairly quickly once abandoned, melting back into the landscape. The great oases, however, have been inhabited for centuries, if not millennia.

There are both Berber and Arab settlements in the Sahara, and at the far end of the road also Tuaregs and Sahrawis, though not everyone wearing a blue robe and turban is a genuine 'blue man' of the desert. Many dress that way just to help sell their souvenirs or camel treks.

While the areas covered in the following pages are mostly a kind of Sahara Touristique, the desert can still be dangerous and should be treated with respect. Don't venture off the road unless you know where you're going or have a local guide with you.

WHEN TO GO

The best time to visit any of these places is in the spring (mid March to May), when all is lush and the almond trees are in bloom. October and November are fine temperature-wise too, though you don't get the greenery. But forget the Sahara between June and September: it's unbearably hot and there are sandstorms. In

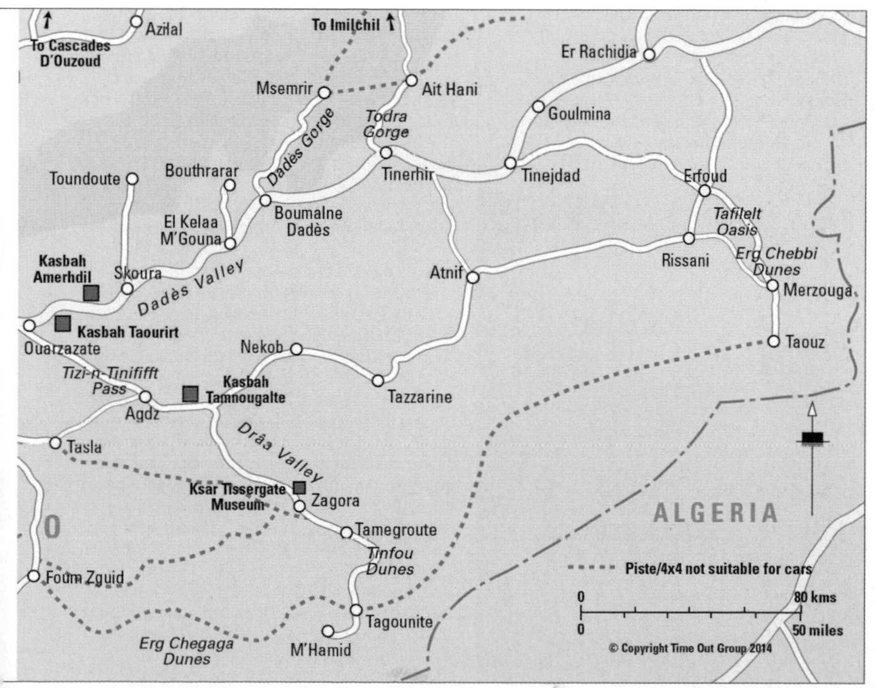

ADVENTURE!

Ways to explore the great outdoors.

The whole of southern Morocco is ripe for adventure and outdoor activities. In the Atlas, Sahara and Drâa regions try **Trekking with Mountain Travel Morocco** (www.mountain-travel-morocco.com) or **Trek In Morocco** (www.trekinmorocco.co.uk) for multi-day treks. For day-hiking seek out the local *bureau des guides* or arrange a guide through your hotel.

For cycling tours try **Maroc Nature** (www.bike-morocco.com) and **Argan Xtreme Sports** (www.argansports.com), which also hires out bikes by the day. Horse-riding is possible in Ouirgane (*see p154*), Lalla Takerkoust (*see p153*) and Skoura (*see p163*) and on multi-day treks through **Sport Travel** (www.sporttravel-maroc.com). There's rafting & canoeing in Ourika with **Splash Morocco** (www.moroccoadventuretours.com); rock-climbing in Todra Gorge and Oukaimeden with **Climb Morocco** (www.climbmorocco.com). Oukaimeden (*see p156*) is Morocco's ski resort, and, of course, there's camel trekking in the Sahara (*see p173* **Hump-backed Holidays**). And, for a variety of sports and activities, there's the outdoor adventure centre **Terres d'Amanar** (www.terresdamanar.com) near Asni (*see p151*).

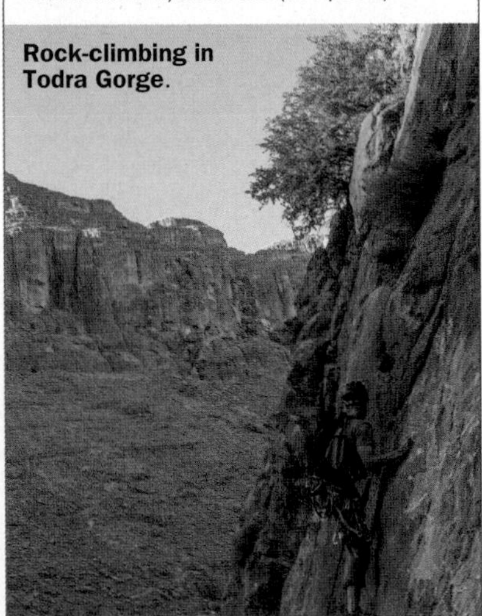

Rock-climbing in Todra Gorge.

winter the nights can be cold but the days are clear, warm and bright. The Atlas is wonderful in the summer, however: Marrakchis scoot up there just to escape from the heat of the city, and you may well want to follow their example. There is sometimes snow in winter, and there's even skiing between February and April at Oukaimeden (*see p156*). Snow will also occasionally close both the Tizi-n-Tichka and the Tizi-n-Test, and in winter it's best to check the situation before setting out.

WHERE TO STAY

Accommodation ranges from basic *gites* to boutique guesthouses and five-star hotels. Most will insist on half-board – room plus dinner – and more often than not this is a good idea as in the remote areas there are almost no decent restaurants. In the desert dunes you can camp in simple, or even luxurious, nomad-style bivouac camps with tents woven from camel-wool. Standard camps have shared washing facilities.

GETTING AROUND

It's possible to reach most places mentioned in these chapters by bus, but we'd recommend travelling that way only if you have time to juggle timetables and wait for a connection to your next destination. It's not suitable for anybody in a hurry, and the safety record of the public buses is far from exemplary. If possible, travel on the more comfortable Supratours and CTM buses (*see p228*). For the High Atlas valleys, grand taxis are your best bet.

The grand taxi network is a little more flexible, and shared taxis aren't much more expensive than buses. You can get to everywhere along the main roads this way. To go to places off the main road you can hire your own private taxi. Make sure the price is agreed beforehand.

The best way to explore is by either renting a car in Marrakech or Ouarzazate, or renting a 4x4 with driver. Car hire isn't cheap: from 350dh per day for a basic small car; and from 1,300dh per day upwards for a 4x4 with driver and fuel included. The driver knows the desert tracks, mountain roads and off-the-beaten-track places to visit. If hiring a standard car, a private driver costs an extra 300dh per day, but you must stay on tarmac roads. Filling stations are infrequent so top up whenever possible and ensure that a spare tyre and jack are in the back. Pack a torch, bottled water and some toilet paper.

A recommend guide for trips from a half day to several days is Hassan Boumezgour. He speaks good English and fluent Japanese, and has private cars, people carriers and 4x4s to ensure comfortable, stress-free adventures.

Transport Touristique Atlas Sahara Prestige

Hassan Boumezgour (mobile 0628 803 075, 0632 508 900, http://jasmin-tours.com).

SPECIALIST TOURS

Independent travel in southern Morocco is manageable and inexpensive, but if time is short and you want to incorporate activities en route, it can be worth enlisting the experts.

Lawrence of Morocco

+44 1672 500 555, www.lawrenceofmorocco.com. A long-established UK-based bespoke tour operator organising travel throughout Morocco – coastal regions, mountains, imperial cities and desert. Caters largely for a mid- to high-end clientele. Also offers bird-watching, cycling, golfing and surfing holidays.

Naturally Morocco

+44 1239 710 814 www.naturallymorocco.co.uk. This UK-based tour operator has a responsible travel ethos and a special focus on the region of Taroudant, where it offers wildlife-watching, bird-watching, trekking and other activity holidays.

Sheherazad Ventures

0524 44 85 18, www.sheherazadventures.com. A boutique English-Moroccan company based in Marrakech specialising in private cultural tours of southern Morocco and the Sahara desert, with English-speaking local guides on all tours. Activities include day hikes, camel treks, rock-climbing, horse-riding, cooking classes, henna classes, pottery-making and photography tours.

Tizi-n-Test to Taroudant

The road to Taroudant heads directly south out of Marrakech, winds over the Tizi-n-Test pass, and snakes down to the Souss Valley. It then cruises west through argan country (*see p156* **Argan: Elixir of Everything**) into Taroudant – a distance of 223 kilometres (138 miles). That's about a five-hour drive. If simply getting to Taroudant is your aim, it's quicker to take the motorway A7 west from Marrakech towards Agadir and take the exit after Ameskroud. But you would be missing out on one of the most spectacular drives in North Africa.

About 100 kilometres (62 miles) or two hours' drive from Marrakech, **Tin Mal** is also doable as a day trip. On the way, **Moulay Brahim** (*see right*) sports a shrine to Moulay Brahim (who else?), **Asni** (*see right*) hosts a Saturday morning souk, and **Ouirgane** (*see p154*) offers a couple of good hotels and some fine dining. An alternative trip is to bear left at Asni up to **Imlil** and maybe enjoy mule-trekking or even a two-day climb to the summit of **Mount Toubkal**.

Heading towards the Tizi-n-Test, after Tin Mal, the newly formed **Lake Yacoub El-Mansour** sparkles on your right, the result of the Ouirgane dam, constructed in 2008. From here on there's not much but the road itself – but what a road it is. It's a tricky one, though, for drivers without much experience of mountains and should be driven with care. Originally built by the French in 1928, it's well surfaced and contoured, but loops and twists like a sack of serpents and in places is treacherously narrow. The stretch after the pass hairpins around blind corners all the way down on to the plain, and it's only half as wide again as your car. The **Gorges of Moulay Brahim** below Asni are another stretch that demands respect. You wouldn't want to come off this road, for precisely the same topographical reasons that make it so worth driving in the first place.

Snow sometimes closes the Tizi-n-Test in winter. There's a sign on the way out of Marrakech that warns if the pass isn't open, and another one just after Tahanaoute. Alternatively just ring one of the hotels (*see p152*) and ask.

GETTING THERE

Buses that run all the way to Taroudant via the Tizi-n-Test tend to leave Marrakech very early in the morning (5am or 6am) and take seven to eight hours. Hotels in these parts can usually arrange a car to collect you from Marrakech.

MOULAY BRAHIM & ASNI

It's a boring administrative sort of town but Tahanaoute is the only feature of note on the plain between Marrakech and the mountains. Just after **Tahanaoute**, on the left, is the eco-friendly outdoor activity centre **Terres d'Amanar** (www.terresdamanar.com), a well-run adventure activity park on a forested hillside laced with zip-wires. It also offers climbing, crafts, horse-riding and archery, and is ideal for a family day out from Marrakech. After Tahanout, the road winds uphill through the Gorges of Moulay Brahim. Drive carefully.

Moulay Brahim also has a village named after him, which is off up to the right just before Asni, and in the middle of the village he has a green-roofed shrine – entry forbidden to non-Muslims. Nearby stalls sell charms, incense, nougat, chameleons and other esoteric supplies. Moulay Brahim is said to sort out female fertility problems, if asked nicely. This is a popular summer day-trip destination for Marrakchi families and it can get quite busy at weekends.

Asni is a few kilometres beyond the gorges. Its approach is lined with poplar and willow trees. The lively Saturday souk draws people from all over the area and it's worth a look if you're here on the day, but expect hassle from trinket-sellers. Beyond Asni the road continues up towards Ouirgane and Tin Mal; *see p154*. The road for Imlil forks off to the left.

IMLIL

The road to **Imlil** hugs the side of a broad valley, its bottom a wide bed of shale. Not far out of Asni, surrounded by high walls and cypresses, is the restored Kasbah Tamadot (*see below*). Further up the valley, across on the far side and perched above green pastoral enclosures and walnut groves, is the hilltop hamlet of **Aksar Soual**, also known as 'Clintonville' since Hilary Clinton swooped in unannounced in 1999, accompanied by a convoy of SUVs and helicopter escort in order to visit her niece who was living up here and married to a local Berber guide.

The tarmac road splits at Imlil branching left over the bridge to Tacheddirt, where it abruptly ends. Imlil serves as the centre for trekking in the region, lying, as it does, at the foot of **Jebel Toubkal** – at 4,167 metres (13,667 feet), North Africa's highest peak. Certified trekking guides (and mules too) can be hired at the Bureau des Guides d'Imlil (0524 48 56 26) in the centre of the village. There are also several small café/restaurants and souvenir shops.

Where to stay

Perched on a rocky outcrop overlooking the valley, the **Kasbah Du Toubkal** (0524 48 56 11, www.kasbahdutoubkal.com, doubles from 1,760dh) is the fashionable place to stay. British tour operator Mike McHugo bought it in ruins in 1990 and subsequently had village craftsmen restore it in vernacular style. The result today is an award-winning hotel with loads of character and touches of luxury. Guests arrive by mule from the village and the company's commitment to responsible tourism is more than just lip service. A five per cent levy is charged on all bookings and goes directly to the Village Association & Education For All foundation. You can also just stop here for lunch on the magnificent terrace with 360-degree panoramic views.

There are a few simple mountain *gites* in surrounding valleys for trekkers and at the top of the village, the stone-built **Riad Imlil** (0524 48 54 85, www.riadimlil.com, 440dh double, no credit cards) has 23 rather garish rooms, but is comfortable and clean.

Further up the road leading to Tacheddirt is **Kasbah Douar Samra** (0524 48 40 34, www.douar-samra.com, half board 520dh per person, no credit cards) offering pretty accommodation in the hamlet of Tamatert. There are seven cosy rooms and a treehouse, a small hammam, and a dining room in the main house. Owner Jacqueline Brandt describes it as a 'hobbit house', built around rock and with lots of slightly rickety wooden stairs and candlelight.

Back down towards Asni, Richard Branson's **Kasbah Tamadot** (0524 36 82 00, www.kasbahtamadot.virgin.com, doubles from 4,750dh) feels like another world. Built in the 1920s as the residence of the caid of the valley, it's kitted out with every luxury amid four hectares of landscaped gardens. There are

Domaine Malika. *See p154*.

AWAY DAYS

Trips within easy reach of the city.

There are plenty of destinations within easy reach of Marrakech. Along the routes covered within this section, Imlil, Ouirgane and Tin Mal on the Tizi-n-Test road (*see p151*), Telouet on the Tizi-n-Tichka road (*see p158*) and the whole of the Ourika Valley (*see p156*) can be done as day trips. Otherwise, there are decent excursions in two other directions – to the south-west, and to the east.

ROUTE D'AMIZMIZ

Leave Marrakech as if heading for Asni, and then fork right soon after Oasiria water park. After ten kilometres take a right turn for Tamesloht, home of a potters' co-operative. The village also boasts ancient olive oil presses with gigantic grindstones until recently driven by mules. There's also a rambling kasbah still partially occupied by descendants of the village founders, and next to it a Shrine of Moulay Abdellah with a minaret that appears to be toppling under the weight of an enormous storks' nest. Call in at the offices of the Association Tamesloht (place Sour Souika) for additional information and directions.

South of Tamesloht, the fertile landscape becomes a brilliant patchwork of greenery. Visible to the left is Kasbah Oumnast, a location for films *The Last Temptation of Christ* and *Hideous Kinky*. Eight kilometres (five miles) further south, the road swings on to a narrow bridge over the Oued N'fis before looping around to hug the shore of the Barrage Lalla Takerkoust, a sizeable reservoir with the mountains as backdrop. A number of lakeside restaurants line the road; **Relais du Lac** (0524 48 49 43, www.relaisdulacmarrakech.com) is the most popular (and noisy) and from here you can also arrange horse-riding with Les Cavaliers de L'Atlas (*see p107* **Enjoy the Outdoors**). Next door is **Le Flouka** (0664 49 26 60, www.leflouka.com), which also has tastefully decorated rooms ideal for a weekend stay (from 660dh double).

Jet-skiing on the lake can be booked with **Jet Atlas** (0524 30 30 22, www.jet-atlas.com). The road ends at Amizmiz (pronounced 'Amsmiz'), 55 kilometres (34 miles) south-west of Marrakech. The luxurious **Capaldi Hotel** (0524 48 47 59, www.thecapaldi.com) has a fine restaurant open for visitors and can arrange guided hiking in the nearby foothills (doubles from 1,900dh). The town has a ruined kasbah and a former mellah (Jewish quarter), as well as a Thursday market that's one of the biggest in the region. There are regular buses and grand taxis between Marrakech (from Bab Er Rob) and Amizmiz. The journey takes just over an hour.

CASCADES D'OUZOUD

The route de Fes runs east out of Marrakech. After ten kilometres (six miles) there's a right- hand turn on to the road for Demnate and Azilal. After 40 kilometres (24 miles) skirting the foothills of the Atlas, look for a right turn down to the village of Timinoutine, which is on the edge of the Lac des Aït Aadel. Also known as the Barrage Moulay Youssef, this is another large reservoir with a High Atlas backdrop. The scenery is gorgeous and it's a popular picnic spot for Marrakchis. At Demnate, a side road runs south to Imi-n-Ifri, which scores with a natural rock bridge, a slippery grotto and fossilised dinosaur footprints. Boutique guesthouse **Tizouit** (0658 34 61 48, www.tizouit.ma, 600dh double) is nearby, offers lots of activities, and is an ideal base for a longer stay. East from Demnate on the way to Azilal is a signposted turn-off north for the Cascades d'Ouzoud: the biggest waterfall in Morocco, it plunges 110 metres in three tiers down to a picturesque pool overlooked by cafés. You arrive at the top, where people will want to 'guide' you down, though help isn't really necessary. For anyone who doesn't fancy going straight back to Marrakech, the **Riad Cascades d'Ouzoud** (0523 42 91 73, www.ouzoud.com, 600dh double) is rustically tasteful. Two buses a day run from Marrakech to Azilal, and from here you can hire a grand taxi for the 20-minute backtrack to the falls. Market day is Thursday.

pools and tennis courts, luxury safari tents and talented international chefs, and the Eva Branson Foundation shop provides money for community projects. Yet, tucked behind high walls with guarded gates, it's totally removed from local life.

OUIRGANE

Ouirgane ('weer-gan') at first seems like the tiniest place, along either side of the Oued N'Fis. But after a while you realise that the houses are hidden in forest and scattered up the valley sides, safe from occasional flash flooding. It's a pretty location, in a basin surrounded by wooded mountains, with glimpses of Toubkal towering highest of all. There's a Jewish hamlet (deserted) nearby to the south-east, and a primitive salt factory (operational) back down the main road and off to the west. You'll need a guide to find either. To visit Tin Mal (*see below*) involves commandeering a taxi unless you have your own transport. But Ouirgane is a place for chilling rather than sightseeing, with a little easy hiking on the side. It's also a good lunch stop as some hotels, including **L'Oliveraie de Marigha** (0524 48 42 81, www.oliveraie-de-marigha.com) have decent restaurants and pool access for day visitors.

La Roseraie (0524 43 91 28, www.la roseraiehotel.com, from 1,350dh double half-board) is a peaceful place set among rose gardens and groves of lime and lemon. It has two restaurants, indoor and outdoor pools, a hammam, tennis courts and its own horse-riding stables. The restaurant is open to all for lunch and dinner. **Domaine Malika** (0661 49 35 41, www.domaine-malika.com, doubles from 1,550dh, minimum stay two nights; *photo p152*) is a French owner-managed contemporary themed guesthouse. There are just seven stylish rooms and suites, all with fireplaces. The modern architecture sits easily among pine and olive trees. There is a pool and lawns and an excellent restaurant that combines fresh organic produce and herbs from their own kitchen garden. Mule-trekking and hiking are available direct from the front door.

TIN MAL

Beyond Ouirgane, the twisting road climbs high up the valley sides, with riverside cultivation glowing green far below. Flat-roofed Berber villages blend into the stony background above the fertile stretches. Just after the village of **Ijoujak**, on the right, is the kasbah of **Talaat-n-Yacoub**. This, and the other kasbahs that crown strategic heights in the area, were all fortresses of the Goundafi tribe, who ran the Tizi-n-Test until 'pacified' by the French. Though they look ancient, the kasbahs mostly date from the late 19th and early 20th centuries – a reminder that the feudal era is still a living memory around here.

About three kilometres past the kasbah, a track to the right leads down and across the river to **Tin Mal**. The ancient **mosque**, built in 1153, stands above the undistinguished modern village. Soon after you arrive, someone will appear with a key to let you in.

Despite such a remote location, it became the spiritual heart of the Almohad Empire in the 12th century. Around 1120, one Ibn Toumart arrived after much wandering to make a pest of himself in Marrakech with criticism of the ruling Almoravids. He was banished and retreated up here to seek the support of local tribes for his militant version of Islam. In 1125 he established his capital at Tin Mal, creating a sort of Moroccan Lhasa – a fortified religious community run with a pitiless, puritanical discipline. Ibn Toumart and his supporters called themselves El-Muwahhidun ('the monotheists') – hence their European name, the Almohads.

Ibn Toumart died in 1130 but his right-hand man, Abdel-Moumen, kept up his work. Tin Mal proved a good base, as the Almoravids' strength was in cavalry, and horses couldn't get up here. In 1144 Abdel-Moumen laid siege to Marrakech and went on to conquer the rest of Morocco, most of North Africa and much of Spain. Back here, in 1153, they used some of the loot to build the mosque that stands today. It was modelled after that of Tata, near Fès, and in turn provided the prototype for the Koutoubia in Marrakech, almost certainly built by the same craftsmen.

Tin Mal was a monument to Ibn Toumart and his doctrines. It also accommodated his tomb and that of other Almohad leaders. When the dynasty fell around the mid 13th century, Tin Mal was their last line of defence. It was taken by the Merenids in 1276, but even after that remained a place of pilgrimage. When the French turned up centuries later, the crumbling remnants of the mosque were home to a strange cult that worshipped the Stone of Sidi Wegweg.

Restoration had to wait until the 1990s. There is no roof but the framework of sandy-coloured transverse arches is complete. For the non-Muslim visitor it's a rare chance to see inside a Moroccan mosque, but note that in mosque architecture the minaret is almost never above the mirhab, as it is here. Normally it's on the north wall, rather than the one facing east towards Mecca; no one knows why it's different at Tin Mal. The roofless structure is currently used for prayers on Friday, which is the one day you can't visit. Tip the attendant with the key as you leave.

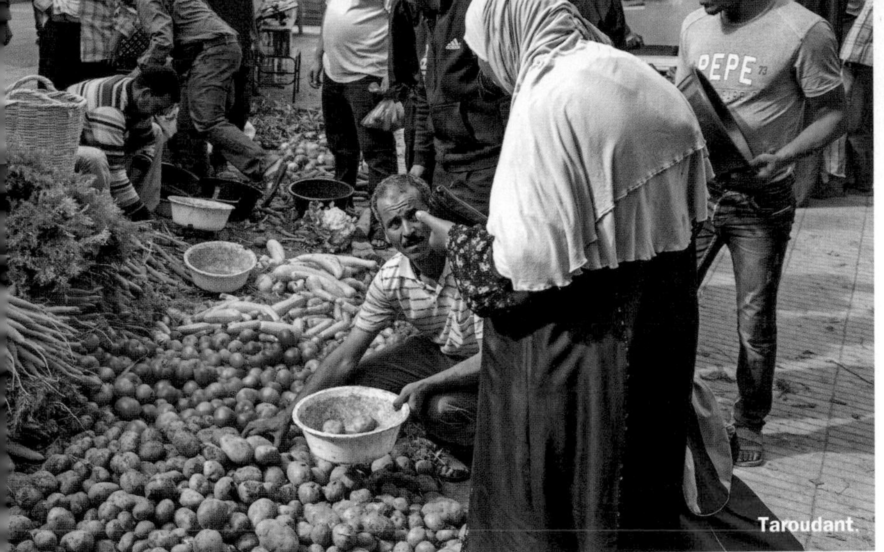

Taroudant.

THE TIZI-N-TEST

This pass (2,092 metres) is about 40 kilometres (25 miles) beyond Ijoujak. The final stretch is beautiful as the road curls up to the heights, and then suddenly reveals the most amazing view south across the plain of the Souss valley. There's a couple of small cafés on the pass where you can stop and enjoy the panorama, as well as the view back towards Toubkal.

On the other side, the road loses height recklessly, descending 1,600 metres in little over 30 kilometres (18 miles). The twists and loops aren't too dangerous, but this is not a stretch to hurry. Take your time and enjoy the views that continue to present themselves until shortly before the road joins the P32, the main east–west route across southern Morocco, for the final run across prosperous farmland to Taroudant.

TAROUDANT

Enclosed by reddish ramparts, with a backdrop of the High Atlas, commanding the trade routes across a plain, kitted out with souks – **Taroudant** is often dubbed the 'little Marrakech'. It has its pretensions. In the early 16th century it was the Saadian capital. They, and the gold they hauled up from the Sahara, built the well-preserved pisé walls that remain the town's most prominent feature. Later the Roudanis, as the inhabitants are called, joined a rebellion against Moulay Ismail. In 1787 Ismail took the town, destroyed the Saadian palaces, slaughtered the locals, and brought in a whole new Berber population from the Rif.

He left behind his own fortress – what is now the Kasbah, one of the town's poorest and most crowded quarters – and the walls. A ride around their crenellated five-kilometre (three-mile) circumference in a horse-drawn calèche costs about 100dh per hour and is Taroudant's only standard tourist activity. On the way, check out the foul-smelling tanneries, on the western side, outside Bab Targhount.

There are two souks: the **Marché Berbère**, where the locals buy groceries; and the **Arab Souk**, more focused on traditional crafts. Local guides may show you an ancient *foundouk* (merchants' hostel) 'used in the French film *Ali Baba*' (we've never heard of it either) or lead you to one of the local sculptors who work with limestone. It's also a good place to buy Berber jewellery.

The Arab Souk is west of **place Assareg**, the town's main square. Settling at a café and watching the laid-back daily life of this modest pre-Saharan market town, you realise that really it's nothing much like Marrakech at all.

Where to stay

A few kilometres out of town is the exclusive **Gazelle d'Or** (0528 85 20 39, www.gazelledor.com, doubles from 5,500dh half board). It was built in 1961 as a Belgian baron's hunting lodge and has been a hotel since 1972. There are 30 grand bungalows set in enormous grounds, with tennis, croquet and an organic farm. This shining jewel was a haven for royals and celebrities in its heyday, but now faces stiff competition from boutique eco-guesthouse **Dar Al Hossoun** (0665 02 82 74, www.alhossoun.com, doubles from 1,200dh) at a fraction of the cost. Within the medina, **Palais Oumensour** (0528 55 02 15, www.palaisoumensour.com, doubles 770dh) is a tasteful riad-style hotel with ten rooms, a small pool and cloistered courtyard and a jacuzzi and hammam designed to soothe. **Riad El Aissi** (0661 17 30 89, www.riadelaissi.com, doubles from 600dh; no credit cards) is three kilometres out of town. On a converted family farm, the place has loads of character with old-fashioned but spacious rooms. There's a pool, and bananas and papaya grow in the extensive garden.

The Ourika Valley

Ourika is a spectacular valley cut deep into the High Atlas and an easy way to get a taste of mountain air. It's not a pass as such – the road stops at **Setti Fatma**, 63 kilometres (39 miles) from Marrakech – and it's an easy day trip for the Marrakchis who nip up here for a break from the summer heat. There are also places to stay if you want to experience the peace of the valley after the daytrippers have all gone home. With rivers, valleys, winter snow and rugged mountains it's also ideal for adventure activities, trekking and skiing at nearby Oukaimeden, Morocco's best ski resort.

The twisting mountain tracks from village to village make cycling is a popular sport. Operator **Epic Morocco** (www.epicmorocco.co.uk) runs an exhilarating six-day High Atlas Traverse on mountain bikes and mules. Trekking in both the Ourika and Imlil valleys can be booked with local mountain guide, Mohammed Aztat of **Atlas Trek Shop** (www.atlastrekshop.com), or alternatively book a day-hike and lunch direct from Auberge le Maquis (*see p157*) or Kasbah Bab Ourika (*see p158*). There is also a *bureau des guides* at both Setti Fatma (0668 56 23 40) and Imlil village (0524 48 56 26).

For skiing head to **Oukaimeden** and hire your own equipment, instructor or guide at the base of the slopes or at Chez Juju (*see p158*).

ARGAN: ELIXIR OF EVERYTHING

A botanic relic from a remote era.

Goats clambering about in argan trees is part of tourist mythology in south-west Morocco. And you may actually see them doing it. Round here grow the world's only argan trees. A botanical relic from a remote era, the fussy argan flourishes only inland between Essaouira and Sidi Ifni, in an area that has been declared a UNESCO Biosphere Reserve.

Thorny and knotted argan trees look similar to olive trees and they too bear a fruit from which oil can be extracted. This is where the goats come in – or at least used to. Some grazed in the trees, others were fed the fruits after harvesting. The goat's digestive system was the means by which the tough fruit was stripped from the recalcitrant nut. The nuts were then collected from goat droppings before being split to expose the kernel, which was pulped and pressed – it takes 30 kilogrammes of nuts to make one litre of oil. Thankfully these days the process is mechanical and hygienic and the goats have been sidelined. The resulting quality of 'goat-free' oil is much better for both culinary and cosmetic use.

Argan oil is highly prized. Berbers have long used the oil to help to heal scars and ease rheumatic pain. Rich in vitamin E, it's good for the skin and has become a staple of Moroccan massage and beauty treatments.

Modern research has pronounced argan oil efficacious in reducing cholesterol and countering arteriosclerosis. The culinary variety, where the kernels are toasted, is very tasty – sweet and rich, great for drizzling or bread-dunking. Moroccan 'peanut butter' is called *amlou* and the best mix is with almonds, argan oil and honey; culinary argan oil costs around 400dh per litre.

Cosmetic oil should be a clear pale yellow, odour-free and absorbed easily into the skin. Expect to pay around 150dh per 100ml.

Professionally organised canyoning and rafting in the rivers and gorges of Ourika can be booked through **Splash Morocco** (*see p150*) and usually include transport from Marrakech.

GETTING THERE

Buses and grand taxis leave from Marrakech's Bab Er Rob. Make sure you're getting one that goes all the way to Setti Fatma, as some head only as far as Arhbalou, 24 kilometres (15 miles) short. The journey takes about two hours. Buses head to Oukaimeden in winter, but if you want to go at another time of year you'll have to hire a taxi or car for the day from Marrakech.

Berber Eco-Museum.

TO ARHBALOU

The route d'Ourika begins at the fountain roundabout of Bab Jedid, by the Mamounia Hotel. The road follows that stretch of the walls which encloses the Agdal Gardens before crossing 34 kilometres (21 miles) of hotel developments and agricultural flatland.

There are two possible side excursions. Firstly, **Aghmat** (signposted as Jemaa D'Rhmat) was the first Almoravid capital of the region. It is now a small village, and has a 1960s mausoleum dedicated to Youssef Ibn Tachfine, founder of Marrakech. Secondly, **Tnine de l'Ourika** has a Monday souk and is home to **Nectarome** (0524 48 21 49, www.nectarome.com, open 9am-5pm daily, no credit cards), an organic garden of aromatic plants with a shop selling wellness products made from their essential oils. On arrival you're invited to take a tour of the gardens, where the properties of plants are explained. Afterwards, browse the selection of soaps, shampoos and bath, massage, skin treatment and aromatherapy oils. Call ahead to book a foot bath (80dh) or foot massage (250dh), and also for a better chance of getting an English-speaking guide.

Six kilometres before reaching Arhbalou from Marrakech, you will find the 'pottery' village of **Tafza**. Leave your car at the roadside by the mosque and then walk 150 metres, following signs, to the centre of the old village and you will find the carefully curated **Berber Eco-Museum** (0610 25 67 34, www.museeberbere.com, open 9am-7pm daily, admission 20dh). Housed inside an old restored village kasbah, the museum is a treasure trove of artefacts, pottery, ceramics, carpets and rare antique photographs depicting local Berber culture and traditions from the past century. The brainchild of Patrick Man'ach and Hamid Mergani, the project aims to promote sustainable tourism and cultural understanding in the village. The museum is a partnership project with their exquisite collection at La Maison de la Photographie, in Marrakech (*see p53*). On-site guide Khalid speaks excellent English and will bring the whole exhibition to life with his thoughtful interpretation.

Beyond here, Berber villages cling to steep valley sides, camouflaged against a red-earth backdrop that forms a brilliant contrast with the deep, luminous greens of the valley floor.

There's nothing much at **Arhbalou**, except for the turn-off to Oukaimeden. On the stretch beyond it, there are a few decent hotels that also double as lunch spots, notably the **Auberge Le Maquis** (0524 48 45 31, www.le-maquis.com, 580dh per room) and **Chez Larbi** (0661 34 23 92, www.chezlarbi-ourika.com) which has a shaded garden terrace and rooms from 700dh.

SETTI FATMA

After a final gorge-like stretch, with cafés and houses along the opposite bank, the road peters out at **Setti Fatma**. The village is nothing special – lots of cafés and souvenir shops, with satellite dishes on breeze-block houses – but the setting is wonderful, ringed by mountains with lots of streams and grassy terraces. If you arrive in mid August there's a big four-day *moussem*, an event that's both a religious celebration and sociable fair. The village also has a *bureau de guides* where you can arrange local hikes.

The shortest and simplest hike is the Walk of the Seven Waterfalls. On the other side of the river from the main body of the village – reached by precarious footbridges made of bundled branches – are a number of small tagine and brochette joints. Concealed behind these cafés is a steep-sided valley, and a climb up it will bring you to the first of the seven cascades. It's quite a strenuous scramble, over big river boulders and up a cliff or two. Anyone will point (or lead) the way, and there is a basic café at the foot of the first waterfall where you can rest with a cool drink. The other six are a more serious climb.

Accommodation ranges from the rustic charm of **Au Bord de L'Eau** (0661 22 97 55, www.obordelo.com) near the falls (rooms from 400dh; no credit cards), to the boutique chic of the fully-licensed **Kasbah Bab Ourika** (0668 74 95 47, www.kasbahbabourika.com, doubles from 1,650dh). Ideal for a few days' escape or even just for an afternoon, it's located around 12 kilometres beyond the turn-off to Oukaimeden. The hotel can arrange a variety of day treks with picnics.

OUKAIMEDEN

Oukaimeden is 70 kilometres (43 miles) south of Marrakech and can be approached from the road that heads out towards the Ourika Valley or from the road that leads to Ouirgane and the Tizi-n-Test mountain pass. Either way, the road hairpins all the way in a fairly gentle fashion, rising eventually to a height of 2,650 metres. The principal attraction here is skiing – this is Morocco's best ski resort, though facilities are old-fashioned and conditions unreliable, even in peak season. It was recently voted by CNN News into its Top 100 Resorts in the world, which commented: 'the resort is one of the world's most bizarre places to ski or snowboard.' The season runs from December to April but snow is most likely to be found between January and March. The ski lift, once the highest in the world, is still, at 3,273 metres, the highest in Africa. It operates all year round, affording spectacular views from Jbel Attar across the surrounding High Atlas summits and beyond to Marrakech. A round trip on the chairlift for non-skiers costs 30dh. There are also drag-lifts serving around ten different ski-runs, of which the steep mogul field, La Grande Combe, is the best. Boots, skis and poles can be hired for around 100dh for the day. Ski passes cost 100dh. Despite ambitious plans heralded a number of years ago to build a full-scale ski and golf resort with UAE money, the 2008 financial crash has put development on hold and the resort remains poorly serviced. However, it's still a very popular day out in winter months for Marrakchi families, who flock to the area to play, toboggan, snowboard and ski before a hearty tagine lunch in one of the small cafés.

The **CAF Réfuge** (0524 31 90 36, 250dh per person with dinner) has both dorms and private rooms, and is a good place to find ski guides. The hotel **Chez Juju** (0524 31 90 05, www.hotelchezjuju.com, doubles from 900dh, no credit cards) has a bar, restaurant and homely en-suite rooms with central heating. It can also arrange a ski guide or instructor if needed.

The terrain in Oukaimeden is also ideal for rock-climbing much of the year and expert instruction is available from Marrakech-based **Climb Morocco** (*see p150*)

In summer, the area below Oukaimeden becomes what is known as an alpine prairie. The pastures become crowded with Berber tents and grazing livestock. Compared to the ski resort, it's a scene not just from another season, but from another age.

The area's other attraction is the prehistoric rock carvings – of animals, weapons, battle scenes, and symbols with forgotten meanings – that can be found nearby with the help of a guide. Look for the book *Gravures Rupestres du Haut Atlas* by Susan Searight and Danièle Hourbette, which might be on sale at the CAF Réfuge or in Marrakech bookshops.

If you're travelling to Oukaimeden by taxi you will need to hire a driver for the day, as it is almost impossible to find a free taxi in the resort itself at any time of year.

IN THE KNOW BIKE RIDE

Every April, an annual charity bike ride, the **Marrakech Atlas Etapes** (www.marrakech-atlas-etape.com) takes place, with a choice of routes: either from Marrakech to Ourika (60 kilometres) or Marrakech to Oukaimden (140 kilometres). The purpose is to raise funds for the Education For All project – founded by Mike McHugo, owner of the Kasbah du Toubkal in the neighbouring Imlil valley. The association provides opportunities for girls in these rural communities to further their education beyond primary school.

Tizi-n-Tichka to Ouarzazate

Running south-east out of Marrakech, the P31 courses across the plain, then cuts into the High Atlas to snake spectacularly over the range's loftiest pass – the **Tizi-n-Tichka**. It then

Tizi-n-Tichka

descends into the arid pre-Sahara and down to Ouarzazate (*see p161*), rightly considered the gateway to the desert, as well as being the centre of Morocco's film industry. Along the way, there are interesting side trips to the kasbahs of **Telouet** and **Aït Benhaddou**.

It's only 196 kilometres (122 miles) to Ouarzazate, and it's a pretty decent road, built by the French Foreign Legion in 1931, but the mountains demand respect so leave a good four hours for the journey – longer if you decide to stop at Telouet or Aït Benhaddou. And if you're not in a hurry, there are places to stay on the way.

GETTING THERE

There are several Ouarzazate buses daily from Marrakech with either Supratours or CTM (*see p228*). Journey time is about four hours. One bus a day leaves Bab Ghemat (map p253 F6) in Marrakech for Telouet at 1pm; the return journey is at 7am, but to reach Aït Benhaddou by public transport it's necessary to go to Ouarzazate and then backtrack by taxi.

THE TIZI-N-TICHKA

About 50 kilometres (31 miles) south-east of Marrakech, the road begins to climb into the mountains. It's a spine-tingling journey, each bend revealing a new panorama. On the way up, the fertile slopes are shrouded in forest or terraced for cultivation, and mud-built Berber villages seem to cling to the rock. The mountains here are full of semi-precious stones and roadside sellers angle melon-sized geodes, broken in half, to show you the glittering coloured crystals within – though beware, as many are often artificially enhanced.

There are various places to take a breather. About 15 kilometres (nine miles) before the pass, the village of **Taddert** is the busiest halt. It's divided into two parts; the higher of the two has a better choice of cafés, some of which overlook the valley below. A barrier is lowered here when the pass is closed, and this is where the snow plough is garaged.

Beyond Taddert it's all much more barren and the road gets quite hairy in places – looping and twisting and running along the knife's edge of exposed ridges. Small shops selling minerals and fossils are perched in some seemingly impossible places. There's a point where you can stop and look back down over the hairpins you have just ascended. At the top, the road levels across a grassy plain and under a stand of conifers is **Assanfou Café** (0661 13 21 30) – a great stop for coffee or a snack, with clean toilets and outdoor space for kids to wander. The pass, at 2,260 metres (7,415 feet), is reached with little fanfare. There are a couple of masts and a few more stalls selling rocks. Beyond it there's an immediate and dramatic change to a more arid landscape, leaving little doubt that the desert is where you're headed. The turn-off to **Telouet** is just a few kilometres further on the left and this minor road continues, though still very rough in places, right through the **Ounila Valley** and on to **Ait Benhaddou**.

TELOUET

The village and kasbah of **Telouet** (*photo p160*) is a 21-kilometre (13-mile) detour deep into the remote heart of the mountains. Scattered settlements hang between barren peaks and luminous green valleys. In spring

Telouet kasbah. *See p159.*

there is almond blossom everywhere. Kestrels and vultures weave in the blue skies above. The village of Telouet is tiny, dominated, as is the whole valley, by the slowly crumbling kasbah of the Glaoui clan.

For centuries, before the French built the Tichka road, this was the southern side of the main pass over the High Atlas. In the late 19th century, control of that pass was in the hands of the Glaoui clan – one of three tribes that dominated the ungovernable south of Morocco. After coming to national prominence following their assistance to Sultan Moulay Hassan in 1893, the Glaoua greatly expanded this kasbah, which remained their stronghold and last line of defence. However, while Thami El-Glaoui (*see p184* **Glaoui Power**), as pasha of Marrakech, ran the South on behalf of the Protectorate, the kasbah passed into control of his obstinately anti-French in-law Hammou. This was enough to stall French 'pacification' of the South until the 1930s, and they built the Tichka road, following a much trickier route, simply to avoid the fortress. It was abandoned upon Thami El-Glaoui's death in 1956. There have been several failed attempts to rescue the kasbah – all foiled by complicated inheritance laws (the site is jointly owned by all the descendants of the Glaoui, whose myriad permissions would be needed for any transfer of ownership).

The kasbah is reached by following the road around the edge of the village. Entry is by donation (20dh) and someone will appear with a bunch of keys to let you in and show you around. Much of the fortress is in advanced disrepair and out of bounds for safety reasons. The main thing to see is the reception hall, built in 1942 and, alongside the ornately traditional decoration in cedarwood, stucco and mosaic, equipped with sockets for electrical appliances – odd, among such apparently medieval surrounds. At the end of the hall is a delicate iron window grille that frames a commanding view.

Where to stay & eat

Right by the kasbah, the tiny **Lion d'Or** (0524 88 85 07) has a pretty terrace restaurant. It's a great lunch stop, serving fruit smoothies and some of the best tagines in the High Atlas. There is only basic, overpriced accommodation in the village itself, but 11 kilometres beyond is **Kasbah Tigmi N'Oufella** (0668 45 00 12, www.kasbah-haut-atlas.blog4ever.com, 450dh double, no credit cards) in Anguelz. It's the family home of a highly regarded and learned local, Lahoucine Ouchou, with three delightful rooms for visitors and lovely views across the valley. The road between here and Telouet was rough in mid 2014, but just manageable in an ordinary car. Aït Benhaddou is 35 kilometres further on, but the road has recently been paved and is a scenic drive through the unspoiled Ounila valley.

On the main Tizi-n-Tichka road to Ouarzazate, **Dar Irocha** (0667 73 70 02, www.irocha.com, 920dh double incl dinner, no credit cards) is an excellent base for exploring this region. This small *maison d'hôte* is in a quiet spot, perched above the P31 (from which it's well signposted) at Tisselday, halfway between the Telouet turn-off and Aït Benhaddou. The simple rooms have a number of tasteful touches, tadelakt walls, nice rugs and en suite showers. There's also a swimming pool, a terrace overlooking the lush valley and a cosy dining room serving excellent food. They will also arrange guided treks in the area.

AIT BENHADDOU

It is possible to drive from Telouet all the way to **Aït Benhaddou** via **Anmiter** (last stop for buses). The surfacing of the road is a work in progress, and the section between Telouet and Anmiter is hazardous for several kilometres, though still just about manageable by car. Allow two hours in 4x4, four hours in a standard car from Telouet to Aït Benhaddou.

Sticking with the main P31, the turn-off for Aït Benhaddou is 11 kilometres (seven miles) south of Amerzgane. If you're already exhausted from your trip over the Tichka pass, it may make sense to do Aït Benhaddou and Telouet together as a full day tour from Ouarzazate (24 kilometres) to the south, or as a scenic detour back to Marrakech.

Whichever, it shouldn't be missed. The fortified village (*ksar*) and complex of kasbahs is one of the most striking and best preserved in southern Morocco, appearing to tumble down a slope above the Oued Mellah. It's also probably the most famous, used as a location in David Lean's *Lawrence of Arabia*, Franco Zeffirelli's *Jesus of Nazareth* and Ridley Scott's *Gladiator*. But the film and tourist industries have only slowed Aït Benhaddou's decline from the importance it formerly had for its position on the old Saharan caravan route. The population is dwindling fast and the village is now under the protection of UNESCO. There are two entrances to the kasbah – one requires crossing stepping stones over the river below and is reached from the main car park by Hotel La Kasbah. Further up the road, by the post office, there is access on a newly constructed footbridge. Recent restoration work has improved the access and footpaths through the kasbah. The ancient fortified granary (*agadir*) at the top of the complex is also worth the uphill clamber. Some families have opened their homes to visitors as living museums and will invite you for tea. You'll be asked to make a cash donation of some sort, so make sure this is clear before entering. Entry to the kasbah in general is 20dh per person.

There's another kasbah, this one dating from the 17th century, ten kilometres (six miles) up the road at **Tamdaght**. You can look around but it's not in very good condition and there's little to see inside. From here the road loops and twists for around 45 kilometres (28 miles) to Telouet.

Where to stay & eat

The cluster of businesses on the other side of the river testify to the importance of Aït Benhaddou on the tourist route, if no longer on the trade route. There isn't much reason to hang about but if you do want to stay then the upmarket **Riad Ksar Ighnda** (0524 88 76 44, www.ksar.ighnda.net, double 1,200dh) is nearby with 19 rooms, a pool, bar, restaurant and hammam. In Tamdaght, the characterful guesthouse **Kasbah Ellouze** (0524 89 04 59, www.kasbahellouze.com, double 950dh with dinner) has a maze of higgledy-piggeldy, homely rooms and a pool in the heart of the village. Terraces overlook almond orchards and the kasbah next door. Either of these hotels are well-placed for exploring the Ounila Valley and Telouet also. For friendly service, good food and a cold beer head to **Bagdad Café** (0524 88 25 06, www.auberge-bagdad-cafe.com, menus from 80dh, doubles from 500dh).

OUARZAZATE

Pronounced 'wa-zah-zat', this doggedly unpicturesque town sits in prime position where the Dades and Drâa valleys fork off from the High Atlas route, and where the route de Taroudant winds in from the west.

It was founded by the French in 1928 as a regional capital and Foreign Legion outpost and still retains both a garrison and a drably functional air, with concrete buildings all along avenue Mohammed V, its one main street. Films are still occasionally made in the region and while crews will be put up in local guesthouses, cast will probably be in the only remaining five-star hotel. Ouarzazate's size and strategic position as gateway to the Sahara means that if travelling in the south you're almost bound to end up spending a night here sooner or later.

The mid 18th-century **Taourirt Kasbah** (8am-6pm daily, admission 20dh), at the eastern end of town, is Ouarzazate's one historical sight and the only thing remaining from before the Protectorate. During the 1930s, when the Glaoua were at their prime, this was one of the largest kasbahs in the area, housing lots of the clan's lesser-known members, plus hundreds of servants and slaves. These days much of it is ruined, although some has been restored under UNESCO auspices. The part that faces the main road has been maintained, and this is what gets shown to visitors – the principal courtyard, the former harem, and a few other rooms around a central airwell.

Some of the town's poorest inhabitants live in the ramshackle old quarter behind the kasbah – all there was of the town before the French built the rest – and here you can wander freely if you don't mind acquiring a small entourage of kids hassling for dirhams and would-be guides.

The **Ensemble Artisanal** is a cluster of stalls and shops opposite the kasbah entrance selling fixed-price arts and crafts. **Tifoultoute** (open 8am-7pm, admission 20dh; *photo p162*) is another Glaoui kasbah, outside town on the road to Marrakech, turning left at the El-Baraka Complex and petrol station. Only the rather unremarkable 19th-century section is accessible, while the rest is crumbling and used as a scenic backdrop for private events.

The other face of Ouarzazate is its connection to the film industry, which dates back to David Lean shooting some of *Lawrence of Arabia* around here. Bertolucci's *The Sheltering Sky*, Martin Scorsese's *Kundun*, Ridley Scott's *Gladiator* and *Kingdom of Heaven* and Oliver Stone's *Alexander* have been among the many blockbusters to make use of the area's good light, cheap labour and variety of mountain and desert locations.

Opposite the Taourirt kasbah is the **Museum of Cinema** (0524 89 03 46, open 8am-6pm daily, admission 30dh), which displays props and sets left over from various film productions shot here during the booming 1990s. The Roman jail, throne room and cloistered patio are all from films you've never heard of and there's also a collection of old movie cameras and period costumes. It's worth a visit on a hot day, if not just to get into the shade.

The **Atlas Corporation Studios** (0524 88 22 23, www.studiosatlas.com, open 8.15am-5.15pm daily, admission 50dh), seven kilometres (four miles) west of town, were the first Moroccan film studios and built in 1983. You can look at the Tibetan monastery built for *Kundun*, a fighter plane made for *Jewel of the Nile*, a fake medina alley and Egyptian temple sets from the *Asterix* movie. A little further out of town, the working **CLA Studios** (www.cla-studios.com), owned by Dino de Laurentis and Cinecittà, also offer guided visits for 40dh. The Jerusalem set for *Kingdom of Heaven* might be worth a look.

Getting there

See p159.

Where to stay

Ouarzazate has hotels for all budgets, with some large chain hotels and a smattering of character guesthouses. **Dar Daif** (three kilometres off the Zagora road, 0524 85 42 32, www.dardaif.ma, 1,200dh double incl dinner) is a rambling converted kasbah guesthouse overlooking a cemetery and palm groves outside town. There are 14 rooms adopting a 'typical Sahara' theme plus a hammam, library, Wi-Fi and a pool. Bring your own beer or wine. Nearby **Riad Dar Barbara** (0524 85 49 30, wwwriaddarbarbara.com, double 700dh with dinner, no credit cards) has huge rooms built in a kasbah style, with English-speaking staff and great food. The 234-room **Berbère Palace** (Quartier Mansour Eddahbi, 0524 88 31 05, www.hotel-berberepalace.com, from 2,500dh double, breakfast 150dh) is the only remaining five-star, with air-conditioned bungalows, a big pool, hammam, gym and tennis courts. Budget hotel **Les Jardins de Ouarzazate** (0524 85 42 00, www.lesjardinsdeouarzazate.com, double 500dh with dinner, no credit cards) is ideal for a short stay. It's simple and clean with pleasant gardens and a tented restaurant, but perhaps a little worn out. Ask for a new bungalow near the pool and away from noisy tour groups.

Tifoultoute. *See p161.*

Kasbah des Sables.

Where to eat & drink

Ouarzazate's restaurant scene is very sparse, but there are a few places worth tucking into. **Chez Dimitri** (22 avenue Mohammed V, 0524 88 73 46, mains 120dh, open daily) is a Ouarzazate institution, serving Greek, French and Moroccan dishes since 1928. **Accord Majeur** (opposite Berbere Palace, 0524 88 24 73, mains 100dh, open Mon-Sat) offers a bistro-style international and a Moroccan menu. **Douyria** (next to Kasbah Taourirt, 05 24 88 52 88, www.restaurant-ouarzazate.net, mains 80dh, open daily) has excellent modern Moroccan cuisine at fair prices. For a sumptuous dining experience book ahead for **Kasbah des Sables** (0524 88 54 28, www.lakasbahdessables.com, mains 120dh, open daily) on the road leading to Skoura. **Côté Sud** (0540 01 93 87, www.cotesud-maroc.com, mains 80dh, open daily, no credit cards) is a restaurant with an art gallery and cinema. It's just beyond Tifoultoute kasbah and specialises in Spanish cuisine as well as cookery classes.

The Dadès Valley & the Gorges

Stretching east from Ouarzazate, the Dadès Valley runs between the High Atlas to the north and the bare, jagged formations of the Jebel Sahro to the south. It's sometimes referred to as the Valley of the Kasbahs, which is appropriate – there are dozens of them. And almost every valley here is dubbed the Valley of Something Or Other.

The Dadès is also the most barren of the southern valleys, but the juxtaposition with such rugged surrounds just makes the oases seem all the more beautiful. North of the main road, from **Boumalne du Dadès** and **Tinerhir** respectively, are the **gorges** of **Dadès** and **Todra**, dramatic cuts into the Atlas that are well worth detouring for.

Skoura, at the westernmost end of the Dadès Valley, can be done in a day trip from Ouarzazate. The Dadès Gorge too. But trying to pack in the Todra Gorge as well is pushing it. There's decent accommodation along the route, and all this can be done with overnight stops on the way to the Tafilelt (*see p168*).

GETTING THERE

Infrequent buses run along the main road and grand taxis shuttle between the bigger towns. If you don't have your own transport and want to visit the gorges, you can commandeer taxis at Boumalne or Tinerhir, and hotels can also arrange transport. But this is an area where it really does make sense to have a 4x4 to explore a little of the Atlas beyond the various valleys or gorges, or to detour into the strange, sculpted landscapes of the Jebel Sahro.

SKOURA

About 40 kilometres (25 miles) east of Ouarzazate, **Skoura** is a big oasis but a small settlement. The main road bypasses what there is of the town centre – just one street with a few basic shops and cafés. Most of the population is scattered about the extensive palmeraie, which is beautiful, and sprinkled with kasbahs. If you want to explore some of these, hire a guide for the day (easily arranged through your hotel).

WHO ARE THE BERBERS?

The original inhabitants of North Africa.

The Berbers were resident from Egypt to the Atlantic for millennia before the Arabs began heading west from the Arabian peninsula in the seventh century. They were probably around as long ago as the Upper Paleolithic era; they were first mentioned in writing around 3000 BC, by the ancient Egyptians.

Invaders and traders came and went – Phoenicians, Romans, Vandals, Byzantines, Alans – some leaving their mark on the Berbers, but none managing to eradicate their languages and traditions altogether. The name 'Berber' was probably given to them by the Romans – it's the same word as 'Barbarian', originally a Greek term. The Berbers call themselves the Imazigen ('free men'; singular Amazigh).

Before the Arabs arrived, most Berbers were Christian. St Augustine was a Berber, as were several Roman emperors. The Arab newcomers weren't able to conquer the Berbers (they settled for living beside them), but they were able to convert them. By the eighth century most had become Muslim, though communities of Berber Jews survived in North Africa right up until the 1950s and 1960s, when most of them moved to Israel.

The Moors who conquered Iberia in 711 were mostly Berbers, as was their leader, Tariq ibn Ziyad, who gave his name to Gibraltar ('Jebel Tariq' – the mountain of Tariq). The dynasties who presided over Morocco's golden age were all Berber: the Almoravids, who founded Marrakech, and the Almohads and Merenids who succeeded them. It wasn't until the 16th century and the coming of the Saadians that Morocco was first ruled by Arabs.

Today there remain significant Berber populations in Algeria, Libya, Tunisia, Mauritania and Egypt, as well as emigrant communities in Belgium, France, the Netherlands and Israel. But the biggest Berber population of all is in Morocco, where they comprise anything between 30 and 40 per cent of the population.

Of course, in reality, it's all got mixed up. Arab intermarriage with Berbers down the centuries means that most Moroccans have at least some Berber ancestry. Berbers have survived more as a culture than a race, and their traditions are most strongly rooted in the regions too remote for anyone to conquer.

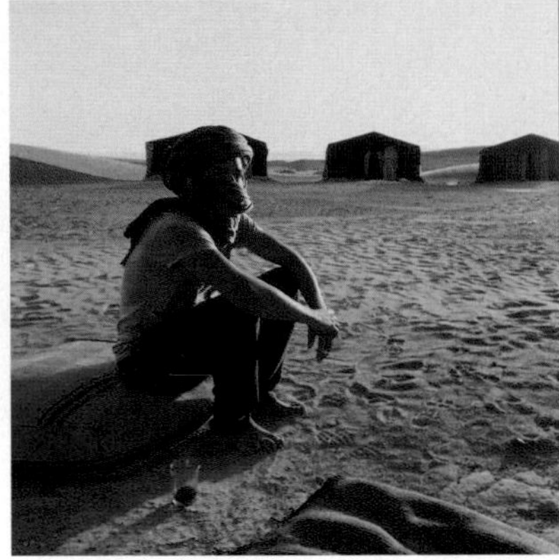

Though many have moved to the cities, the three main Berber groups in Morocco are based in the Rif mountains, the Middle Atlas, and the High Atlas and Sahara. And there's no one physical type. Riffian Berbers from the north are often pale-skinned with fair or reddish hair, high cheekbones and green eyes. Southern Berbers are usually dark-haired and brown-eyed, with skin shading from olive to black.

During the Protectorate, the French favoured the Berbers – the Glaoui, for example, who ran southern Morocco as colonial proxies, are a Berber tribe. But after independence, Berber traditions were ignored or suppressed in the interests of forging a Moroccan national identity. However, in recent decades Berber culture has been experiencing a revival. King Mohammed VI, whose mother is a Berber, appointed the Berber Driss Jettou as prime minister and founded a Royal Institute for Amazigh Culture. A written form of the Berber language, Tamazight, has been standardised using the ancient Tifinagh alphabet. Berber activists agitated for Tamazight to join Arabic as an official language, and in 2011 King Mohammed VI announced that this had become law. There are Amazigh associations, films, books, festivals, newspapers and websites. The Berbers are very much back.

One of the kasbahs, on the far side of the *oued* (wadi, or dry river bed) from the road, to the west of the centre behind Kasbah Ben Moro (*see below*), is the famous **Amridil** (open dawn-sunset daily, admission 20dh). Built by a Middle Atlas tribe in the 17th century, it's been restored recently with local labour and foreign donations. Resident guide Toufik will show you around the inner rooms and museum (call him on 0613 04 34 13; 50dh for a guided tour).

Another dramatic old kasbah, **Dar Aït Sidi El-Mati**, is ten minutes' walk to the south-west of Amridil. Look for the nearby **Musée Theatre Skoura** (0524 85 32 68, open daily, admission 20dh) on the main road, an enterprising project by former teacher, Abdelmoula El-Moudahab, whose family have lived in the area for centuries. The museum displays manuscripts, costumes, and household gadgets retrieved from his ancestral home. He also offers guided tours around the other kasbahs and marabouts (saints' tombs) in the oasis.

The road that heads north out of Skoura up to the village of **Toundoute** is a beautiful drive through what's known locally as the **Vallée des Amandes** (Valley of the Almonds). Beyond, there are also salt mines and the Berber village of **Tamsoulte** to explore on foot. On the road to Toundoute is **Skoura Equestrian Centre** (0661 43 21 63, www.sporttravel-maroc.com) for horse-riding lessons, half-day rides or multi-day treks between September to May.

Where to stay & eat

Kasbah Ait Ben Moro (0524 85 21 16, www.kasbahaitbenmoro.com, 770dh double) is on the Ouarzazate road, two kilometres short of Skoura proper. It was founded by a Spanish exile in the 18th century and is now a modern 16-room hotel owned by a Spanish expat from Cádiz. The rooms are cosy but dark – but that's a kasbah for you. There's also a small pool.

Deep in the palmeraie, the luxurious **Dar Ahlam** (0524 85 22 39, www.maisondes reves.com, from 5,390dh double) is the kasbah as designer labyrinth – the ground floor is a maze of corridors and salons. There are nine tasteful suites and three sumptuous garden villas, and every evening you are escorted from the enormous lounge to your elusive private dining table – somewhere different each evening, with different place settings and a different menu. The kitchen is excellent and you can add half-board for an extra 800dh per person. Also thrown in is a gorgeous hammam, professional masseur and swimming pool set in lush gardens.

Out on the far edge of the oasis, **Sawadi** (0524 85 23 41, www.sawadi.ma, from 750dh double) offers kasbah-styled eco-lodge accommodation. It's a great option for families with large suites for up to six people. There are four hectares of grounds and farm to explore, a swimming pool, library, table tennis and a climbing frame. With panoramic views over the oasis is **Chez Talout** (0524 85 26 66, www.talout.com, doubles 600dh, no credit cards). Rooms are cheerful, with carpets and colourful blankets, and there's a large pool. The English-speaking manager, Soufiane, is extremely helpful and can set up guided tours in the oasis or to Almond Valley.

Nestled within the palm groves is French-run boutique guesthouse **Les Jardins de Skoura** (0524 85 23 24, www.lesjardins deskoura.com, from 880dh double) with superb rooms, some with fireplaces and all kitted out in kilims, throws and pouffes. Shaded gardens and pool make this very popular. Book ahead.

EL-KELAA M'GOUNA

Fifty barren kilometres (30 miles) east of Skoura, the oasis resumes at **El-Kelaa**, which ribbons along the road. It's famous for its rose products. All over the country, women rub rosewater into their face and hands, and most of it comes from here. It seems the most Moroccan of things, yet it was French perfumiers who, in the early 20th century, realised that this area offered ideal growing conditions for the leafy *rosa centifolia*. You'd barely notice them among the palms when they're not blooming, but there are hundreds of thousands of rose bushes around here. The harvest is celebrated on the first weekend of May by a Rose Festival with dances, processions and lots of petal-throwing.

Essences are distilled at two factories and every other shop sells rose soap, rose skin cream, rose shampoo, rose shower gel and, of course, rosewater. It's not otherwise a very interesting place, though there's also a dagger-making co-operative.

You can drive north towards Tourbist through what's known, naturally, as the **Vallée des Roses**. From **Bouthrar** you can follow the road as far as the **Gorge M'Goun**. Alternatively, with 4x4 only, you can loop around to the east on piste, to join the tarmac road at **Ait Youl**, at the foot of the Dadès Gorge. The town of **Kelaa M'Gouna** has little to recommend by way of restaurants or guesthouses, but **Kasbah Itrane** (0524 83 71 03, www.kasbahitran.com, 450dh double, no credit cards), just over three kilometres north on the road to Tourbist, has plenty of traditional features in a converted kasbah with commanding views over the valley. Most rooms have private bathrooms. Service can be a little patchy.

DADÈS GORGE

Leaving El-Kelaa and continuing east, ribbon development continues for another 20 kilometres (12 miles) or so, with kasbahs left to crumble among new buildings made from concrete rather than pisé. There's not much of interest at the next major settlement, **Boumalne Dadès**, but it does mark the mouth of the **Dadès Gorge**.

The road into the gorge swoops and twists, climbing high up the steep valley sides through curvaceous formations of red rock and old kasbahs on rugged outcrops. The valley is at its most dramatic and gorge-like after the village of **Aït Oudinar**, about 27 kilometres (17 miles) along, where it turns into a deep, reddish canyon – though only for a couple of hundred metres.

It's a good road up to this point, but from here it gets more difficult. You'll need a 4x4 to proceed beyond **Msemrir**, but could then take the spectacular piste that runs east over the mountains to **Aït Hani**, whence you can come back down through **Todra**. This is also excellent hiking territory, and any hotel can arrange guides and excursions.

Back on the main Dadès Valley road, just east of Boumalne Dadès, is the turning for the **Vallée des Oiseaux** (Valley of the Birds), signposted to Iknioiun. Here, amateur ornithologists can spot Houbara bustards, Egyptian vultures, eagle owls and bar-tailed desert larks.

Where to stay & eat

Clambering up the steep valley side for 26 kilometres (16 miles) from Boumalne Dadès and shortly before the canyon, **Chez Pierre** (0524 83 02 67, www.chezpierre.org, 600dh double, no credit cards) is the most sophisticated option for either sleeping or eating. It has nine spacious rooms with tadelakt bathrooms, a small pool and a licensed restaurant serving excellent food that includes vegetarian options. Moroccan brothers Lahcen and Ismail took over in 2011 from 'Pierre' and maintain impeccable standards. Dinner is the best in the region. A little further south of the canyon is **Hotel Auberge le Panorama** (Ait Ibrahim, 10km from Boumalne, 0524 83 15 55, www.aubergepanorama.com, 500dh with dinner, no credit cards). No frills, simple rooms and stunning terrace views to the 'monkeys fingers' rock formations.

Just on the other (north) side of the canyon, 34 kilometres (21 miles) up the Dadès Valley road is the **Berbére de la Montagne** (0524 83 02 28, 560dh double incl dinner, no credit cards), which has seven whitewashed rooms with showers and three without. All are well furnished and the riverside location is sublime.

For a touch of luxury and an ideal base from which to explore on foot, bike or in 4x4 is **La Perle du Dadès** (0524 85 05 48, www.perledudades.com, from 825dh double, no credit cards). The restored kasbah sits on the southern side of the Dadès river, about seven kilometres before Boumalne Dadès if travelling from El-Kelaa M'Gouna. There's a large garden, pool, cinema, library and outdoor games, and the spaces are decorated with African art, rugs and masks collected by the owners. In addition there are underground 'troglodyte' rooms and a Mongolian yurt if you've grown tired of kasbahs. Bikes are available for hire.

TINERHIR

There's another desolate stretch beyond Boumalne, but after about 50 kilometres (30 miles) the road arrives in the town of **Tinerhir**, which has been recently upgraded to provincial capital and, in mid 2014, was getting a makeover of widened boulevards, roundabouts and fountains. The new part of it ribbons east and west along the road; the old part stretches out in huge kasbah-dotted palmeraies to the north and south. There's a pocket-sized medina where you can find rug-weavers from the Aït Atta tribe at work on their looms. The carpets these women make are brilliantly coloured and of high quality, but you'll need an interpreter to negotiate as few speak anything but Berber. The small mellah (Jewish quarter) on the far side of the medina, closed off behind a big wooden door, is these days occupied by about 20 Berber families.

The modern part of town has all mod cons – post office, banks, cybercafés, and a small supermarket. Opposite Kasbah Lamrani is where you'll find Tinerhir's Monday souk.

Where to stay & eat

Kasbah Lamrani (0524 83 50 17, www.kasbahlamrani.com, 840dh double with dinner) has 22 rooms kitted out with air-conditioning, heating, telephones, fridges, TVs and nice bathrooms. There's also a pool and three restaurants. It's popular with tour groups travelling the southern valleys route from Merzouga, but slightly charmless and not a place to spend more than one night. Midway between the Dadès and Todra gorges, on the main route is the five-roomed **Riad Timadrouine** (0615 93 39 80, www.riadtimadrouine.com, 715dh double, no credit cards), with a small pool, library, a sauna and possibly the only working 1900s pianola in all Morocco.

Tinerhir.

TODRA GORGE

The road up to **Todra** winds north around the edge of the lush palmeraie of **Tinerhir**. Once in the valley, the road runs along the bottom, never climbing the sides as the road does in Dadès. After about ten kilometres (six miles) of palmeraie and campsites, the road fords the river. It's worth getting out and walking to enjoy the canyon-like stretch if you are not continuing further – it's not as narrow as at Dadès but it's much grander and more spectacular. Here the cliffs rise to about 300 metres, and provide a habitat for assorted birdlife, including Bonelli's eagles. Todra is a popular destination for rock-climbing in the high limestone walls of the gorge. You need to bring your own gear or alternatively **Climb Morocco** (*see p150*) can set you up with instruction and equipment. By car it is possible to head on up beyond the gorge and follow the tarmac road, past **Tamtattouchte**, as far as Imilchil, although this is not recommended in winter. If you have a 4x4 then you can take the mountainous piste east from Aït Hani to Msemrir, and then enter the Dadès Gorge from the north.

Going back down the road towards Tinerhir, notice the **Source des Poissons Sacrés**, a spring-fed pool full of 'sacred' fish, these days on the grounds of a rather tawdry campsite where you can pull in to admire the fish. According to local folklore, bathing in here on three successive Friday afternoons will help women to conceive.

Where to stay

This enclosed section of the gorge is an atmospheric place to stay the night, and feels remote despite being just 15 kilometres (nine miles) north of busy Tinerhir. Most of the hotels here are basic, but **Dar Ayour** (0524 89 52 71, www.darayour.com, 660dh double with dinner, no credit cards), just before the narrowest part of the gorge, is a small guesthouse a few notches above the rest. Its five storeys tower over the river below and quaint rooms have wrought iron bedsteads, Berber carpets and jaw-dropping views. There are two budget hotels, **Yasmina** (0524 89 52 71, 400dh double with dinner, no credit cards) and **Les Roches** (0524 89 52 71, 400dh double with dinner, no credit cards), at the bottom of the cliffs on the other side of the river – each of them unremarkable and worn out. The **Hotel Kasbah Amazir** (10km along the route de Todra, 0524 89 51 09, 650dh double with dinner, no credit cards) is an alternative. It has functional, clean accommodation with the bonus of Wi-Fi, great service and an outdoor swimming pool.

TINEJDAD

Beyond Tinerhir the road continues in the direction of **Er Rachidia**. After about 50 kilometres (30 miles), just short of Tinejdad, there's an eccentric roadside attraction on the left-hand side. The **Sources de Lalla Mimouna** (8am-sunset daily, admission 50dh) is a walled garden housing an assortment of small 'museums' (of agriculture, manuscripts and horses), each built around a gurgling spring. It's the pet project of Zaïd Abboa, who also owns the Galerie d'Art (really more of a museum and antique shop) in downtown Tinejdad. It's on the main road, which is otherwise full of shops selling chickens. There are also some antiques and paintings on sale at the Sources. The springs themselves are disappointingly devoid of special significance.

On the outskirts of Tinejdad, a right turn (if coming from Tinerhir) at the sign for the Musée des Oasis leads, after a few twists and turns, to the beautiful 18th-century **Ksar El-Khorbat**. Part of this fortified village has been transformed into a fascinating museum of oasis life (admission 20dh). It's the best exhibit this side of the Atlas: well organised with informative captions in five languages, supplied by Spanish writer Roger Mimó.

Just after Tinejdad there's a turn-off to Erfoud and the Tafilelt (*see below*), which takes you through towns inhabited by members of the once widely feared Aït Atta tribe.

Where to stay & eat

To go with the museum, Mimó and his Moroccan partners have opened a restaurant and converted some village houses into a warren-like eco-hotel, **El Khorbat** (0535 88 03 55, www.elkhorbat.com, 550dh double, no credit cards). The ten rooms, all with en suite bathrooms, are big and dark and cool – great in the dizzying heat of summer. There is also a small, rather murky, pool in the heart of the old kasbah and the whole place lives the sustainable tourism ideal. The hotel contributes a percentage of all its trade to provision of local schooling and improving facilities for the local community. The restaurant (menus 80dh-150dh) serves both Spanish and Moroccan dishes in a shaded terrace under palm trees and if you're ever going to try camel tagine, this is probably the place to do it.

The Tafilelt, Merzouga & beyond

Historically, the Tafilelt Oasis was the most important area south of the Atlas. Taroudant, Telouet and the Drâa Valley might all have had their moments, but it was the Talifelt that in 1893 sent Moulay Hassan and his tax-collecting expedition scurrying back over the Atlas with its tail between its legs, thus inadvertently hastening the end of independent Morocco and giving the Glaoui a leg-up to power. And it was from here that the Alaouites, three centuries ago, sallied forth to become the dynasty that still rules Morocco today.

Tahiri Museum.

You wouldn't guess any of this from a quick look at the area's two major settlements today, bureaucratic **Erfoud** and impoverished **Rissani**. The area long ago stopped being on the way to somewhere and started being the end of the line. (The Algerian border isn't far away to either south or east.) But the Tafilelt does retain a kind of brooding quality, thanks to its decaying kasbahs, ancient palm groves and vague royal connections. This last has meant that traditionally it was a place to dispatch the more troublesome members of the ruling family to, out of sight and far from the centre of power.

Most travellers who get this far carry straight on through to **Merzouga** and the dunes of **Erg Chebbi**, which are one of the great sights of Morocco. This should be your plan too. But Rissani is worth spending some time in, either coming or going, and there is life to the south of Merzouga too.

GETTING THERE

You can get here by road from the Dadès Valley via the turn-off at Tinejdad (*see p167*). Buses run from Tinehrir to Tinejdad, and from Tinejdad to Erfoud, but you will not be able to do much around here without your own transport. Driving to or from the Drâa Valley there's a road that runs east–west through the empty quarter south of the Jebel Sarho, connecting with the Drâa Valley between Agdz and Zagora.

ERFOUD

Erfoud is a mostly French-built administrative town that has the most mod cons within striking distance of the photogenic Merzouga dunes. It's a desultory sort of place – a frontier town with a gridlike street pattern and ideas above its station. But it's where you'll find essential facilities such as banks, a supermarket, a hospital and a pharmacy. There's a Sunday souk and an October date festival.

The one unique local item is a kind of fossil-rich black marble. This is polished up and used for tabletops and bar counters. By another process, the stone is sculpted to bring the fossils into relief on everything from ashtrays to washbasins. The results are mostly quite kitsch, as can be seen at **Manar Marbre** (0535 57 81 26, www.manarmarble.com, open daily) a few hundred metres up the Tinehrir road. On the road between Erfoud and Rissani, a far more interesting collection of fossils and minerals is on display at **Tahiri Museum** (0535 57 68 74, www.tahirimuseum.com, open 8am-6pm daily). You can't miss it – there's a gigantic brontosaurus skeleton parked outside.

Erfoud has a few hotels and the best is probably the former Hotel Salam, now **Hotel Erfoud le Riad** (0535 57 66 65, www.mahdsalam.com, double 800dh), which has a pool, gardens, bar and sauna and is just about the first thing you'll see arriving from the Dadès as it sits on the Erfoud-Tinejdad junction. Six kilometres to the north of Erfoud, passing the Royal Palace, is the Spanish-owned **Kasbah Xaluca** (0535 57 84 50, www.xaluca.com, 1,080dh double). Rooms have air-conditioning and bathrooms with sculpted fossil fittings. Apart from the poolside bar and buffet restaurant open to non-guests, there's every kind of excursion, trek, rental, hike, adventure and experience on offer. For any overspill, **Kasbah Hotel Chergui** (0535 57 85 04, www.hotelchergui.com, 1,400dh double with dinner), is a monster of a place with a pool shaped like the African continent. Rooms are enormous and well equipped, but the gaudy interiors and tacky paintings makes it look cheaper than it is. Sadly, Erfoud lacks any charming mid-price guesthouses.

RISSANI

Around 20 kilometres (12 miles) south of Erfoud, **Rissani** is an untidy village with a small modern central core, and *ksour* (villages) and kasbahs scattered throughout its extensive palmeraie. This is the home town of the Alaouite dynasty, which started feeling expansive in the early 17th century and had taken power by 1664.

Before that it was the site of Sijilmassa, founded in the mid eighth century by Berber heretics. At the heart of such a fertile oasis, and at the nexus of trade routes connecting West Africa to Morocco and Europe – and Morocco to the rest of North Africa and the Middle East – Sijilmassa quickly became a great trading centre and dominated the South for five centuries. Huge caravans would set out from here heading first for the Saharan salt mines in what today is Mali, then to the Niger region, where salt was traded for gold, then back across the Sahara, laden with gold, ebony,

TELL IT TO THE TOURISTS

In any tourist economy, locals have their little jokes for the visitor. They're the common currency of cross-cultural exchange, designed to throw light upon their traditions, foster international understanding, affirm shared humanity through the precious gift of laughter – and sell you some useless damn thing you don't need. The gag in southern Morocco is to translate the function of everyday items into terms the foreigner will understand. Once you've wandered around a few souks and kasbahs, you'll have heard these many times, but no harm in being ahead of the game.

Berber massage Sex.

Berber Mercedes A donkey. *See also* Berber taxi.

Berber pharmacy A herbalist's shop; the place to buy Berber viagra.

Berber taxi A donkey. *See also* Berber Mercedes.

Berber telephone The narrow airwell that's an architectural feature in Berber kasbahs. Apart from admitting light and air to lower levels, these allow communication between different floors.

Berber viagra Ginseng. *See also* Berber pharmacy.

Berber whisky Mint tea. Sometimes used with scarcely a hint of irony, as Moroccans credit their national hot beverage with powers that, to the foreigner, it simply does not seem to possess. 'I've drunk too much Berber whisky,' you may hear someone moan.

IN THE KNOW
WHATEVER HAPPENED TO SIJILMASSA?

Reasons for the demise of the wealthy medieval trading city of Sijilmassa (*see below*) are lost in the sands. Andalusian traveller and diplomat Leo Africanus was the first to record the destroyed condition of the once-glorious city in the early 16th century. He reported that residents had killed an evil ruler and then dispersed to the surrounding area. Others cited the more prosaic cause of a lack of resources, especially after the Portuguese opened maritime routes to sub-Saharan Africa. Whatever the reason, the city was rebuilt in the 18th century, but destroyed again by the warlike Aït Atta clan in 1818.

ostrich feathers and slaves. Meanwhile, coins from Sijilmassa have been found as far away as Akabar in Jordan.

Sijilmassa long ago sank back into the sands (*see above* **In the Know**). Such ruins as there are can be found on the north side of Rissani, near the outlying hamlet of **El-Mansouria**, where a gate known locally as the Bab Errih probably dates from the Merenid period. The other faint traces of Sijilmassa are really only of academic interest. A few archaeological finds are on display at the small museum of the **Centre d'Étude et de Recherches Alaouite** (open 8.30am-6.30pm Mon-Fri) on the north side of Rissani's main square – basically a handful of dusty pots. It also hosts temporary exhibitions and seminars.

The ancestors of the current ruling Alaouite dynasty in Morocco settled in the region in the 13th century. Off the road running towards Merzouga, just after the village peters out into the desert, there are signposts directing you to the **Mausoleum of Moulay Ali Cherif**, founder of the dynasty, who was buried here in 1640. It's a modern building, an older one having been destroyed by flash flooding in the mid 1950s, and entrance is forbidden to non-Muslims.

Beyond the mausoleum is a signposted turn on to the Circuit Touristique, a 21-kilometre (13 mile) loop around the *ksour* and kasbahs of the palmeraie. The first point of interest is the 19th-century **Ksar Akbar**, once used to house disgraced members of the Alaouite family. About two kilometres (one mile) further on is the grand **Ksar Ouled Abdelhalim**, built for Moulay Hassan's brother around the turn of the 20th century and touted as the 'Alhambra of the Tafilelt'. Its remains include imposing towers, cloistered courtyards and ornate gateways that give a flavour of former grandeur. The whole circuit takes in a number of other kasbahs and *ksours* – some in an advanced state of erosion, others still housing a substantial part of Rissani's population.

If you carry along the Merzouga road past the Mausoleum turn-off and take the next left, the first big, intact structure on the right is the 19th-century **Ksar El-Fida**. It was formerly an Alouite residence, then a short-lived museum, but it now sits vacant since exhibits were sent to other collections. The architecture of the *ksar* still makes it worth stopping for a look inside.

Back downtown, Rissani has a lively souk on Sunday, Tuesday and Thursday, drawing people from all over the area to buy and sell everything from dates to doorknobs. There's also an animal market behind it, with donkeys, sheep and camels for sale. Souk days are good for people-watching and there are some strategically placed cafés with terraces. We wouldn't recommend staying in Rissani, but if you do, the **Kasbah Ennasra** (0535 77 44 03, www.kasbahennasra.net, 700dh double) is certainly the best place. Constructed in traditional materials of mud and straw – pisé – all rooms have en-suite bathrooms and suites have romantic four-poster beds. You can also eat here on the poolside terrace even if you're not staying the night.

MERZOUGA & ERG CHEBBI

There's good paved road from Rissani all the way to Merzouga village, the Erg Chebbi dunesline, and beyond to Taouz near the Algerian border.

There's nothing much at **Merzouga** itself but squat, flat-roofed houses, a few general stores and some extremely basic café-hotels. The real attraction here are the dunes looming over to the east of the road and to the north of the village. About 27 kilometres (17 miles) from north to south and eight kilometres (five miles) from east to west, **Erg Chebbi** is a huge, shifting expanse of pink sand that looks exactly how the desert always looks in the movies – probably because many of them were shot right here. But the celluloid image doesn't quite prepare you for the precise beauty of the sand, its contours and peaks picked out by shadow, its colours shifting from pink to gold against a backdrop of clear blue sky and particularly vivid at either dawn or sunset.

But it's not the world's quietest piece of desert. This area has long been a big tourist attraction. Around two dozen hotels nudge up to the western edge of the sands, and in the late afternoon there are both tourists and locals running around on quads and motorbikes, as well as camel-trekking trains setting off to overnight at the small oasis that lies out of sight among the dunes. *See p173* **Hump-backed Holidays**.

Camels aren't the only wildlife here. Birders should look out for Egyptian nightjars, fulvous chatterers and blue-cheeked bee-eaters. Best of all, however, is when there's been enough rainfall for a shallow seasonal lake to appear to the north-west of the village, usually in late spring, which sometimes attracts large flocks of pink flamingos – a particularly exotic sight out here in the arid wilderness.

Where to stay & eat

There are hotels dotted all along the western fringes of the dunes, and getting to the more northerly of these involves a rattle across bumpy piste from the road between Rissani and Merzouga. Individual establishments are well signposted.

All the hotels sell half-board, which makes sense around here as there aren't any cafés or restaurants. The **Kasbah Hotel Tombouctou** (0535 57 84 50, www.xaluca.com, double 1,400dh with dinner) fulfills an extravagant Arabian nights fantasy with luxury trimmings at the dunesline. It's part of a Spanish chain that also owns hotels in Erfoud and Dadès. This one has a pool, bar and 72 brightly coloured tadelakt rooms in faux-kasbah style. It backs directly on to the dunes, and you can also take a camel trek to the hotel's luxury bivouac and spend the night there for 1,800dh per person, with dinner included.

If you're looking for something cheaper, then the **Auberge Café du Sud** (0661 60 28 85, www.aubergedusud.com, 800dh double incl dinner, no credit cards) is a good bet. The hotel has recently been entirely renovated, a swimming pool added and all rooms upgraded with new decor and air-conditioning. The accommodation is comfortable and clean, with typical Sahara themes and Berber motifs carved into the walls. You can also sleep in a nearby tent for 250dh per person with dinner and use the bathroom facilities of the auberge. Stylish eco-lodge **Ksar Sania** (0535 57 74 14, www.ksarsaniahotelmerzouga.com, double 600dh, no credit cards) has quirky hexagonal mud-and-straw huts far away from tourists. There's a pool, garden and tasteful music too.

SOUTH OF MERZOUGA

The road from Rissani continues all the way to Taouz. About eight kilometres (five miles) south of Merzouga is a gnawa village called

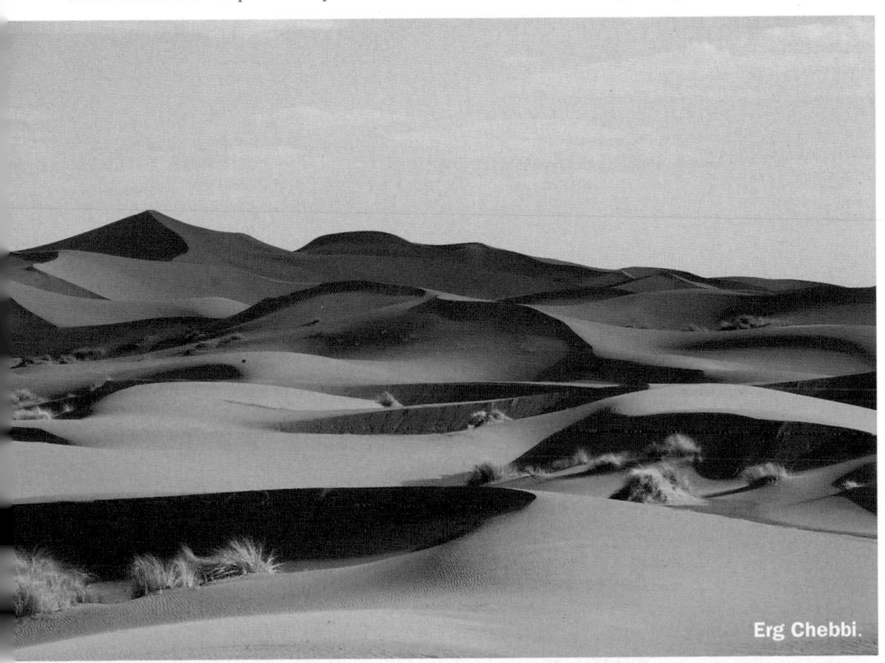
Erg Chebbi.

Khamlia, populated by the Berber-speaking descendants of black African slaves (*see p123*). The sun-blasted scattering of poor, flat-roofed pisé houses feels like it could have been lifted whole from the other side of the Sahara. Music is one of the locals' main pursuits and there are several family bands here. You can often find them playing at the village's small cultural centre or at the home of **Zaid Oujeaa** (0667 51 07 14) on Khamlia's south-east side. Go in, say hello, and settle on cushions in the room to the left. Within minutes musicians in white robes will appear to perform – drummers, castanet players and a guy on a gimbri. It's excellent entertainment. Tip them 100dh or buy their CD.

Sixteen kilometres (ten miles) further on, past salt flats and dry lake beds, is the village of **Taouz**. It's little more than a military outpost by the Algerian border, but if you like being stared at then this is the place. A piste from Taouz interconnects this region of the Sahara with Tagounite at the foot of the Drâa Valley, near M'Hamid. It's a tough motoring challenge for at least eight hours non-stop and there are no services or cafés en route. It should only be tackled in a sturdy 4x4, with a local driver who knows both the terrain and how to handle the unpredictable Sahara sandstorms.

The Drâa Valley

The River Drâa begins where the Oued Dadès, Oued Mellah and other streams come together at Ouarzazate, and theoretically it runs all the way to the Atlantic Ocean, some 750 kilometres (465 miles) distant. But the last time it actually managed that feat was in 1989. More usually, it vanishes into the sand near **M'Hamid**, the town that marks the end of the Drâa Valley route, some ten kilometres (six miles) short of the Algerian border.

Beyond M'Hamid, all travel is by camel or 4x4. But before that, the **Drâa Valley** between **Agdz** and **Zagora** is a truly beautiful drive past palm groves, kasbahs and geology in the raw.

GETTING THERE

Buses run south from Ouarzazate with reasonable frequency as far as Zagora, but from there onwards services are spotty. Only CTM runs a once-daily bus as far as M'Hamid. Grand taxis run between the bigger villages and are the best way of getting around, but any kind of traffic gets sparse towards M'Hamid. It's ideal off-road biking country and Maroc Nature (www.bike-morocco.com) run a Southern Morocco tour from Marrakech to Zagora.

IN THE KNOW MARABOUTS

Marabouts are local saints and holy men. Their tombs, also referred to as marabouts, are dotted around rural areas of Morocco and serve as places of reflection.

THE VALLEY

The arid, stony plains south of Ouarzazate are breathtakingly bleak – flatlands of brown rubble as far as the eye can see. The road does get quite dramatic, though, as it winds up through the layered rock formations of the **Jebel Sarho** to the 1,600-metre (5,250-foot) **Tizi-n-Tinififft pass**.

On the other side of the pass, **Agdz** is a small market town with a few carpet shops and a Thursday souk. The boutique hotel **Kasbah Azul** (0524 84 39 31, www.kasbahazul.com, 880dh double) in the Agdz palm groves is idyllic – great food, swimming pool, beautifully designed rooms and lush gardens.

The kasbah at **Tamnougalte** is the oldest in the Drâa Valley and well worth stopping for a guided visit. The road to it is six kilometres (four miles) past Agdz, and the kasbah is down a further three kilometres of piste. The more palatial **Glaoui Kasbah Timidarte** (0668 68 00 47, www.kasbahtimidarte.com, 330dh double) is eight kilometres (five miles) further south and has been restored and opened as a guesthouse.

Agdz is overlooked by the 1,500-metre (4,921-foot) **Jebel Kissane**, which looks like a single mountain until you draw abreast and realise it's actually one end of a long, brooding range. This is also where the Drâa Valley oasis begins. The next 100 kilometres (62 miles) is a long, verdant strip cut into the desert. Every last scrap of fertile land is planted to grow olives, lemons, oranges, almonds, cereals and, most of all, dates, which are the valley's principal crop. Dates like lots of water and are sweetest and plumpest where it is hottest. A Moroccan saying has it that date palms have 'their heads in fire and their feet in water'. Dense with such trees, the Drâa Valley produces some of the finest dates in North Africa. Local kids stand by the road trying to sell boxes of them to passing motorists.

On the other side, where nothing will grow, there are dozens of red-ochre *ksour* – fortified Berber villages. The last stretch runs through the **Jebel Azlag** gorge before emerging on to the palm-filled plain that is the **Zagora oasis**.

About eight kilometres north of Zagora is the fortified village of **Tissergate** and here can be found the **Museum of Drâa Valley Arts and Traditions** (0661 34 83 88, open daily,

HUMP-BACKED HOLIDAYS

Travel on the 'ship of the desert'.

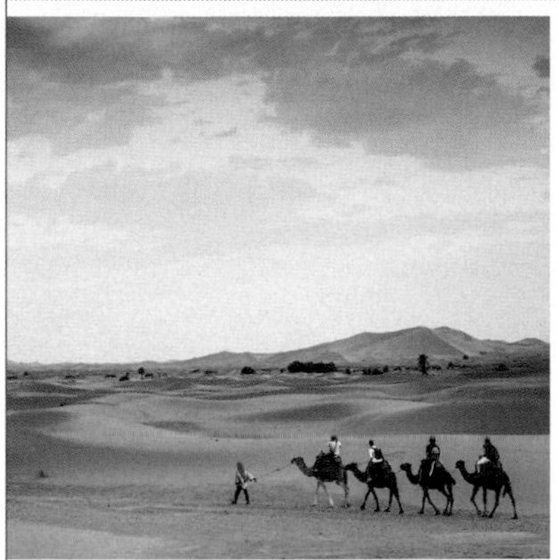

Here's a challenge. In the region of Erg Chebbi, or on the lower reaches of the Drâa Valley road, see if you can find anyone at all who *can't* help to arrange a camel trek. It sometimes seems as if everybody is touting some kind of hump-backed experience. The camel-trek business has been booming to the point where extra camels were brought in from Mali.

Camels aren't native to the region; they were introduced from Asia around 2,000 years ago. The 'ship of the desert' is a remarkable beast. Camels can last up to seven days with little or no food or water and, when they do drink, slurp up 20 gallons (91 litres) in ten minutes. They can carry huge loads, their wool is used to make tents, and their dung can be used as fuel for fires even without being dried.

It was these special talents that made trans-Saharan trade routes possible. That trade is now long gone. You do sometimes see small camel trains moving stuff around within the bigger oases, and there are still some genuine nomads knocking about between the smaller ones, but the only volume item camels carry into the desert these days is tourists.

And why not? You didn't come this far just to sit in a hotel. And while oases are cool, a taste of the desert's shattering stillness is what's needed to complete the experience. And on board a camel is a good way to find it.

They're easy enough to ride. It's a small surprise when you first clamber aboard and the beast stands up, rocking you forward and back as it hoists you disconcertingly high. But after that it's steady going, if a little jolting on a downhill stretch.

Camel treks can involve anything from a sandy sleepover to a fearsome 14-day lurch between Merzouga and M'hamid. Most hotels have their own permanent encampments – bivouacs – out in the dunes, and a night in one of these offers the quickest desert fix. You'll typically find a horseshoe arrangement of semi-permanent structures – often mud-sided with a woven camel-wool canopy and with carpets spread out to cover the sand. While you watch a desert sunset, your guides will be preparing tagines. After eating, just gaze into the clearest night sky you've ever seen.

Camel treks cost around 400dh per person per day with guide. Don't think of going on one between June and September, when the heat is too intense. The trek organisers below have good reputations and speak English. They also do 4x4 excursions at around 1,200dh per day. Standard desert camps cost from 300dh per person with dinner to 2,500dh per person for the ultra-deluxe camps, where clients often arrive by helicopter.

Adventures With Ali
Nomad Palace, Merzouga (0661 56 36 11, www.adventureswithali.com). **No credit cards.**
Ali Mouni can sort everything from a three-hour ride and a night at an oasis in the Erg Chebbi dunes, to tailor-made treks accommodating specialist interests. His camp is about an hour and a half by camel from the auberge Nomad Palace and has solar power.

Zbar Travel
Next to Hotel El-Ghizlane, M'Hamid (0668 51 72 80, www.zbartravel.com).
No credit cards.
Ahmed Hajja runs a very comfortable bivouac in Erg Chegaga's remote dunes and also arranges camel treks in nearer M'Hamid. Four-day treks to the 'Screaming Dunes', desert 4x4 safaris and sand-boarding are its fortes, as well as all-inclusive tours from Marrakech.

Azalai Desert Lodge.

admission 20dh). Park near the museum, follow the signs and head into the narrow covered streets of the old *ksar* to locate the entrance. It's one of the few collections where artefacts are labelled in English, and a guidebook explaining the history of the five regional tribes is also available. It's well worth stopping here.

ZAGORA

Zagora is a colonial creation, built by the French as a garrison and administrative centre. But the oasis has been inhabited for millennia. There's an 11th-century **Almoravid fortress**, built to guard the Sahara trade route, on top of **Jebel Zagora** at the end of town. And the Saadians would set out from around here at the beginning of the 16th century to conquer first Taroudant, then the rest of Morocco.

This trading history is acknowledged in the town's famous sign that shows a camel train and the legend 'Timbuktu, 52 days'. It used to stand outside the Préfecture, facing traffic as it left Zagora heading south. But a few years ago the original was replaced and moved over the road to an obscure position. Pretty much anything you might want to find is along the main **boulevard Mohammed V**: post office, banks, cafés, petrol stations, pharmacies and army barracks. There's a large souk on Wednesdays and Sundays, at which the biggest section is given over to dates, compressed and packed into plastic sacks.

There's not much else going on in Zagora. Over the river, the adjacent hamlet of **Amazrou** is more interesting. The palmeraie is wonderfully dense and lush, and crossed by paths that afford a good stroll. The nearby **Kasbah des Juifs** was, as its name suggests, built and formerly inhabited by Jews. They all left in the 1960s and local Berbers now make silver jewellery by old Jewish methods, using clay moulds. You can visit them at work making fibulas, brooches worn by Berber women (one below the right shoulder if yet to be married, one below each shoulder if married or divorced). Any local will guide you round the kasbah, which has underground passageways that are still partially inhabited.

The existing desert piste between Zagora and Foum Zguid is currently undergoing an upgrade to tarmac the minor road. When it's completed, it will open up the whole of the southern Sahara regions to new tourist routes, bypassing Tazenakht and skirting south of the Anti-Atlas mountains.

Where to stay & eat

La Fibule du Drâa (0524 84 73 18, www.casbah-fibule.ma, doubles 675dh) is a small and budget-friendly complex built around a pool on the edge of the Amazrou palmeraie. It has basic but clean rooms, a restaurant and a bar. Nearby, among the palms (take the path along the irrigation canal), is the **Riad Lamane** (0524 84 83 88, www.riadlamane.com, doubles 1,200dh incl dinner). The boutique hotel has seven rooms, five small bungalows and seven stunning tented rooms, each with a huge bed and tadelakt bathrooms. There's an indoor restaurant or you can eat in the garden under the pretty canopy by the small swimming pool. Nestled in the oasis, near to the Tissergate museum (8km north of Zagora), is **Azalai Desert Lodge** (0661 16 43 94, www.azalaidesertlodge.com, doubles 1,450dh with dinner). It's a boutique retreat par excellence with individually decorated rooms, vintage oddments and leather sofas, conjuring up a bygone era. A cosy winter lounge with fireplace, a library, gardens and a pool complete the picture. They also run a luxury safari-style desert camp in Erg Chegaga.

TAMEGROUTE & TINFOU

Around 18 kilometres (11 miles) south of Zagora, the town of **Tamegroute** has long been an important religious centre. Its green-roofed *zaouia* (shrine) was founded in the 17th century and is headquarters of the Naciri Islamic brotherhood, whose leaders, known as 'peacemakers of the desert' have traditionally been called upon to settle disputes between tribes or rival traders.

There's a *medersa* (Qur'anic school) along with the tomb of the Brotherhood's founder, a place of pilgrimage, but these are off-limits to non-Muslims. The main thing to see is the wonderful **library** (8am-3pm, 20dh donation), up a side street on the left of the main road. It was once much larger but 4,000 volumes remain, carefully stored in glass-fronted cases, including an 11th-century gazelle-skin Qur'an as well as old books from as far afield as Egypt and Mali.

Back by the minaret, there's also a cloistered courtyard that acts as a sanctuary for the infirm or mentally ill. People huddle in blankets, waiting for miracles or donations, or just for the next square meal. Around the corner on the left as you head south is a clutch of pottery shops selling cups, plates and tagines in the distinctive green glaze native to Tamegroute.

About five kilometres (three miles) south of Tamegroute, at a place called **Tinfou**, is an isolated patch of sand dunes. It's only the size of a few football pitches and you'll be sharing this Saharan experience with any number of tour groups who haven't time to go all the way down to M'Hamid (*see below*) or across to Merzouga (*see p170*).

M'HAMID

Beyond Tamegroute the road narrows and runs through mostly arid landscape for the next 70 kilometres (42 miles), crossing the barren **Jebel Bani** before coming back into oasis country at **Tagounite**. Before M'Hamid it's worth stopping off to see the small, private museum (open 6am-8pm, admission 20dh) in **Ouled Driss**. Follow the 'Musée' sign from the main road. It's a beautiful 17th-century Berber house, once owned by the village chief, containing an exhibition of costumes, jewellery and tools.

M'Hamid is a tiny town that really does feel like the end of the line, fighting a losing battle against the sand. The locals, a mix of Berber and Sahrawi, will stare like they've never seen a tourist before – although the entire town seems to be involved in the camel-trekking business (*see p173* **Hump-backed Holidays**). You'll be beating away touts from the various agencies as soon as you step out of the car and it's advisable to book a trek in advance of arriving.

If you're here in March or November, it's worth checking out one of the music festivals (*see p121*): the International Nomads Festival in March or the Taragalte Festival in November. A new generation of Saharwis are striving to bring their nomadic culture and traditions into the spotlight and attract tourism. Events are staged in the town and out in the nearby dunes.

If you're not heading straight off to the dunes of **Erg Chegaga**, there isn't much to do except sit in a scruffy café and wonder how the locals survive. There's a Monday souk, and quad-biking can be arranged from some of the hotels in Ouled Driss. A new '*piste touristique*' has also been carved out, leading through the picturesque palmeraie of 'old M'Hamid' via several kasbahs and mud-built villages. The 18th-century 'Jewish' kasbah is still inhabited by the descendants of African slaves who built it. The Algerian border isn't far away; in the 1970s some of the kasbahs were destroyed by Polisario guerillas.

Where to stay & eat

Accommodation and dining in the town are limited. It's best to opt for the guesthouses and hotels scattered along the edge of the palm groves at Ouled Driss, five kilometres before M'Hamid centre. **Chez le Pacha** (0524 84 82 07, www.chezlepacha.com, doubles 900dh with dinner) is a popular spot with poolside bar, terraces, and tastefully decorated rooms all at ground level. The restaurant is open to all. Since early 2014, Chez le Pacha has also run a boutique hotel, **Dar Azawad** (0524 84 87 30, www.darazawad.com, doubles 1,000dh with dinner) across the road. The hotel has had a few ups and downs recently and only time will tell if the new management can live up to the old owner's reputation for first-rate service and fine dining. **Jnan Lilou** (0671 51 74 77, www.jnanlilou.com, double 1,450dh with dinner) is French-run and owner-managed. It's more expensive and has just four cute one- or two-roomed bungalows set in private gardens with a pool. Cuisine is a mix of Moroccan and French.

In the town itself, the budget **Dar M'Hamid** guesthouse (main street, 0652 11 80 78, 300dh double) has five basic rooms with shower. **Kasbah Azalay** (0524 84 80 86, www.azalay.com, doubles 1,100dh) has good facilities but not much atmosphere. It's just across the bridge towards the palmeraie. Rooms are huge and some have private terraces overlooking the oasis. There's a bar, restaurant and magnificent indoor pool (though it's rarely heated). Umpteen bivouac camps are dotted in the desert near M'Hamid and if you don't have time to head deep into the Sahara, then an overnight in **Erg Lehoudi** dunes might just hit the spot.

In Context

History

From desert outpost to international playground.

In the beginning, were the Berbers. Before the Arabs, Carthaginians, Romans and Phoenicians, they were here. Their origins are lost in time. Over the centuries, the Berbers dug into the Rif and Atlas mountains. There they remained unconquered, no matter what happened down on the plains. The Romans couldn't dislodge them. Neither could the Arabs, who ended up living alongside them. But though many Berbers had been unimpressed by Christianity, Islam took their fancy and proved to be the glue that held Morocco together. It condemned petty interests and local loyalties, and enabled a central authority to draw legitimacy from respect for its teachings. From here on, the history of Morocco is one of dynastic rule, but also of tension between central government and tribal independence, between the relatively orderly plains and coast – known as the Bled El-Makzhen – and the ungovernable areas of mountain and desert – the Bled Es Siba. And, as tribe after tribe forayed out of the Atlas or Sahara to found dynasties in the north, Marrakech would watch history from the border between the two.

نعم

Tin Mal.

THE ALMORAVIDS (1062-1147)

The first such was the Almovarid dynasty. In the ninth and tenth centuries, trans-Saharan trade routes were established, mostly for gold – exchanged for salt in the Niger region. The main staging-post at this end was Sijilmassa, which stood near present-day Rissani in the Tafilelt oasis and thrived until the 14th century. There was ferocious competition for control of the caravan routes, but one tribe of nomadic Berbers came out on top. They ranged across the western Sahara from fortified religious settlements, known as ribat, and this gave them their name – El-Mourabitoun, or Almoravids.

One of their leaders went off to Mecca and returned preaching against palm wine and having more than four wives. Newly fired with missionary fervour, the Almoravids subdued the south, crossed the Atlas and paused for breath. Being nomads, they'd never done much in the way of founding cities, but as their dominions grew they saw the wisdom in having a central store of weapons and food, and as a pious people they wanted somewhere to build a great mosque. It was 1062. At a location offering control of the most important Atlas passes, they founded Marrakech.

It began as a military outpost – no more than an encampment circled by thornbush – but, well placed on the route between Sahara and Atlantic, it soon also became a trading post. The original name was Marra Kouch. No one knows what it meant but the name lives on in both 'Marrakech' and 'Morocco'.

From this new base, the Almoravids quickly went on to conquer the whole of Morocco. In 1086 they landed in Spain, defeated the Christians and absorbed much of the Iberian peninsula. By the early 12th century their empire stretched from Lisbon to West Africa and from the Atlantic to Algeria. Back in Marrakech, the Almoravids built a spectacular city. Sadly, nothing survives except one little piece of their great big mosque – the small but exquisite Koubba El-Badiyin (*see p53*). How grand must the Ali Ben Youssef Mosque have been if this was just its ablutions fountain?

The Almoravid legacy in Marrakech can still be felt in the city walls they erected and the palm groves they planted. They used their Saharan expertise to establish the water supply, building long underground pipes that conveyed Atlas meltwater to the fountains, pools and gardens of Marrakech.

THE ALMOHADS (1147-1269)

By the mid 12th century, the Almoravids had overstretched themselves. There were reverses in Spain and unrest at home. A rival confederation of Berber tribes, the Almohads, scented blood.

The Almohads had their own ribat, the mountain fastness of Tin Mal (*see p154*) in the High Atlas. Armed with interpretations of Islam even more strict than their predecessors, the Almohads, whose name means 'unitarians', galloped out of the hills and placed Marrakech under siege. It took 11 unpleasant months, but in 1147 the city was theirs.

So they knocked it all down and rebuilt it – and, to be fair, did a beautiful job. The monumental architecture of this period still dominates Marrakech. The most stunning achievement was their own big mosque, the Koutoubia (*see p42*). Other significant period pieces include the Kasbah Mosque (*see p76*) and Bab Agnaou (*see p76*) and the Agdal and Gardens (*see p83*) and Menara Gardens (*see p105*).

The greatest Almohad leader, Abdel Moumen, reconquered southern Spain and was victorious in Tunis, Tripoli and southern Algeria. During his reign, Marrakech became a bastion of Islamic civilisation and culture, a haven for scholars and philosophers.

THE MERENIDS (1248-1554)

Like the Almoravids before them, the Almohads had overreached, losing their religious drive and running into trouble in Spain. Another nomadic Berber tribe was waiting to charge in, this one the Beni-Merens – Merenids – from the empty lands between Tafilelt and Algeria. Fès fell to them in 1248; Marrakech in 1269.

The Merenids ruled from Fès and, compared to the glory of the Almohad period, Marrakech fell upon hard times, reduced to a provincial outpost. This is the era of the great Muslim geographers and explorers such as Ibn Khaldun and Ibn Batuta (the Muslim Marco Polo). But it was a golden age in which Marrakech played little part except as a bastion against attacks from the south.

Following the pattern established by previous dynasties, by the 15th century the Merenids too were in decline and Europe was on the attack. This was the epoch of the great discoveries. The Portuguese explored the African coast, grabbing Mogador (Essaouira) and other ports. The Christian incursions, which the Merenids had proved unable to resist, spawned a new kind of Islamic movement, based around leaders called cherifs, who claimed descent from the Prophet. The Saadians were one such movement.

THE SAADIANS (1549-1668)

The Saadians arrived from Arabia in the 12th century and settled in the Drâa Valley. They lived peacefully among the palm groves and bothered no one for several hundred years. But when the 16th century rolled around, with the Portuguese all over the coast, rebellious Berber tribes roaming the interior and the Merenids pretty much confined to Fès and Marrakech, the Saadians decided it was time to restore order and repel the Christians.

In 1510 they took the Sous valley and used Taroudant as their capital. In 1541 they defeated the Portuguese at nearby Agadir. And in 1549 they dethroned the Merenids at Fès.

The Saadians then returned the court to Marrakech and essentially refounded the city, which once more acquired the atmosphere of an imperial capital. Sultan Moulay Abdellah built a new Ali Ben Youssef Mosque and developed the similarly named medersa (*see p53*) into North Africa's biggest Qur'anic school. He gave the Jews their own quarter (*see p81*), the Christians their own trading centre at the heart of the Medina (roughly where Club Med is today), and sprinkled the city with fountains and hammams.

To celebrate victory over the Portuguese at Battle of the Three Kings (1578) – remembered as such because that's how many rulers lost their lives before it was over – the succeeding Sultan Ahmed El-Mansour oversaw the construction of the lavish Badii Palace (*see p78*), importing some 50 tons of marble from Italy. Another extravagance was the opulent mausoleums now known as the Saadian Tombs (*see p78*).

Much of this was paid for with gold from the Niger. In 1590 Ahmed led an army across the Sahara, reviving the trade routes, securing the salt mines, grabbing the gold and enslaving the locals. The whole area of the Western Sahara, Mauritania and Mali became a protectorate run by the Saadian pashas from Timbuktu.

ALAOUITE LONGEVITY

After Ahmed died in 1603, Morocco descended into civil war. Saadian rulers clung on to the Sous and Marrakech, another tribe grabbed Fès and the strange pirate republic of the Bou Regreg briefly flourished in Rabat and Salé. It was clearly time for another dynasty to enter from the south.

The Alaouites were cherifs from Rissani in the Tafilelt, the same oasis that 600 years previously had nurtured the Almoravids. Like the Saadians before them, the Alaouites' route to power was a slow one; they took Taza and Fès before seizing Marrakech in 1668. Moulay Rachid was the first Alaouite Sultan, and though his reign was uneventful, his legacy lives on: the Alaouites still rule Morocco today.

As in any family, there are the members no one likes to talk about – in this case, Rachid's younger brother and successor Moulay Ismail (1672-1727). Ismail hated Marrakech and built a new imperial capital at Meknès. He stripped the Badii Palace and, such was the wealth there, this took a team of labourers 12 years to complete. Marrakchis must have been glad to see the back of him, particularly as he turned out to be one of the most cruel and depraved rulers imaginable. He is said to have personally killed 30,000 people, chopping off heads and doing a bit of disembowelling when he felt like it. He also sired 888 children, ensuring succession problems. But there was method as well as madness. He kept at bay the Europeans and the Ottomans, by now in Algeria, and one way or another made Morocco strong again.

Until, after a 54-year reign, he died. Ismail's authority had been enforced by his Black Guard, an army of descendants of slaves taken by the Saadians on their Timbuktu expeditions. With Ismail gone this force owed loyalty to no one and spent 30 years on the rampage, rendering Morocco ungovernable.

Somehow the Alaouite ruler Sidi Mohammed Ben Abdellah (1757-90) managed to get the Black Guard under control. He also rebuilt the Atlantic port of Mogador and renamed it Essaouira. But chaos resumed when he died, followed by a period of isolationism towards Europe.

ISOLATION AND DECLINE

By the early 19th century, Marrakech still hadn't progressed much beyond the Middle Ages. Dynasties had come and gone and it still made its living the same way it had done for 1,000 years, trading olive oil, corn, livestock, tanned leather, slaves and woven goods.

Meanwhile, the end of the Napoleonic Wars left European powers free to get on with colonial expansion. The French moved into Algeria in 1830 and defeated the Moroccan army at the Battle of Isly in 1844, the Spanish conquered Tetouan and grabbed what is now Western Sahara, and the British forced Sultan Abdel Rahman (1822-59) to sign a preferential trade treaty in 1857. But amazingly, Morocco remained just about the only bit of Africa that wasn't under some form of colonial rule.

Sultan Moulay Hassan (1873-94), the last pre-colonial ruler with any real power, used Marrakech as his southern capital. By this time the city had long been in decline – the 1875 Encyclopaedia Britannica noted holes in the walls big enough for a horseman to ride through and a Medina 'defaced by mounds of rubbish and putrid refuse'.

But Moulay Hassan was a moderniser. He tried to stabilise the currency, play off the Europeans against each other and shore up national defences. For funds he had no recourse save the traditional *harka* – the Sultan would set off somewhere with an army and entourage, collecting tribute in the manner of a swarm of locusts. In 1893, he returned from such an expedition in the Tafilelt dying and with his forces in disarray. Crossing the Atlas towards Marrakech via the Tizi-n-Tichka pass, he was offered sanctuary at Telouet, the fortress of the Glaoua tribe.

Hassan's arsenal included an aged but still functional Krupp assault cannon. Such weapons had acquired a bizarre symbolic role as representative of the Sultan and his cherifian powers. People swore by them, prayed to them, kissed their barrels, brought them offerings of severed enemy heads, and believed them to possess healing powers.

Madani El-Glaoui somehow fed and sheltered the Sultan's entire army for several days. In gratitude, Hassan declared him his personal representative in the Atlas and Sahara and left behind most of his armoury, including the 77mm bronze Krupp cannon. The Glaoua tribe thus acquired both a weird legitimacy and a fearsome arsenal. They set about subjugating the south.

DEBT AND UNREST

Moulay Hassan was succeeded by his young son, Abdel Aziz (1894-1908), but for the first few years Hassan's powerful vizier, Ba Ahmed Ben Moussa, carried on pulling the strings. He also spent the next six years building for himself the Bahia Palace (*see p82*). When Ba Ahmed died in 1900, Abdel Aziz was barely 20 years old.

Walter Harris, the *Times* correspondent whose *Morocco That Was* is a court insider's account of this period, paints a vivid picture of a country ripe for imperialist plucking. While his advisers feathered their nests, and the European powers contemplated a colonial carve-up, Abdel Aziz amused himself with games of cricket and bicycle polo, frittering away millions on toys and gadgets. These included a lift for a one-storey palace and a state coach for a country with no roads. Morocco was now heavily in debt to European banks.

European powers met to discuss matters at the 1906 Conference of Algeciras. his established Tangier's status as an international free port and affirmed the independence of the Sultan, but it also paved the way for the Protectorate by giving Spain and France a mandate to restore order, if necessary.

In March 1907, Emile Mauchamp, a doctor sent by the French to set up a clinic in Marrakech, planted a pole on his roof. He did this as a joke. Moroccan authorities were so worried about foreign powers establishing a wireless telegraph network, that a mass paranoia about radio antenna had been spreading across the country. Mauchamp's provocation worked too well – he was lynched outside his house by an angry crowd. The French used this as an excuse to move troops across the Algerian border and into the Moroccan town of Oujda.

Later, other Europeans were killed in Casablanca. The French stepped in and occupied that city too. Aziz was deposed by his brother, Moulay Hafid (1908-12), but faced with unrest, crippling debts and European aggression, Hafid had little choice but to accept French rule, formalised in the 1912 Treaty of Fès. He abdicated soon afterwards.

INTO THE 20TH CENTURY

The first French Résident Général (later Maréchal) of Morocco was Louis Lyautey. He was to have an enormous effect on the country, building roads and railways, the ports of Casablanca and Kenitra, and adding new French-style towns to the old Medinas of Rabat, Fès, Meknès and Marrakech. The French dragged Morocco into the 20th century – except some of it didn't want to come along.

The old Bled El-Makzhen became what the French called *Maroc Utile* – the useful bits of Morocco whose resources they would set about exploiting. The rest of the country – the old Bled Es Siba of mountains and

Battle of Isly.

desert – remained unruly. Hardly was the ink dry on the Treaty of Fès than a tribal warlord called El-Hiba appeared from the south and camped an army of 12,000 outside the walls of Marrakech. The French turned up to massacre them with machine-guns and mortars.

Machine guns and mortars would soon also be firing in Europe, and the likelihood of war with Germany meant Lyautey would never have the forces to subdue the south. Instead he struck a deal with the ruler of the powerful Glaoua tribe, Thami El-Glaoui, who, with his brother Madani, had recently backed the coup that placed Moulay Hafid on the throne. Thami was installed as *bacha* (lord) of Marrakech, while Madani was given command of all lands to the south. They were allowed to rule as they saw fit and in return gave their full support to the occupying power. Madani died in 1918, but Thami was to carry on as bacha for the next 42 years. *See below* **Glaoui Power**.

EXTRAVAGANT DESPOT

Ensconced in Dar El-Bacha ('House of the Lord'), Thami El-Glaoui took his place among the despots of Moroccan history, ruling Marrakech like a Mafia boss. He hung the heads of his enemies from the gates, while his secret agents brought in suspects to be tried in his own personal *salon de justice*.

GLAOUI POWER

The despot installed by the French.

When the French first encountered Thami El-Glaoui in the early 20th century, he was little more than an uncouth tribal warlord with a mountain base in Telouet. Installing him as boss of Marrakech in 1912, the French seemed to take the view that he might be a ruthless despot, but at least he was *their* ruthless despot.

European society took a similar tack. Although at first he didn't speak a word of French, within 20 years 'the Glaoui' had become one of the most fashionable names to drop, imbued with the mystique and exoticism of an Indian maharajah. While his political enemies rotted in dungeons below the opulent Dar El-Bacha, the Glaoui threw sumptuous banquets and lavished gifts on international guests – maybe a diamond ring, maybe a cute Berber boy or girl. While his subjects went hungry, the Glaoui diverted water from farmland to maintain a golf course.

Europeans were less appalled by the Glaoui's excesses than they were suckered by his manners, generosity and *bons mots*. At one dinner party, the Glaoui overheard a young Parisian woman – who thought he understood no French – call him a pig, but admit to coveting his emerald ring. At the end of the meal, the Glaoui pulled her aside and said, in immaculate French, 'Madame, a stone like this emerald was never made for a pig like me. Permit me to offer it to you.' His comment on the French war minister, Daladier, was often quoted: 'He is like a dog without a tail – there is no way to tell what he is thinking.'

The Glaoui's refined exterior hid a voracious sexual appetite. His enormous harem – 96 women at his brother Madani's death in 1918, from whose harem he poached a further 54 – wasn't distraction enough and he put great effort into the pursuit of European women. A network of talent scouts scoured Morocco for likely conquests. White-skinned belles would be invited to tour the palace. If they took his fancy, the Glaoui would make a 'surprise' appearance and invite them to dinner – and further seductions.

As the dungeons filled with prisoners and the coffers with cash, the Glaoui threw sumptuous banquets for European dignitaries while his henchmen combed the countryside for girls to stock the harem. The Glaoui funded his extravagant lifestyle by grabbing local monopolies in hemp, olives, almonds, saffron, dates, mint and oranges. Soon, he enjoyed greater power than the puppet Sultan and Marrakech rivalled in importance the new capital, Rabat.

But there was one snag. Madani had handed control of the lands beyond the Atlas to his son-in-law, Hemmou, who now sat in Telouet between Thami and the rest of the South. Wealthy, ruthless and equipped with an arsenal greatly expanded since the original Krupp cannon, he was also obstinately anti-French. For this reason the south was never 'pacified' – and the Protectorate not fully established – until after his death in 1934. It's also why the French Foreign Legion built the Tizi-n-Tichka road over a difficult route avoiding Telouet.

But despite all this, the Glaoui enjoyed the wholehearted support of the French administration. His despotic regime left them free to exploit Morocco's phosphates, iron, anthracite, manganese, lead and silver. Agriculture also flourished, as French companies turned traditional olive groves and orchards into industrialised enterprises.

COLONIALS AND LOCALS

Lyautey was on a civilising mission. 'I have always had two passions,' he said, 'policies regarding the natives and town planning'. Thus Marrakech acquired a *nouvelle ville* just outside the Medina, later to become known as Guéliz. Lyautey was explicit that this new quarter – like similar projects in other Moroccan cities – had to be separate from the Medina in order to 'protect the autonomy of each'. This can be read two ways: on the one hand, a respect for Moroccans and a desire not to interfere with the traditional organisation of their cities; on the other, an enforced segregation with nice new quarters for the white folks and the natives confined to crowded and unsanitary medinas.

For the new Marrakech a town planner named Henri Prost laid out a scheme of large *rondpoints* connected by broad, leafy avenues. Camp Guéliz, just north of the new town, provided security. Prost was one of the architects behind the Mamounia hotel, built in 1922 by the Moroccan national rail company. Thus Guéliz received all the roads, railway connections, hospitals and schools; the Medina remained squalid.

Lyautey's town planning formalised the gulf between Moroccans and Europeans. By the 1930s there were 325,000 Europeans in the country. The staggering inequality between the locals and colonialists was a major factor in stoking support for a nationalist movement. This found political voice in the Istiqlal (Independence) Party. World War II provided further momentum. The French army had included 300,000 Moroccan soldiers. These acquitted themselves so ably that Franklin D Roosevelt, who had travelled to Casablanca to meet Winston Churchill for a conference, hinted to the new Sultan, Mohammed V, that, after the war, the country would become independent.

WORKING FOR THE CLAMPDOWN

Mohammed V had succeeded his father in 1927. He was young but not content to be a puppet. He began to press for independence. With membership of the Istiqlal Party mushrooming, the French got nervous. In 1953, with the help of the Glaoui, they sent Mohammed V into exile. This proved a mistake, confirming him as a nationalist figurehead. His expulsion sent the country into turmoil, triggering riots in Marrakech and Casablanca. There was a clampdown on both cities, with curfews, arrests and interrogation under torture. A week after the Sultan's expulsion, 13,000 Moroccans were arrested for treason.

By the summer of 1955 a campaign for the Sultan's return had escalated into armed rebellion. Terrorists tossed a bomb into a Casablanca café, killing seven Europeans. In Marrakech, a bomb was lobbed into the Berima Mosque where Ben Arafa, France's new puppet Sultan, was praying.

The Glaoui advised the French to 'do as the British did with the Mau Mau' – a reference to Kenya, where nationalists were slaughtered in the thousands. (It's perhaps not surprising that, when being driven around in his Bentley, the Glaoui only felt safe on the floor with a submachine gun on his chest.)

Hands already full with a bloody nationalist revolt in Algeria, the French decided to cut their losses. In November 1955 Mohammed V was permitted to return. The Glaoui was furious, but kissed the Sultan's feet and begged for mercy. Punitive measures were unnecessary as the Glaoui died of cancer on 30 January 1956.

What should have been a joyous occasion for Marrakech quickly turned ugly. A rampaging mob chanted 'Death to the traitors!'. Old allies of the Glaoui were hunted down, stripped, stoned and dragged outside the city walls to be doused in petrol and set alight. Children gathered around, laughing and cheering as victim upon victim was thrown on the bonfires.

The new governors of Marrakech did nothing to halt the rioting but placed guards round the smouldering bodies so that women could not take pieces of them for black magic. The corpse of the Glaoui himself was spared any indignities and interred, with full French military honours. Three months later, with France fully engaged in a bloody war in Algeria, Morocco was granted independence.

MOHAMMED V AND INDEPENDENCE

On 2 March 1956, the Sultan restyled himself as King Mohammed V, a modern constitutional monarch. But not too modern: the monarchy was still at the centre of political life, and the King kept the military on a short leash. He was rightly worried that the jubilation following independence would be short-lived; the nationalist movement quickly disintegrated into rival factions. The left-wing of the Istiqlal Party broke away to set up the socialist UFSP, with the King lending his support to the more moderate Mouvement Populaire.

Mohammed V never lived to see the first democratic election. Presided over by his son, King Hassan II, in 1963, it was won by a coalition of royalists and the Mouvement Populaire. The socialists claimed that the polls had been rigged. Their leader, Ben Barka, denounced the monarchy and was exiled to Paris, where he was assassinated by secret agents. So much for the new Morocco. Much of the period's civil unrest was the result of poverty compounded by a series of natural disasters. In 1961 locusts devastated crops around Marrakech. That same year there was a severe drought and a catastrophic earthquake in Agadir, which killed 15,000. Hassan II nationalised much of the economy, expropriating land from French companies. But most of this land was reserved for export crops and did nothing to feed the domestic population. By the mid 1960s Morocco – once called 'the bread basket of the Roman Empire' – had become a net importer of cereals.

As poverty increased, mass migration to the cities followed. Sprawling, overcrowded shanty towns or *bidonvilles* sprang up on the edge of Marrakech and other cities. An informal economy developed. Marrakech was packed with illegal taxi drivers, street peddlers and hustlers. The rise of hashish farming also fuelled the black economy and helped to spawn a new kind of tourism.

JOHN, PAUL, MICK AND KEITH

North Africa had long held romantic resonance for European intellectuals: a haven for 19th-century bohemians, it had been a source of inspiration for writers and painters from Gustave Flaubert and Eugène Delacroix to André Gide and Henri Matisse.

The bohemian tradition continued into the 20th century when the licentious enclave of Tangier – designated an International Zone – attracted the likes of Paul Bowles and William Burroughs. In 1956 the International Zone was absorbed into independent Morocco and the expats began drifting south to Marrakech, lured by its balmy climate and colourful exoticism. According to Beat philosophy, the spiritual went hand in hand with the sexual. The Marrakech brothels were infamous, particularly among gays. And, of course, there was the kif, or cannabis, which was smoked openly.

Brian Jones of the Rolling Stones made his first trip in 1966 with Anita Pallenberg. He brought the rest of the band with him on the next visit; they drove from Tangier to Marrakech and checked into the Hotel Es Saadi. There they tripped on LSD and ran into Cecil Beaton, who photographed Mick and Keith by the pool. At the centre of the scene were the American oil heir John Paul Getty Jr and his wife Talitha. The Gettys owned a place in the Medina, where they were photographed in kaftans up on the roof terrace. Here they hosted parties that went on for days. An entry in John Hopkins's *Tangier Diaries* for 1 January 1968 reads: 'Last night Paul and Talitha Getty threw a New Year's Eve party at their palace in the Medina. Paul McCartney and John Lennon were there, flat on their backs. They couldn't get off the floor let alone talk.'

COUPS AND MARCHES

While the foreigners carried on, members of the royal court were plotting to get rid of their ruler. In 1971 the King's 42nd birthday party was gatecrashed by 1,400 army cadets who fired machine guns at the 800 or so diplomatic guests lounging around the pool. The coup leader was accidentally killed in the crossfire and the cadets panicked, at which

MARRAKESH EXPRESS

Morocco on the countercultural map.

Jimi Hendrix might have been Morocco's most celebrated visitor from the Woodstock generation, but it was Crosby, Stills and Nash who released the hippie holiday anthem. Graham Nash wrote 'Marrakesh Express' after a 1966 train journey from Casablanca, recording postcard impressions of clear skies, snake-charmers, and djellebas 'we can wear back home'.

In the decade between 1965 and 1975, tourism revenue doubled. And the main reason was the hippie generation. Even before *Casablanca* in 1942, Morocco had been Hollywood shorthand for 'exotic', but it was the Beats who put it on the countercultural map. William Burroughs' association with Tangier, and visits by Allen Ginsberg, Jack Kerouac and Timothy Leary, drew the first curious bohemians.

What became known as the Hippie Trail led from London to Istanbul, India and Nepal. Morocco was a side trip, a quicker and more convenient blast of Third Worldliness, alien spirituality and cheap marijuana. Its culture impenetrable to the casual visitor, it was a blank wall on which the hippies could daub their own psychedelic mural. Tangier and Marrakech were the principal hippie destinations, but so too were Asilah, Chefchaouen and other towns in the Rif. To this day, further down the coast, the occasional longhair can be found nodding to Bob Marley tunes in the village of Taghazoute.

It's impossible to say just how many made the trip, but Ed Buryn's guidebook for the love generation, *Vagabonding in Europe and North Africa*, had 50,000 copies in print by 1973. By that time the Moroccan authorities were getting sick of the hippies, refusing to let in some and forcing many others to make a trip to the barber at Casablanca airport. Hippies were widely perceived as contributing little to the local economy. Anti-drug laws that were usually ignored or enforced only loosely were used to harrass the hippies by authorities increasingly worried about their effect on the local youth.

It's a sad paradox that the very decade during which western youth was acting out a Maghrebi fantasy of freedom was also the most heavy-handed and repressive period in Morocco's post-Independence history. Moroccans call it Les Années de Plomb – the 'Years of Lead'. Students were ruthlessly repressed, with the army killing over 1,000 people after the 1965 riots in Casablanca, and closing down Mohammed V University in Rabat after strikes in 1971 and 1972. The period included two failed coups and came to an end only with the 1975 Green March into Western Sahara, when the monarchy managed to channel dissent into a resurgent nationalism.

The hippies never connected with any of this at all, smoking kif and staring out of the train windows. Graham Nash sang of seeing 'ducks and pigs and chickens' – there are hardly any ducks in Morocco and you could live your whole life there without ever seeing a pig. The hippies' detachment was absolute and, eventually, they went home.

point the King, who had hidden in a bathroom, emerged and coolly stared down his would-be assassins, who dropped their weapons and rushed to kiss his hands and feet. The failed coup left 98 guests dead.

Thirteen months later the King's Boeing 727 was attacked in the air by six F5 fighters from his own airforce. One of the jet's engines was destroyed but the pilot managed to land at Rabat. As the King and his party ran for cover three more rebel aircraft continued to strafe the runway and the officials who had been waiting to greet the plane. Eight people on the ground were killed and close to 50 wounded. The minister of defence committed suicide, there were summary executions, the pilot was promoted – and the King got back to ruling the country.

In 1975 he seized the Spanish colony of Rio del Oro in the Western Sahara. He did so by organising the 'Green March', in which 350,000 citizens marched into the territory from Marrakech. General Franco had just died and Spain relinquished the colony without much fuss. But the colony's residents had other ideas. Polisario, a nationalist group comprised of the indigenous Sahrawi tribe, proclaimed a republic. Backed by the Algerians, they waged a guerrilla war of independence against Morocco until a ceasefire in 1991. The situation remains unresolved today.

The same year as the Polisario ceasefire, the King dispatched 1,200 troops to Saudi Arabia as a gesture of support to the US-led Gulf War operation. It was not a popular move and resulted in rioting and worse: in 1994 Islamic extremists attacked a hotel in Marrakech, killing two Spanish tourists. Hassan II reacted with the ruthless suppression characteristic of his reign, involving arbitrary arrests, 'disappearances' and widespread abuses of human rights and judicial norms. It's a darker side to the King's rule that has only recently been aired in public, most notably in the furore surrounding 2004's publication of a novel by Moroccan writer Tahar Ben Jelloun (*see p240*) that focused on the fate of detainees in Hassan II's desert concentration camps.

MOHAMMED VI AND HUMAN RIGHTS

Hassan II died of a heart attack in July 1999 and was succeeded by his 36-year-old eldest son, who became King Mohammed VI. Popular approval greeted his pledge to a multi-party political system, respect for human rights and improved rights for women. Some progress has been made towards these goals. The King dismissed his father's much-feared interior minister, political exiles were allowed to return and political detainees were released.

'The country straddles a narrow tightrope between autocracy and democracy, East and West, old and new.'

In 2004 a Justice and Reconciliation Authority was set up to investigate the human rights abuses of the past. The same year, the rights of women were improved by a rewriting of the *moudawana* (the laws governing personal rights) to restrict polygamy and give women equal rights to men in marriage, divorce and the custody of children. Meanwhile, the May 2003 Islamist suicide-bomb attacks on various targets in Casablanca helped to gather support for a crackdown on this new breed of dissident. In April 2007, there were several more explosions in Casablanca, as terrorists blew themselves up rather than be taken prisoner in a massive police operation.

Marrakech has prospered under the influence of the new King. Although his official residence is in Rabat, Mohammed VI spends as much time as he can in the Red City – and built himself a new, more modest palace rather than occupy the gigantic old one that sprawls across half of the kasbah district. Mohammed VI removed the red tape obstructing foreign investment, triggering the current property boom in the Medina, and cracked down on the touts and hustlers.

The young King remains popular, despite press revelations that he costs taxpayers £144.6 million a year – 18 times more than Queen Elizabeth II. But it's hard not to warm to someone who speaks with such frankness: *Time* magazine asked him what advice his father gave him; the King answered: 'He told me that the most important thing was "to last". I do not know what he meant.'

THE ARAB SPRING

When a Tunisian street seller, Mohamed Bouazizi, set himself on fire in December 2010, he did not realise that he would set in motion an awakening that would spread across North Africa and the Middle East. The Arab Spring would lead to the collapse of regimes in Tunisia, Egypt and Libya but, notably, not Morocco.

There seem to be several possible explanations as to why Morocco didn't have a revolution. The first is that across the Arab world, monarchies seem to have endured and fared better than military or dictatorial regimes that lack legitimacy in the eyes of their people. On top of that, Mohammed VI, still a relatively young man and in touch with Morocco's population, has been very adept at anticipating change and keeping one step ahead. He seems to have done just enough to release the social pressure valves in order to sidestep the sort of social explosions or 'youthquakes' seen in other Arab nations.

Protests did, however, break out across Morocco. On 20 February 2011 thousands marched in Rabat, Casablanca, Marrakech and Tangier, shouting slogans such as 'down with autocracy' and 'we are not slaves.' The activists were largely students who mobilised via Facebook and Twitter and became known as the February 20 movement. But in the end, despite prompting some concessions, the movement failed.

Protests on 20 February 2011.

Later that year Mohammed VI introduced a new constitution that prevented the lid from blowing off the pressure cooker. Now the prime minister is no longer chosen directly by the king, parliament has greater power and the monarchy has less. By allowing a moderate Islamist party (the PJD) to win elections at the end of 2011, Mohammed VI managed to sideline more extremist Islamist views. Berber was also made an official language and parliament now has the power to grant amnesties.

Another factor keeping Morocco from revolution is that it still has a successful economy, built around manufacturing, agriculture, tourism and other service industries such as telephone call centres. Again, the king astutely gave people subsidies for their food and energy bills and this took the wind out of the sails of revolt.

It may also be that Moroccans have seen the carnage that occurred in Egypt, Libya and Syria and thanked their lucky stars that they did not have a revolution.

But that is not to say that everything is rosy in the Red City or Morocco generally. Millions are unemployed and living in poverty. The gap between rich and poor has been described as obscene. Critics say the reforms are cosmetic and that parliament is just a fig leaf for an undemocratic system in which the king still pulls the strings of power.

Islamic extremism is not dead either. In April 2011 a bomb ripped through the terrace of the Argana Café, which overlooks the Jemaa el Fna, killing 17 people, most of them tourists. The attack was blamed on the Al Qaeda affiliate in North Africa, and a young Moroccan was convicted and sentenced to death. However some think his conviction was unsafe and that the bombing may even have been a government plot to warn people of the dangers of opting for revolution.

The Argana bombing, combined with the global economic downturn, had a devastating impact on tourism in Marrakech, though the situation is now improved. Meanwhile the country continues to straddle a narrow tightrope between autocracy and democracy, East and West, old and new. It is difficult to predict where it will go from here but a Moroccan phrase seems to sum it up well: 'nothing is certain,' they will tell you here, 'but everything is possible.'

Architecture

Unique use of colour, natural materials, distinctive design: it can only be Marrakech.

When the Arab commander Oqba Ben Nafi spurred his horse into the surf of the Atlantic in AD 682 and swore, 'O God, I take you to witness that there is no ford here. If there was, I would cross it', it marked the completion of the Islamic conquest of North Africa, confirmed when Idris II established the wholly Islamic city of Fès. In 818, a failed rebellion in Córdoba sent a flood of Arab refugees to Fès, and a decade later a similar rebellion in Tunisia brought more. In just a few decades, Morocco had gained its defining architectural influences and the communities of craftsmen that would give them shape and form.

Kasbah Mosque.

ANDALUCIAN INFLUENCE

Morocco became the inheritor of the architectural and craft traditions of Muslim Spain and the Córdoban empire (whose glory was enshrined in the marvellous Mezquita, Córdoba's Great Mosque). The Almoravids (1062-1147), who were the next dynasty to reunite Morocco after the country dissolved into principalities on the death of Idris II, further opened the doors to the influx of Spanish Muslim culture. They founded Marrakech (1062) as their capital and, under the influence of the Spanish, built some monumental structures, importing into Morocco the horseshoe arch and cusp arch (the one that looks like a broccoli section). Under the Almoravids the fine carving of stucco also first appears. Incredibly, some of those earliest designs (stylised, paisley-like flowers), which appear in the *mihrab* (prayer niche) of the Karawiyin Mosque in Fès and are reproduced in the erudite *A Practical Guide to Islamic Monuments in Morocco* by Richard Parker, are still being reproduced in Marrakech by craftsmen furiously chiselling swirls and flourishes into bands of damp plaster.

In terms of surviving monuments, the only complete Almoravid building in the whole of Morocco is Marrakech's **Koubba El-Badiyin** (*see p53*), which displayed for the first time many of the elements and motifs that have since come to characterise Moorish building.

During the reign of the successors to the Almoravids, the Almohads (1147-1269), the Spanish-Moorish synthesis reached its peak. Moroccan architectural styles were developed dramatically. Building materials of choice remained mud brick and *pisé* (reinforced mud), but stone was employed for certain structures, notably the **Bab Agnaou** (*see p76*), the splendid Marrakech gate. Decoration was simplified and made more masculine: whereas the Almoravids went in for flowers, their successors favoured geometric patterns. But these austere rulers eventually softened: witness the lovely trellis-like brickwork and faience tiling lavished on the minarets of the **Koutoubia Mosque** (*see p42*) and the **Kasbah Mosque** (*see p76*).

Under the Merenids (1276-1554), Marrakech may have languished as attention switched to the northern imperial cities of Fès, Meknes and Salé, but artistic interchange continued with Spain. Some of the Merenids' finest monuments – including the Karaouiyine Mosque and Bou Inania Medersa, both in Fès – share similarities with the other great Moorish architecture of the time, the extraordinary Alhambra palace complex, across the Strait in Granada.

ARABESQUE INTERIOR DESIGN

It was the Merenids who introduced most of today's familiar interior design repertoire into Morocco, including carved stucco and carved wood, and *zelije*, the creation of intricate mosaic design using hand-cut tiles.

Islamic tradition forbids any representation of living things, a policy defined in the formative years of the religion when the Prophet Mohammed first started preaching against the idol worshippers of Mecca. Hence, creativity flourished in more abstract forms. The tradition of tiling was carried west by the Arabs, who had been inspired by the bright turquoise domes and mausoleums of ancient Persia and Samarkand. The Central Asians, in their

COLOUR CODES

The Marrakchi spectrum

A bit of enlightened ordinance set down during the time of French rule specifies that all buildings in Marrakech must be painted pink. Except it's not really pink. The colour is more ochre, the natural hue of the earth on which the city is founded. Earth has always been the prime building material, mixed with crushed limestone and straw to make *pisé*. No painting required. It's already the right colour.

It was only when the French began building the *nouvelle ville* now known as Guéliz in the early 20th century, and introduced new building materials such as concrete, that colour became an issue. Even so, most newer buildings stay somewhere in the pink palette. There's no prescribed paint number or swatches to match, and as a result the tones vary from pale flesh to fiery vermilion. It's all highly practical, as the colour takes much of the glare out of the sunlight (by contrast, Casablanca, which frequently labours under overcast skies, is, as its name suggests, uniformly white). Doors, woodwork and trim are usually done in a complementary shade of pale green. Some recent buildings in the new town, however, have begun contrasting Marrakech pink with Majorelle blue – the intense, luminous blue developed by French artist Jacques Majorelle.

turn, had picked up the idea from Chinese porcelain, hence the devotion to blue. The Moors of Morocco and Andalucía widened the colour palette courtesy of the Berber influence. Tribal inhabitants of the Atlas Mountains, the Berbers added pink, purple, orange, red and yellow to the existing blue, green and white palette of Islamic culture.

Zelije takes the form of complex geometrical patterns executed in small glazed tiles like a massive jigsaw puzzle. The tiles are formed in large sizes and then cut to shape. This remains the case today. Visit a building under construction and there will be a group of craftsmen employed to do nothing but cut tiles, which are then stockpiled awaiting the attention of the *zelayiya*, the zelije master craftsman, who will assemble them according to designs passed from father to son and retained in memory only.

Dar Si Said Museum.

'Unfortunately, Moroccan dynasties have been inclined to destroy whatever had been created by their predecessors.'

There are, it's claimed, 360 shapes of cut-clay pieces, called *fourma*, and permutations of colour and pattern are endless. The craft has always been a speciality of the artisans of Fès, but Marrakech has no shortage of kaleidoscopic tiling either, exhibited in its various palaces and religious monuments.

The other great Merenid addition to architecture is woodworking. Wood has rarely been used as a primary structure (walls and floors are made of stone and mudbrick) but it was frequently employed for ceilings, lintels, capitals and, of course, doors – frequently massive and imposing pieces of work, and decorated with carving, incising and inlays. Unfortunately, much of the best woodworking has traditionally been reserved for holy institutions such as mosques, shrines and medersas (Koranic schools; a building type also introduced by the Merenids), most of which are off-limits to non-Muslims. However, some impressive examples of historic craftsmanship can be seen in Marrakech at the **Dar Si Said Museum** (*see p83*).

PALACES AND HOUSES

Post Merenid, Moroccan architecture went into a period of stagnation. The Moors had retreated from southern Spain in the late 15th century and the Moroccan empire had collapsed inwards. Under the Saadians (1549-1668), Marrakech became the capital again and was embellished with grand new monuments, including the delightful **Ben Youssef Medersa** (*see p53*) and the dazzling **Saadian Tombs** (*see p78*). The former is notable for its acres of carved stucco and wood, the latter for floor-to-ceiling zelije. Architectural historians dismiss these buildings as inferior repetitions of

Badii Palace.

earlier techniques and motifs. That may be so, but at least through them visitors gain an idea of the glorious old buildings that have disappeared.

What the Saadians excelled at were palaces. Sultan Ahmed El Mansour (1578-1607) took 25 years to build the **Badii Palace** (*see p78*). Unfortunately, Moroccan dynasties have not only had a habit of shifting the centre of power around, they've also been inclined to destroy whatever had been created by their predecessors. Right at the start, the Almohads pulled down the original founding fortress of Marrakech to replace it with the Koutoubia Mosque, and, later, Moulay Ismail, who succeeded the Saadians, dismantled the Badii Palace – all that remains are impressive ruins.

Essentially the palaces echoed the design of a traditional house or *dar*. Both followed the principle of an anonymous exterior of blank walls with an entrance leading via a passage – kinked, so that anyone at the door or gate couldn't see directly inside – to a central open-air court. The whole building looks inward rather than outward, with windows and terraces addressing the courtyard, which serves to introduce light and air into the rooms around it. On the ground floor are public reception rooms and salons; the private quarters are on the floor above. The central open spaces are also rooms in themselves, used for eating and entertaining. In larger houses the courts often have *bahou*, small recessed seating areas. A *douiriya*, or annex, contains the kitchens and servants' rooms. At roof level, flat terraces provide space for storage, drying washing or keeping goats and chickens.

BERBER HERITAGE

All that has been described so far is essentially Arab architecture, imported into Morocco since the arrival of Islam. But Marrakech is different to the imperial cities of the north because of the influence of the indigenous Berbers.

These desert and mountain tribal people were the original inhabitants of Morocco long before the Arabs and their city of Fès, long even before the Romans established their outpost at Volublis. Their architecture is quite literally of the earth. The typical fortified Berber village, known as a *ksar or ksour*, has traditionally been built of soil reinforced with lime, straw and gravel, mixed into a thick mud paste and applied by hand to a wooden frame. It dries so hard that it takes a hammer and chisel to mark it. At the same time, it has a beautifully organic quality; if another house or extension is needed it's simply welded on and the village grows like a bees' nest.

Similar to the *ksour* is the *kasbah*, which can be described variously as a castle, a fortress, a palace or a garrison – but essentially it is the residence of a tribal ruler. These ancient structures predominate in southern Morocco, built as much to protect the Berbers from one another as from invaders. They are often sited on a hill, with towers at each corner serving as lookout posts. The interiors are simple, often claustrophobic, with narrow windows (terraces and courtyards bring in light). They might rise to five storeys, with the living quarters and grander reception rooms on the upper floors. Decoration comprises bold geometric motifs – the Berbers were early converts to Islam so share the Arab aversion to figurative representation. At the same time, they held on to many pre-Islamic superstitions and adorned walls with simple carved motifs, designed to ward off evil.

'The Berbers added pink, purple, orange, red and yellow to the existing blue, green and white palette of Islamic culture.'

A guaranteed method to breach the defences of a kasbah was to reroute a river and let the water wash away the foundations. Sadly, many kasbahs and ksours have been abandoned over the decades as tribal power has waned. The south of Morocco, particularly the High Atlas region, is studded with grandly decaying hilltop ruins, most spectacularly at **Telouet**, the former stronghold of the Glaoui tribe. On a brighter note, there are also impressive partially and wholly restored kasbahs at **Aït Benhaddou**, **Taouirt**, **Tifoultoute** (for all of the above, *see p161*) and **Skoura** (*see p163*).

Telouet.

Bahia Palace.

MAURESQUE MODERNISM

Following the Saadian dynasty, Marrakech and Morocco endured a succession of weak, ineffectual imperial figureheads who were largely unable to halt the country's descent into intermittent civil war. Architecture rarely flourished. Marrakech briefly grew wealthy during the reign of free-trade fan Sultan Abdel Rahman (1822-59), with the wealth accrued resulting in the building of the **Bahia Palace** (*see p82*). Half a century later the Glaoui's rapacious taxes financed the **Dar El Bacha** (*see p67*). However, if the Saadian monuments were just imitations of greater glories past then these later buildings are third-hand pastiche, only sporadically enlightened by the skills of local artisans.

The arrival of the French in 1912 drew a line under all that had gone before. With foreign rule came a new style of architecture, a mix of European modernistic and Moorish, dubbed 'Mauresque'. Marrakech gained a new town but few buildings of distinction.

In Marrakech, the Protectorate was a mixed blessing. The city was introduced to new architectural ideas, but traditional forms and crafts were largely sidelined. It's only recently, just over 50 years after the departure of the French, that architecture in the city has begun to move on. Gratifyingly, the inspiration for much of what is happening is Berber simplicity, with high-profile architects such as Charles Boccara and Elie Mouyal looking to the logic, economy and organic-stylings of mud building.

According to Boccara, when he first began working in Marrakech in the 1980s there was 'no competition'; now he estimates there are maybe more than 50 small architectural practices. He singles out for attention Mohammed Amine Kabbaj, originally from Casablanca, trained in Strasbourg with a diploma from Paris and resident in Marrakech since 1980. Along with two partners, Kabbaj balances big-bucks projects with riad rebuilds in the Medina and a project to revitalise the small Berber town of Tamesloht and conserve its kasbah.

At the same time, thanks to the patronage of a new wave of designers and decorators, the traditional skills of the city's artisans (zelije workers, the wood and stucco carvers) are back in vogue. After what has been the best part of four centuries of lassitude, a new Marrakech style finally looks set to shake things up.

Essential Information

Hotels

The piecemeal conversion of the Medina into a vast complex of boutique hotels continues apace. Marrakech probably boasts more boutique hotels per square mile than any other city in the world. The current number of riads, as they're now generically known, weighs in at almost 1,000. In some districts, such as the R'mila area in the north-western Medina – more developed than most because of good vehicle access – there already appear to be more guesthouses than houses. Although rocketing property prices means that there are few real bargains left on the market, all the signs are that this trend is set to continue. And it all makes a certain sense. If your city is low on conventional sights, then make the accommodation the destination. It's just that Marrakech has taken this further than most places.

STAYING IN MARRAKECH

'Riad' means garden house, though for 'garden' you can usually read 'courtyard'. The city's riad guesthouses are organised around one or more of these courtyards, reflecting the traditions of Moroccan domestic architecture, which are inward-looking with thick blank walls to protect the inhabitants from heat, cold and the attentions of the outside world. Grander riads involve two or more houses knocked together, but many consist of just half a dozen or so rooms around a single courtyard. Most are privately operated affairs, which generally means excellent personal service and a high degree of individuality.

Rooms feature en suite bathrooms in all but the cheapest riads, but in many places TVs, telephones and other mod cons are often dispensed with in the name of authenticity and getting away from it all.

Marrakech can be decidedly chilly during the winter and many riads offer chimneys, central heating and hot water bottles – if you feel the cold, check exactly what's available. Breakfast is commonly taken on a roof terrace shielded from the sun beneath tent-like awnings (and is, in the majority of cases, included in the room price), while lunch and dinner are provided on request. Many riads have excellent cooks, producing food as good as, if not superior to, anything dished up in the city's restaurants.

In deference to local aesthetics, most riads forgo any kind of tell-tale frontage, signboard or even nameplate. Given that they often lie deep within the obscure twists of narrow alleys, this makes them a swine to locate. Guests are generally met at the airport (for which there may or may not be an additional charge), but after that it's just you and your sense of direction. With that in mind, it's always wise to carry your riad's business card to show locals in case you get lost.

Gaining in favour of late is the out-of-town retreat. There are a growing number of villas and new-build compounds on the outskirts of the city – scattered throughout the Palmeraie and further afield – that serve as semi-private retreats dedicated to indolence and pampering, with teams of cooks, masseurs, manicurists, maids and assorted flunkies to obviate the need for any exertion on the part of the guest. Marrakech is on hand simply to provide blasts of colour and exoticism between early afternoon waxings and evening cocktails. One way to holiday is to spend a couple of days at a riad in the Medina followed by a couple of days in a self-indulgent retreat. Independent tour operators now offer this sort of package.

Whichever way you choose to go, we highly recommend pushing the budget. Marrakech isn't the place to scrimp on accommodation – not when your hotel could turn out to be the highlight of the trip.

RATES AND BOOKING

There are significant seasonal variations in room rates. What constitutes the peak period varies by establishment, but generally speaking you'll pay considerably more (and there'll be a minimum stay) for a room any time over Christmas/New Year and Easter, as well as late September to October, when the fierceness of the summer heat has abated and temperatures are near-perfect. Rooms are scarce at peak times and booking well in advance is a must. Note that some riads close in the summer months.

When it comes to making a reservation, even though most hotels boast websites, bear in mind that Moroccan servers are prone to meltdown. Book through the website by all means, but make sure you receive a confirmation email.

We've divided this chapter by area, then price. For **deluxe** hotels you can expect to pay from 3,450dh (approx £250); **expensive** 2,100dh-3,450dh (approx £150-£250); **moderate** 850dh-2,100dh (approx £60-£150); and **budget** under 850dh (approx £60). Breakfast is usually included. Payment is typically either cash in local currency or by credit card (there's often at least a five per cent surcharge added on to card payments to cover transaction costs). When it comes to paying your bill, you'll also want to know whether VAT (at 20 per cent) and the nightly tourist tax, which varies according to the category of the establishment, are already included.

Let's just reiterate this: Marrakech is not the place to scrimp on accommodation. But for those who simply don't have the cash, there are plenty of budget hotels between rue Bab Agnaou and Riad Zitoun El-Kedim, south of Jemaa El Fna. The very best budget options are listed in this chapter.

JEMAA EL FNA & AROUND

Deluxe

★ La Mamounia

Avenue Bab Jedid (0524 38 86 00, www.mamounia.com). **Map** p252 A6.

La Mamounia is seriously glamorous. In early 2014, Nicole Kidman stayed here while filming Hollywood

La Mamounia.

Royal Mansour.

flick *Queen of the Desert*, joining a long list of celebrities who've graced its fabled rooms. After an almond-scented milk and platter of dates on arrival, walk through the majestic Bar Italien with its original Majorelle ceiling to the lofty gardens. Renovated in 2009, the rooms are smartly elegant with carved stucco horseshoe arches, bands of ziggurat-stacked *zelije*, painted doors, blends of mustard yellow and burgundy threads, and latticed horseshoe windows in the marble bathrooms (with chocolate-brown Havaianas for sun-tanned toes). And then there are the expansive terraces with views of the Atlas mountians and the crisp African light. You can waft around the scented corridors, be pampered in the spa, take tea in the gardens or dine at the multiple restaurants (we love the natty Majorelle blue jacket of the maître d' in Le Français). After a stay here, you'll have a hard time returning to normal life beyond the storied walls.

► *For more on the hotel and its history, see p203 Luxury Lounging.*

Royal Mansour

Rue Abou Abbas El-Sebti (0529 80 80 80, www.royalmansour.com). **Map** p252 A5.

The Royal Mansour is a stunner. It's fit for a king and was built by one (*see p203* **Luxury Lounging**). Morocco's Mohammed VI employed 1,500 craftsmen to fashion the 53 riads, lobby, restaurants and spa within the hotel grounds, all just a ten-minute amble from Jemaa El Fna. Although the Mansour oozes luxury – 45 kinds of marble were used, including a stunning lapis lazuli-hued marble from Brazil that patterns the lobby of the restaurant pavilion – it's an opulence that somehow doesn't overwhelm. The private riads, topped by terraces with plunge pools and reached by paths that meander through the gardens, are very private. If you want to speak to another human being, head for the library with its retractable roof and telescope, the dessert library with its cabinet of sweet confections, or the spa sanctuary with its indoor pool under a pavilion of glass and pretty garden. If you're going to live like a king, you'll want to eat like a king too (you'll need a royal budget, though). Three Michelin-starred chef Yannick Alléno is consultant chef for the restaurants, and La Grande Table Marocaine wows with gourmet treats such as spinach salad with orange blossom foam, royal pigeon *pastilla*, and gold-dusted chocolate fondant dessert.

Villa des Orangers

6 rue Sidi Mimoun, place Ben Tachfine (0524 38 46 38, www.villadesorangers.com). **Map** p252 B7.

Built in the 1930s as a judge's residence, the dreamy Villa des Orangers was acquired by a French husband-and-wife team with a successful hotel business in Paris, and extended in 2008. The style is Moorish palatial, with 27 rooms and suites done out in deep chocolate, bordeaux and stone tones, and arranged

LUXURY LOUNGING

Rest assured at Marrakech's grandest grandes dames.

Morocco's most famous 'destination' hotel, **La Mamounia** (*see p201*) was opened in 1923 to coincide with the arrival of the French-built North African railway network. In the inter-war years, it became more or less synonymous with a trip to Marrakech, and an exclusive clientele of writers, artists, colonial rulers and well-to-do adventurers would sip whisky in the piano bar or stroll around its well-watered gardens. Winston Churchill was a regular, painting a number of watercolours on the balcony of his favourite suite; and Doris Day sang 'Que Sera, Sera' in room 414, in Hitchcock's *The Man Who Knew Too Much*.

For the rich and famous, it carried on being simply the only place to stay well into the late 20th century – until the new boutique hotels started making it feel its age. A kitsch 1986 makeover didn't help, adding a conference centre but eradicating the cool elegance of the past. Nor did a 2001 overhaul of the rooms, with a clutch of tawdry themes (Orient Express, 1930s, Nuptial). And so, in July 2006, it closed again for major renovations, reopening in 2009 following a design revamp by Parisian Jacques Garcia, and boasting no less than 27 fountains, 2,264 doors and 1,000 lanterns. Craftsmen reworked the building's art deco style to a more classically Moroccan one abounding in richly painted wood (*zouaq*) doors, a feast of intricately carved stucco (*ghebs*), walls patterned with *zelije* (coloured decorative tilework) and bathrooms screened with lattice woodwork (*mashrabiya*). Another major change was the conversion of the Moroccan restaurant into a seductive swimming pool chamber.

La Mamounia.

Royal Mansour.

Across town, the Moroccan king's **Royal Mansour** (*see p202*) opened in 2010 close to Jemaa El Fna with a network of service tunnels as intriguing as the hotel itself. No expense was spared on the 53 private riads built within a walled gardened plot that showcases the finest details of Moroccan craftsmanship: *zelije* is patterned in beautiful honey and cream in the public areas, Le Bar is clad with rose gold leaf, the spa pool beneath a glass curved roof is lined with white onyx mosaic, *mashrabiya* screens in dark wood filter the stark light, and intense carved stucco work maps the walls.

Both of these stunning hotels deserve a visit, even if you can't afford to book in for the night. While La Mamounia welcomes visitors, the doormen at the Royal Mansour are somewhat less keen. The best way to feel like royalty at the Mansour is to make a reservation in one of the in-house restaurants, passing through a courtyard entirely adorned with midnight blue Brazilian marble on your way to dinner.

Jardins de la Koutoubia.

around three beautiful courtyards – one filled with the eponymous orange trees, the others lavishly decorated with lacy carved plasterwork. Ten suites have private upstairs sun terraces, and all rooms have access to the roof with matchless views of the nearby Koutoubia minaret – doubly enchanting when the storks come wheeling round at dusk. The subterranean spa and beautifully lit hammam – also open to non-guests – is a draw, as are the three swimming pools. Service is outstanding, and breakfast, a light lunch, non-alcoholic drinks, laundry and airport transfers are included in the price.

Expensive

Jardins de la Koutoubia

16 rue de la Koutoubia (0524 38 88 00, www.lesjardinsdelakoutoubia.com). **Map** p252 B5.

With more than 100 rooms, several gardens, indoor and outdoor pools, a fitness room, and a choice of restaurants including Moroccan, Indian and international, this is the place to stay in the Medina if you crave a hotel rather than an intimate guesthouse. This comfortable, well-run establishment is brilliantly located, two minutes from Jemaa El Fna in one direction, two minutes from the Koutoubia mosque and a steady stream of taxis in the other. The courtyard pool is heated, they can shake a proper cocktail in the Piano Bar, the patio restaurant (*see p39*) is a fine spot for lunch, and everything is nicely spacious. The faux traditional design may not bother the major style supplements, but it isn't too shabby, and both bedrooms and bathrooms are large and welcoming.

Maison MK

14 derb Sebaai, Bab Laksour, Medina (0524 37 61 73, www.maisonmk.com). **Map** p252 B5.

Maison MK oozes class behind its cool walls close to Jemaa El Fna. Indulge in an intense double session of hammam and massage at the in-house Spa MK before sauntering upstairs to the terrace for the nightly Gastro MK supperclub (*see p35*). Canapés are served on the terrace as the sun sets and the call to prayer echoes around the Medina. Then guests head downstairs to the dining room to complete the gourmet adventure. Menu highlights include a rich cauliflower and leek soup laced with argan oil and a clever apple tart tagine. Intrigued by the new-wave Moroccan cuisine? Book into one of the cookery classes (*see p72* **Stir It Up**). After dinner, hit the hookah and cigar snug for a late-night rendezvous under the fabulous papier-mâché sculpture of a mounted camel head smoking a Camel cigarette, or settle into the cinema room (popcorn included) for a late-night screening. Rooms are very comfortable

Maison MK. *See p205.*

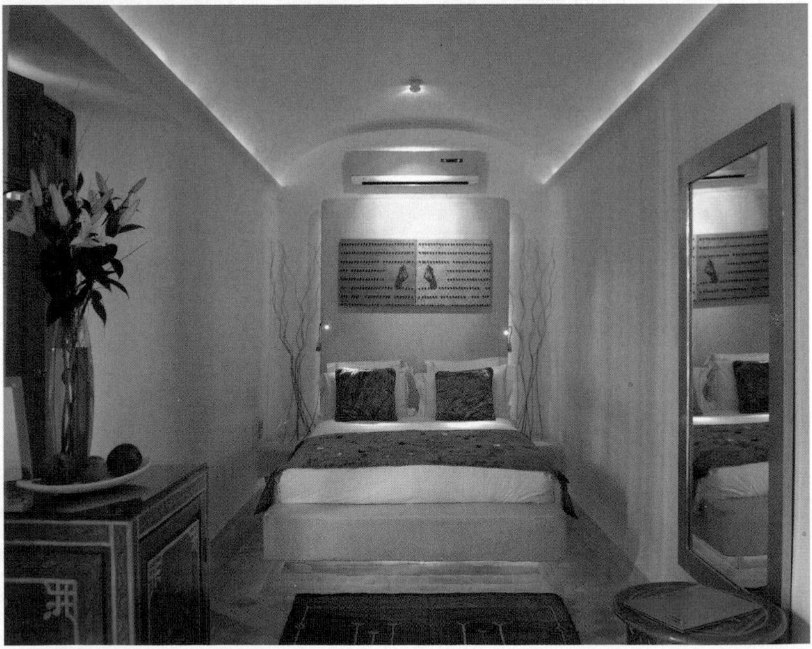

with minibars, iPod docks, large *tadelakt* bathrooms (with an enormous rubber duck for company) and wafting drapes in russet tones.

★ Riad Enija

9 derb Mesfioui, off rue Rahba Lakdima (0524 44 09 26, www.riadenija.com). **Map** p253 D5.

Anyone lacking the pose and hauteur of a Karl Lagerfeld model risks being made to look shabby by comparison with the drop-dead gorgeousness of the surroundings at Riad Enija. Its 15 rooms and suites variously boast glorious old wooden ceilings, beds as works of art (wrought-iron gothic in one, a wooden ship bed in another), some striking furniture (much of it designed by artist friends of Swedish/Swiss owners Björn Conerding and Ursula Haldimann) and grand bathrooms resembling subterranean throne rooms. Central to the three adjoining houses (which originally belonged to a silk trader from Fès and 64 members of his family) is a lush Moorish courtyard garden gone wild, where maroon-uniformed staff flicker through the greenery. Distractions such as TVs and telephones are dispensed with, but alternative services include anything from a visiting aromatherapist and masseurs to cookery classes. The service and food are both excellent, and the riad is just a few minutes' walk from Jemaa El Fna. The only downside to a stay here is the fact that taxis can't get you anywhere very near. Then there's the nuisance of having the latest fashion shoot going on outside your window – we warned you this place was a looker. *Photo p209.*

★ Riad El Fenn

2 derb Moulay Abdallah Ben Hezzian, Bab El-Ksour, Medina (0524 44 12 10, www.riadelfenn.com). **Map** p252 B5.

This riad has received plenty of media attention, partly because it's co-owned by Vanessa Branson (sister of Richard) and partly because it's such a fine place to stay. Several historic houses have been joined together to create 24 spacious, luscious jewel-coloured bedrooms that are happily lost in a warren of staircases and courtyards. The clutter-free rooms are dominated by an Egyptian cotton-swathed bed, standalone baths in some, camel leather-tiled floors and proper-sized desks. The midnight blue courtyard room displays an intriguing scattered collage of Christmas-tree roots that look like small mammal skulls. Despite the grandeur of the architecture and some serious modern art on the walls, the mood is relaxed, with plenty of private spaces, three pools and a glorious rooftop terrace. *'Fenn'* is the local slang for 'cool', and staying here gives you a real sense of tapping into the hip heart of the Red City.

Riyad Al Moussika

17 derb Cherkaoui (0524 38 90 67, www.riyad-al-moussika.ma). **Map** p253 D6.

One reason laid-back Turinese owner Giovanni Robazza opened this former pasha's palace as a guesthouse was to showcase the superb cordon bleu cooking of his son Khalid. This is a riad for gourmands, dedicated 'to the art of good living', with a touch of pretension but a comfortable, worn-in feel. Guests start the day with complimentary breakfast including croissants, a selection of cheeses and home-made jams and even honey from the owner's farm in Italy. The palace has been restored in a relatively traditional style: fountains splash and birds sing in the trees, while six bedrooms are complemented by a hammam, a formal dining room and a small library with some interesting volumes. There are three courtyards, one of which features a long, thin 'Andalucian' pool for swimming, plus two flower-filled roof terraces for dining. The riad also houses the popular Pepe Nero restaurant.

Riad El Fenn.

Moderate

Dar Attajmil

23 rue Laksour, off rue Sidi El-Yamani (0524 42 69 66, www.darattajmil.com). **Map** p252 B5.

With just four bedrooms, Dar Attajmil is one of our favourite small riads. It's run by lovely English-speaking Italian Lucrezia Mutti and her small team of staff. There's a tiny courtyard filled with tropical foliage: banana trees and coconut palms that throw welcome shade on to a small recessed lounge and library. Bedrooms overlook the courtyard from the first floor, and are beautifully decorated in warm,

rustic tones with dark-wood ceilings and handsome *tadelakt* bathrooms. Best of all, though, is the astonishingly peaceful roof terrace, which is scattered with cushions, wicker chairs and sofas – guaranteed to get you in the holiday spirit. Dinner (traditional Moroccan with Italian leanings) is available on request for 220dh per person. It's an easy six-minute walk from the house to Jemaa El Fna, Mouassine and the main souks.

Dar Fakir

16 derb Abou El-Fadal, off Riad Zitoun El-Jedid, Kennaria (0524 44 11 00, www.darfakir.co.uk). **Map** p252 C6.

This riad is for the twentysomething crowd. Dar Fakir's central courtyard and surrounding salons are layered with casually strewn rugs and scattered with inviting sofas for lounging with a drink. The heady scent of incense hangs heavy in the air and tea candles illuminate the riad, while the chilled-out beats humming in the background complete the vibe. The eight guestrooms (two on the ground floor, six upstairs) are very simply done but attractive, including *tadelakt* bathrooms. Owner Noureddine Fakir, an ambitious young Casablancan, also runs the Le Tanjia and Le Salama (*see p39*) restaurants, both within walking distance of the riad.

Budget

Hotel Gallia

30 rue de la Recette, off rue Bab Agnaou (0524 44 59 13, www.ilove-marrakesh.com/hotelgallia). **No credit cards. Map** p252 C6.

The lanes off rue Bab Agnaou – seconds from Jemaa El Fna – are thick with budget options, but Gallia comes top of the class. This small guesthouse ticks all the right boxes: it's smack-bang central, clean and aesthetically pleasing. Nineteen en suite double rooms open on to two picturesque, flower-filled courtyards, where a Moroccan breakfast is served. Bathrooms are big, modern pink affairs with limitless hot water. The well-kept flowery roof terrace is an ideal spot for lounging.

Hotel du Trésor

77 derb Sidi Boulokat, off rue Riad Zitoun El-Kedim (0524 37 51 13, www.hotel-du-tresor.com). **No credit cards. Map** p252 C6.

The Trésor is indeed a little treasure. Restored by its Italian owner, this small hotel blends Moroccan features with mid-century accessories to create a retro look across the building. The chic, white-tiled patio, dotted with Saarinen tulip chairs and tables, has a deep plunge pool and is shaded by a leafy orange tree. The 12 rooms mix and match: a painted ceiling looms over a mezzanine bed, while a mid-century droplet chandelier illuminates the room. At this price, so close to Jemaa El Fna, it's a steal. *Photos p210.*

Jnane Mogador

116 derb Sidi Bouloukat, off rue Riad Zitoun El-Kedim (0524 42 63 24, www.jnanemogador.com). **Map** p252 C6.

The Mogador is a small riad with considerable charm and warmth in a prime location – and all for an unbelievable 380dh per double with en suite bathroom (just don't expect a power shower). The

Riad Enija. *See p207.*

Hotel du Trésor. *See p209.*

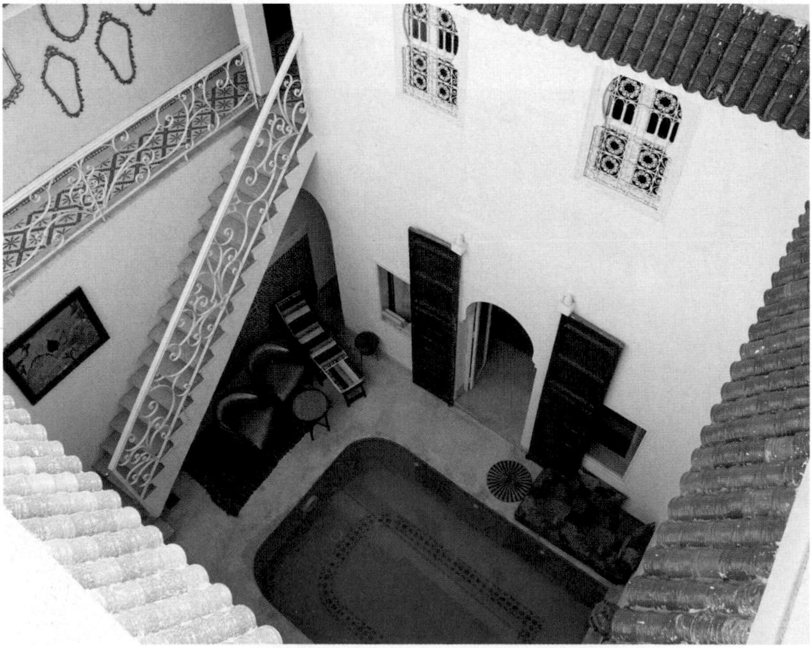

18 rooms are simple and predominantly pink with *tadelakt* bathrooms. All rooms have heating, but a few lack air-conditioning, an important factor when booking in the summer months. Public areas are much more ornate, with fountain courtyards, stucco arches and a large roof terrace used for in-house meals. The spa in the basement is a great place for a cheap and relaxing massage with Rachida. Brush up on your French as spoken English here is limited. Breakfast isn't included in the rates, but it's available for 35dh. Dinner can be served à la carte or from the *menu fixe*.

Riad Linda

93 derb Jamaa, derb Dabachi (0645 91 27 78, UK +44 7812 365 712, www.riadlinda.com). **Map** p253 D5.

This bright and breezy guesthouse is run by the very welcoming Linda, who hails from Edinburgh. The six rooms are named and themed by colour and feature cheery accents, paintings by Linda's husband Gordon Davidson, and plenty of shelf space. One downstairs room is wheelchair-accessible with an adaptable lavatory and shower chair available. Meals are taken on the top terrace with its candy-pink sunloungers, potted bougainvillea and Bedouin tent, or around the central dining table. Staff are very friendly and helpful.

Riad Omar

22 rue Bab Agnaou (0524 44 56 60, www.riadomar.com). **No credit cards. Map** p252 B7.

Omar's cramped but clean, no-frills rooms are the trade-off for budget prices and an excellent location on pedestrianised rue Bab Agnaou, a short stroll south of Jemaa El Fna. This is a hotel rather than a *maison d'hôte*, with 17 rooms and four suites set around a central courtyard with a small fountain. They're all air-conditioned and have decent-sized bathrooms (though only seven of them have baths). The four suites have small sitting areas.

THE SOUKS & AROUND

Aka the Old City. A room here puts you right in among the souks and sights, and the nearer to Jemaa El Fna the better. Remember that much of the Medina is inaccessible by car, so accommodation close to a taxi-friendly main street is always preferable.

Deluxe

★ Riad Farnatchi

2 derb El-Farnatchi, Kat Benahid (0524 38 49 10, www.riadfarnatchi.com). **Map** p251 D4.

Farnatchi is the creation of Jonathan Wix (42 The Calls in Leeds, the Scotsman in Edinburgh and Hôtel de la Trémoille in Paris). Originally intended as his private residence, it's now an intimate, top-class hotel run by his son, James. Suites are set around four courtyards, one of which has a modestly sized heated pool. The suites are vast and supremely luxurious, with large sunken baths, shower rooms, underfloor heating, desks, armchairs and private sun terraces. Standout features include a funky patchwork kilim bedspread in one room, and a bathroom with an art deco-style black marble sunken bath and accompanying circular pink marble sinks in another. The hotel is superbly run and right in the middle of the Medina, just north of Ben Youssef Medersa; taxis can get to within 200m. A spa and standalone restaurant are in the pipeline. The hotel is closed during August.

Expensive

Maison Arabe

1 derb Assehbe, Bab Doukkala (0524 38 70 10, www.lamaisonarabe.com). **Map** p250 A4.

Maison Arabe began life in the 1940s as a restaurant run by two raffish French ladies. It rapidly gained fame through its popularity with illustrious patrons such as Winston Churchill. The last tagines were served in 1983, and the place lay dormant for more than a decade before reopening under Italian ownership in January 1998 as the city's first *maison d'hôte*. Today, it has expanded considerably and houses 12 rooms and 14 suites, with a hotel feel. Inside, the prevailing style is Moroccan classic with French colonial overtones – lots of Orientalist paintings and antiques, high-backed armchairs and an elegant cedarwood library. The rooms and suites are

Jnane Mogador. *See p209.*

Maison Arabe. *See p211.*

supremely comfortable, most with their own private terraces and a couple with fireplaces. Our favourite is Sabah, which is ingeniously fitted around the curve of a dome. In addition to the on-site pools, including a heated outdoor pool, guests can venture out to the large swimming pool at Coin Caché (under separate management), in a luxurious garden setting, a 15-minute ride from the hotel (a free shuttle service is provided). Back at the hotel, there's live Arab-Andalusian music to accompany dinner in the Moroccan restaurant (*see p71*). Downstairs, there are two large hammams and a wellness area. Guests can also sign up for the hotel's Moroccan cookery workshops (*see p72*).

Riad Kniza

34 derb l'Hôtel, Bab Doukkala (0524 37 69 42, www.riadkniza.com). **Map** p250 A3.

This grand, well-located 18th-century house has belonged to the family of current owner Mohammed Bouskri for two centuries, but it only opened as a *maison d'hôte* in 2004. It's the most Moroccan of upmarket riads, decorated entirely in a conservative and traditional style. There are seven suites and four rooms, and even the smallest is pretty spacious. The suites all have separate sitting rooms and there are working fireplaces throughout. The Bouskri family are antiques dealers, and there are a lot of old pieces in alcoves and cabinets. Mohammed Bouskri has also been a professional guide for more than 30 years, so it's a useful place for anyone who wants to 'do' Marrakech in an old-school way. Rates include a free half-day tour of the Medina and airport transfer. The in-house hammam is large enough for two people – the perfect way to spend a romantic afternoon. Kniza deserves its reputation as a well-run establishment – the only downside is a slightly staid atmosphere. No children under 12 allowed.

Riad Noir d'Ivoire

31 derb Jdid, Bab Doukkala (0524 38 09 75, www.noir-d-ivoire.com). **Map** p250 A3.

Riad Noir d'Ivoire has that gratifying combination of looking spectacular while feeling exceedingly comfortable. Interior designer and former co-owner Jill Fechtmann mixed specially commissioned Moroccan elements with assorted curiosities from sub-Saharan Africa (inspired by years in Swaziland), Europe (years more in Paris and the Dordogne) and India. Six rooms and three suites set around two courtyards have huge beds imported from the US, Egyptian cotton sheets, big bathrooms and pleasingly eccentric furnishings that vaguely exude an animal theme. Our favourite is the Chameau suite, with its open fire, golden masks in alcoves, divinely comfortable armchairs, and a sculpted wooden camel as big as a mule. Off the chandeliered winter courtyard with plunge pool there's a hammam in Tiznit marble, plus a lounge/library, small boutique, dining area and cosy bar. The vibe is sociable, especially around the summer courtyard pool, but it's also enchantingly serene. Riad Noir d'Ivoire is slightly buried in the Medina, but Couscous the donkey is on permanent hoof to assist with luggage.

Moderate

★ Dar Doukkala

83 Arset Aouzal, off rue Bab Doukkala (0524 38 34 44, www.dardoukkala.com). **Map** p250 B4.

A handsome mix of English country mansion and Moroccan townhouse pepped up with 1960s and art deco vintage pieces, Dar Doukkala is a very chic, slightly unkempt, homely place to stay. Its five bedrooms and two suites are filled with gorgeous period details and furnishings, including claw-foot tubs and pedestal basins in the bathrooms. Other wonderfully eccentric touches include Guimard-like glass canopies projecting into the central, lusciously overgrown garden courtyard, and an artful array of lanterns patterning the wall behind the terrace-level pool. It's one of the most fun and delightful *maisons d'hôtes* in town. Both suites have two extra beds for kids, while one of the doubles also comes with an extra bed. The location is good, too, opposite the wonderland warehouse of Mustapha Blaoui (*see p73*) and close to the main Dar El-Bacha road and its taxis.

Riad Adore

97 derb Tizouagrine, Dar El-Bacha (0524 37 77 37, www.riadadore.com). **Map** p250 B4.

This, the latest in the Pure Riads collection of sleek little properties, is in the most fashionable part of the Medina. The contemporary design is the result of Stuart Redcliffe's passion for interiors, and he's used clean lines and soothing, muted tones as a frame for eye-popping souk finds such as hand-embroidered bedlinens and bespoke lanterns. Unusually, each of the individually decorated rooms has cable TV, and you'll find stacks of lifestyle magazines scattered throughout the various living areas. There's also a well-stocked library, television lounge with fireplace, courtyard plunge pool, top-notch hammam (book at least one session, it's one of the best in town) and romantic canopied roof terrace with outside fireplace for dining. The food here is excellent.

Riad Azzar

94 derb Moulay Abdelkader, off derb Debbachi (0661 15 81 73, www.riadazzar.com). **Map** p253 D5.

Owned by a friendly, English-speaking Dutch couple, Azzar is a neat little six-room riad with the feel of a B&B. It's distinguished by a small, emerald-green heated plunge pool in the middle of the courtyard. Walls are whitewashed and the decor is understated: it's a very tasteful place. Three of the rooms are suites and come with fireplaces and air-conditioning (as does the twin room); of these, the Taznarth suite also boasts a beautiful *mashrabiya* (wooden lattice) window overlooking the courtyard and a particularly lovely grey *tadelakt* bathroom. Riad Azzar supports a local orphanage; guests are encouraged to contribute by bringing children's toys and clothing or school materials for donation.

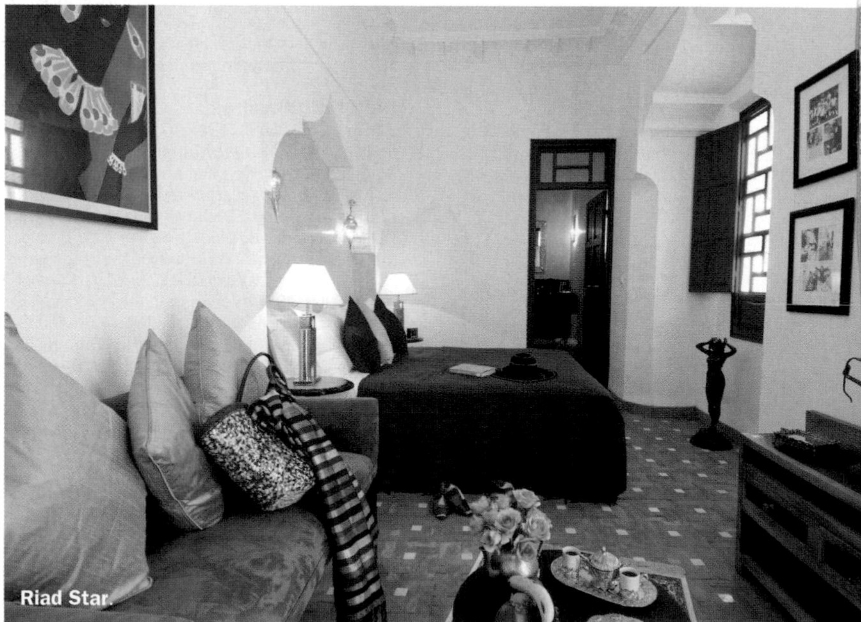

Riad Star.

Riad Noga

78 derb Jedid, Douar Graoua (0524 37 76 70, www.riadnoga.com). **Map** p253 D5.

Noga is one of the homeliest of Marrakech's riads. Behind salmon-pink walls lies a bougainvillea- and orange tree-filled courtyard (complete with chatty grey parrot), serving as an antechamber to an inner, more private courtyard centred on a shimmering, tiled, solar-heated swimming pool. Noga is very spacious (it's made up of three old houses knocked into one), and shared by just seven rooms. All of the rooms are bright, bold and cheery, displaying the hospitable touch (small libraries of holiday-lite literature, for instance) of the garrulous German owner, Gaby Noack-Späth. Expansive roof terraces filled with terracotta pots and lemon trees offer terrific views over the Medina and make for the perfect spot to enjoy aperitifs or fine cooking.

Riad 72

72 derb Arset Aouzal, off rue Bab Doukkala (0524 38 76 29, www.riad72.com). **Map** p250 B4.

Italian-owned, this is one sleek and good-looking place – Marrakech has it away with Milan. The result is a traditional townhouse given a black, white and grey *tadelakt* makeover. The structure, space and detailing are Moroccan, the furniture and fittings imported. There are just four guest bedrooms, all up on the first floor and set around the central courtyard. Rooms include a master suite that's laugh-out-loud large, five metres or more in height and crowned by an ornate octagonal fanlight. The personal service here is the cherry on top: guests have the choice of scented toiletries and each room has its own Italian espresso machine. The roof terrace has one of the best views in town, with the green-tiled roofs of Dar El-Bacha in the foreground and a jagged mountain horizon beyond. Being that much higher than the neighbours means sunbathing is no problem (many riads are overlooked and modesty can be an issue). Milanese owner and designer Giovanna Cinel is currently expanding the riad and plans to open three more rooms in 2014. Superior vehicle access is a further bonus.

★ Riad Star

31 derb Alailich, Kaat Benahid (UK +44 20 7193 7357, www.marrakech-riad.co.uk/riad-star). **Map** p251 D4.

A glittering homage to American starlet Josephine Baker, who stayed in this Medina home in the 1940s while entertaining Allied troops, Riad Star is managed by the charming Abdel and Miriam, and oozes a soothingly pared-back luxury. The Star's seven rooms are themed: Josephine's Room is furnished with funky cushions printed with Baker's image, as well as lithographs of Baker framed on the walls. The Lori Park flying wire and monofilament 'Josephine Dancing' sculpture, depicting Baker sporting the iconic banana tutu, makes for a glorious bathroom feature. Downstairs in the dining room, Baker's seductive sequinned gowns are displayed alongside a rail of 1920s clothes for guests to dress up in. Don a wig or a fez, slip into a flapper dress and lounge on the top sun terrace or by the small courtyard fountain amid the silver pouffes, Baker collectibles and silver screen moments projected on to the walls. It's a dreamy place to stay.

★ Riad Tizwa

26 derb Gueraba, Dar El-Bacha (0668 19 08 72, UK +44 7973 115 471, www.riadtizwa.com). **Map** p250 B4.

Relaxed and comfortable, Tizwa is one of the friendliest riads in town. Laid out in the usual fashion on three open-fronted floors around a central tiled courtyard, this place is a great antidote to design excess. The six rooms are white with gull-grey doors and splashes of colour, and some feature wood-beamed ceilings; *tadelakt* bathrooms are in a limestone shade. Design solutions are simple but striking, such as the thick, high azure *tadelakt* headboards that conceal clothing rails behind them in two of the rooms. Each room is equipped with an iPod docking station. There is a hammam, and the roof terrace has a shaded area for alfresco dining. Another advantage of this place is that it's accessible to taxis, just a few yards down a narrow alley off rue Dar El-Bacha. Mornings are a pleasure – early-morning coffee and tea at your door in tasselled Thermoses, and breakfast when and where you want it.

ESSENTIAL INFORMATION

RIAD REVOLUTIONARIES

Modern takes on Moroccan style.

Jnane Tamsna.

Tadelakt walls, carved stucco, colourful *zelije* tiling, rugs on the walls – it sometimes seems like every riad has been designed from the same Marrakech style handbook. The basic forms and materials are native, of course, as is the palette – the pinks and ochres of local earth, lemon yellow, the blue of cobalt skies. But for traditional Moroccan and Berber crafts and methods to result in an internationally recognised style required outside intervention. Enter Bill Willis, the man who ignited the Marrakech interiors explosion.

A native of Memphis, Tennessee, Willis moved to Marrakech in the 1960s and began working for such clients as John Paul Getty, Jr and Yves Saint Laurent. He developed a style based on traditional Moroccan references (arches, painted woodwork, geometric patterns in tiling), but imbued the whole with his own slightly camp sense of humour. Check out his candy-striped, onion-domed fireplaces at **Dar Yacout** (*see p67*) or the palm tree columns at the Tichka hotel on route de Casablanca.

While his particular twists are wholly modern, the techniques are age-old – intricate mosaic work, wood carving, stonemasonry. And because his interiors demanded local craftsmen to adapt and stretch, Willis also helped to revive the city's artisan traditions. He worked on the Tichka with architect Charles Boccara, who also used traditional elements to convey a strong sense of place while striking an unmistakably modern pose. His interiors make stunning use of *tadelakt*, the polished wall finish traditionally employed in hammams, where heat and moisture are a problem. Surfaces are trowelled in a plaster of powdered limestone mixed with coloured dust to provide the requisite hue. The plaster is then polished hard with flat stones, sealed with a glaze of egg white, and polished again with Moroccan black soap. Boccara brought *tadelakt* out of the steam room and into style.

Following the example set by his signature **Les Deux Tours** (*see p224*), completed in the early 1990s, Marrakech has gone *tadelakt* mad. French-Senegalese architect Meryanne Loum-Martin also schooled herself in traditional crafts and methods, then applied the knowledge to a half-built concrete shell in the Palmeraie. The result was Dar Tamsna, the protoype boho-chic villa and the place that really introduced Marrakech to the international lifestyle press. Like Willis, she reinterpreted local ingredients, but with a beautifully restrained simplicity – an approach she refined at **Jnane Tamsna** (*see p225*), which was completed in 2002.

Meanwhile, the riad scene began to boom in the Medina. Low property prices and an abundance of local artisans encouraged designers to buy houses and go to town on them. Each started with the same traditional references, but the beauty of the whole modern Marrakech style is how readily traditional methods lend themselves to experimentation and innovation.

Björn Conerding and Ursula Haldimann took traditional Moroccan into the realm of gothic fantasy at **Riad Enija** (*see p207*); Christian Ferré played heavily on colour and patterning at **Riad Kaiss** (*see p221*); Christophe Siméon developed a Moroccan minimalism with **Riad Mabrouka** (*see p221*); Giovanna Cinel married Marrakech to Milan at **Riad 72** (*see p215*); and Jill Fechtmann and Jean-Michel Jobit mixed local elements with an idiosyncratic eclecticism at **Riad Noir d'Ivoire** (*see p213*). It's astonishing how many riads are now owned by designers turned hoteliers: Marrakech has become their playground.

Riad Enija.

Riad Kaiss.

Riad 72.

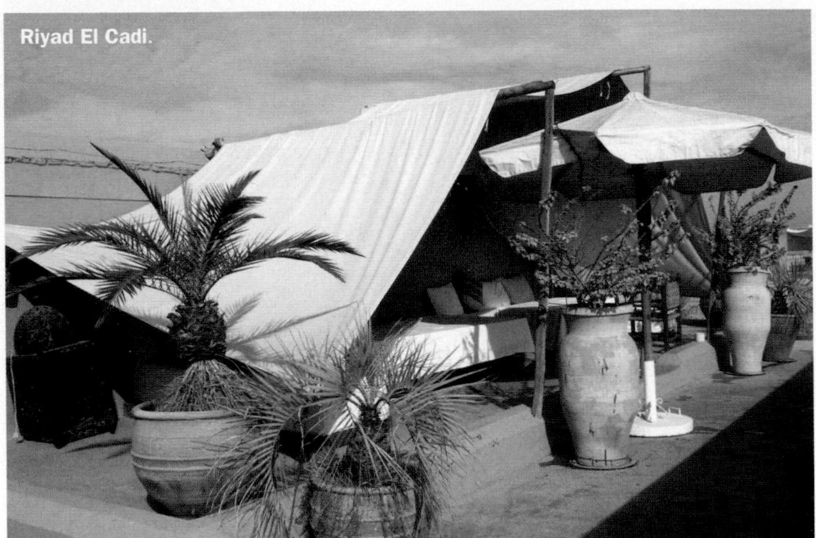
Riyad El Cadi.

Riad Wo

41 derb Boutouil, Douar Graoua (0665 36 79 36, www.riadw.com). **Map** p253 D6.

Working on the premise that guests will get quite enough sensory input from their forays into the Medina, Spanish owner Elsa Bauza designed her five-bedroom riad with a philosophy of simplicity and 'quiet in the head'. The bedrooms – two huge, two big, one small – have white walls, unadorned save for a few framed textiles. Three rooms have fireplaces. Downstairs, zen-like lines are matched by some quietly retro furnishings. It makes a refreshing change in a town where there's often too much colour and clutter. Up top are two roof terraces, one of which is shared by two rooms, perfect for families or friends travelling together. Below is a spacious courtyard, a plunge pool, two sitting rooms (one with a piano), and Bauza and her daughter's apartment. Dinner can be arranged on request.

Riyad El Cadi

87 derb Moulay Abdelkader, off derb Debbachi (0524 37 86 55, www.riyadelcadi.com).
Map p253 D5.

Made up of eight interconnecting houses, El Cadi is a rambling maze of a place in which getting lost is a pleasure – which is lucky as it'll happen quite a lot in your first few days. The 12 well-appointed suites and bedrooms, as well as the various salons, corridors, staircases and landings, also double as gallery spaces for an outstanding collection of art and artefacts gathered by late former owner Herwig Bartels. The reception area alone boasts an ancient Berber textile with a Bauhaus chair and a Rothko-style abstract painting. Despite the rich details, the overall feel is uncluttered, cool and contemporary. Bartels' daughter Julia now runs the riad, with the assistance of a friendly team, and standards remain high. Extensive roof terraces with tented lounging areas further add to the appeal of what, for the money, is some of the classiest accommodation in town. The two-bedroom Blue House is available for groups and is part of the main riad. The only drawback of the place is its distance from taxi dropping-off points, though cars can get quite close at the top end of Jemaa El Fna in the morning.

Talaa 12

12 Talaa Ben Youssef, El-Moqf (0524 42 90 45, www.talaa12.com). **Map** p251 D4.

A serene, minimalist-style riad in the north-east of the Medina, Talaa 12 is owned by Belgian architect Philipe Taburiaux and interior designer Marianne Lacroix. Walls are white and shutters are grey, with judicious bolts of colour provided by rugs, furnishings and hangings. The courtyard is planted with lemon trees, and Arabic chill-out and gnawa-style music plays on the CD player. There are eight comfortable bedrooms, with limestone *tadelakt* bathrooms. Location is another plus factor: Talaa 12 is in the El-Moqf section of the Medina, right next to the souks, a few doors down from the Musée de Marrakech and just a ten-minute walk from Jemaa El Fna. The roof terrace has a 360-degree view of the rooftops of Marrakech and the high peaks of the Atlas mountains.

Tchaikana

25 derb El-Ferrane, Azbest (0524 38 51 50, www.tchaikana.com). **No credit cards. Map** p251 D4.

Tchaikana's four rooms are spacious, particularly the two 11mx5m suites (which can sleep up to four people). The decor is chic, with a nomad/ethnic vibe, and the central courtyard, laid out for dining, is gorgeously lit at night. Soft drinks and orange juice are free for guests, and there's a selection of board games to keep youngsters busy. The owners, Jean-Louis Montilla and Barbara Seine, are French, and Jean-Louis' photographs are displayed throughout the riad. In case you're wondering, a *tchaikana* is a Central Asian teahouse. Closed 15 July to 31 August.

Budget

Dar 18

18 derb El-Ferrane, off rue Riad El-Arous (0524 38 98 64). **No credit cards. Map** p250 C3.

It's barely possible to find anything cheaper in the Medina, but the real attractions of this artists' hub are the pop-up events (*see p93* **Art Explosion**), art installations in the courtyard such as the emerald green threaded balcony weaving by Hermione Skye, and artwork on the walls, plus the knowledge that your stay supports local Moroccan artists. Upstairs are three comfortable bedrooms – think recycled wardrobe doors as mirrors, French dressers, white drapes, and *tadelakt* bathrooms. Lounge about on the roof terrace with its potted cactus and flowers or grab a mint tea from the cool black-and-white tiled kitchen while mingling with the residents and visiting artists.

Equity Point Hostel

80 derb El-Hammam, Mouassine (0524 44 07 93, www.equity-point.com). **Map** p250 C4.

Equity Point has achieved a considerable feat by shoehorning a 147-bed hostel into the heart of the Medina – including a swimming pool for the backpackers. Buried down derb el Hammam behind the Mouassine fountain, Equity has reinhabited the old Riad Amazigh and built a brand new attached property behind. The original riad has private rooms, but it's all a bit dark and uninviting. The best options are the ensuite dorm rooms – girls only or mixed – with lockers that line the pool area in the new building. You'll have to bring your own towel or pay a charge, but with breakfast and Wi-Fi included, and tours and cooking classes that can be booked at the front desk, there's little to complain about – except the awkward location. Sometimes the hostel signs are taken down and once you go under the arch between the Mouassine fountain and the mosque (where there are also signs to the *douiria, see p60*), the signs peter out. If you're arriving at night, you may be best off booking the airport transfer so you're delivered direct to the door.

KASBAH, MELLAH & AROUND

Expensive

Dar Les Cigognes

108 rue de Berima (0524 38 27 40, www.sanssoucicollection.com). **Map** p253 D8.

Dar Les Cigognes (House of Storks) is two properties combined – and reworked by the architect Charles Boccara – facing the walls of the vast Badii Palace. Above the central courtyard, perfumed with

Tchaikana.

orange trees, are several of the Dar's 11 bedrooms. One of the double rooms features an iron four-poster, creamy drapes, carved stucco ceilings, a sparkling *handira* carpet on the floor and an astoundingly beautiful wardrobe inlaid with mother-of-pearl. In summer, breakfast and dinner are taken on the roof terrace of the building that was once a 17th-century merchant's townhouse. The terrace is so close to the palace walls that you can virtually eyeball one of the famous nesting storks. Les Cigognes is well known for its food and cooking classes – Yotam Ottolenghi filmed an episode of his *Mediterranean Feasts* here, and MasterChef Travel has partnered with the property.

Les Jardins de la Medina

21 derb Chtouka, Kasbah (0524 38 18 51, www.lesjardinsdelamedina.com). **Map** p252 C9.
At the southern end of the kasbah, this former royal residence has been a luxurious 36-room hotel since 2001. You enter a beautiful reception area eccentrically decorated with a tree and wooden birds hanging upside down from a painted dome. From there, you emerge into a wonderfully spacious garden with rows of orange trees and a heated swimming pool actually large enough to swim in – which makes it a great place for families. Comfortable rooms, decorated in a Moroccan-international style, come in three categories. Most are in the middle 'superior' class – big enough to have sofas as well as beds – and all of them have DVD players and iPod docks. A large international restaurant, splendid hammam, decently equipped gym, beauty salon and cookery school round off the perks.

★ Riad Hayati

27 derb Bouderba, off derb El-Bahia, Riad Zitoun El-Jedid (UK +44 7770 431 194, www.riadhayati.com). **Map** p253 D7.
Could this be the most tasteful riad in town? It's a little piece of visual perfection, with two bedrooms arranged around the courtyard and two set off the galleried first floor of a white courtyard framed by cascading bougainvillea; intricately carved dark wooden doors complete the look. In an adjoining building, reached through a beautiful and tranquil salon, a small staircase leads up to a private garden suite with plunge pool and sunloungers on its own terrace. Complementing the classic Moorish architecture are subtle references to Ottoman Turkey, Persia and Arabia (a mirror modelled on one seen in Istanbul's Dolmabahçe Palace, a fountain from Damascus), mementos of the British owner's many years in news broadcasting from the Middle East (*hayati* means 'my life'). The location is extremely peaceful but only six or seven minutes' walk from Jemaa El Fna.

Riad Kaiss

65 derb Jedid, off Riad Zitoun El-Kedim (0524 44 01 41, www.riadkaiss.com). **Map** p252 C7.
Renovated by the late architect Christian Ferré, the nine-room Kaiss is small but exquisite. Its Rubik's Cube layout has rooms linked by galleries, multi-level terraces and tightly twisting stairs, all set around a central courtyard filled with orange, lemon and pomegranate trees. The decor is traditional Moroccan: earthy ochre walls with chalky Majorelle-blue trim, stencilled paintwork (including some gorgeous ceilings), jade *zelije* tiling and frilly furniture (including four-poster beds). Guests are greeted by red rose petals sprinkled on the white linen pillows. Modern tastes dictate a handsome, cool plunge pool on the roof and an in-house hammam to relieve aching, souk-sore limbs. *Photo p222.*

★ Riad Mabrouka

56 derb El-Bahia, off Riad Zitoun El-Jedid (0612 41 73 21, www.riad-mabrouka.com). **Map** p253 D6.
The Mabrouka is a vision of cool, understated elegance. Architect Christophe Simeon has gone for a Moroccan minimalist look, with whitewashed walls, black-and-white photography, billowing canvas in place of doors and some fabulous painted ceilings and shutters; kilims add selective splashes of colour. The result is stylish, but also very comfortable.

La Sultana. *See p222.*

ESSENTIAL INFORMATION

Bathrooms are sensuous; all soft corners and rounded edges, they look as if they've been moulded out of coloured clay. With just four suites and two doubles, the place has a very intimate feel. There's a pleasant roof terrace with a canvas-shaded breakfast area, and a good kitchen turning out Moroccan, Mediterranean, French and Italian cuisine.

La Sultana

403 rue de la Kasbah, Kasbah (0524 38 80 08, www.lasultanahotels.com). **Map** p252 B8.

Opened in 2004, the Sultana is astonishing in that it's a completely new-build hotel of considerable size and scale in the middle of the Medina – and you'd never know it was there. It has no frontage to speak of, but beyond the arched street door are 28 guestrooms and suites, seemingly connected by acres of arcaded corridors, courtyards, landings and galleries. There's a good-sized swimming pool with beautiful turquoise fishscale mosaic, a full spa complex, a row of boutiques and a vast roof terrace with a splash pool that overlooks the gardens of the Saadian Tombs. The hotel boasts all the facilities and amenities of a five-star but is packaged to look like a *maison d'hôte*. The architecture (Moorish-gothic) and decoration is sumptuous , mixing Indian, African and Oriental with Moroccan. Serving French and Moroccan cuisine, the restaurant is open to non-guests who reserve in advance, but the basement bar is residents only. Kitted out to resemble a ship's cabin, the bar even has a window into the deep end of the swimming pool. The hotel closes for two weeks in July. *Photo p221.*

Budget

Riad Souika

6 derb Souika, Berima (www.lawrenceofmorocco.com/accommodation/riad-souika). **Map** p253 D8.

This small, quiet riad is close to the Berima mosque in a non-touristy part of town, but it's just a short walk from the monumental Badii Palace and the labyrinthine Mellah. With just three rooms, it's perfect for families or groups of friends who want a place to themselves. The choice room at the prettily tiled Souika faces out out on to one of the top sun terraces, with glass doors leading away from the low-slung bed and cute blue and *tadelakt* grey bathroom with alcove shower. Aziz, the manager, comes in daily to serve breakfast in the dining room or on the terrace, and is a dab hand at cooking dinner if you fancy a night in.

VILLE NOUVELLE

Budget

Hotel du Pacha

33 rue de la Liberté, Guéliz (0524 43 13 27, www.hotelpacha.net). **Map** p254 B2.

Hotel du Pacha is a fairly standard two-star joint. The only indication that this is Morocco comes courtesy of a handful of aged tourist office posters. Better rooms have small balconies overlooking a pleasant central courtyard, but all are clean with air-conditioning, TV and Wi-Fi. There are plenty of female staff around, making it a comfortable option

Riad Kaiss. *See p221.*

ESSENTIAL INFORMATION

Mosaic Palais Aziza.

for solo female travellers. Its position, a stone's throw from the chic shopping street of rue du Vieux Marrakchi and the new Carré Eden shopping centre in Guéliz, is unrivalled. Note that breakfast costs extra (40dh).

THE PALMERAIE

Deluxe

Ksar Char-Bagh

Djnan Abiad, Palmeraie (0524 32 92 44, www.ksarcharbagh.com).

Ksar Char-Bagh takes the whole Moroccan fantasy trip to its absolute extremes. The original French owners recreated an Alhambran palace court that nearly defies belief; it's been built from scratch on a kasbah-sized scale. A moated gatehouse with six-metre-high beaten metal doors fronts an arcaded central courtyard with a pool. Extensive grounds contain herb and flower gardens, an orchard, a subterranean rose marble hammam and a stunning heated 34-metre pool elegantly lined with handsome palms. Lunch or dinner can be served out on the terrace or by the pool; the chef previously worked as a sous-chef to Gérald Passédat at Marseille's Le Petit Nice. A champagne bar, library and cigar salon complete the luxury picture. All these treats are shared by just a handful of sumptuous, not to mention spacious, suites, each featuring its own private garden or terrace, and several with their own exclusive swimming pool.

★ Mosaic Palais Aziza

Mejjat 3/38, Cercle Ennakhil, Commune J'Nanate, Palmeraie (0524 32 99 88, www.mosaicpalaisaziza.com).

Situated in the star-studded roads of the Palmeraie, and surrounded by Moroccan and Saudi Arabian royalty, the charming Mosaic Palais Aziza is run by its equally charming manager Karim el Ghazzawi. What distinguishes the Aziza from the plentiful palaces that now dot the Palmeraie are the inventive dishes from its Morolino Moroccan-Italian restaurant, and its decadent spa. With just 12 rooms, it's also an intimate place with a warm and friendly vibe. Plush white beds are surrounded by soothing aubergine and tangerine tones, and the large grey *tadelakt* bathrooms feature rain-shower cubicles, jacuzzi baths, and luxury chocolate and poppyseed soaps. The centrepiece of the hotel is the pool surrounded by matt gold sunloungers (with an attached section for the kids). When you're not stretched out in the sun, head for the subterranean spa for a hammam and one of the best massages in Marrakech.

Palais Namaskar

Route de Bab Atlas, no.88/69, Province Syba, Palmeraie (0524 29 98 00, www.palaisnamaskar.com).

The modernist villas at this Palmeraie palace are stylish and secluded. Behind thick, heavy doors, a private heated aquamarine pool, set amid olive trees, unfurls in front of the floor-to-ceiling glass windows of your private hideaway. Minimalist in

Peacock Pavilions.

outlook, there's a chimney for winter days, grey velvet chairs, a vast Minotti double beanbag for watching the Bang & Olufsen TV, a super sleek bathroom with double rainshower cubicle and an outdoor bathtub. There are rooms at the hotel, set behind the spa area, but you'll want to opt for a villa if you can. The Namaskar is known for its Moroccan food (*see p108*), but it's a shame they've taken some of the heat out of the Thai food (pandering to requests from guests).

Expensive

Dar Zemora

72 rue El-Aandalib, Ennakhil (0524 32 82 00, UK +44 7913 152 195, www.darzemora.com).

Set in a hectare of lush gardens filled with roses and hibiscus, fragrant bougainvillea and palm trees, Dar Zemora is the Marrakech equivalent of an English country-house hotel – perhaps because it's owned by an English couple, who've remodelled this former private abode beyond all recognition. Apart from two large sitting rooms, a dining room and a library with leather-upholstered armchairs, the main house contains just three rooms and two big suites. The Zahara suite, done out in coffee-coloured tones, boasts a king-size four-poster, a small private terrace with daybed and a sunken marble bath. There's also a two-bedroom pavilion in the garden with a spacious living room and its own private pool. The hotel closes for three weeks in August.

Les Deux Tours

Douar Abiad (0524 32 95 27, www.les-deuxtours.com).

Les Deux Tours (named for its distinctive twin-towered gateway) is the sublime work of leading Marrakchi architect Charles Boccara. It's a walled enclave of earthen-red villas that together offer 37 chic rooms and suites in a lush blossom-, citrus-, fig- and palm-filled garden setting. No two rooms are the same, but all feature glowing *tadelakt* walls and *zelije* tiling with stunning bathrooms, several in pink mud-brick domes seductively lit via glassy punch-holes. Guests share the most attractive of outdoor pools, keyhole-shaped and fringed with perfectly maintained grassy lawns, as well as an alfresco restaurant. After a day in the souks, head for the hammam or a massage. The free shuttle bus service into Guéliz (not always a given with Palmeraie hotels) is a definite bonus.

★ Jnane Tamsna

Douar Abiad (0524 32 94 23, www.jnane.com).

The creation of designer Meryanne Loum-Martin and her ethnobotanist husband Dr Gary Martin, Jnane Tamsna is a 'Moorish hacienda' with opulent suites and 24 gorgeous rooms, set in five buildings scattered around some beautiful, fragrant gardens, each with its own pool. The architecture is vernacular chic, coloured in the palest tones of primrose, peppermint and clay, and enhanced by Loum-Martin's own furniture. The surrounding fruit orchards and herb and vegetable gardens provide organic produce for the kitchen. The combination of rural tranquillity, Zen-like aesthetics and ecological beliefs makes for an almost utopian (no locks on the doors) vibe. There's also an art gallery (ask to see Loum-Martin's Meissen porcelain designs) and boutique, gardening and calligraphy workshops, and magic shows and children's activities during the holidays; non-guests are able to take advantage of 'pool, lunch and tennis' packages or visit for dinner (*see p108*). Donations for guided tours of the gardens go towards a charity project to restore Moroccan school gardens.

FURTHER AFIELD

All of the places listed below are roughly a ten- to 40-minute drive from the Medina – far enough away to be rural, but close enough to head into town for dinner.

Deluxe

Amanjena

Route de Ouarzazate, km12 (0524 39 90 00, www.amanresorts.com).

The Amanjena is part of Amanresorts, one of the world's most luxurious hotel chains. It caters to a very specific and highly pampered clientele: Amanjunkies are not the kind to worry about a few hundred dollars here and there. What they get for their money is an exclusive gated complex a few miles south of town. The architecture is low-rise palatial, rose pink and frilly, trimmed with green-tiled roofs. At the heart of the resort is the *bassin*, a massive fish-filled reservoir of water that feeds two shallow canals running between the 32 *pavillons* and six *maisons*. These are vast private residences oozing pared-back luxury. All come with their own walled gardens, and some have private pools. Services range from hammams to the loan of clubs for use on the Amelkis golf course next door. Yes, that might be Sting lounging by the pool, but if you can afford to stay here you're probably as rich and famous as he is.

★ Peacock Pavilions

Route de Ourzazate, km18 (0664 41 46 53, www.peacockpavilions.com).

This striking, stylish retreat, located just 20 minutes from downtown Marrakech, is set in an olive grove and scented by flourishing rose gardens. Maryam Montague, a writer and human rights specialist, and her husband Chris, an architect, host guests in two large pavilions (which Chris built) set either side of an inviting, sparkling turquoise pool. The Atlas and Medina pavilions house two and three bedrooms respectively. Another pavilion harbours a library, shop and indoor dining room. Peacock Pavilions is decorated with Maryam's eclectic global treasures: Moroccan carpets, skulls sporting goggles, wooden fertility sculptures, Swan chairs fashioned from petrol cans, Frank Gehry's cardboard wiggle chairs,

Selman. *See p226.*

Fellah Hotel.

and primary-coloured vintage Malian bread baskets. The atmosphere is very relaxed: sip a cocktail (we love the gin, jasmine syrup and mint) by the pool before dining on doughy olive bread, tender lamb tagine and poached pear while listening to Maryam's tales of Moroccan magic, legends and myths. The alfresco cinema with its deckchairs is an indulgent perk (and is accompanied by lashings of hot chocolate in winter). Chris and Maryam run outreach Project Soar (www.projectsoarmarrakesh.org) for girls in the local village, run yoga retreats, and also manage an online shop, www.redthreadsouk.com; Maryam's book, *Marrakesh by Design*, is a must-buy for those seeking to recreate the Moroccan look back home.

Selman

Route d'Amziz, km5 (0524 38 67 18, www.selman-marrakech.com).

An extraordinary 80-metre heated pool lined with chic pavilions greets you at the family-run Selman, just a ten-minute drive from the Medina. Kitted out by French designer Jacques García, who was also behind the Mamounia renovation, it's a Moorish-style palace clad with enormous Baccarat chandeliers and luxury fabrics, but it retains an intimate feel. Owners Saida and Abdeslam Bennani Smires are equestrian aficionados and their collection of 12 award-winning Arabian horses, which are paraded for guests on a regular basis, are a real draw. The 56 rooms – think plush suedes in tangerine, taupe and mustard, elegantly lit with Moulay Youssef lanterns, luxury *zelije* bathrooms and in-mirror TVs – overlook the pool, gardens and stables. There are also five individual villas set back behind Assil, the Moroccan restaurant pavilion. The luxury spa, dimly lit and beautiful, pampers with Chenot beauty treatments. *Photo p225.*

Expensive

Chez Max

Douar Tagadert Ait El-Kadi, route du Barrage, Km24, Tameslouht (www.lawrenceofmorocco.com/accommodation/chez-max).

As the hills slope up towards the High Atlas, a scattering of Berber villages colonise the starkly beautiful plains. In the midst of the village of Tagadert lies a stylish country getaway in the form of Chez Max. Set around a huge living-dining space accented with stylish mid-century furniture and books, as well as vintage Berber finds, are five bedrooms split between two adjoining buildings. Wander around the village and the olive groves during your stay before huddling around the open fire in winter or taking a dip in one of the two pools in high summer. Come winter or summer, though, savouring Saida's delicious home-cooked traditional Moroccan dishes will be a highlight.

★ Fellah Hotel

Route de l'Ourika, km13, Tassoultante, Canal Zabara (0525 06 50 00, www.fellah-hotel.com).

This desert-chic retreat blended with urban cool is a big hit with hipsters, artists and young families alike. Banker-turned-entrepreneur Redha Moali has fashioned a funky hotel, with a social responsibility ethos, roaming over land dotted with cactus, herbs, a children's treehouse, sunken gym, gorgeous pool and farmyard. Embedded into the unusual hotel landscape are villas with spacious rooms and fabulous half-egg bathtubs, but it's the restaurant area and pool, the Salon Mahler for films and talks, and the on-site cultural centre (http://dam-arts.org), supported by income from the hotel, that really stand out. The beautiful 2,500-book library, with a children's section, is a centre for translation; one of the villas is dedicated to an artists' residency programme; there's a fabulous kids' club and cooking classes; and Wat Po masseurs from Bangkok can be found at the spa. Most guests are drawn to the central bar, restaurant and pool section heralded by a kitsch Arnold Schwarzenegger *Santería*-style altar, shabby-chic sofas and a pool table. Beyond lie alfresco restaurant Touco (*see p109*) and the alluring pool with its thatched tiki parasols set against the backdrop of the snow-dusted Atlas mountains. All the staff are local, a literary project educates women in the village, and local kids can use the children's pool and gym.

Le Palais Paysan

Douar Akrich, route d'Amziz, km20 (0529 80 16 38, www.lepalaispaysan.com).

The 'Peasant Palace', a 16-room hotel with fabulous views of the Atlas, is anything but peasant-like. This supremely chic modernist countryside hotel designed by Belgian architect Philippe Taburiaux stares out across the undulating green-hued foothills of the Atlas, which eventually rear up to the snowy peaks beyond. There's a joyous simplicity to the rooms, done out in taupes and stone with the odd spash of colour – African cherry-coloured feathered circular headdresses are pinned to the bedroom walls. The unheated, oblong slate-grey mosaic pool unfurls alongside parasols and smart forest-green loungers, while the farmyard is a boon for kids who won't sit still. As the sun sets in the evening, the surrounding countryside is filled with shepherds leading their flocks back home, and it's all just a 40-minute drive from the Medina. A spa, cookery classes, Atlas hikes and falconry complete the bucolic picture.

Tigmi

Douar Tagadert El-Cadi, route d'Amizmiz, km24 (0524 48 40 20, www.tigmi.com).

The ultimate rural retreat, Tigmi is a mud-walled haven of solitude with five suites and 16 rooms lying in the middle of nowhere halfway to the foothills of the Atlas, some 15 miles (24km) south of Marrakech. The hotel's architecture and interiors are rustically simple but fashion-shoot stylish – whitewashed arches, arcades and alcoves, covered walkways and terraces with beguiling views over raw, dusty-pink landscapes; think Sergio Leone with citrus fruits. Most suites have courtyards (one has its own little pool), terraced chill-out areas and sweet, cosy bedrooms with fireplaces that are lit in winter. There's a TV room, hammam, two outdoor pools, food (and wine) when you want it, and a small Berber village for company, but no phones and otherwise little to do but kick back and relax amid the flowers and foliage. A rental car would extend your options, but then again, as David Byrne once sang, 'Heaven is a place where nothing ever happens'.

Moderate

★ La Pause

Douar Lmih Laroussiène, Commune Agafay (0661 30 64 94, www.lapause-marrakech.com).
No credit cards.

La Pause is the closest thing you'll get to a desert experience within the vicinity of Marrakech. At this country retreat it's all about big skies, magnificent sunsets, rolling hills and nothing much else for miles and miles around. Guests are accommodated in beautifully simple, cosy, country-style rooms scattered about an oasis that curves around a river. Lunch and romantic, lantern-lit dinner are served in traditional tents. Owner Frédéric Alaime fell in love with the spot while out riding, and outdoor activities are a big part of the La Pause experience. There's horseriding, mountain biking and camel trekking – not to mention an intriguing form of cross-country golf and a swimming pool buried in the olive grove. There really isn't anything else quite like it in Marrakech.

Le Palais Paysan.

Getting Around

ARRIVING AND LEAVING

By air

Aéroport Marrakech Menara
0524 44 79 10, www.marrakech.airport-authority.com
Marrakech's international airport is located just six kilometres (four miles) west of the city. From the airport to the city centre is a ten-minute drive. There is also an airport information desk in the arrivals hall. There are banks offering currency exchange in both the baggage and arrivals hall, open 8am-6pm daily, plus two ATMs.

Taxis wait outside the arrivals building. There are official fixed rates for taxis from the airport, but drivers rarely adhere to these charges: 70dh for a small taxi, 100dh for a big taxi to the Medina or Guéliz; 100dh for a small taxi, 150dh for a big taxi to the Palmeraie. Expect to pay around 100dh in a *petit taxi* (*see right* **Taxis**) for up to 3 passengers to anywhere in the Medina (15-20 mins) or Guéliz (30 mins); to the Palmeraie expect 150-200dh. Prices go up by 50 per cent from 8pm to 6am. Most will accept payment in US dollars, euros or pounds. There is also a half-hourly airport shuttle bus (no.19) to Jemaa el Fna (about 20 mins), which stops at most of the major hotels in Guéliz and Hivernage. Tickets cost 30dh and the service runs 6.15am-9.30pm daily from the airport.

By rail

Trains are operated by the national railway company **ONCF** (0890 20 30 40, www.oncf.ma). The impressive new train station is on the western edge of Guéliz, on avenue Hassan II. Marrakech is the southernmost terminus of two lines, both of which pass through Casablanca and Rabat; some trains then continue north to Tangier, others north-east to Oujda on the Algerian border via Meknes and Fès. There is a taxi rank outside the station; make sure to get a *petit taxi* (not the big Mercedes grand taxi). The fare into central Guéliz should be no more than 10dh on the meter; (15-20dh to the Medina) but, unless you hail a taxi that is passing by, you will have to pay extra for those that have been waiting at the rank. Alternatively, buses nos.3 and 8 pass by the station on avenue Hassan II, en route to the place Jemaa El Fna (4dh).

By bus

The **gare routière** is just beyond the Medina walls at Bab Doukkala. Most long-distance buses stop here, including those operated by national carrier **CTM** (0522 54 10 10, www.ctm.ma). Both the central Medina and Guéliz are walkable from the station; a *petit taxi* will cost 10dh, or catch a local bus for Place de Foucault (Jemaa El Fna). The main CTM terminus and ticket office is in Guéliz, near the Theatre Royal, on Rue Abou Bakr Seddiq.

Supratours (0890 20 30 40, www.oncf.ma), is another quality long-distance bus service run by the ONCF train operators. Its terminus and ticket office are next to the main train station on avenue Hassan II. The Supratours bus timetable is shown on its website along with the train information.

PUBLIC TRANSPORT

Marrakech has a city bus network radiating from the Medina out to the suburbs. Other than along avenue Mohammed V, no buses operate within the confines of the city walls, where streets are prohibitively narrow. Few local bus services are of much use to visitors. The possible exceptions are those services that run between the Medina and Guéliz, which is a fairly long walk, but it's much less hassle (and still relatively inexpensive) to take a taxi.

Buses

ALSA buses (0524 33 52 70, www.alsa.ma) are regular city buses with no air-conditioning. They charge a flat fee of 4dh payable to the driver. Beware: the drivers never have any change. All the following buses leave from the main terminus on Place de Foucault, 100m west of the Jemaa El Fna:

Local bus routes

No.1 to Guéliz along avenue Mohammed V.
No.2 to Bab Doukkala for the gare routière.
No.3 to Douar Laskar via avenue Mohammed V, avenue Hassan II and the train station.
No.4 to Daoudiate (a northern suburb) by avenue Mohammed V.
No.8 to Douar Laskar via avenue Mohammed V, avenue Moulay Hassan and the train station.
No.10 to boulevard de Safi via Bab Doukkala and the gare routière.
No.11 to the Menara Gardens and passing by the airport.
No.14 to the train station.
No.19 to the airport terminal.

TAXIS

Taxis are plentiful and easy to find, whatever the time of day or night. They are also cheap enough that it makes little sense bothering with buses. The standard ride is known as a **petit taxi** and is usually a little khaki-coloured four-door Dacia Logan or Peugeot 205. By law, they can carry a maximum of three passengers. Drivers are reluctant to use the meter. Asking for them to switch it on sometimes works, otherwise it's just a question of knowing the right fare. From Jemaa El Fna to Guéliz costs around 10dh; from Jemaa El Fna to the Palmeraie 60dh-100dh, depending on distance. Expect to pay about 50 per cent more after about 8pm. You can flag a taxi if it is passing. If there are already passengers aboard, you first tell the driver your destination and he will let you know if he is headed in that direction. The first passenger in is the first to be dropped off. If the taxi is empty, then you just hop in and command your destination. The driver may then pick up other passengers along the way. He should re-set the meter for each new passenger.

Grand taxis are Mercedes cars that can squeeze in six people and are normally more expensive. They loiter outside hotels and the railway station. Avoid them, unless you are a group of four or more, or are travelling long distance: some *grand taxis* operate like minibuses running fixed routes to outlying suburbs, villages and towns.

Taxi Vert (0524 40 94 94) is an excellent new dial-a-cab system. You can order a *petit taxi* by phone

and be guaranteed a pick-up at any location at any time. The cost is the metered rate plus an extra 15-20dh and tip.

TRAMS

At time of writing a new urban development plan is in progress and roadworks are underway to install a tram system in Marrakech. It will link the train station, bus station, suburban areas, football stadium and the industrial zone of Sidi Ghanem.

DRIVING

A car can be useful for venturing out of the city, especially for trips to the south, but unless you are a resident a car is of limited use within Marrakech itself. For short-term visitors, taxis are cheap and plentiful and easily hired by the day for around 400dh in and around the city; ask your hotel for help in finding a reputable driver.

Vehicles drive on the right in Morocco. The old French rule of giving priority to traffic from the right is observed at roundabouts and junctions: in other words cars coming on to a roundabout have priority over those already on it. Speed limits are 40km/h (25mph) in urban areas, 100km/h (62mph) on main roads, 120km/h (74mph) on autoroutes. There are on-the-spot fines for speeding and other traffic offences. It is compulsory to wear seatbelts front and back.

Be very wary when driving at night as cyclists and moped riders often have no lights. Neither do sheep, goats and pedestrians, and street lighting can be poor. In the case of an accident, report to the nearest gendarmerie to obtain a written report, otherwise insurance will be invalid.

Car hire

To hire a car, you must be over 21, have a full current driving licence and carry a passport or national identity card. Rental isn't cheap; daily rates with a local agency start at about 300dh for a small, basic no-frills car with unlimited mileage. At the international companies like **Avis**, **Budget** or **Hertz**, expect to pay about 25 per cent more. All companies have agents in the arrivals hall at Marrakech airport.

The drawback with many of the local hire firms is the back-up service – cars may be old and may not be very well maintained. Breakdown support is lacking and replacement vehicles are not always forthcoming.

Be aware that payments made in Morocco by credit card often incur an additional five per cent fee. This is one of several reasons why it works out cheaper to arrange your car rental in advance.

The major companies allow you to rent a car in one city and return it in another. Rental cars in Morocco are delivered empty of petrol and returned empty. Almost all agencies will deliver cars to your hotel and arrange pick-up at no extra charge.

If you are heading south over the mountains, note that you are responsible for any damage if you take a car off-road or along unsuitable tracks. Four-wheel drives are available from most hire companies and start at around 1,200dh per day.

Avis
Marrakech airport (0524 43 31 69, www.avis.com). **Open** 8am-11pm daily.

Hertz
154 avenue Mohammed V, Guéliz (0524 43 99 84, www.hertz. com). **Open** 8.30am-12.30pm, 2.30-6.30pm Mon-Sat. **Map** p254 B2.
Other locations: *Aéroport Marrakech Menara (0524 44 72 39).* **Open** 8am-11pm daily.

Sixt
9 rue el Mansour Eddahibi, Guéliz (0524 43 31 84, www.sixt.com). **Open** 8.30am-12.30pm, 2.30-6.30pm Mon-Fri; 8.30am-12.30pm Sat.

Parking

Wherever there's space to park vehicles you'll find a *gardien de voitures*. They're licensed by the local authority to look after parked vehicles and should be tipped about 10dh (the local rate is 4dh during the day, 10dh at night, but as a visitor you're not going to get away with paying that). Street-side parking is easy enough in the nouvelle ville but troublesome in the Medina: there is a car park behind the Koutoubia (off avenue Mohammed V) and at the bottom of Rue Fatima Zahra across from the Koutoubia. Some areas now have ticket machines for pay-and-display. The hourly rate is 2dh and you will be clamped if you overstay or park illegally. If you get clamped, a notice will be left on your windscreen with a number for you to phone. One quick call and a man will appear to release you at a cost of 40dh.

Repairs & services

The garage below should be able to help get you back on the road.

Auto Speedy
6 avenue Abdelkrim Elkhatta, route de Casablanca – next to Marjane supermarket (05 24 30 59 58).

CYCLING

Bicycles, mopeds and motorbikes are hugely popular modes of local transport – despite the inconvenience of widespread potholes, choking bus fumes and the perils of having to share the road with the average lunatic Marrakchi motorist. If you fancy taking to the streets on two wheels, try one of the places listed below for bike rentals.

Note that most rental places do not offer any kind of lock so if you want to leave the bike or scooter anywhere it'll have to be with a *gardien de voitures* (*see below* **Parking**). Wearing a helmet on a scooter or motorbike is compulsory and you risk getting fined or having the bike confiscated without one.

Argan Sports
Rue Fatima Al Fihria, near Agdal gardens (0524 40 02 07, www.argansports.com).
Bicycle rental – city bikes, mountain bikes and road-bikes from 250dh per day, with 12 hours notice required.

Marrakech Roues
3 rue Bani Marine, Imm Roux, Medina (0663 06 18 92, www.marrakech-roues.com).
Motorbikes, scooters and bicycle hire with insurance, helmet and lock included.

WALKING

Walking is the only way to get around the Medina, which is where most visitors spend the bulk of their time. It's a compact area, perfect for exploring on foot. Many of the streets and alleys are too narrow for anything bigger than a motorcycle or donkey cart anyway.

Be sure to pack a pair of comfortable, flat-soled shoes because the streets in the Medina are rarely paved and full of ruts and potholes. Visitors coming any time from November to April should bring cheap and/or waterproof footwear because the slightest bit of rain turns the whole of the Medina into a mudbath.

Resources A-Z

TRAVEL ADVICE

For up-to-date information on travel to a specific country – including the latest on safety and security, health issues, local laws and customs – contact your home country government's department of foreign affairs. Most have websites with useful advice for would-be travellers.

AUSTRALIA www.smartraveller.gov.au	**CANADA** www.voyage.gc.ca	**NEW ZEALAND** www.safetravel.govt.nz
REPUBLIC OF IRELAND foreignaffairs.gov.ie	**UK** www.fco.gov.uk/travel	**USA** www.state.gov/travel

ADDRESSES

In the newer quarters of the city, streets are well signposted in both French and Arabic. This is not the case in the Medina: major streets do have dual-script signs but the majority of smaller alleyways have signs in Arabic only, or simply no signs at all. Most of the time, when looking for a specific street or place, the only option is to ask the locals. It's best to ask a shopkeeper so you don't end up with a 'guide' who will want to be paid.

BUSINESS

Casablanca is the country's economic centre, Rabat is the political capital and Marrakech is a modestly sized provincial city with a massive tourist trade. Big business is generally absent from the local scene, meaning that facilities for the powerbroker are few. If you are here doing business, don't expect deals to be closed in a single meeting, partly because of red tape, partly because haggling and hedging are standard practice, but also because getting to the point is often considered rude. Neither should you expect anyone to show up on time; why hurry when, as the local saying has it, 'A chance encounter is worth a thousand appointments'?

Business centres

If your business meeting requires more than just a quiet corner with Wi-Fi, then there are conference facilities in many of the large hotels.

Hivernage Business Centre (0524 42 41 00, www.hivernage-hotel.com) is set up to provide a full range of audio-visual, technical, secretarial and catering services for running larger meetings and conferences. Internet cafés (*see p233*) usually have scanners and printers for simpler needs.

Couriers

Within Marrakech, businesses use *petits taxis*. Note the number of the taxi (painted on the door) so if there's any problem later the police can track down the cabbie through the drivers' register. Pay as you would if the taxi was carrying a passenger. The following international couriers have offices in Marrakech:

DHL
133 avenue Abdelkarim El-Khattabi, Guéliz (0524 43 76 47, www.dhl-ma.com). **Open** 8.30am-6.30pm Mon-Fri; 8.30am-12.30pm Sat. **Map** p254 A2.

FedEx
113 avenue Abdelkarim El-Khattabi, Guéliz (0524 43 01 76, www.fedex.com). **Open** 8.30am-6.30pm Mon-Fri; 8.30am-12.30pm Sat. **No credit cards. Map** p254 A2.

CONSUMER

There are no such things as consumer rights. You haggled for it and set your own price, in the course of which you examined the object in question. However, if you do have a genuine grievance, take it to the tourist police, who are good at settling matters promptly (and usually in the favour of the visitor).

CUSTOMS

The following allowances apply to people bringing duty-free goods into Morocco: 250g of tobacco, 200 cigarettes or 25 cigars and 1 litre of spirits. There is no limit to how much foreign currency you can bring in to Morocco, but you are limited to changing back a maximum of 50 per cent of the amount you arrived with. For this reason it is best to keep all transaction receipts in case of questioning on departure. Moroccan dirhams are not legal tender outside the country and can only be paid into a Moroccan resident bank account.

Moroccan customs officials can be sensitive about electronic and photographic equipment. If it's just one or two items, obviously for your personal use, then you should be OK, but if you have significant amounts of camera or electrical gear, for example, you may have it written into your passport. Anything that can't be presented on leaving will be assumed to have been 'sold' and liable to a heavy duty tax. If the property has been stolen, you need police documentation to prove it. Any items you bring in that are deemed to be 'new' (less than six months old) will be taxed, so keep proof of purchase date. If you are bringing in a lot of cameras or filming equipment you will almost certainly be questioned and have to prove that you are not working in a professional capacity, which requires a permit from the **Moroccan Cinematographic Centre**.

Pets may be taken into Morocco as long as they have a medical certificate no more than ten days old and an anti-rabies certificate no more than six months old.

DISABLED

Marrakech is tough on anyone with a mobility problem. Roads

and pavements are uneven and pitted, and frequently rutted. Routes through the Medina are narrow and crowded and it's necessary to be nimble. Outside of the bigger hotels (the **Mamounia** and the **Sofitel** all lay claim to disabled facilities), few buildings make concessions to the disabled. In smaller hotels and riads, while facilities may be lacking, it's a given that people will try to make your stay as easy as possible but steps, if not stairs, are pretty much unavoidable. Problems may be compounded by the fact that banisters do not exist in traditional Moroccan homes, and you won't find them in most riads and small hotels.

DRUGS

Morocco is the world's largest cannabis producer and most of it is exported. Discreet use is tolerated and a significant minority still consume the stuff. It's smoked as *kif* (grass) in a long pipe called a *sebsi* or less traditionally as hash mixed with tobacco in European-style joints. It's also eaten in the notoriously hallucinogenic jam- or cake-like form of *majoun*.

However, Moroccan law maintains stiff penalties for sale or consumption, so be careful. Some dealers double as police informers, angling for a share of the *baksheesh* you'll later pay to buy yourself out of trouble. If you are going to partake, never buy more than a small amount for personal use, and don't travel with any in your possession.

ELECTRICITY

Morocco operates on 220V AC. Plugs are of the European two-pin variety. If you forget to bring an adapter, they're available from electrical shops for around 50dh. Visitors from the USA will need to bring a transformer if they intend to use appliances from home.

EMBASSIES & CONSULATES

British Embassy
28 avenue S.A.R.Sidi Mohammed, Souissi, Rabat (0537 63 33 33, www.gov.uk/government/world/organisations/british-embassy-rabat **Open** 8.30am-12.30pm, 1.30-4pm Mon-Thur; 8.30am-12.30pm Fri.
In the event of an emergency in Marrakech contact the Honorary Consulate (*see above*).

British Honorary Consulate Marrakech
47 avenue Mohammed V, Guéliz (0524 42 08 46) **Open** 8.30am-12.30pm Mon-Thur; 8.30-11.30am Fri.
Britain also has consulates in Casablanca and Tangier.

Canadian Embassy
13 rue Jaafar Es Sadiq, Agdal, Rabat (0537 68 74 00, www.canadainternational.gc.ca).
Also handles Australian consular affairs.

French Consulate
Rue Camille Cabana, Hivernage, Marrakech (0524 38 82 00, www.consulfrance-ma.org). **Open** 8.30-11.30am Mon-Fri. **Map** p254 A4.
There's an emergency 24hr hotline (0661 34 42 89).

US Embassy
2 avenue de Mohamed El Fassi, Rabat (0537 76 22 65, www.morocco.usembassy.gov). **Open** 8am-5.30pm Mon-Fri.
The US also has a consulate in Casablanca (8 boulevard Moulay Youssef, 0522 26 45 50).

EMERGENCIES

Police 19 or 112 from a mobile.
Fire service 15.
Ambulance service 15 or 0524 40 40 40.

HEALTH

Morocco has no reciprocal health care agreements with other countries, so taking out your own medical insurance is advisable. No vaccinations are required for Marrakech, although inoculation against hepatitis is a good idea. Bring anti-diarrhoea capsules, such as Imodium, and avoid tap water: bottled water is inexpensive and available at all restaurants and cafés.

Should you become ill, be warned: the Moroccan healthcare system is ropey. While good doctors can be found and pharmacies are well stocked and knowledgeably staffed, for anyone afflicted with serious illness the best route to take is the one leading straight to the airport and home.

Contraception & abortion

You can purchase condoms as well as birth control pills over the counter at any pharmacy. If you aren't using birth control, bring an emergency morning-after pill kit with you if you think you might need one, as this is not available in Morocco.

Abortion is not openly discussed. It is unavailable to unmarried women; any doctor practising an abortion on an unmarried woman can be arrested and disbarred. However, married women who already have children seem to be able to have abortions discreetly without any problems. For non-Moroccans, revert to your home country health-care service.

Dentists

Dental care in Marrakech is of a reasonable standard – discounting the wizened old guys on Jemaa El Fna with the trays of pliers and loose false teeth. Offices and equipment may not be state of the art, but the practitioners are usually competent and some speak English. Most will send you to an external radiology clinic if X-Rays are required.

Docteur Houriya Eljai Oubaaz
Residence Caroline, apartment 3, 2nd floor, Junction of Avenue Mohammed VI and Route de Targa, Guéliz, near Lycee Victor Hugo (0524 42 24 37). **Office hours** 9am-noon, 3.30-6pm Mon-Fri. **No credit cards**.
Female dentist who speaks good English and is popular with expats.

Doctors

There's no shortage of doctors and specialists in Marrakech, but the trick is to find a good one. We can recommend the following:

Docteur Samir Bellmezouar
6 rue Fatima Zohra Rmila, 1st floor Imm Benkirane, opposite Hammam Al Bacha, Medina (0524 38 33 56 or 0661 24 32 27 emergency). **Office hours** 10.30am-12.30pm, 4.30-6.30pm Mon-Fri. **No credit cards**. **Map** p250 B4.
Doesn't speak English but does make house calls.

Doctor Frederic Reitzer
Above Café Zohra, Immeuble Moulay Youssef, 4th floor, rue de la Liberté, Guéliz (0524 43 95 62 or 0661 17 38 03 emergency). **Office hours** 9.30am-noon, 3.30-7pm Mon-Fri; 10am-noon Sat. **No credit cards**. **Map** p254 B2.
Speaks English.

Hospitals

There are two private clinics in Marrakech, frequented by the expat community and wealthier

Moroccans. They are used by most insurance companies if their clients experience problems. Avoid public hospitals, where conditions are shocking.

Polyclinique du Sud
rue Yougoslavie, Guéliz (0524 44 79 99). **Open** 24hr emergency service. **Map** p254 A2.
International Clinic
Bab Ighil, route de M'Hamid, (0524 36 95 95, www.clinique-internationale-marrakech.com).

Pharmacies

Pharmacies are clearly marked with a green cross and/or green crescent. There's at least one in every neighbourhood. The drugs may have strange names, but staff can usually translate. Most pharmacies are open 9am to 6-7pm Monday to Friday. Some may also open on Saturday mornings or afternoons. When closed, each pharmacy should display a list of alternative pharmacies open after hours.

For a map showing pharmacies and a list of pharmacies open at night, see http://www.syndicat-pharmaciens-marrakech.com.

Pharmacie Centrale
166 avenue Mohammed V, corner of rue de la Liberté, Guéliz (0524 43 01 58). **Open** 8.30am-12.30pm, 3.30-7.30pm Mon-Thur; 8.30am-noon, 3.30-7.30pm Fri; 8.30am-1pm, 3.30-7.30pm Sat. **Map** p254 B2.
The most conveniently central pharmacy in the New City. On the door is a list of the city pharmacies which are on 24-hour duty that particular week.
Pharmacie du Progrès
Jemaa El Fna, Medina (0524 44 25 63). **Open** 8.15am-12.30pm, 2.15-6.30pm Mon-Sat. **Map** p252 C5.
Knowledgeable, qualified staff will advise on minor ailments and suggest medication. English is spoken.

Prescriptions

Next to anything can be bought over the counter without a prescription; about the only thing that raises eyebrows are condoms (these can be bought in large supermarkets and some small general stores).

ID

You are meant to carry ID at all times. Moroccans have identity cards but a passport is fine for foreign visitors, or better still, a photocopy, so you can leave the original at the hotel. Valid ID is essential when checking into a hotel, hiring a car, changing foreign currency and collecting poste restante.

INTERNET

Computers are expensive in Morocco and many people, particularly in the poorer rural areas, still resort to internet cafés for accessing email, chatting online, web-surfing or working. But they are dying out rapidly with the advance of mobile internet technology. Smartphones, tablets, 3G and free Wi-Fi zones have changed the face of daily life. The few remaining internet cafés are the domain of gadget-free tourists, college students and those needing to print out documents.

Most hotels and cafés offer free Wi-Fi.

Internet service providers (ISPs)

For anybody intending to stay a long while in Morocco, **ADSL** broadband internet is available through **Ménara** (Maroc Télécom's ISP, www.menara.ma). You need a landline, with a modem and router for Wi-Fi. To subscribe, visit the **Maroc Télécom office** (*see p235* **Telephones**). For short-term internet access there are free Wi-Fi zones in most hotels, riads, cafés and restaurants. You can also purchase mobile 3G USB dongles from **Meditel** (www.meditel.ma), **Maroc Telecom** (www.iam.ma) and **Inwi** (www.inwi.ma) with various pay-as-you-go packages. Micro-SIM cards can also be purchased from all three ISPs for use inside tablets and iPads.

Internet access

Cyber Hassna
Rue Beni Marine, Medina (no phone). **Open** 10am-11pm Mon-Thur, Sat, Sun.
10dh per hour. Printing available.
Cyber Efet
183 avenue Mohammed V, Hivernage (no phone). **Open** 8.30am-8.30pm daily.
10dh per hour. Printing, scanning and photocopying also available.

LEFT LUGGAGE

There are no left luggage facilities at Marrakech's international airport nor at the train station. The hotel where you are staying may be able to store your bags for a short time.

LEGAL HELP

Embassies and consulates (*see p232*) can assist nationals in emergencies and provide a list of English-speaking lawyers.

LOST PROPERTY

In general, if you've lost it, forget it. If you've lost something on public transport, call the transport operator, who should, in principle, hang on to lost property.

MEDIA

Foreign publications

English language publications are easy to come by. Newspapers are usually only the weekly international digests put out by some of the broadsheets. There will also usually be the *International New York Times*, *Time*, *Newsweek* and *The Economist* plus sundry fashion, style and interiors magazines. The kiosks next to Café France on Jemaa el Fna, next to the main Post Office in Guéliz, and next to the Tourist Information Office in Guéliz have the best selection.

Magazines

Most magazines are in French, the best being *Telquel* (www.telquel-online.com) and *Couleurs Maroc* (www.art-pour-art.com): the former is a Morocco current affairs magazine, the latter is a bi-monthly lifestyle, travel and culture magazine. *La Tribune* is a Marrakech-focused quarterly publication in French. *Marrakech MAG* is a glossy bi-lingual quarterly in English and French covering fashion, culture and events (www.anothereditions.com).

Newspapers

There are both French and Arabic papers. National dailies tend to restrict their coverage to the goings-on of the royal family, sports and local events. If you read French, the best daily paper is *Le Matin* (www.lematin.ma).

Television

Most hotels and riads that offer TV have satellite with BBC World and Al Jazeera English. Some places will have a subscription service that accesses the major UK channels.

Websites

Moroccan news in English can be found at www.moroccoworld news.com. Events are listed on www.madeinmarrakech.co.uk and at www.marrakechpocket.com. For local life and tips follow **Maryam Montagu** on http://moroccan maryam.typepad.com/my_ marrakesh; **Mandy Sinclair** on http://whymorocco.wordpress. com and **Amanda** on http:// marocmama.com.

MONEY

Local currency is the Moroccan dirham, abbreviated as dh (in this book) and sometimes MDH, or MAD. There are 100 centimes to a dirham. Coins come in denominations of 5, 10, 20 and 50 centimes (all useless) and 1, 2, 5 and 10dh. Small change is useful for things like tips and taxi fares and should be hoarded. Banknotes come in denominations of 20 (being phased out), 25, 50, 100 and 200dh.

Excess dirhams can be exchanged for euros or dollars (pounds sterling are often not available) at a bank. You may be asked to show the exchange receipts from when you converted your hard currency into dirhams – this is because banks will only allow you to change back up to half the amount of Moroccan currency originally purchased.

At the time of writing, conversion between currencies was £1 = 13dh.

ATMs

Cashpoints, or *guichets automatiques*, are common in most Moroccan towns and cities, and it's perfectly possible to travel on plastic – although it's always wise to carry at least a couple of days' 'survival money' in cash. Most ATMs are connected to the international banking systems and issue dirhams on most European and US debit and credit cards. If the ATM carries only a Visa symbol, don't go there; it will only process locally issued Visa cards and may well swallow the international variety. Instead, look for machines bearing the Cirrus, Link and Maestro symbols.

Most banks set a daily withdrawal limit of 2,000dh (currently around £154) per card, per day on ATM withdrawals. It's advisable to exchange extra currency on arrival or to carry multiple ATM cards.

ATMs are concentrated along rue Bab Agnaou in the Medina and around place Abdel-Moumen in Guéliz. Beware of Monday mornings when machines are often empty.

Banks

The main local banks are Banque Marocaine du Commerce Extérieur (BMCE), Banque Marocaine du Commerce et de l'Industrie (BMCI), Société Générale and Banque Polulaire. All have agreements with major international banks. The heaviest concentration of bank branches is around place Abdel-Moumen in Guéliz or rue Bab Agnaou in the medina. Most are open 8.30am-3.30pm.

Bureaux de change

Almost all banks have a bureaux de change counter, as do most major hotels of three stars and up. The exchange rate is set by the Bank of Morocco and is uniform. No commission is charged. When changing money you will usually be asked to show your passport. Travellers' cheques are rarely accepted.

Credit cards

MasterCard and Visa are accepted at larger shops, supermarkets, up-market artisan emporiums, restaurants, nightclubs and hotels; American Express less so. Credit card payments may often incur an extra 5 per cent charge. It's wise to carry cash back-up because management will often claim that the machine is 'broken' or that your card won't go through – they aren't keen on the delay in payment that comes with credit cards. Outside of the city centre, few shops and many smaller hotels will not accept credit cards. You can use your credit card to withdraw cash from ATMs. Credit-card fraud is also a problem in Morocco, so keep all receipts to check against your statement.

Lost/stolen credit cards

All lines of the companies listed below have English-speaking staff and are open 24hrs daily.

American Express +44 1273 696 933 (UK)
Barclaycard +44 1604 230 230 (UK)
MasterCard +1 636 722 7111 (reverse charge call to USA)
Visa 00 211 0011, await second dial tone and enter 866-654-0163 (USA based call centre for all Visa card holders)

Travellers' cheques

Travellers' cheques are virtually obsolete in Morocco. The only place that exchanges them still is the **Banque El-Maghrib** on avenue Mohammed VI.

OPENING HOURS

Opening times listed in this book should be taken more as guidelines than gospel (many places close in the afternoon for a siesta, which is not always reflected in the times we have given). As a rule of thumb the working week is Monday to Friday, with a half-day on Saturday. Note that hours vary during Ramadan (*see p25*), when businesses open and close later.

Banks 8.30am-3.45pm Mon-Fri.
Shops 9am-1pm, 3-7pm Mon-Sat.
Museums & tourist sights 8am-6pm daily.

PHOTOGRAPHY

Morocco's medinas, landscapes and architecture are a photographer's dream, but there are places where photography is not permitted – government buildings, royal palaces, mosques, airports and airfields, bridges, army barracks, checkpoints, and military and police personnel. Also avoid anything that can be deemed a military asset, for example, hydro-electric dams, solar farms or industrial complexes. If you are photographing a person you should always ask their permission, which will often be declined or they may ask for money instead. In Marrakech the locals can be quite aggressive towards snap-happy tourists who take their picture without asking. Women and elderly folk in rural areas especially do not like to be photographed.

Wrédé et Cie
142 avenue Mohammed V, Hivernage (0524 43 57 39).
Open 9am-noon, 3-9pm Mon-Sat.
Sells tripods, digital cameras, batteries and memory cards. Also has a digital printing service and can do passport photos.

POLICE

Crime against visitors is rare and physical violence almost unheard of. You do need to watch your pockets and bags, though, particularly around Jemaa El Fna. If you are robbed or have a complaint against an unscrupulous taxi driver or souk merchant, go to the office of the **Brigade Touristique** (*see below*).

Note, if you are the victim of crime outside Marrakech, then you must make a report to the local police wherever the incident occurred – do not wait until your return to the city.

Police stations

The main police station, the **Prefecture de Police** (0524 33 03 63), is on the Route de Fes, near Bab el Khemis and next to the large local government administration building – the wilaya. There's also an office of the **Brigade Touristique** (Tourist Police; 0524 38 46 01) on the north side of Jemaa El Fna. The Tourist Police are plain-clothed officers watching out for the safety and security of tourists. They patrol the medina undercover and will be quickly on the scene if you have a problem. If you need assistance, alert a local shopkeeper or official guide, or go to one of the blue-uniformed policemen that are easily visible – a member of the Tourist Police will not be far away.

POSTAL SERVICES

The main post office (**PTT Centrale of Poste Maroc**) is on place du 16 Novembre, Guéliz, halfway along avenue Mohammed V (across from McDonald's). It's open 8am-8pm Mon-Fri, 8.30am-6pm Sat. There is a second, smaller PTT in the Medina on rue Moulay Ismail, between Jemaa El Fna and the Koutoubia Mosque. Stamps are sold at a dedicated *timbres* counter, but can also be bought at a *tabac* or at the reception desks of big hotels. Parcels should be taken unwrapped for examination.

Mail delivery is painfully slow. Post offices provide an express mail service (**EMS**), also known as *poste rapide*. For really urgent mail, it's safer to use an international courier company, *see p231*.

RELIGION

Islam underpins society, places of worship are prominent and religious festivals are a highlight of the annual calendar. Sex before marriage is taboo. Islam may be tough on alcohol, but the Moroccans are more liberal when fit comes to drugs (*see p232*). Although every district has its mosque, few Moroccans perform the required five daily cycles of prayer. Many attend the mosque only at noon on Friday, the main weekly prayer session. But most Moroccans make an effort to observe Ramadan; *see p25*.

Christian

Church of Holy Martyrs
rue El-Imam Ali, Guéliz (0524 43 05 85). **Map** p254 B3.
Catholic services are held in French at 6.30pm Mon-Sat; 10am Sun. There is a service in English at 8pm Sat.

SMOKING

Morocco is firmly in thrall to nicotine. Few cafés and restaurants recognise the concept of a clean-air environment. Foreign cigarette brands cost 40dh, or about £3, for 20, while the best of the domestic product goes for even less.

STUDY

Classical and Moroccan Arabic can be studied in structured three-week intensive modules during the summer at the American-run **CLC**. Each module costs around 6,500dh for 45-60hrs group tuition. Moroccan-run study programme **Study Arabic Marrakech** also offer holiday classes and online courses as well as longer-term conversation classes for ex-pats.

Center for Language and Culture
Rue Sourya, Guéliz (0524 44 76 91, www.clcmorocco.org).

Study Arabic Marrakech
Sidi Abud 2 Residence Amal 3, on route de Casablanca (0672 86 90 36, www.studyarabic marrakech.com).

TELEPHONES

Telephoning abroad from a public phone in Marrakech is no problem. Either use the cardphones that are dotted around town (cards are bought from post offices, *tabacs* or news vendors) or one of the numerous *téléboutiques*.

Dialling & codes

To call abroad dial 00, then the country code followed by the telephone number. When calling within Morocco you need to dial the area code even if you are calling from the same area. For instance, to make a local call within Marrakech, you must still dial 0524. Mobiles begin with the prefix 06; landlines begin with 05.

Information 160
International assistance 130
Morocco country code 212

Area codes

Casablanca 0522
Essaouira 0524
Fès 0535
Marrakech 0524
Ouarzazate & the south 0524
Rabat/Tangier 0537

Mobile phones

There are three main mobile service providers offering a pay-as-you-go option: the national operator **Maroc-Télécom**, **Méditel** and **Inwi**. Most European networks have arrangements with one of the first two so that visitors can use their mobiles in Morocco (note: it's expensive). Alternatively, mobile users can buy a pre-paid SIM card from any of the Moroccan network operators for around 20dh and then buy additional credit top-up at booths or shops around town. As long as your phone is unlocked, you insert the SIM and have a local number from which calls can be made at standard rates. Skype and Viber are also cheaper options in Wi-Fi areas.

If you are using your own mobile and are staying for a few weeks it is worth buying a Moroccan SIM card with Inwi and opting for their Zen International package. For 150dh you get 3 hours of national and international calls, valid for a month.

Inwi
Marrakech train station, Avenue Hassan II, Guéliz (0529 80 01 98, www.inwi.ma). **Map** p254 A3.
Look for the purple kiosks on most major intersections in Guéliz or visit their shop at Marrakech train station.

Maroc-Télécom (Agence Guéliz Mobile)
Avenue Mohammed V (opposite McDonald's), Guéliz (0524 43 44 53, www.iam.ma). **Map** p254 B2.

Méditel
279 avenue Mohammed V, Guéliz (0664 82 58 25, www.meditel.ma). **Map** p254 B2.

TIME

Morocco follows GMT all year round (it's on the same time as Britain and Ireland) and in recent times has synchronised with Europe to follow the same daylight savings winter and summer time changes. The time changes are not well publicised and the changes always create confusion as to whether you mean 'new' time or 'old' time. In rural areas they often don't bother to alter the clocks at all. To add to the confusion, there is another time adjustment at the start and end of Ramadan if it falls in the hot, long summer days – but not always! Allow an extra hour if you are catching a flight to avoid problems.

TIPPING

Tipping is expected in cafés and restaurants (round up the bill or add 10-15 per cent), by guides and porters, and by anyone else that renders you any sort of small service. Five or ten dirhams is sufficient. Tip taxi drivers around 10 per cent if they have been honest enough to use their meter, otherwise do not bother.

TOILETS

Public toilets are a rarity – use the facilities when in bars, hotels and restaurants. They're usually decent enough. It's a good idea to carry tissues as toilet paper is not always available. At cafés the toilet attendant expects a few dirhams as a tip; it's bad form not to oblige.

TOURIST INFORMATION

The **ONMT** (Office National Marocain du Tourisme) has a presence in Marrakech. Basic tourist information can also be found at its website, www.visitmorocco.com.

ONMT
ONMT, place Abdel-Moumen, Guéliz (0524 43 61 31). **Open** 8.30am-noon, 2.30-6.30pm Mon-Fri; 9am-noon, 3-6pm Sat. **Map** p254 A1.

International offices

London *205 Regent Street, W1R 7DE (+44 20 7437 0073).*
New York *104 West 49th Street, suite 1820, 10018 (+1 212 221 1583).*
Paris *161 rue Saint Honoré, 75001 (+33 1 42 60 63 50).*

VISAS & IMMIGRATION

All visitors to Morocco need a passport to enter (it should be valid for at least six months beyond the date of entry). No visas are required for nationals of Australia, Britain, Canada, Ireland, New Zealand, the US and most EU countries. If in doubt check with your local Moroccan embassy.

Travellers can stay in Morocco for three months from the time of entry. Long-term extensions mean applying for the official residence permit or *carte de séjour* – a tedious and bureaucratic procedure involving trips back and forth to the **Bureau des Etrangers** at the Préfecture de Police. You need to prove you have sufficient funds and a regular income deposited into a Moroccan account, provide bank statements, proof of address in Morocco, obtain a police security check from your home country, a medical certificate and more. The cost is officially 100dhs, but requirements often change and it can take several weeks to process.

For a simpler option, leave the country for a few days and re-enter, gaining a new three-month stamp. Alternatively, if it's a one-off short-term extension there should be no charge, but plenty of strong reasons are required. You should report to your local police station or to the Bureau des Etrangers no later than two weeks before the expiry of your current visa. If you overstay your visa, you will be stopped at the airport on leaving and will be fined. The amount is decided by the local court.

Bureau des Etrangers
Prefecture de Police, route de Fès, Daoudiate – behind the Wilaya de Marrakech administration building (0524 33 03 63). **Open** 9.30am-3pm Mon-Thur; 9.30-11.30am Fri.

WHEN TO GO

Though Marrakech gets lots of sunshine, December and January can be overcast and rainy. Still, Marrakech makes for a good winter retreat with daily temperatures of around 15-20°C (59-68°F). Evenings can be chilly though (you need to stay in a hotel that has heating).

March to May is the perfect time to visit but beware of price hikes at Easter. Summers can be oppressive with temperatures averaging 30-35°C (86-95°F), peaking at 40°C (104°F). Things cool off in September. Hotel rates soar over Christmas.

WOMEN

Though Marrakech is a Muslim country, the dress code for women is not strict – with a few provisos. Leave the minis and micros behind. Shorts are out too. Wear trousers or dresses and skirts that reach the knee or lower; baggy is the way to go. It's a good idea to keep shoulders covered with a light shawl or scarf.

In touristy areas such as Jemaa El Fna and the souks, you may get hit on, so avoid direct eye contact and don't smile at men. Ignore come-ons or obnoxious comments. If a man is persistent, raise your voice so others can hear; someone may intervene on your behalf.

THE LOCAL CLIMATE

Average temperatures and monthly rainfall in Marrakech.

	High (°C/°F)	Rainfall (inches/mm)
Jan	21/70	1.1/28
Feb	22/72	1.2/30
Mar	23/73	1.2/30
Apr	26/79	1.1/28
May	29/84	0.7/18
June	30/86	0.3/7.6
July	33/91	0.1/2.5
Aug	36/97	0.1/2.5
Sept	31/88	0.3/7.6
Oct	28/82	1.0/25
Nov	24/75	1.3/33
Dec	21/70	1.3/33

Glossary

ARCHITECTURE

bab gate
dar house
fundouk medieval merchants' inn arranged around a central courtyard with stabling on the gound floor, sleeping quarters above
hammam traditional bathhouse
kasbah traditional Berber fortress/palace
koubba domed tomb
mashrabiya fretworked wooden screens traditionally used for windows
Mauresque French colonial version of neo-Moorish architecture
méchouar parade ground
medersa Koranic school for the teaching of Islamic law and scriptures
mihrab prayer niche facing towards Mecca in a mosque
minbar pulpit in a mosque for the reading of the Koran, usually free-standing
muqarna Moorish ceiling ornamentation resembling stalactites
pisé mud reinforced with straw and lime, and the primary building material of Marrakech
riad house with a central courtyard garden
tadelakt moisture-resistant polished plaster wall surface
zaouia shrine of a holy man, usually also doubling as a theology school
zelije coloured tilework typical of Moorish decoration

AROUND TOWN

agdal walled garden
arset quarter
calèche horse-drawn carriage
derb alley
hôtel de ville city hall
jnane market garden
maison d'hôte guest house
medina Arabic for 'city', often used to mean the 'old city'
marché market
mellah traditional Jewish quarter
place square
souk bazaar or market

CULTURE

babouche traditional leather slippers, typically yellow
baksheesh a tip or kickback
baraka blessings
ben son of (also spelled ibn)
Berber the indigenous tribes people of southern Morocco
bidonvilles unplanned slum dwellings on the outskirts of town
douar tribe
Fassi adjective for someone from Fès
gnawa semi-mystical brotherhood of muscians descended from black African slaves. Also the name of the music they play
haj pilgrimage to Mecca which observant Muslims are expected to perform at least once during their lifetime. Also the honorific title of someone who has made the pilgrimage
hijab headscarf warn by some Muslim women
jellaba traditional men's robe
jinn souls without bodies, usually malevolent (also spelled djinn)
kif the local marijuana, cultivated extensively in the Rif Mountains
leila all-night gnawa music performance (the word literally means 'night')
maalim master craftsman or master of any profession, including musician
majoun a cake or jam of marijuana
Marrakchi adjective for someone from Marrakech
muezzin the man who makes the call to prayer
oud musical instrument, like a lute
oued wadi or dried river bed
sidi saint
Souari adjective for someone from Essaouira
wali regional governor appointed by the king

FOOD

briouettes little envelopes of paper-thin ouarka (filo) pastry wrapped around ground meat, rice or cheese and deep fried, served as an hors d'oeuvre
chakchouka dessert of light pastry filled with fruit couscous coarse-ground semolina flour. Also the name of the cooked dish harira vegetable soup
pastilla ouarka (filo) pastry typically filled with a mixture of shredded pigeon, almonds and spices, served as an hors d'oeuvre
tajine slow-cooked stew of meat (usually lamb or chicken) and/or vegetables. Also the name of the conically lidded dish it's cooked in trid shredded pigeon wrapped in a crêpe soaked in broth

HISTORY

Almohads Berber dynasty (1147-1269) that ruled out of Marrakech before relocating to Rabat
Almoravids Berber dynasty (1062-1147) that founded Marrakech
Green March action by which Morocco seized the Spanish colony of Rio del Oro in the western Sahara in 1975
Merenids Berber dynasty (1248-1554) that ruled from northern Morocco
Saadians Arab dynasty (1549-1668) that oversaw a brief renaissance of imperial Marrakech
Treaty of Fès The act that formalised the imposition of French rule over Morocco in 1912

Vocabulary: French

In French, as in other Latin languages, the second person singular (you) has two forms. Phrases here are given in the more polite vous form. The tu form is used with family, friends, young children and pets; you should be careful not to use it with people you do not know sufficiently well, as it is considered rude. You will also find that courtesies such as monsieur, madame and mademoiselle are used much more often than their English equivalents.

GENERAL EXPRESSIONS

good morning/hello bonjour
good evening bonsoir
goodbye au revoir
hi (familiar) salut
OK d'accord; **yes** oui; **no** non
How are you? Comment allez vous?/vous allez bien?
How's it going? Comment ça va?/ça va? (familiar)
Sir/Mr monsieur (M)
Madam/Mrs madame (Mme)
Miss mademoiselle (Mlle)
please s'il vous plaît; **thank you** merci; **thank you very much** merci beaucoup
sorry pardon; **excuse me** excusez-moi
Do you speak English? Parlez-vous anglais?
I don't speak French Je ne parle pas français
I don't understand Je ne comprends pas
Speak more slowly, please Parlez plus lentement, s'il vous plaît
how much?/how many? combien?
Have you got change? Avez-vous de la monnaie?
I would like... Je voudrais...
it is c'est; **it isn't** ce n'est pas
good bon (m)/bonne (f); **bad** mauvais (m)/mauvaise (f)
small petit (m)/petite (f);
big grand (m)/grande (f)
beautiful beau (m)/belle (f);
well bien; **badly** mal
expensive cher; **cheap** pas cher
a bit un peu; **a lot** beaucoup;
very très; **with** avec; **without** sans; **and** et; **or** ou; **because** parce que
who? qui?; **when?** quand?;
which? quel?; **where?** où?;
why? pourquoi?; **how?** comment?
at what time/when? à quelle heure?
forbidden interdit/défendu
out of order hors service/ en panne daily tous les jours (tlj)

GETTING AROUND

When is the next train for...? C'est quand le prochain train pour...?
ticket un billet; **station** la gare;
platform le quai
bus/coach station gare routière
entrance entrée; **exit** sortie
left gauche; **right** droite;
interchange corréspondence
straight on tout droit; **far** loin;
near pas loin/près d'ici
street la rue; **street map** le plan; **road map** la carte
bank la banque; **is there a bank near here?** est-ce qu'il y a une banque près d'ici?
post office La Poste;
a stamp un timbre

BEHIND THE WHEEL

no parking stationnement interdit/stationnement gênant;
speed limit 40 rappel 40
petrol essence; **unleaded** sans plomb **diesel** gasoil

SIGHTSEEING

museum un musée
church une église
exhibition une exposition;
ticket (for museum) un billet; **(for theatre, concert)** une place
open ouvert; **closed** fermé
free gratuit; **reduced price** un tarif réduit

ACCOMMODATION

Do you have a room (for this evening/for two people)? Avez-vous une chambre (pour ce soir/pour deux personnes)?
full complet; **room** une chambre
bed un lit; **double bed** un grand lit; **(a room with) twin beds** (une chambre) à deux lits
with bath(room)/shower avec (salle de) bain/douche
breakfast le petit déjeuner
included compris
lift un ascenseur
air-conditioned climatisé

AT THE CAFÉ OR RESTAURANT

I'd like to book a table (for three/at 8pm) Je voudrais réserver une table (pour trois personnes/à vingt heures)
lunch le déjeuner;
dinner le dîner
coffee (espresso) un café;
white coffee un café au lait/ café crème; **tea** le thé
wine le vin; **beer** la bière
mineral water eau minérale;
fizzy gazeuse; **still** plate
tap water eau du robinet/ une carafe d'eau
the bill, please l'addition, s'il vous plaît

NUMBERS

0 zéro; **1** un (m), une (f);
2 deux; **3** trois; **4** quatre;
5 cinq; **6** six; **7** sept; **8** huit;
9 neuf; **10** dix; **11** onze;
12 douze; **13** treize; **14** quatorze;
15 quinze; **16** seize; **17** dix-sept;
18 dix-huit; **19** dix-neuf;
20 vingt; **21** vingt-et-un;
22 vingtdeux; **30** trente;
40 quarante; **50** cinquante;
60 soixante; **70** soixante-dix; **80** quatre-vingts;
90 quatre-vingt-dix;
100 cent; **1,000** mille;
1,000,000 un million.

DAYS, MONTHS & SEASONS

Monday lundi; **Tuesday** mardi; **Wednesday** mercredi;
Thursday jeudi; **Friday** vendredi; **Saturday** samedi;
Sunday dimanche.
January janvier; **February** février; **March** mars; **April** avril; **May** mai; **June** juin;
July juillet; **August** août;
September septembre;
October octobre;
November novembre;
December décembre.
Spring printemps; **summer** été; **autumn** automne;
winter hiver.

Vocabulary: Arabic

Within Marrakech (and other main towns and cities) you can get by in French, which is widely spoken by all educated Moroccans. However, a little effort with Arabic goes a long way, even if it is just a few stock phrases like 'hello' and 'goodbye'.

Moroccan Arabic is a dialect of the standard Arabic language and is not the same as that spoken elsewhere in North Africa and the Middle East, although there are some words and phrases in common.

We should point out that transliteration from Arabic into English is a highly inexact science and a wide variety of spellings are possible for any given word (for example Koran vs Quran). In this guide we've tended to plump for whatever seemed the most straightforward. You are also likely to encounter Berber, which comes in three distinct dialects. Most Berber speakers will also be fluent in Arabic.

Arabic pronunciation

Arabic has numerous sounds that non-speakers have trouble in pronouncing but nobody is going to knock you for trying.
gh – like the French 'r', slightly rolled
kh – like the 'ch' in loch

EMERGENCIES

leave me alone esmahli la
help! tekni!
help me, please awenni afak
call the police ayyet el bolice
thief sheffar
I'm lost tweddert

GENERAL EXPRESSIONS

good morning/hello sabah el kheir/salaam aleikum
good evening masr el kheir
goodbye masalaama
please min fadlak (to a male); min fadlik (to a female)
yes aywa/anam; **no** la
How are you? labas/kifhalak (to a male)/kifhalik (to a female)
thank you shukran
no thanks la shukran
sorry/excuse me esmahli
Do you speak English? Itkelim Ingleezi?
I don't speak Arabic Metkelimsh Arabi
I don't understand Mafayimtish
who? shkun?; **why?** lash?; **which?** ashmen?;
where? feyn?
today el youm; **tomorrow** ghedda; **yesterday** imbara
God willing inshalah
never mind/so it goes malish tips baksheesh
let's go yalla
passport passeport

SHOPPING

how much?/how many? bekam?
Do you have...? Wahesh andakum...?
Have you got change? Maak sarf?
credit card kart kredi
travellers' cheques shek siyahi
good mleah; **bad** mish imleah
small seghir; **big** kebir
beautiful jameel
that's expensive ghali bezzaf
enough kafi

GETTING AROUND

Where is...? Feyn keyn...?
Where is the hotel? Feyn keyn el otel?
airport el mattar
station el mahatta
bus/coach station mahatta d'el ottobisat
ticket office maktab el werka; **ticket** werka
train station el gar
bus stop plasa d'el ottobisat
museum el mathaf
embassy el sifara
pharmacy farmasyan
bank el banka
post office el busta;
stamp etnaber
restaurant el mattam
mosque jamaa
left yassar; **right** yemeen
stop here haten hinayer
here hina; **there** hinak

ACCOMMODATION

Do you have a room? Andak beit?
key srout
room beit
sheet eyzar
shower doush
toilet vaysay
breakfast iftar

AT THE CAFÉ OR RESTAURANT

table for... tabla dyal...
what's that? shnu hada?
I'm a vegetarian makanakulsh elham
I don't eat... makanakulsh...
meat leham
chicken dzhazh
fish elhut
bread elkhobz
coffee qahwa; **tea** atay
beer birra; **wine** shshrab
mineral water sidi ali
the bill, please lahsab afak

NUMBERS

0 sifer; **1** wahid; **2** itnehn; **3** telata; **4** arbaa; **5** khamsa; **6** setta; **7** seba; **8** tamanya; **9** tesa; **10** ashra; **11** hadasha; **12** itnasha; **13** teltash; **14** arbatash; **15** khamstash; **16** settash; **17** sebatash; **18** tamantash; **19** tesatash; **20** eshreen; **21** wahid w'eshreen; **22** itnehn w'eshreen; **30** telateen; **40** arba'een; **50** khamseen; **60** setteen; **70** seba'een; **80** tamaneen; **90** tesa'een; **100** mea; **1,000** alef.

DAYS & MONTHS

Monday el itnehn; **Tuesday** el teleta; **Wednesday** el arbaar; **Thursday** el khemis; **Friday** el jomaa; **Saturday** el sebt; **Sunday** el ahad.
January yanayir; **February** fibraiyir; **March** maris; **April** abril; **May** mayu; **June** yunyu; **July** yulyu; **August** aghustus; **September** sibtimber; **October** oktobir; **November** nufimbir; **December** disimbir.

Further Reference

BOOKS

Fiction

Ben Jelloun, Tahar *This Blinding Absence of Light* (2004) Novel concerning the desert concentration camps in which King Hassan II held his political enemies, by Morocco's most acclaimed writer.
Binebine, Mahi *Welcome to Paradise* (2002) A ragtag group of the hopeful and the hopeless cower on a north Atlantic beach waiting for the boat that's to smuggle them into Europe. Highly moving.
Bowles, Paul *The Sheltering Sky* (1949) There's little in the writings of Morocco's most famous expat writer that relates to Marrakech, but his best-known novel hauntingly portrays the tribal life and deserts of North Africa.
Burroughs, William *The Naked Lunch* (1959) Compiled in Tangier from hoarded scraps of stories and typed up in a hotel room by Kerouac, who suggested the title.
Freud, Esther *Hideous Kinky* (1992) A child's view of hippie life in the Marrakech of the early 1970s; mum wants to be a Sufi, her two young girls just want to go home.
Goytisolo, Juan *Makbara* (1980) 'Spain's greatest living writer' is a long-standing resident of Marrakech. He also exhibits a cavalier way with grammar and punctuation.
Grimwood, Jon *Courtenay Stamping Butterflies* (2004) A would-be assassin holed up in a future version of Marrakech plots to kill the US president. Cutting edge Moroccan-tinged sci-fi from Britain's answer to William Gibson.
Hopkins, John *All I Wanted Was Company* (1999) This enjoyable short novel about love and solitude is mostly set in Tangier, but with sections of the story in Marrakech, the Atlas and the Sahara – all conveyed with a keen sense of place.
Taylor, Debbie *The Fourth Queen* (2003) Scots lass rises through the ranks of the harem in 18th-century Marrakech and has sex with a dwarf called Microphilius. Based on a true story, apparently.
Watkins, Paul *In the Blue Light of African Dreams* (1990) Lyrical tale of Foreign Legion flyers based in Mogador (Essaouira) who desert desert patrols to attempt the first aerial crossing of the Atlantic.

Non-fiction

Bowles, Paul *Their Heads Are Green* (1963) Short anthology of travel writings includes accounts of music-collecting in the Rif and a drive from Tangier to the Sahara via Marrakech.
Canetti, Elias *The Voices of Marrakech* (1967) A Nobel Prize winner's highly impressionistic tales and thumbnail sketches of the city.
Edwards, Brian T *Morocco Bound* (2005) Interesting deconstruction of America's cultural take on Morocco, from the movie *Casablanca* through Bowles and the Beats to the Marrakesh Express.
Hamilton, Richard *The Last Storytellers* (2011) As the oral tradition of the Place Jemaa El Fna storytellers is on the brink of extinction, the tales are captured and translated into English by a former BBC correspondent.
Harris, Walter *Morocco That Was* (1921) Correspondent of *The Times* who witnessed the downfall of the sultans and arrival of the French (1912) and documented all in a wickedly funny style.
Hopkins, John *The Tangier Diaries 1962-1979* (1997) 'Bill Willis calls my house "Scorpion Hall" there are so many. I keep viper serum and scorpion serum in the ice box in case someone gets bitten.' Magic stuff.
Howe, Marvine *Morocco: The Islamist Awakening and Other Challenges* (2005) Well-informed recent history of a Morocco torn between modernity and fundamentalism, by veteran foreign correspondent returning to the country where she learned her trade.
Katz, Jonathan G *Murder in Marrakesh* (2006) Heavyweight history of how the 1907 lynching of Dr Émile Mauchamp in Marrakech was exploited by the French in establishing the Protectorate.
Maxwell, Gavin *Lords of the Atlas* (1966) The single best book on Marrakech – an account of the rise and fall of the despotic Glaoui clan.

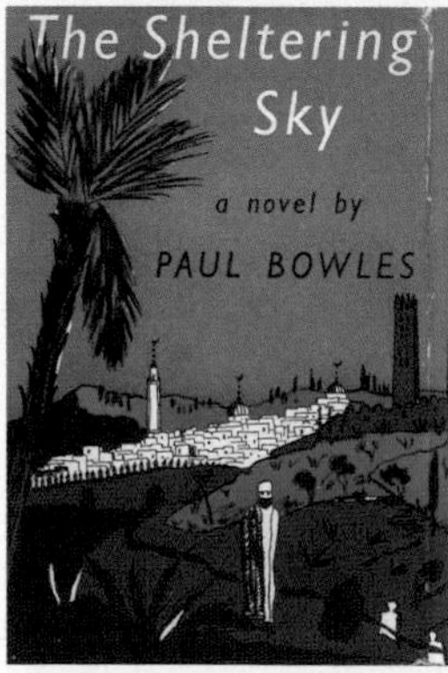

Mayne, Peter *A Year in Marrakesh* (1953) Account by a loafing Englishman of local alley life with drugs, casual sex and garden picnics. A bit of a wheeze.
Milton, Giles *White Gold* (2004) Action-packed popular history of white slaves in 18th-century Morocco, based on the memoirs of a Cornish cabin boy who became a personal slave of tyrannical sultan Moulay Ismail.
Rogerson, Barnaby *Marrakesh, Through Writers' Eyes* (2003) Terrific anthology of non-fiction writings on the city, from Ibn Battuta in 1325 to BBC radio reporters chasing down storytellers on the Jemaa El Fna in 2002.
Shah, Tahir *In Arabian Nights* (2009) By a British-Afghani travel writer who lives in Casablanca. He unearths the exotic wisdom of classic fables by meeting with storytellers on a journey through Casablanca, Fès and Marrakech. Enchanting.

FILM

For more on Moroccan film, *see pp114-117.*

Babel
Alejandro González Iñárritu (2006)
Brad Pitt and Cate Blanchett star in the Moroccan section of a globalised narrative mosaic. Marrakech is only glimpsed; the film is mostly set in the Saharan village of Tazarine.
Hideous Kinky
Gillies Mackinnon (1998)
Solid adaptation of the novel, in which Kate Winslet romanced by Moroccan-born Said Tagmaoui and loads of gorgeous local scenery.
The Man Who Knew Too Much
Alfred Hitchcock (1955)
Hitchcock's second take on the title begins with 30 minutes shot entirely on location in Marrakech. There's a murder at the Mouassine fountain and scenes featuring James Stewart and Doris Day at the Mamounia.
Moroccan Chronicles
Moumen Smihi (1999)
Haunting portmanteau of three fables: shot in Marrakech, Essaouira and Tangier.
Othello
Orson Welles (1951)
Shot in fits and starts over four years, on a dozen locations including Essaouira, where the film crew's prolonged stay was a huge boost to the local economy.

Our Man In Marrakesh
Don Sharp (1996)
Light-hearted, stereotypical 1960s comedy spy romp concerning fixed UN votes and starring the excellent Terry-Thomas as a Moroccan caid. Almost entirely shot on location in Marrakech.
The Road to Morocco
David Butler (1942)
Like Webster's dictionary Bing (Crosby) and Bob (Hope) are Morocco bound, quipping and gagging as they vie for the hand of Dorothy Lamour.
The Sheltering Sky
Bernardo Bertolucci (1990)
Adaptation of the Bowles novel. American couple go down the drain in the desert.

DISCOGRAPHY

For more on Moroccan music, *see pp121-123.*

Classical

Amina Alaoui *Alcaneara* (Auvidis Ethnic)
The great diva of Arab-Andalous music accompanied by three classical musicians. Ethereal and beautiful.
Moroccan Ensemble of Fès *Andalucian Music from Morocco* (Harmonia Mundi)
Good recordings of Moroccan classical music performed by one of Morocco's finest orchestras.

Berber & gnawa

Aziz Sahmaoui *University of Gnawa* (Naïve)
Marrakchi *guimbri* master brings the gnawa tradition slapping and banging into a new generation with original compositions, electronic effects and West African instrumentation.
Jil Jilala *Chamaa* (Blue Silver)
One of the most revered of all North African bands; this album shows why.
Lemchaheb *La Chanson Populaire Marocaine* (Club Du Disque Arabe)
A CD that captures the band raw before they went West.
Najat Aatabou *The Voice Of The Atlas* (Globestyle)
Outspoken female Berber vocalist who sings in Berber, Arabic and French and has risen to major star status.
Nass El Ghiwane *Le Disque d'Or* (Blue Silver)
Classic album from the early 1970s features Nass at their finest.
Various *Gnawa Music of Marrakech: Night Spirit Masters* (Axiom US)
Great recording of gnawa musicians in the Medina, featuring Brahim El Belkani.
Various *Morocco: Jilala Confraternity* (Ocora)
An important recording of a small Jilala ensemble who perform rituals in rural Morocco on request.
Various *Rough Guide to Music of Morocco* (World Music Network)
A cross-section of traditional and contemporary, funk and hip hop Moroccan music. Old favourites Master Musicians of Joujouka rub shoulders with new kids Mazagan.

Modern Morocco & fusion

Oum *Soul of Morocco* (LOF Music)
Contemporary Casablanca chanteuse, mixing Western jazz and Saharwi influences in an eclectic style. The song 'Taragalte' is dedicated to the Taragalte Festival and people of M'Hamid El-Ghizlane (*see p121*).
Majid Bekkas *Chalaba* (ACT)
Stylish jazz-gnawa collaboration from trio of gnawa master Majid Bekkas, German avant-garde pianist Joachim Kuhn and Spanish percussionist Ramon López.
Hoba Hoba Spirit *Trabando* (Moroccan Music Division)
From Casablanca, one of the most popular live bands on the festival circuit – mixing hip hop, rock, reggae and gnawa.

Index

INDEX

INDEX

INDEX

INDEX

مراكش
MARRAKECH
414

Maps

Marrakech Overview

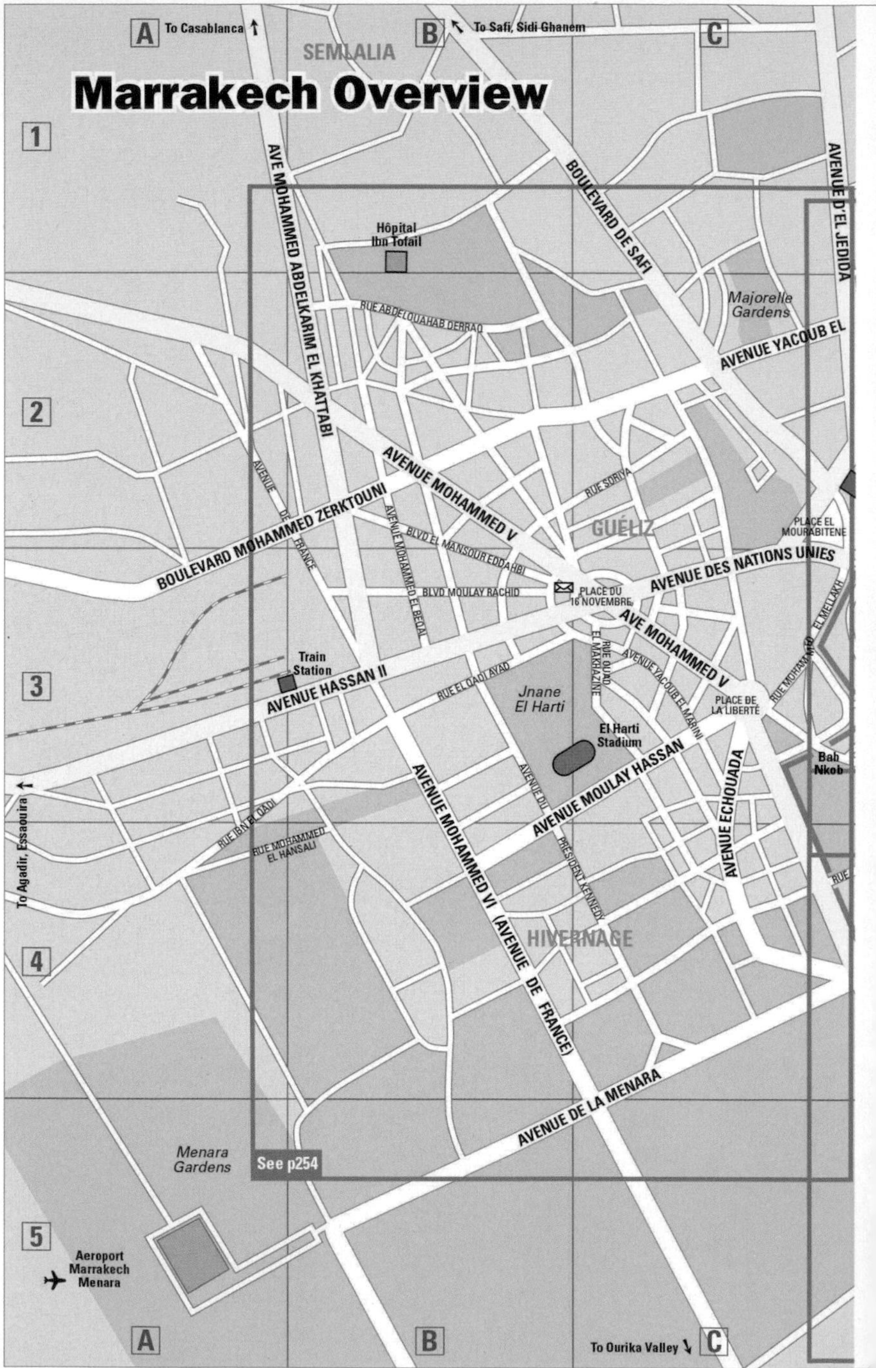

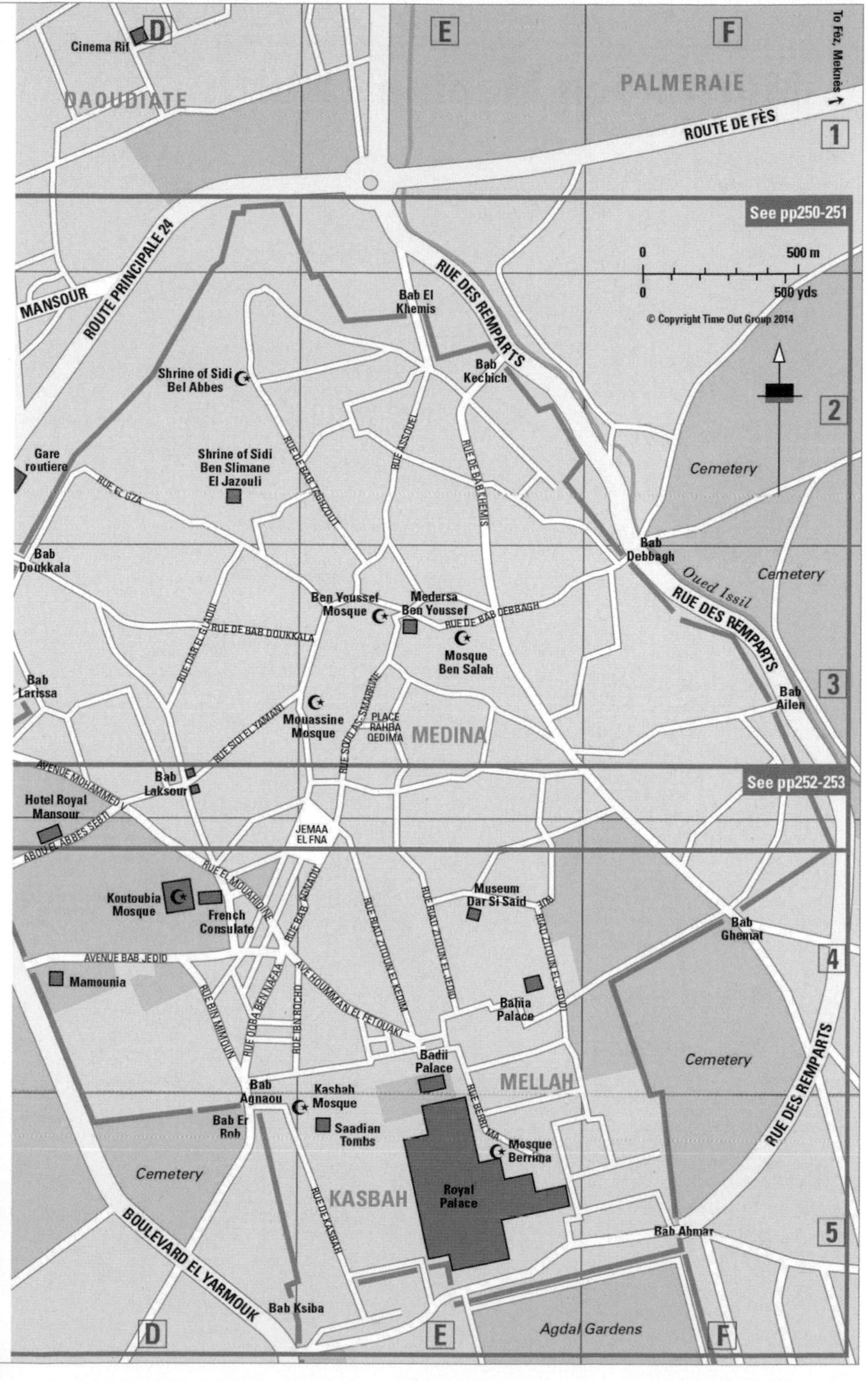

D
E
F
Cinema Rif
DAOUDIATE
PALMERAIE
To Fèz, Meknès
ROUTE DE FÈS
1
See pp250-251
0
500 m
0
500 yds
© Copyright Time Out Group 2014
MANSOUR
ROUTE PRINCIPALE 24
RUE DES REMPARTS
Bab El Khemis
Bab Kechich
Shrine of Sidi Bel Abbes
2
Gare routiere
Shrine of Sidi Ben Slimane El Jazouli
RUE EL GZA
RUE DE BAB TAGHZOUT
RUE ASSOUEL
RUE DE BAB KHEMIS
Cemetery
Bab Debbagh
Bab Doukkala
Oued Issil
Cemetery
RUE DES REMPARTS
Ben Youssef Mosque
Medersa Ben Youssef
RUE DE BAB DEBBAGH
RUE DE BAB DOUKKALA
RUE DAR EL GLAOUI
Mosque Ben Salah
Bab Larissa
3
Bab Ailen
Mouassine Mosque
RUE SOUQ AS-SMARINE
PLACE RAHBA QEDIMA
MEDINA
RUE SIDI EL YAMANI
AVENUE MOHAMMED V
Bab Laksour
See pp252-253
Hotel Royal Mansour
ABOU EL ABBES SEBTI
JEMAA EL FNA
RUE EL MOUAHIDINE
RUE BAB AGNAOU
Koutoubia Mosque
French Consulate
Museum Dar Si Said
RUE RIAD ZITOUN EL KEDIM
RUE RIAD ZITOUN EL JEDID
Bab Ghemat
AVENUE BAB JEDID
4
Mamounia
RUE BIN MIMOUN
RUE OQBA BEN NAFAA
RUE IBN ROCHD
AVE HOUMMAN EL FETOUAKI
Bahia Palace
Cemetery
RUE DES REMPARTS
Badii Palace
MELLAH
Bab Agnaou
Kasbah Mosque
RUE BERRIMA
Bab Er Rob
Saadian Tombs
Mosque Berrima
Cemetery
RUE DE KASBAH
KASBAH
Royal Palace
BOULEVARD EL YARMOUK
Bab Ahmar
5
Bab Ksiba
Agdal Gardens
D
E
F

MAPS

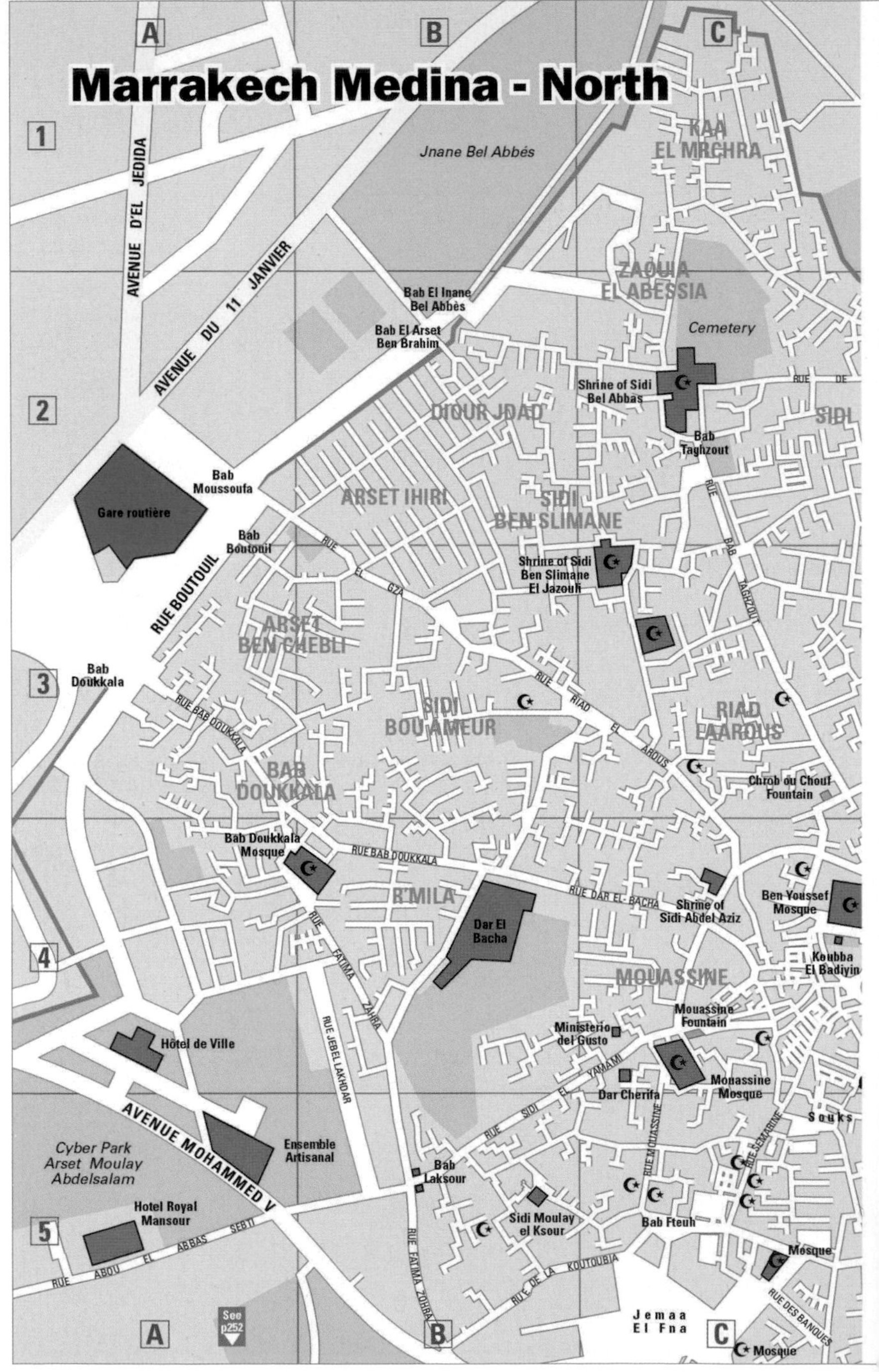
Marrakech Medina - North
A
B
C
1
2
3
4
5
Jnane Bel Abbés
KAA EL MRCHRA
ZAOUIA EL ABESSIA
Cemetery
AVENUE D'EL JEDIDA
AVENUE DU 11 JANVIER
Bab El Inane Bel Abbès
Bab El Arset Ben Brahim
Shrine of Sidi Bel Abbas
Bab Taghzout
DIOUR JDAD
SIDI
RUE DE
Bab Moussoufa
Gare routière
ARSET IHIRI
SIDI BEN SLIMANE
Bab Boutouil
RUE EL GZA
Shrine of Sidi Ben Slimane El Jazouli
RUE BAB TAGHZOUT
RUE BOUTOUIL
ARSET BEN CHEBLI
Bab Doukkala
RUE BAB DOUKKALA
SIDI BOU AMEUR
RUE RIAD EL AROUS
RIAD LAAROUS
BAB DOUKKALA
Chrob ou Chouf Fountain
Bab Doukkala Mosque
R'MILA
Dar El Bacha
RUE DAR EL BACHA
Shrine of Sidi Abdel Aziz
Ben Youssef Mosque
Koubba El Badiyin
RUE FATIMA ZAHRA
MOUASSINE
RUE JEBEL LAKHDAR
Hôtel de Ville
Ministerio del Gusto
Mouassine Fountain
RUE SIDI EL YAMAMI
Dar Cherifa
Mouassine Mosque
Souks
AVENUE MOHAMMED V
Ensemble Artisanal
Cyber Park Arset Moulay Abdelsalam
Bab Laksour
RUE MOUASSINE
RUE SEMARINE
Hotel Royal Mansour
Sidi Moulay el Ksour
Bab Fteuh
RUE ABOU EL ABBAS SEBTI
RUE FATIMA ZOHRA
RUE DE LA KOUTOUBIA
Mosque
RUE DES BANQUES
See p252
Jemaa El Fna
Mosque

MAPS

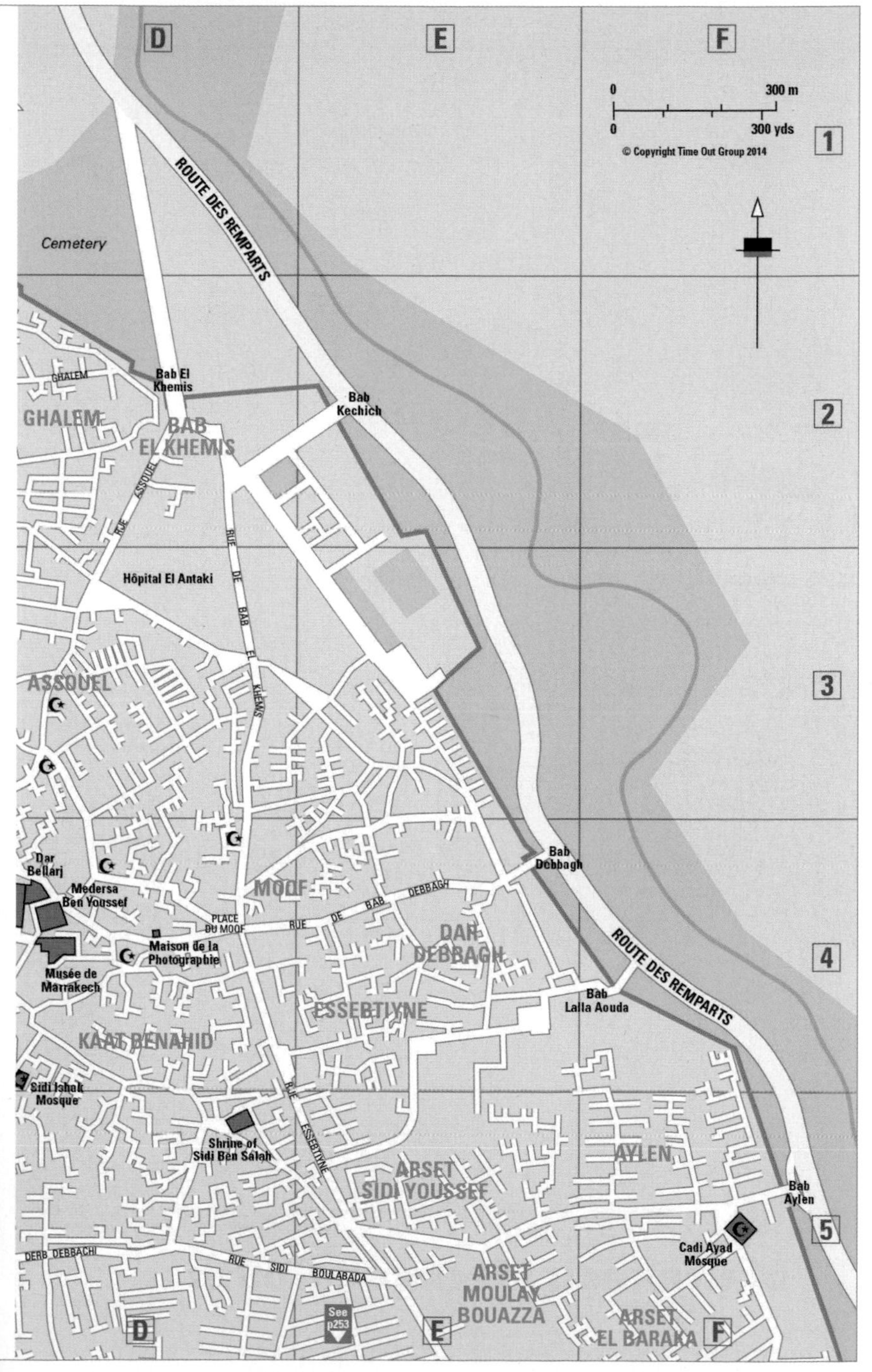
D
E
F
0
300 m
0
300 yds
© Copyright Time Out Group 2014
1
2
3
4
5
Cemetery
ROUTE DES REMPARTS
GHALEM
Bab El Khemis
GHALEM
BAB EL KHEMIS
Bab Kechich
RUE ASSOUEL
RUE DE BAB EL KHEMIS
Hôpital El Antaki
ASSOUEL
Bab Debbagh
Dar Bellarj
Medersa Ben Youssef
MOUF
PLACE DU MOUF
RUE DE BAB DEBBAGH
DAR DEBBAGH
Maison de la Photographie
Musée de Marrakech
ROUTE DES REMPARTS
Bab Lalla Aouda
ESSEBTIYNE
KAAT BENAHID
Sidi Ishak Mosque
Shrine of Sidi Ben Salah
RUE ESSEBTIYNE
AYLEN
ARSET SIDI YOUSSEF
Bab Aylen
Cadi Ayad Mosque
DERB DEBBACHI
RUE SIDI BOULABADA
ARSET MOULAY BOUAZZA
ARSET EL BARAKA
See p253
D
E
F

MAPS

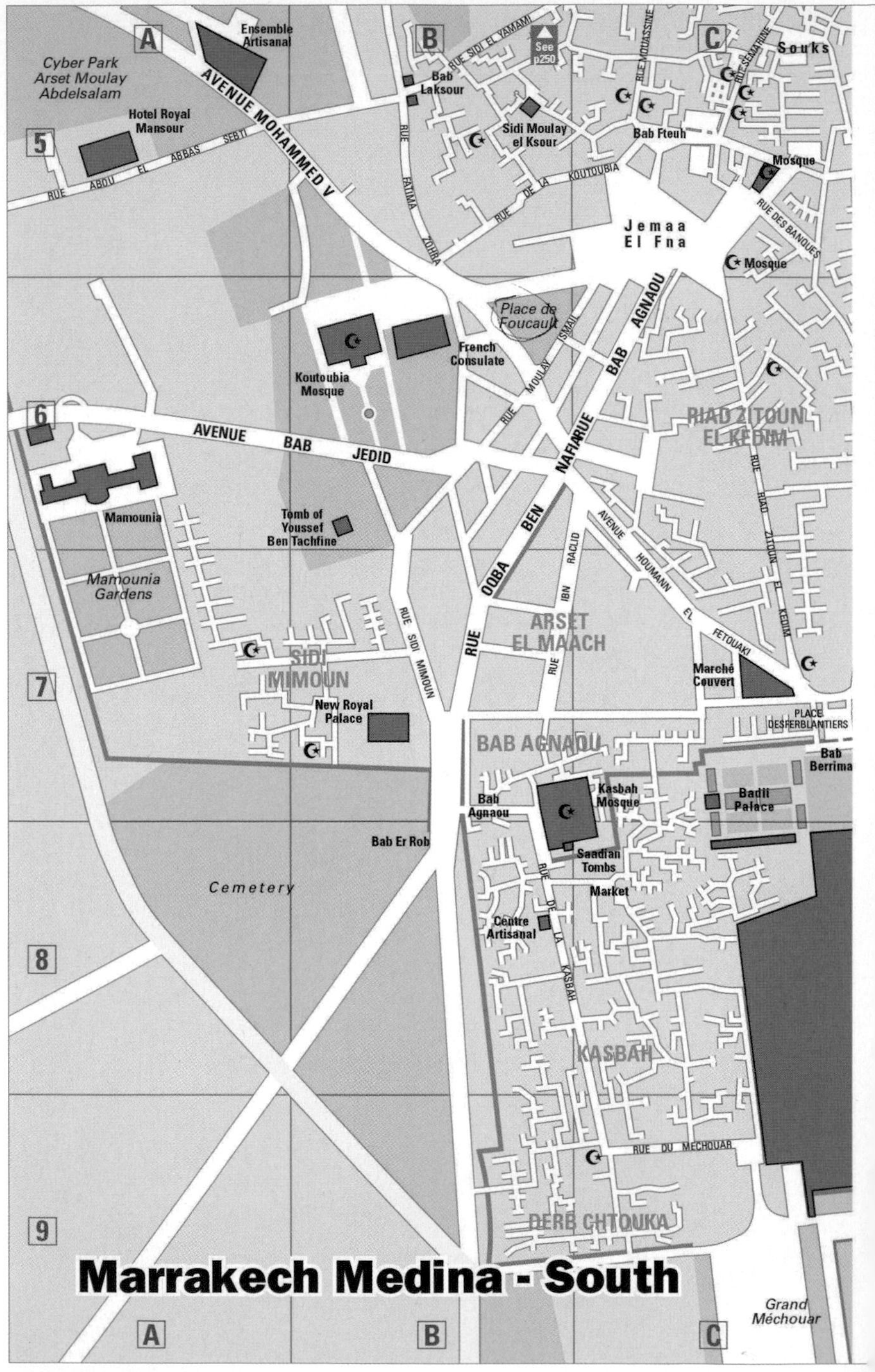

Marrakech Medina - South
A
B
C
5
6
7
8
9
Ensemble Artisanal
Cyber Park Arset Moulay Abdelsalam
Hotel Royal Mansour
Avenue Mohammed V
Rue Abou El Abbas Sebti
Bab Laksour
Rue Sidi El Yamami
See p250
Sidi Moulay el Ksour
Rue Fatima Zohra
Rue de la Koutoubia
Bab Fteuh
Souks
Mosque
Rue des Banques
Jemaa El Fna
Place de Foucault
French Consulate
Koutoubia Mosque
Rue Moulay Ismail
Bab Agnaou
Riad Zitoun el Kedim
Avenue Bab Jedid
Rue Nafia
Mamounia
Tomb of Youssef Ben Tachfine
Mamounia Gardens
Rue Ooba Ben
Rue Ibn Raclid
Avenue Houmann El Fetouaki
Rue Riad Zitoun El Kedim
Rue Sidi Mimoun
Sidi Mimoun
Arset el Maach
Marché Couvert
New Royal Palace
Place Desferblantiers
Bab Agnaou
Bab Berrima
Kasbah Mosque
Badii Palace
Bab Agnaou
Bab Er Rob
Saadian Tombs
Cemetery
Market
Rue de la Kasbah
Centre Artisanal
Kasbah
Rue du Mechouar
Derb Chtouka
Grand Méchouar

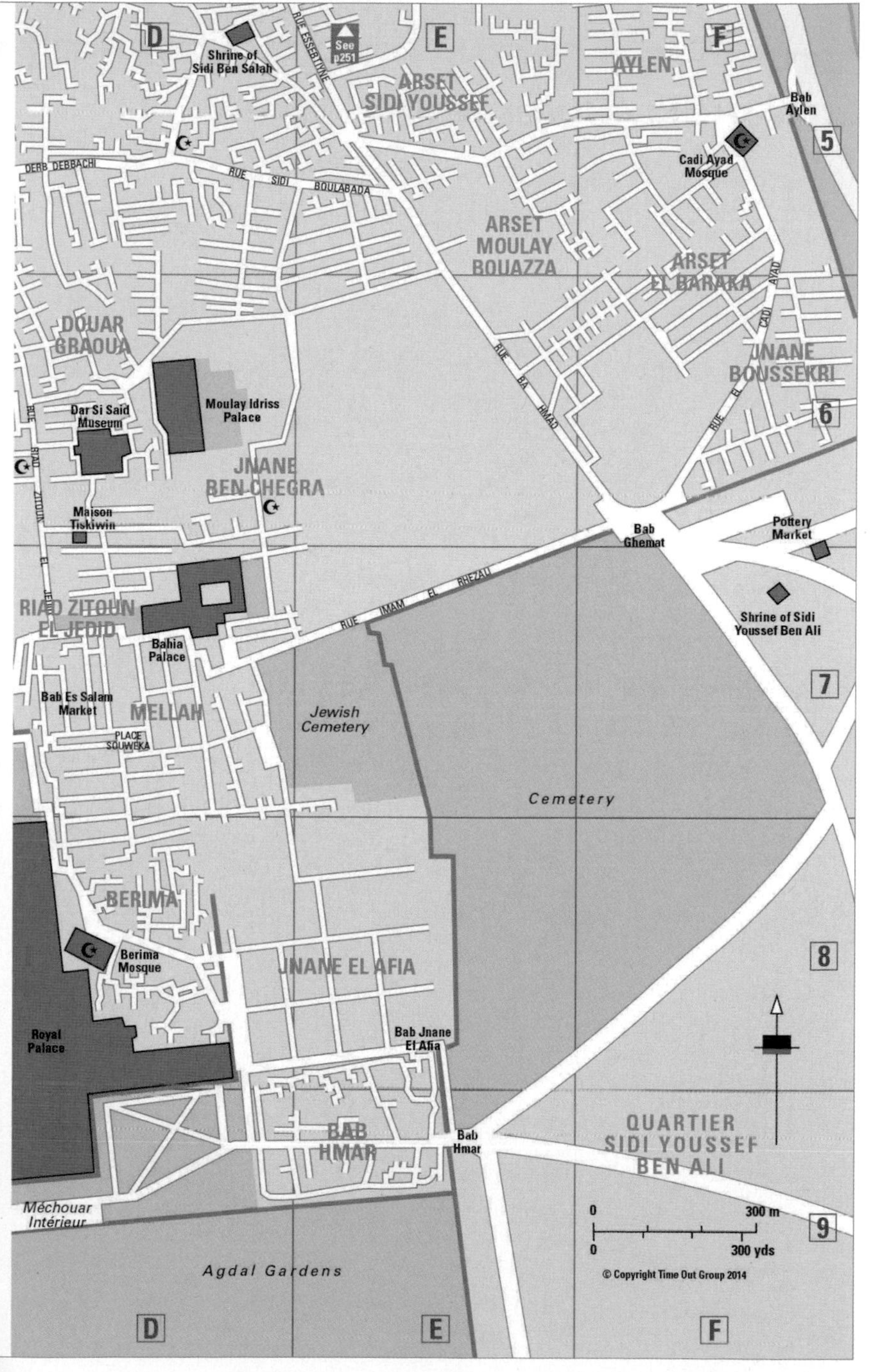
D
E
F
Shrine of Sidi Ben Salah
RUE ESSEBTIYNE
See p251
ARSET SIDI YOUSSEF
AYLEN
Bab Aylen
5
Cadi Ayad Mosque
DERB DEBBACHI
RUE SIDI BOULABADA
ARSET MOULAY BOUAZZA
ARSET EL BARAKA
RUE CADI AYAD
DOUAR GRAOUA
RUE BA HMAD
JNANE BOUSSEKRI
Dar Si Said Museum
Moulay Idriss Palace
6
RUE RIAD ZITOUN EL JEDID
JNANE BEN CHEGRA
Maison Tiskiwin
Bab Ghemat
Pottery Market
RUE IMAM EL RHEZALI
RIAD ZITOUN EL JEDID
Shrine of Sidi Youssef Ben Ali
Bahia Palace
7
Bab Es Salam Market
MELLAH
Jewish Cemetery
PLACE SOUWEKA
Cemetery
BERIMA
8
Berima Mosque
JNANE EL AFIA
Royal Palace
Bab Jnane El Afia
BAB HMAR
Bab Hmar
QUARTIER SIDI YOUSSEF BEN ALI
Méchouar Intérieur
0
300 m
0
300 yds
9
© Copyright Time Out Group 2014
Agdal Gardens
D
E
F

MAPS

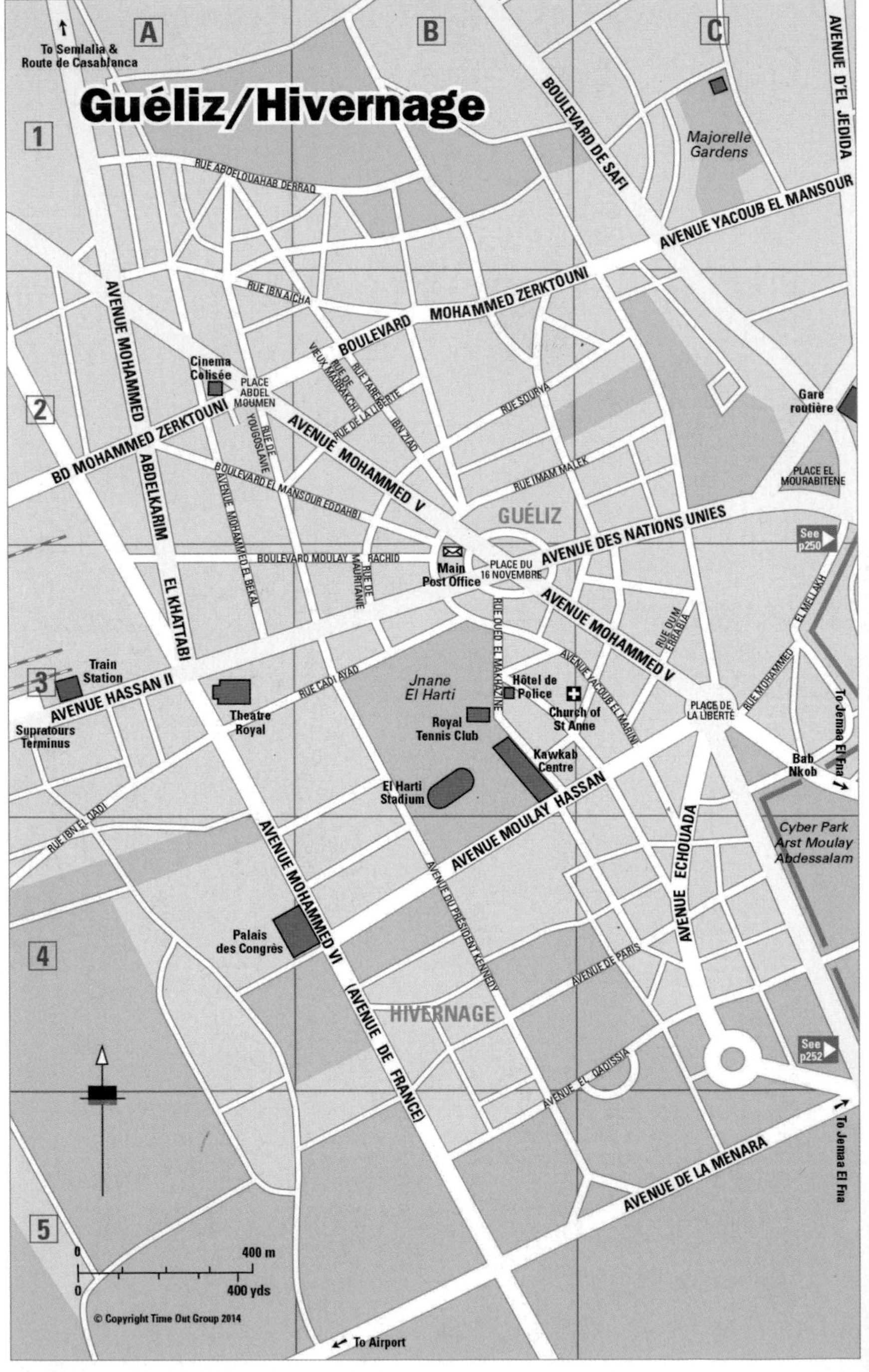
Guéliz/Hivernage
A
B
C
1
2
3
4
5
To Semlalia & Route de Casablanca
Majorelle Gardens
Boulevard de Safi
Avenue d'El Jedida
Avenue Yacoub El Mansour
Rue Abdelouahab Derraq
Rue Ibn Aicha
Boulevard Mohammed Zerktouni
Avenue Mohammed Abdelkarim El Khattabi
Cinema Colisée
Place Abdel Moumen
BD Mohammed Zerktouni
Rue de Vieux Marrakchi
Rue Tarek Ibn Ziad
Rue de la Liberté
Rue de Yougoslavie
Avenue Mohammed V
Rue Sourya
Rue Imam Malek
Boulevard El Mansour Eddahbi
Avenue Mohammed El Bekal
Gare routière
Place El Mourabitene
Guéliz
Avenue des Nations Unies
See p250
Boulevard Moulay Rachid
Rue de Mauritanie
Main Post Office
Place du 16 Novembre
Rue Oued El Makhazine
Avenue Mohammed V
Rue Oum Errabia
El Mellakh
Train Station
Avenue Hassan II
Supratours Terminus
Theatre Royal
Rue Cadi Ayad
Jnane El Harti
Royal Tennis Club
Hôtel de Police
Church of St Anne
Avenue Yacoub El Marini
Place de la Liberté
Rue Mohammed
To Jemaa El Fna
Kawkab Centre
Bab Nkob
El Harti Stadium
Avenue Moulay Hassan
Rue Ibn El Qadi
Avenue Mohammed VI (Avenue de France)
Avenue du Président Kennedy
Avenue Echouada
Cyber Park Arst Moulay Abdessalam
Palais des Congrès
Avenue de Paris
Hivernage
See p252
Avenue El Qadissia
To Jemaa El Fna
Avenue de la Menara
0
400 m
400 yds
© Copyright Time Out Group 2014
To Airport

MAPS

Street Index